ENVIRONMENTAL LAW

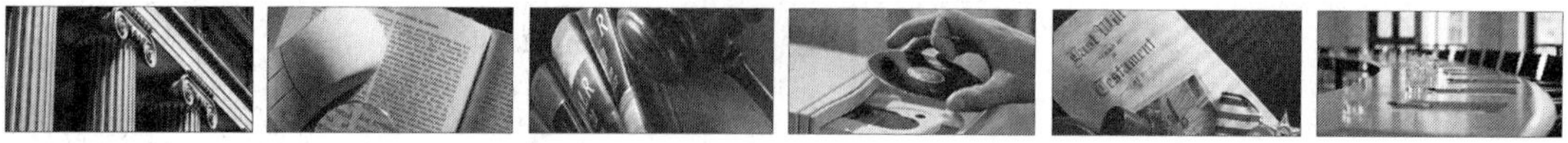

ENVIRONMENTAL LAW

KATHRYN L. SCHROEDER

THOMSON
DELMAR LEARNING™

AUSTRALIA CANADA MEXICO SINGAPORE SPAIN UNITED KINGDOM UNITED STATES

THOMSON
DELMAR LEARNING

WEST LEGAL STUDIES

ENVIRONMENTAL LAW
Kathryn L. Schroeder

Career Education Strategic Business Unit: Vice President:
Dawn Gerrain

Director of Learning Solutions:
John Fedor

Managing Editor:
Robert L. Serenka, Jr.

Acquisitions Editor:
Shelley Esposito

Senior Product Manager:
Melissa Riveglia

Editorial Assistant:
Melissa ZaZa

Director of Production:
Wendy A. Troeger

Senior Content Project Manager:
Betty L. Dickson

Technology Project Manager:
Sandy Charette

Art Director:
Joy Kocsis

Director of Marketing:
Wendy Mapstone

Marketing Manager:
Gerard McAvey

Marketing Coordinator:
Jonathan Sheehan

Cover Design:
Dutton and Sherman Design

Printed in the United States
1 2 3 4 5 XXX 11 10 09 08 07

For more information contact
Delmar Learning, 5 Maxwell Drive,
P.O. Box 8007, Clifton Park,
New York 12065.

Or find us on the World Wide Web at
http://www.westlegalstudies.com

Library of Congress Cataloging-in-Publication Data

Schroeder, Kathryn L.
Environmental law /
Kathryn L. Schroeder.
p. cm.
Includes index.
ISBN-13: 978-1-4018-5714-1
ISBN-10: 1-4018-5714-0
1. Environmental law—United States.
2. Environmental protection—United States. I. Title.

KF3775.S37 2008
344.7304'6—dc22

2007019015

NOTICE TO THE READER

CONTENTS

PREFACE

INTRODUCTION

Welcome to the study of one of the most varied and intricate areas of law in the U.S. legal system. While environmental law is a complex field of study, it also is a fun field of study and is relevant to the everyday lives of all citizens of planet earth. Since the body of environmental laws is one of the most dynamic and developing areas of law in the United States, this subject is especially relevant to students who are seeking a greater understanding of growing areas of the law. There is room in the environmental legal field for practitioners at all levels, including attorneys and paralegals. Environmental law is primarily about document creation, analysis, and management, as well as the litigation that inevitably flows from complex and controversial legal issues.

ABOUT THIS TEXT

This text is written as a basic introduction to the study of environmental law. Intended as an overview, it does not go into great detail about any one subject or issue. It offers curious students the resources necessary to explore subject areas or issues more fully by providing citations and resources that allow students to dig deeper into specific environmental laws or related issues if they so choose. There is no prerequisite to the study of environmental law as found in this text. Chapter 1 provides all of the legal subject matter background necessary to understanding the material presented in the text. The text is generally organized around primary federal environmental laws such as the Clean Water Act, Clean Air Act, and National Environmental Policy Act. This structure is common among environmental law texts; but beyond the similar organizational choice, this text varies significantly from other environmental law texts on the market today. The study of environmental law can be extremely boring and confusing when a text consists only of a summary of the relevant laws. The reason? Because environmental laws tend to be even more convoluted and full of exceptions than most areas of the law. Many environmental law texts can be described as dry. In comparison, this is not a law school text filled with thousands of case citations that explore the intricacies of the more subtle points of the law on a given subject. This text provides a survey of relevant case law, but it is not overly infused with case citations.

To further combat the likelihood of students' minds wandering or, worse yet, students dozing off, this text includes special features on people, events, and organizations connected with the study and practice of environmental law. It is exciting to learn, for example, that the 2004 Nobel Prize winner, a woman from South Africa, received the prize for her environmental efforts. Many of the cases highlighted in the text were chosen for their interesting facts as well as for their significance to the body of law. An example of this philosophy of text authorship is a case in Chapter 1 that explores the question of whether a cetacean (in this case, a whale) has standing to bring an environmental action against the president of the United States. Significantly, this text is written in language that a nonlawyer can follow, understand, and enjoy.

The author believes that environmental law can be an exciting and energizing subject if the proper learning resources are provided. This text is intended to be a balance between providing students with the basic knowledge required for understanding the subject and offering interesting material to motivate students to become engaged in this field of study.

Each chapter of this text provides learning objectives, subject matter exposition, key terms, and questions and exercises to test students' knowledge of the facts of a particular subject and students' ability to apply that knowledge beyond the pages of the text. Web sites are provided for further exploration. Each chapter summary is designed to remind students of key material covered in the chapter. In addition, ethical considerations for environmental law practitioners such as paralegals are provided to remind students that the job duties of anyone working in the legal arena involve more than just the application of knowledge; those duties also require the application of ethical principles.

ABOUT THIS SUBJECT

It would be difficult to find anyone who would admit that he or she was opposed to keeping the planet's waters and air clean or to protecting the human habitat and the ecosystems of all living things. No issue is that one-dimensional, however. Problems inevitably arise when growth and development (and the economics to which they relate) begin to have a negative effect on the physical world, forcing governments at all levels to put laws and regulations in place to ensure that any environmental damage is minimized and remediated as much as possible.

In essence, every person is an "environmentalist" because he or she lives in and exerts dominion over the environment. The United States is a comparatively new country; but it has developed at an accelerated rate, which has magnified the effects of that development on the surrounding environment. In her book *Silent Spring*, Rachel Carson describes an imaginary American town and what was happening to it as a result of pollution.

A Fable for Tomorrow

> There was once a town in the heart of America where all life seemed to live in harmony with its surroundings. The town lay in the midst of a checkerboard of prosperous farms, with fields of grain and hillsides of orchards where, in spring, white clouds of bloom drifted above the green fields. In autumn, oak and maple and birch set up a blaze of color that flamed and flickered across a backdrop of pines. Then foxes barked in the hills and deer silently crossed the fields, half hidden in the mists of the autumn mornings. . . .
>
> Then a strange blight crept over the area and everything began to change. Some evil spell had settled on the community: mysterious maladies swept the flocks of chickens; the cattle and sheep sickened and died. Everywhere was a shadow of death. . . .
>
> There was a strange stillness. The birds, for example—where had they gone? . . . The roadsides, once so attractive, were now lined with browned and withered vegetation as though swept by fire. These, too, were silent, deserted by all living things. Even the streams were now lifeless. . . .
>
> No witchcraft, no enemy action had silenced the rebirth of new life in this stricken world. The people had done it themselves. . . .

> This town does not actually exist, but it might easily have a thousand counterparts in America or elsewhere in the world. I know of no community that has experienced all the misfortunes I describe. Yet every one of these disasters has actually happened somewhere, and many real communities have already suffered from a substantial number of them. A grim specter has crept upon us almost unnoticed, and this imagined tragedy may easily become a stark reality we all shall know. . . .

Silent Spring was emblematic of the environmental wake-up call that eventually occurred in the United States. Once government leaders became aware of what was happening, a strong push was made to enact laws to remedy the damage already done and prevent further damage to the "spacious skies," "amber waves of grain," and "purple mountain majesties" of this beautiful land. The body of environmental law found in this text is the result of that continuing quest.

There has been recent speculation that "environmentalism" is losing momentum. In 2004, two environmentalists, Michael Shellenberger and Ted Nordhaus, wrote a thesis entitled "The Death of Environmentalism." Although their contentions did not prompt much interest initially, a perceived anti-environmentalism result in the November 2004 presidential election caused a reevaluation of their assertions. The authors proposed "abolishing the category" of environmentalism in favor of including the same objectives in a broader agenda addressing "progressivism" in a positive way. These views gave voice to a concern that to a debatable degree, some of the momentum evidenced by the spate of environmental laws in the 1970s seems to have dissipated. Shellenberger and Nordhaus are "convinced that modern environmentalism, with all of its unexamined assumptions, outdated concepts and exhausted strategies, must die so that something new can live." There is no doubt that the environmental laws in this text will change as physical and political circumstances change because laws are never perfect. Laws are never without controversy. Environmental laws are no exception. Many find them cumbersome, overly technical, political, ineffective, or simply superficial.

Whatever their efficacy, environmental laws represent an effort to address a growing problem in America. The environmental laws in the United States are but one part of a worldwide effort to maintain the integrity of the environment. As these laws are read and studied and as they are modified to adapt to the changing circumstances of existence, the hope is that the laws will evolve into a system that serves the purposes for which they were intended. Whether these laws are adequate to serve those purposes, whether there is a proper balance between development and preservation, whether money and nature can find common ground, and whether humans are intelligent and unselfish enough to find a legal way to solve the problem are yet to be determined. In any event, it is likely that, in some modified form, environmental laws will survive; therefore, they are fitting subjects for the education of today's students of the law.

THE AUTHOR'S PERSPECTIVE

Having practiced law in private practice and in local government for more than 23 years, I believe that environmental laws intersect with virtually everyone, especially every legal practitioner. If an individual does not know the basics of environmental law, he or she should. If a person knows a little something, he or she should know more.

Through teaching Environmental Law at various educational levels, including paralegal students in undergraduate school and master's level students, it became obvious that existing environmental law texts were inadequate to provide an effective learning experience. No effort was made to bring the subject to life for the lay student. There are few areas of law that touch our lives more than environmental law. It is my hope that students will read and evaluate the materials in this text, and enjoy the study of this fascinating system of laws.

DEDICATION

This book is dedicated to my parents, William and Nadine Schroeder, career educators whose wonderful love, knowledge, guidance, and faith in me have allowed me to become the person I am: an attorney, a teacher, an author, and someone very proud to be their daughter.

ACKNOWLEDGMENTS

The author wishes to thank Rebecca Parker, Attorney and Chair of the Paralegal Program at Arapahoe Community College in Littleton, Colorado, for her advice, research assistance, legal expertise, and friendship, without which this text could not have been written.

Thanks also go to the Arapahoe County Sheriff's Office, ably led by Sheriff Grayson Robinson and Carol Tomaszewski of the Environmental Crimes Unit, for providing information and materials about the Emergency Planning and Community Right-to-Know Act and its implementation in law enforcement and firefighting communities. Thanks also go to George Rosenberg, who assisted in obtaining permissions for use of the cartoons included in this text. Attorney Howard Kennison, who practices Environmental Law in Denver, Colorado, provided assistance and support for this effort. Melissa Riveglia of Delmar Learning has been a wonderful editor, providing excellent guidance and feedback to a nervous and insecure author.

I have been fortunate to have had excellent teachers, beginning, of course, with my parents, but also at every level of my education. I owe a great deal to all of them. I also have been fortunate to have worked in great organizations and with wonderful colleagues. Thanks to all of you for your professionalism, integrity, and faith in me.

Personally, the author wishes to thank her husband, Michael Hume, for his love, support, and patience with the process of getting a textbook published, and her brother, Richard Schroeder, and her sister, Laurie Healy, for always being there when needed.

The author and Delmar would like to thank the following reviewers for their valuable comments and suggestions:

Erin Calkins
College of St. Mary
Omaha, NE

Lynne Dahlborg
Suffolk University
Boston, MA

Stephanie Delaney
Highline Community College
Des Moines, WA

Bob Diotalevi
Florida Gulf Coast University
Ft. Myers, FL

Regina Dowling
Brandford Hall Career Institute
Windsor, CT

Kathryn Myers
Saint Mary of the Woods College
Saint Mary of the Woods, IN

Wendy Vonnegut
Methodist College
Fayetteville, NC

Kathryn L. Schroeder

WEST LEGAL STUDIES

SUPPLEMENTAL TEACHING MATERIALS

- The **Instructor's Manual with Test Bank** is available on-line at **http://www.westlegalstudies.com** in the Instructor's Lounge under Resource. Written by the author of the text the *Instructor's Manual* contains suggested syllabi, lecture notes, answers to the text questions, useful web sites, and a test bank.
- **On-line Companion™**—The Online Companion™ Web site can be found at **http://www.westlegalstudies.com** in the Resource section of the Web site. The On-line Companion™ contains the following:
    - Chapter Summary
    - Trivia
    - Internet Resources
    - Appendices
- **Web page**—Come visit our Web site at **http://www.westlegalstudies.com** where you will find valuable information specific to this book such as hot links and sample materials to download, as well as other West Legal Studies products.
- Westlaw®—West's on-line computerized legal research system offers students "hands-on" experience with a system commonly used in law offices. Qualified adopters can receive ten free hours of Westlaw®. Westlaw® can be accessed with Macintosh and PC.

Please note that Internet resources are of a time-sensitive nature and URL addresses may often change or be deleted.

Contact us at westlegalstudies@delmar.com

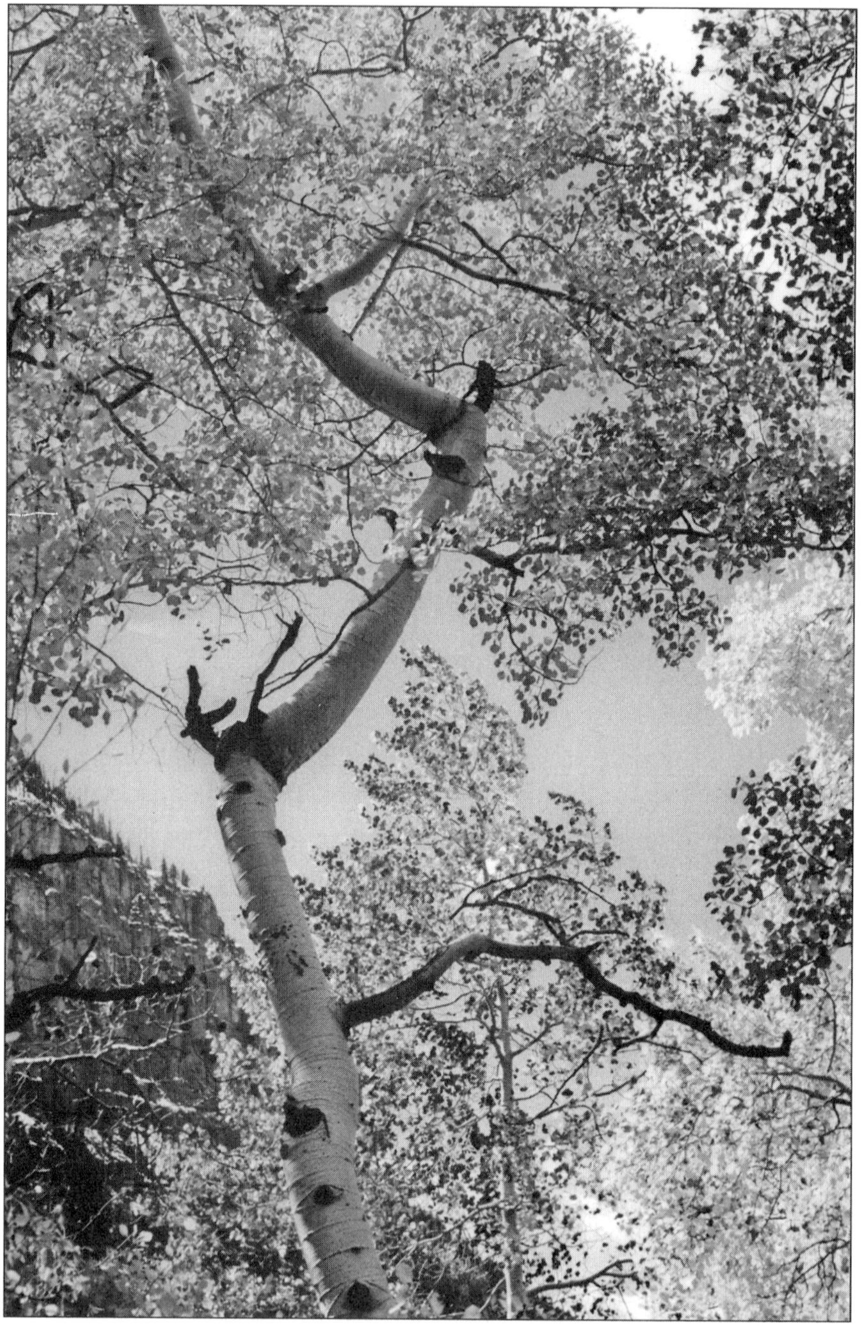

TABLE OF CASES

CHAPTER 1

LEGAL FOUNDATIONS OF ENVIRONMENTAL LAW

The legal system in the United States deals with various issues necessary to an organized society: criminal behavior, family relations, regulation of business and industry, employer-employee relationships, and many others. Certainly, one of these important issues is environmental law. What is environmental law? Environmental law, in a broad sense, is the regulation of actions that threaten or actually harm the natural world, including people or the environment (animals, plants, air, water, etc.).

REVIEW

Environmental law is the regulation of actions that threaten or actually harm the natural world, including people, animals, plants, air, and/or water.

LEARNING OBJECTIVES

After studying this chapter, the reader should be able to

- describe the sources of law.
- explain the legal foundations of environmental law, including:
  constitutional law.
  civil law (including common law).
  administrative law.
  tort law.
  criminal law.
- describe the litigation process, including the concept of standing.
- practice helpful tips in reading and understanding the body of environmental law.

FOUNDATIONS OF ENVIRONMENTAL LAW

For several reasons, the study of environmental law is one of the most complex areas in the legal field. First, the laws regulating the environment come from a number of sources: federal courts, Congress, various federal administrative agencies, and international treaties, as well as regulation from state legislatures, state courts, state administrative agencies, and local government (cities, towns, and counties). While environmental law is a relatively new field of legal study (having developed primarily within the last 50 years), the involvement of these many different entities sometimes makes it difficult to study the laws and regulations that govern environmental law.

Second, a number of different substantive areas of the law are involved. The study of environmental law involves some knowledge of administrative law, criminal law, tort law, the court system, civil and criminal procedure, and constitutional law, in addition to others. The relationships among these areas are not always easy to see or understand, but they all play a part in environmental law and regulation.

Finally, science plays a major role in many environmental law issues. In a discussion of the maximum contaminant levels for drinking water or the rules concerning sulfur dioxide emissions (a contributing factor to acid rain), science plays a major role in the development and enforcement of environmental statutes and regulations.

The study of environmental law also can be complicated by the many acronyms and technical phrases used in the field. The student of environmental law may puzzle over MPRSA (Marine Protection, Research and Sanctuaries Act, which regulates transporting material to be dumped into the ocean) or SNUR (a Significant New Use Rule for new uses of chemicals issued by the Environmental Protection Agency, EPA). A glossary of many of these acronyms and phrases is a part of this textbook.

The remainder of this chapter discusses how major substantive areas of the law are involved in the field of environmental regulation and how they originated.

QUESTION

You may have eaten organic food, but do you know what an organic law is? An organic law is the fundamental law, or constitution, of a state or nation, written or unwritten. The organic law or system of laws or principles defines and establishes the organization of that government and sets the limits of that government's power. For the United States and each individual state, their constitutions are their organic laws. An organic act is the statute by which a municipal corporation is organized, such as a home rule charter.

SOURCES OF LAW

In the United States, the form of government was created by the Constitution. Since the Constitution forms the basis of all other laws, it is known as an organic law. The federal Constitution set up three branches of government (legislative, judicial, and executive); each branch creates a different type of law. In addition to creating the form of government, the federal Constitution specified the powers of each branch, while guaranteeing many important rights to individual citizens.

The legislative branch (Congress or state legislatures) passes **statutes**, which are rules of general applicability. Congress has the authority to regulate interstate commerce because of the **commerce clause** of the Constitution (U.S. Const. art. I, § 8). This clause gives the federal legislature broad powers to prevent states from "unreasonably burdening" interstate commerce by passing laws that hinder interstate commerce. Some environmental initiatives by states have been invalidated as a result of this provision on the theory that the initiatives unreasonably restrict the free conduct of commerce. However, where courts have found that the benefits of the state laws outweigh their effect on interstate commerce, the state environmental provisions have been upheld.

statute A rule of general applicability passed by the legislative branch of a government.

commerce clause A section of the Constitution that allows regulation of commerce between the states.

The judicial branch decides specific disputes between or among parties (who may be individuals, the government, corporations, etc.). The resulting body of case law, which is based on generally accepted legal principles adopted from England and modified over the years, is referred to as **common law**. Common law often interprets statutes and sometimes creates legal principles to "fill in the gaps" where no statutory law exists.

common law A body of case law based on generally accepted legal principles adopted from England and modified over the years.

Finally, the executive branch passes rules and regulations, which are designed to carry out the processes of government, primarily as set forth by the legislature in the statutes it enacts. The executive branch also makes decisions concerning the application of regulations. These regulations, rules, and decisions are collectively referred to as *administrative law* and also have the force of law.

ASSIGNMENT

Look up some of the old English common laws and see where you can find parallels in the laws of the United States.

ADMINISTRATIVE LAW

Executive agencies at the federal level and at most state levels are required to comply with laws concerning how regulations and administrative decisions are made. The federal **Administrative Procedure Act (APA)**, 5 U.S.C. § 500 *et. seq.*, which has been the model for many similar state acts, sets forth the procedures that executive agencies must follow when adopting regulations and making administrative decisions. These procedures generally include requirements of prior notice and opportunity to be heard before a rule is adopted or a decision is made.

Administrative Procedure Act (APA) A federal act that sets forth the procedures that agencies must follow in adopting regulations and making administrative decisions.

The following key concepts about administrative law are worth remembering.

- Administrative agencies have only "delegated" authority; they have no ability to create their own authority.
- Administrative agencies must abide by the provisions of the Administrative Procedure Act or other applicable external procedural requirements, as well as whatever rules the agency itself adopts concerning its activities.
- Administrative agencies must maintain a record of their activities that can be reviewed by the public or a court.
- In rendering decisions, an administrative agency may not act in an "arbitrary and capricious" manner; in other words, there must be a legal and evidentiary reason for the action taken.
- The decisions of administrative agencies may be appealed once the decision is final and there are no other administrative avenues of relief for a party; that is, a party must "exhaust its administrative remedies" prior to any appeal.
- If proper administrative procedures are followed, the decisions of administrative agencies will be given great deference by the courts.

One case in which there was an appeal under the APA of an environmental law administrative decision is *Citizens to Preserve Overton Park v. Volpe*.[1] In that case, plaintiff citizens' groups filed suit against the Secretary of Transportation, alleging that he violated federal law by authorizing expenditure of public funds to build a highway through a public park.

CASE LAW

CITIZENS TO PRESERVE OVERTON PARK V. VOLPE, 401 U.S. 402 (1971).

SUMMARY OF CASE: Petitioners sought judicial review of an order that affirmed a decision of the Secretary of Transportation to build an interstate highway through a public park.

Justice Marshall delivered the opinion of the court.

In 1956, the Bureau of Public Roads approved a route for construction of an interstate highway in Memphis, Tennessee, which route would have destroyed 26 acres of a 342-acre park located near the center of Memphis and which would have severed that area of the park containing the zoo from the remainder of the park, which contained a golf course, an art academy, 170 acres of forest, and other recreational areas. This route was again approved in 1966 by the Federal Highway Administrator. However, in 1966, Congress passed the Department of Transportation Act, section 4(f) of which declared it to be the national policy that special effort should be made to preserve, inter alia, public park and recreational lands and which ordered the Secretary of Transportation not to approve any program or project which required the use of any publicly owned land from a public park or recreation area unless (1) there was no reasonable and prudent alternative to the use of such land, and (2) there was included in any such program all possible planning to minimize harm to any park or recreational area used for such purposes. . . . [T]he state in 1969 acquired the right of way inside the park from the city. Final approval of the route and design for the road was not announced until late in 1969. . . . The announcements approving the route and design of the highway were not accompanied by formal findings of fact, nor did the Secretary state why he believed there were no feasible and prudent alternative routes or why design changes could not be made to reduce harm to the park. Petitioners . . . brought suit . . . seeking to halt construction of the highway through the park and arguing that the Secretary's action in approving the route and design was invalid without formal findings. . . . [T]he District Court held that the statutes did not require the Secretary to file formal findings, and, construing its review powers narrowly, decided that the Secretary had not exceeded his authority in approving the route.]

The growing public concern about the quality of our natural environment has prompted Congress in recent years to enact legislation designed to curb the accelerating destruction of our country's natural beauty. We are concerned in this case with . . . the Department of Transportation Act of 1966. [This statute] prohibit[s] the Secretary of Transportation from authorizing the use of federal funds to finance the construction of highways through public parks if a "feasible and prudent" alternative route exists. If no such route is available, the statutes allow him to approve construction through parks only if there has been "all possible planning to minimize harm" to the park.

Petitioners . . . contend that the Secretary has violated these statutes by authorizing the expenditure of federal funds for the construction of a six-land interstate highway through a public park in Memphis, Tennessee. [They] contend that it would be "feasible and prudent" to route [the highway] around Overton Park, either to the north or to the south. And they argue that if these alternative routes are not "feasible and prudent," the present plan does not include "all possible" methods for reducing harm to the park. . . . Respondents argue that it was unnecessary for the Secretary to make formal findings, and that he did, in fact, exercise his own independent judgment which was supported by the facts.

The threshold question—whether petitioners are entitled to any judicial review—is easily answered. Section 701 of the Administrative Procedure Act . . . provides that the action of "each authority of the Government of the United States," which includes the Department of Transportation, is subject to judicial review. . . .

Despite the clarity of the statutory language, respondents argue that the Secretary has wide discretion. . . . But no such wide-ranging endeavor was intended. It is obvious that in most cases considerations of cost, directness of route, and community disruption will indicate that parkland should be used for highway construction whenever possible. . . . [T]here will always be a smaller outlay [of funds] required from the public purse when parkland is used since the public already owns the land and there will be no need to pay for right-of-way. And since people do not live or work in parks, if a highway is built on parkland no one will have to leave his home or give up his business. Such factors are common to all highway construction.

Congress clearly did not intend that cost and disruption of the community were to be ignored by the Secretary. But the very existence of the statutes indicates that protection of parkland was to be given paramount importance. The few green havens that are public parks were not to be lost unless there were truly unusual factors present in a particular case. . . . If the statutes are to have any meaning, the Secretary cannot approve the destruction of parkland unless he finds that alternative routes present unique problems.

The court is first required to decide whether the Secretary acted within his scope of authority. . . . As has been shown, Congress has specified only a small range of choices that the Secretary can make. . . . Scrutiny of the facts does not end, however, with the determination that the Secretary has acted within the scope of his statutory authority. Section 706(2)(A) requires a finding that the actual choice was not 'arbitrary, capricious, an abuse of discretion or otherwise was not . . . in accordance with law.' . . . The court is not empowered to substitute its judgment for that of the agency.

Undoubtedly, review of the Secretary's action is hampered by his failure to make [specific] findings, but the absence of formal findings does not necessarily require that the case be remanded. . . . [The statutes] do not require that there be formal findings.

Thus it is necessary to remand this case to the District Court for plenary review of the Secretary's decision. That review is to be based on the full administrative record that was before the Secretary at the time he made his decision . . . in order to determine if the Secretary acted within the scope of his authority and if the Secretary's action was justifiable under the applicable standard. ■

QUESTION

1. Do you think the act discussed in this case would be effective in preventing destruction of parkland? Why or why not?

To ensure that the public has adequate information concerning administrative proceedings, the notices, written decisions, and records of other administrative action are published in the *Federal Register*, which is a periodical published by the federal government. Appendix A in this text contains sample pages from the *Federal Register* about environmental actions the EPA has taken. These sample pages demonstrate the form that noticing and reporting takes in the *Federal Register* and show the detail and particularity with which the information is provided.

For environmental law, the chief federal administrative agency involved in the application of federal law through the drafting, adopting, and enforcing of environmental regulations is the **Environmental Protection Agency (EPA)**. Often in administrative proceedings, as in litigation, there is significant disagreement concerning the facts related to a particular matter. In environmental law, this is particularly true because of the voluminous amount of scientific information necessary for the proper resolution of an environmental issue. The APA requires the EPA, if the EPA intends to promulgate a regulation or rule, to issue an administrative order finding a company in noncompliance with an environmental law or take any other action within its authority to provide notice to the public and the affected parties, hold public hearings, and issue a written decision concerning its action. These administrative proceedings are, essentially, trials at which testimony and evidence are presented, legal argument is provided, and a decision is rendered. The only difference between these often protracted administrative proceedings and typical litigation is that in an administrative proceeding, the decision is made by the appropriate administrative agency and in court litigation, the decision is made by a judge or jury.

Environmental Protection Agency (EPA) The federal agency tasked with administering and enforcing most of the federal environmental acts.

Freedom of Information Act (FOIA) A federal act giving the public access to records kept by governmental bodies and agencies.

environmental assessment (EA) The beginning of the process found in the National Environmental Policy Act (NEPA) to determine the impact of certain proposed federal actions.

environmental impact statement (EIS) A detailed analysis of the environmental impact of a proposed federal action. Follows the environmental assessment (EA) as part of the NEPA process.

ASSIGNMENT

FOIA is a product of federal law, but every state has similar laws that require all levels of government in that state, including the state itself, counties, and municipalities, to allow access to government records like the access required by FOIA. These state laws are typically called "open records" laws. Look at the statutes in your state and find out what governments must provide and what the procedures are for obtaining open records.

In addition to the information provided through the public notice and opportunity to participate provisions guaranteed by the administrative process and the information contained in the *Federal Register*, citizens also are able to acquire information concerning environmental matters through the use of the federal **Freedom of Information Act (FOIA)**, 5 U.S.C. sec. 552, *et seq.* With very few exceptions for certain confidential information, all records of the EPA and other federal agencies are available to the public for inspection and copying (at the expense of the requesting party, of course). Often factual information is sought by entities preparing an **environmental assessment (EA)** or **environmental impact statement (EIS)**. A FOIA request is made in writing to the agency from which the records are sought, and the agency must respond within a set period of time or explain why a response cannot be provided within that time period. If an agency refuses to provide the information requested, that agency must explain in writing why the documents are being withheld so the requester can appeal the decision of the administrative agency if it so desires. FOIA is an excellent tool for obtaining environmental information on almost any subject or case.

The types of law created by the three branches of government often act together to govern a problem. For example, suppose Congress passes a statute giving a federal administrative agency (such as the EPA) the authority to enact rules governing the discharge of pollutants into navigable waters. The EPA would then promulgate regulations to execute, or carry out, the terms of the statute. These regulations might require a business to get a permit from the EPA to dispose of industrial waste into a stream. If the business disputed whether the regulation applied (perhaps because there was a dispute over whether the stream was "navigable water"), the business could sue the EPA in court for a judicial determination of whether the regulation applied. The statute, the regulation, and the court decision would all be part of the body of environmental law.

Of course, the Constitution also preserves many important rights for individual citizens. U.S. citizens have the right to due process of law (U.S. Const. amend. XIV), equal protection of the law (U.S. Const. amend. XIV), and the right to be free from unreasonable searches and seizures (U.S. Const. amend. IV). Each of these important constitutional concepts may play a role in environmental law cases.

The body of environmental law, then, consists of items from all of these sources: federal constitutional, statutory, common, and administrative law; state constitutional, statutory, common, and administrative law; and local laws. The complex relationships between these laws are a major component in the study of environmental law.

TORT LAW

One area of law outside the field of environmental law that has a considerable impact on environmental law is tort law. A **tort** is sometimes referred to as a "civil wrong" ("civil" to distinguish it from a "criminal" wrong). Tort law is concerned with the general legal responsibility of private parties toward each other. If a person violates this general legal responsibility and injures another, the injured party may sue in court to receive **damages**. Damages are money payments for injuries, such as medical bills and lost profits. The tort can be committed intentionally or negligently or, in some cases, without any intent at all ("strict liability" torts).

tort A civil, as opposed to a criminal, wrong.

damages Money payments for injuries.

There are many types of torts recognized by the law. Several of these torts have particular significance for students of environmental law.

The most common type of tort is **negligence**. Negligence is a breach of a duty to another person that causes an injury. Negligence results when someone has a responsibility; fails in that responsibility; and, as a result, causes the injury. The standard of care used in determining whether someone owes a responsibility to another is the **reasonable person test**: whether a person of ordinarily prudent care would have exercised that care under the circumstances. In addition, the failure to exercise reasonable care must be the **proximate cause** of the injury. Proximate cause is the act (or failure to act) without which the injury would not have occurred; it is the event that produces the injury without an intervening cause. If a company carelessly disposed of hazardous waste and another person was injured as a result of the careless disposal, the injured person could sue the company for negligence.

negligence A breach of a duty to another person that causes an injury.

reasonable person test This is part of the test for negligence, and is based upon whether a person of ordinarily prudent care would have exercised that care under the particular circumstances of a case.

proximate cause The act (or failure to act) without which an injury would not have occurred; the event that produces an injury without an intervening cause.

In some cases, courts have determined that a violation of a statute or regulation was **negligence per se**. Negligence per se occurs when conduct is treated as negligence even where there is no actual evidence concerning the breach of duty. In the previous example, if no evidence were available concerning how the disposal of hazardous waste occurred but the injured person could prove that the company violated a statute prohibiting the disposal, the injured person might be able to prevail on a negligence per se argument; that is, violation of the statute is, in and of itself, evidence of the negligence of the company. Of course,

negligence per se A situation where conduct is treated as negligence even when there is no actual evidence concerning a breach of duty.

the injured person would still have to prove that the disposal was the proximate cause of his or her injury.

In other situations, the common law is that persons engaging in specific "hazardous activities" are liable for the damages he or she caused as a result of that activity even when there is no proof that there was a breach of duty. This tort is **strict liability**; the person engaging in the hazardous activity is strictly liable for the damages they cause. The theory behind this tort is that persons who are performing these especially dangerous activities should be liable for any damage whether or not they were exercising reasonable care or regardless of what they intended to happen. A traditional example of a hazardous activity is the use of explosives. This tort (strict liability) is often used in environmental law situations to impose liability without regard to the principles of negligence.

strict liability A liability for damages as a result of engaging in an activity even when there is no proof that the liable party breached a duty while engaging in that activity. This is a very common liability standard in environmental law due to the hazardous nature of many activities related to environmental law.

Another tort applied in environmental law situations is **nuisance**. Nuisance is a tort that results from an annoyance or a disturbance that unreasonably interferes with the enjoyment of property. While, generally, owners may use their private property as they wish, the law limits this right to uses that do not unduly interfere with the enjoyment of other property owners. A use that results in injury or unreasonable annoyance to a neighboring property owner would be nuisance.

nuisance A tort that results from an annoyance or a disturbance that unreasonably interferes with the enjoyment of property.

Many activities could result in nuisance: excessive noise, odors, smoke or dust, discharges of pollutants into water, or disposal of hazardous wastes, to mention a few. The court will consider the facts of each case to determine whether the degree of harm or annoyance rises to the level of nuisance and whether the landowner was using his or her property reasonably. In performing this analysis, the court will use a "balancing test," by which the reasonable interests of the parties will be balanced to determine who should prevail. See *Harrison v. Indiana Auto Shredders Co.*[2]

A final tort relevant to the study of environmental law is **trespass to land**. Trespass to land occurs when there is an unlawful entry onto another's real property. This entry need not be a person setting foot on the property; courts have held that sending noxious orders or water onto someone else's land constitutes trespass.

trespass to land This tort occurs when there is an unlawful entry onto another's real property. The tort does not require that a person set foot on someone else's property; sending noxious odors or water onto someone else's property can be considered trespass to land.

CRIMINAL LAW

Another major area of law that has a significant impact on the field of environmental law is criminal law. A criminal prosecution differs from a tort case in that in a criminal case, the suit is always brought by the government (federal, state, or local) against a specific defendant or defendants for an alleged violation of a specific criminal statute. Persons convicted of violations of criminal statutes can be penalized by fines, imprisonment, or both. Most environmental statutes have civil and criminal consequences for violation of their provisions.

A related but noncriminal remedy for violation of certain environmental laws is an **injunction**. An injunction is a court order to do (or refrain from doing) a specific act. If the injunction is violated, the individual violating the order is guilty of **contempt of court**; while this is not a criminal action, the court can punish the person committing contempt by fine and/or jail. Finally, a number of environmental regulations permit the government to seek substantial fines for violations of regulations; fines of $50,000 per day are not uncommon in these situations.

injunction A court order to do (or refrain from doing) a specific act.

contempt of court When a party to a court proceeding fails or refuses to abide by an order of court, that party may be held in contempt of court.

LITIGATION PROCESS

In any lawsuit brought before a court, there are at least two parties: the party bringing or initiating the action and the party against whom the action is brought. The party bringing the action is generally called the **plaintiff** (although in criminal cases, the party bringing the action is usually referred to as the government or the "People"); the party against whom the action is brought is called the **defendant**. A civil lawsuit is begun when the plaintiff files a **complaint** or petition with the court, claiming that the defendant has violated a law and has injured the plaintiff. The defendant has the opportunity to file an **answer** to the complaint, and the parties then exchange information in a process known as **discovery**. The parties may settle the case between them or proceed to a **trial** before a judge or a jury. The losing party at the trial has the right to **appeal** to a higher court, asking the higher court to review the lower court's decision for errors. Almost every case a student reads is a written decision by an appeals court concerning the specific lawsuit in question.

One of the legal requirements for a lawsuit that is relevant to the student of environmental law is the issue of **standing to sue**. To bring a lawsuit, a plaintiff is required to have standing. Standing may be defined as "an appropriate individual interest in the outcome of the suit." Plaintiffs cannot sue defendants just because they believe the defendants are wrong; the plaintiffs must have real interests in the suit that affects them. Under the APA mentioned previously, for example, to sue an administrative agency, the plaintiff must demonstrate standing

plaintiff The party bringing a litigation action.

defendant A party against whom a legal action is brought.

complaint The initial pleading in a litigation proceeding.

answer A pleading filed in response to a complaint in a judicial proceeding.

discovery Information exchanged by parties to a legal proceeding.

trial The forum in which a lawsuit is adjudicated.

appeal A request that a higher court or another authority review a decision by a lower court or an administrative tribunal.

standing to sue No person may bring an action in court unless that person has standing to sue, which is determined by the application of numerous criteria, such as whether the person has a personal stake in the outcome of the litigation.

injury in fact A showing that a person has suffered from individual, concrete harm rather than a speculative future harm.

by showing that the agency's action will cause an **injury in fact** to the plaintiff. The plaintiff cannot claim that he is worried about a possible future injury (say, possible cancer caused by improper disposal of hazardous waste). To have standing, the plaintiff must show that he or she suffers from individual, concrete harm rather than a speculative future harm. Chapter 2 of this text explores the concept of standing as it relates specifically to the unique concepts of environmental law.

SPECIAL ETHICAL CONCERNS FOR PARALEGALS

Paralegals often have substantial responsibilities during major litigation, including during the typical environmental lawsuit. Paralegals frequently have contact with clients, employees of clients, experts, and other witnesses in environmental cases. As a result, paralegals should be meticulous about the following issues:

- Paralegals should be clear about their status as paralegals in their initial communication with a client or witness. Misunderstandings about whether a client or witness believed that a paralegal was an attorney are frequent.
- Paralegals should be aware of the issues of miscommunication, especially with lay witnesses or clients, and should communicate in writing or be careful to document conversations in writing whenever possible.
- Paralegals should be aware of issues of confidentiality in all dealings with clients.
- Paralegals should be conscious of the prohibition on giving legal advice and be prepared to refer the client to the appropriate attorney at any time.

BURDEN OF PROOF

burden of proof The responsibility of one or the other parties to litigation to produce evidence to prove a fact in dispute.

beyond a reasonable doubt The standard of proof in criminal cases.

preponderance of evidence A standard of proof that requires a party to produce slightly more evidence than their opponent.

Another significant element in the litigation process relates to the **burden of proof**. This refers to the responsibility of one or the other parties to produce evidence to prove a fact in dispute. If a party has the burden of proof, he or she must actually meet his or her duty to affirmatively demonstrate the existence of the fact in question. In criminal cases, the government has the burden of proof to show that the defendant is guilty **beyond a reasonable doubt**. Normally, in civil cases, the plaintiff has the burden of proof to show that the defendant is liable by a **preponderance of evidence**. However, specific statutes or rules may make defendants responsible for the burden of proof in some situations, such as the strict liability torts.

RULES OF EVIDENCE

The information that may be presented to a court is governed by rules that specify what information can be presented and in what form. All courts are bound by these **rules of evidence**, which are the procedural rules that address items such as expert witnesses, physical evidence, and other matters concerning admissibility of information to the court.

rules of evidence The rules governing the information that may be presented to a court or an administrative tribunal. These rules specify what information can be presented and in what form.

HELPFUL STUDY TIPS

At this point, studying environmental law might seem a bit daunting. This text provides a broad overview of environmental law—just enough to teach the basics and whet the appetite of those who read it. Every environmental law can be better understood by breaking it down into components. As you read each new act or regulation, you may find it helpful to consider the following questions:

- Who made the law or enacted the regulation?
- If the analysis is of a law, is it an organic law? a federal, state, or local law?
- What is the subject matter?
- What is the stated purpose, if any? If the purpose is not stated, what is it?
- How is the law or regulation structured?
    - Is it divided into appropriate sections?
    - Is it logically or systematically structured?
    - What constructive changes, if any, could be made to its structure? Are there too many acronyms?
- What requirements are imposed?
- Upon whom are the requirements imposed?
- How is compliance monitored?
- What are the enforcement provisions of the law?
- What are the penalties for failure to comply?

  - civil penalties?
  - criminal penalties?
- Against whom may the penalties be enforced?
- Is the subject matter overly broad? too narrow?
- Could the subject matter be combined with that of another subject to simplify the system?

When beginning the study of environmental law, it is important to realize that not everyone believes environmental laws successfully serve the purposes for which they are intended. In Philip K. Howard's book *The Death of Common Sense (How Law Is Suffocating America)* (1994), the author presents the viewpoint that the body of environmental laws occasionally results in the exact opposite of that for which it is intended: the laws maximize cost to the owner/operator while minimizing the benefit to the public. Howard writes:

> . . . When the Environmental Protection Agency (EPA), after years of hearings, passed a rule requiring that specific equipment be put in smokestacks to filter benzene, a harmful pollutant, Amoco [Oil Company] complied and spent $31 million at its Yorktown, Virginia refinery. In 1989 a chance encounter on an airplane between James Lounsbury of EPA and Debora Sparks of Amoco led to a discussion about the frustrations and inadequacies of environmental law. One thing led to another, and with some trepidation, Amoco let a team from EPA into the Yorktown plant to see how the environmental rules, written in windowless rooms in Washington piled high with scientific evidence and legal briefs, actually worked in practice.
>
> EPA found that its precisely drawn regulation almost totally missed the pollution. The Amoco refinery was emitting significant amounts of benzene, but nowhere near the smokestacks. The pollution was at the loading docks, where gasoline is pumped into barges. Just as fumes escape when you use an old-style nozzle when filling up your car at the gas station, large quantities of benzene were escaping as Amoco pumped several hundred millions of gallons of gasoline every year into barges. Once EPA and Amoco officials actually stood on the dock together and realized the problem, the solution was easy and relatively inexpensive. Meanwhile, pursuant to the rigid dictates of a thirty-five page rule that many government experts had spent years fine-tuning, Amoco had spent $31 million to

capture an insignificant amount of benzene at the smokestack. The rule was almost too perfect in its failure: It maximized the cost to Amoco while minimizing the benefit to the public.

The Amoco incident brought to the surface a long-simmering suspicion that, in the words of EPA administrator Carol Browner, there are "really serious problems" with environmental regulation in this country. Environmental laws and rules, now seventeen volumes of fine print, often seem to miss the mark or prove counterproductive. Under one requirement, before industrial land with any toxic waste can be used, it must be cleaned up to almost perfect purity. It sounds great, but the effect is to drive industry out to virgin fields, where it encounters no such costs. Instead of cleaning up one dirty lot, the strict law creates a second dirty lot. Then, of course, jobs are moved away from cities, to places that workers can only reach by driving long distances, which causes yet more pollution. A final irony is that whoever cleaned the polluted land would often be required to incinerate it, literally burning tons of dirt, a process that itself generates significant pollution. Environmental laws have accomplished much, but not because the laws were generally sensible. Spending a trillion dollars in the last twenty years was bound to clean some things up, however inefficiently.

On a more positive note, in 2004, the Nobel Peace Prize was awarded to an African woman primarily for her environmental efforts.

ENVIRONMENTAL LAW CITIZEN PROFILE

Wangari Maathai

In 2004, the Nobel Peace Prize was awarded to an African woman named Wangari Maathai. In the Nobel Prize Presentation Speech for Dr. Maathai, it was stated that:

> Peace on earth depends on our ability to secure our living environment. . . . This year, the Norwegian Nobel Committee has evidently broadened it's definition of peace still further. Environmental protection has become yet another path to peace. . . . Most people would probably agree that there are connections

(continued)

> between peace on the one hand and an environment on the other in which scarce resources such as oil, water, minerals or timber are quarreled over. . . . Another thing that needs to be said in this context is that sooner or later, in order to meet environmental problems, there will have to be international cooperation across all national boundaries on a much larger scale than we have seen up to now. We live on the same globe. We must all cooperate to meet the world's environmental challenges. Together we are strong, divided we are weak.

Thus, innovatively connecting the global environment to world peace, the Nobel Peace Prize was awarded to Dr. Maathai.

Dr. Maathai was born in Nyeri, Kenya, in 1940. A highly educated woman, Dr. Maathai earned her bachelor's degree in Biology from Mount St. Scholastica College in Atchison, Kansas, in 1964, a Master of Science degree in Biological Sciences from the University of Pittsburgh in 1966, and a PhD in Anatomy from the University of Nairobi in 1971. She was the first woman in East and Central Africa to earn a doctorate degree. Dr. Maathai taught in the Department of Veterinary Anatomy at the University of Nairobi and was the department chair.

This background in the academic world explains why Dr. Maathai had the intellectual tools to change the world, but not why she chose to use her gifts to aid the environment. In her acceptance speech, Dr. Maathai said:

> My inspiration partly comes from my childhood experiences and observations of Nature in rural Kenya. It has been influenced and nurtured by the formal education I was privileged to receive in Kenya, the United States and Germany. As I was growing up, I witnessed forests being cleared and replaced by commercial plantations, which destroyed local biodiversity and the capacity of the forests to survive. . . . Throughout Africa, women are the primary caretakers, holding significant responsibility for tilling the land and feeding their families. As a result, they are often the first to become aware of environmental damage as resources become scarce and incapable of sustaining their families. The women we worked with recounted that, unlike in the past, they were unable to meet their basic needs. This was due to the degradation of their immediate environment as well as the introduction of commercial farming, which replaced the growing of household food crops. . . . I came to understand that when the environment is destroyed, plundered or mismanaged, we undermine our quality of life and that of future generations.

In response to her observations about the African environment and the changes that were negatively affecting her and other women, Dr. Maathai decided to take affirmative steps to change the course of environmental degradation in Africa. Dr. Maathai's solution was to start the Green Belt Movement in 1977. This movement is a grassroots, non-governmental organization dedicated to the use of tree planting to affect community development in Africa as well as other developing countries. Through this movement, Dr. Maathai has assisted women in planting more than 30 million trees and has promoted environmental consciousness, volunteerism, conservation of local biodiversity, self-empowerment, community development, and accountability.

Through the Green Belt Movement and her other activities, including serving as Assistant Minister for the Environment, Natural Resources and Wildlife for the Republic of Kenya, Dr. Maathai has made significant strides in her attempts to educate and motivate the people of Africa to respect and enhance their environment.

This, then, is how a concern for the environment can be seen as making a significant contribution to world peace and why it is appropriate to recognize the efforts of Wangari Maathai in an environmental law text.

SUMMARY

The study of environmental law is complex, requiring an understanding of many federal and local laws, as well as regulations, constitutional provisions, and case law. While environmental law as a field of study is relatively new (see Chapter 2), dynamic scientific advances in analyzing and monitoring substances and releases have altered the development of environmental laws. The science of the environment plays a major role in understanding the legal responses to the variety of environmental issues facing the world today. Administrative law and administrative procedure are an integral part of the process of making and enforcing environmental laws. The requirements of the Administrative Procedure Act (APA) permeate the processes of environmental law. Federal agencies including the Environmental Protection Agency (EPA) use administrative law and procedure to perform their required functions as set forth in substantive environmental laws. A familiarity with certain tort concepts, including negligence, strict liability, nuisance, and trespass, is an important foundation for understanding environmental law. Most environmental laws have criminal penalties for certain types of violations, so criminal law is one of the steps on which environmental law was built. A good understanding of the litigation process is crucial to having an effective understanding of environmental law. The concept of "standing" to bring a lawsuit is essential to the study of environmental law, and its application to environmental law is explored more fully in Chapter 2 of this text. Environmental laws exist as their own separate body of law, but they are intimately connected with other areas of the law. Together, these laws make up the system of laws that are designed to protect human health and the environment.

KEY TERMS

- Administrative Procedure Act (APA)
- Answer
- Appeal
- Beyond a reasonable doubt
- Burden of proof
- Commerce clause
- Common law
- Complaint
- Contempt of court
- Damages
- Defendant
- Discovery
- Environmental assessment (EA)
- Environmental impact statement (EIS)
- Environmental Protection Agency (EPA)
- Freedom of Information Act (FOIA)
- Injunction
- Injury in fact
- Negligence
- Negligence per se
- Nuisance
- Plaintiff
- Preponderance of evidence
- Proximate cause
- Reasonable person test
- Rules of evidence
- Standing to sue
- Statute
- Strict liability
- Tort
- Trespass to land
- Trial

REVIEW QUESTIONS AND HANDS-ON ACTIVITIES

1. Describe three different categories of laws that relate to the study of environmental law.

2. Name three torts that are part of the body of environmental law.
3. Outline the procedures and proceedings that make up an administrative action under the Administrative Procedure Act. Describe the review process once an administrative decision has been made, including the standard of review upon appeal.
4. Review your state statutes relating to administrative procedure. Outline the procedures required and the appeal criteria.
5. Describe the basic procedures involved in civil and criminal litigation. What are the standards of proof in each type of proceeding?
6. Is strict liability the appropriate standard to apply to environmental issues? Why or why not?
7. Do you think it is appropriate that the Nobel Peace Prize was awarded for the environmental efforts of Wangari Maathai? Describe how preserving the environment and the concept of "peace" are related.
8. Make an initial analysis of the complexity of environmental laws. Be prepared to amend that analysis as you study more of the text.

HELPFUL WEBSITES

http://www.gpoaccess.gov/cfr/about.html (Government Printing Office, Code of Federal Regulations)

http://www.earthisland.org (Earth Island Institute)

http://www.earthjustice.org (Earthjustice, an environmental legal defense fund)

http:www.sej.org (Society of Environmental Journalists)

http://www.eli.org (Environmental Law Institute®)

http://www.lawvianet.com (Environmental Law Net(SM))

http://www.archives.gov/federal_registerindex.html (The Federal Register)

http://www.sso.org/ecos (The Environmental Council of the States)

http://www.progressiveregulation.org (Center for Progressive Reform)

http://www.ombwatch.org/regs (OMB Watch)

ENDNOTES

1. *Citizens to Preserve Overton Park v. Volpe,* 401 U.S. 402 (1971).
2. *Harrison v. Indiana Auto Shredders Co.,* 528 F.2d 1107 (7th Cir. 1975).

CHAPTER 2

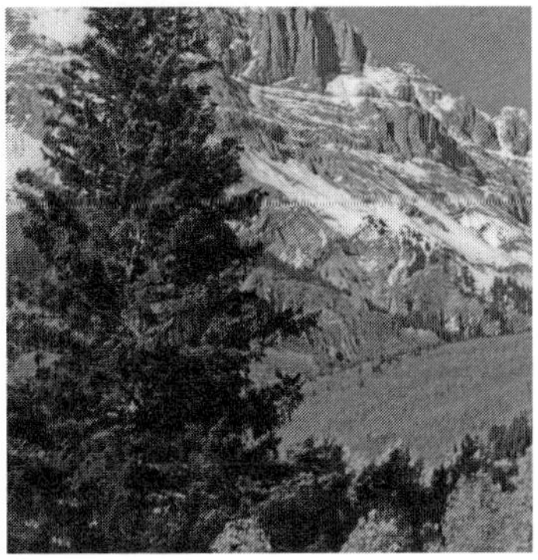

HISTORY, STANDING, LOCAL GOVERNMENT REGULATION, RISK MANAGEMENT, AND WORKPLACE SAFETY

Environmental law is a relatively new body of law in the United States. As this new body of law has developed over the past few decades, traditional legal concepts such as standing have been revisited to ensure that they are appropriately applied to environmental issues. All levels of government, including local governments, have begun to enact environmental laws and regulations to protect their boundaries and their citizens. Within the workplace, concepts such as risk management are utilized to control the workplace environment, along with laws such as the Occupational Safety and Health Act (OSH Act), which established the Occupational Safety & Health Administration (OSHA).

LEARNING OBJECTIVES

After studying this chapter, the reader should be able to

- outline the history of environmental law.
- explain how the concept of "standing" is applied in environmental litigation.
- explain how and why local governments make environmental laws.
- describe what *environmental justice* means.
- describe how risk management concepts apply to environmental law.
- describe the provisions of the Occupational Safety and Health Act (OSH Act) and the Occupational & Safety Health Administration (OSHA).

HISTORY OF ENVIRONMENTAL LAW

In 1963, an American named Rachel Carson wrote a book called *Silent Spring* that led many people to think seriously about environmental issues. At about the same time, there was a historic lawsuit known as *Scenic Hudson Preservation Conference v. Federal Power Commission*.[1] That case was brought to try to stop a power plant from being constructed at the entrance to the gorge of the Hudson River at Storm King Mountain, a beautiful, scenic site. This was one of the first cases that was part of the new "environmental movement" in the United States. Prior to this time, scattered laws in the United States provided relief for environmental problems; but what had existed before was nothing compared to what was about to happen in the area of environmental law.

CASE LAW

SCENIC HUDSON PRESERVATION CONFERENCE V. FEDERAL POWER COMMISSION, 354 F.2D 608 (2D CIR. 1965).

SUMMARY OF CASE: The Federal Power Commission (Commission) entered an order that granted Consolidated Edison a license to construct a hydroelectric project. The petitioners sought judicial review of this order.

Hays, Circuit Judge.

In this proceeding the petitioners . . . ask us, pursuant to § 313(b) of the Federal Power Act, 16 U.S.C. § 825(b), to set aside three orders of the respondent, the Federal Power Commission, [including] an order of March 9, 1965 granting a license to the intervener, the Consolidated Edison Company of New York, Inc., to construct a pumped storage hydroelectric project on the west side of the Hudson River at Storm King Mountain in Cornwall, New York.

A pumped storage plant generates electric energy for use during peak load periods, using hydroelectric units driven by water from a headwater pool or reservoir. The contemplated Storm King project would be the largest of its kind in the world. Consolidated Edison has estimated the cost . . . at $162,000,000. . . . Transmission lines would run under the Hudson to the east bank and then underground for 1.6 miles to a switching station which Consolidated Edison would build. . . . [T]hereafter, overhead transmission lines would be placed on towers 100 to 150 feet high and these would require a path up to 125 feet wide through Westchester and Putnam Counties for a distance of some 25 miles until they reached Consolidated Edison's main connections with New York City. . . .

To be licensed by the Commission, a prospective project must meet the statutory test of being 'best adapted to a comprehensive plan for improving or developing a waterway. . . .' If the Commission is properly to discharge its duty in this regard, the record on which it bases its determination must be complete. The petitioners and the public at large have a right to demand this completeness. It is our view, and we find, that the Commission has failed to compile a record which is sufficient to support its decision. The Commission has ignored certain relevant factors and failed to make a thorough study of possible alternatives to the Storm King project. While courts have no authority to concern themselves with the policies of the Commission, it is their duty to see to it that the Commission's decisions receive that careful consideration which the statute contemplates.

The Storm King project is to be located in an area of unique beauty and major historical significance. The highlands and gorge of the Hudson offer one of the finest pieces of river scenery in the world. . . . The Federal Power Act was the outgrowth of a widely supported effort on the part of conservationists to secure the enactment of a complete scheme of national regulation which would promote the comprehensive development of the nation's water resources. . . . Congress gave the [Commission] sweeping authority and a specific planning responsibility. . . . In recent years the Commission has placed increasing emphasis on the right of the public to 'out-door recreational resources.' The Commission has recognized generally that members of the public have rights in our recreational, historic and scenic resources under the Federal Power Act. . . .

Respondent argues that 'petitioners do not have standing to obtain review' because they 'make no claim of any personal economic injury resulting from the Commission's action. . . .' Section 313(b) of the Federal Power Act reads:

> Any party to a proceeding under this chapter aggrieved by an order issued by the Commission in such proceeding may obtain a review of such order in the United States Court of Appeals for any circuit wherein the licensee or public utility to which the order relates is located.

The Commission takes a narrow view of 'aggrieved party' under the Act. . . . [T]he Supreme Court has not made economic injury a prerequisite where the plaintiffs have shown a direct personal interest. In order to insure that the . . . Commission will adequately protect the public interest in the aesthetic, conservational, and recreational aspects of power development, those who by their activities and conduct have exhibited a special interest in such areas, must be held to be included in the class of "aggrieved" parties under § 313(b). We hold that the Federal Power Act gives petitioners a legal right to protect their special interests. . . . Moreover, petitioners have sufficient economic interest to establish their standing. . . . [Petitioner] has some seventeen miles of trailways in the area of Storm King Mountain. Portions of these trails would be inundated by the construction of the project's reservoir.

The primary transmission lines are an integral part of the Storm King project. The towns that are co-petitioners with Scenic Hudson have standing because the transmission lines would cause a decrease in the proprietary value of publicly held land, reduce tax revenues collected from privately held land, and significantly interfere with long-range community planning. . . .

We see no justification for the Commission's fear that our determination will encourage 'literally thousands' to intervene and seek review in future proceedings. . . . We rejected a similar contention [in another case], noting that 'no such horrendous possibilities exist. Our experience with public actions confirms the view that the expense and vexation of legal proceedings is not lightly undertaken.'

The Federal Power Commission argues that having intervened 'petitioners cannot impose an affirmative burden on the Commission.' But, as we have pointed out, Congress gave the [Commission] a specific planning responsibility. . . . The totality of a project's immediate and long-range effects . . . are to be considered in a licensing proceeding. . . . In this case, as in many others, the Commission has claimed to be the representative of the public interest. This role does not permit it to act as an umpire blandly calling balls and strikes for adversaries appearing before it; the right of the public must receive active and affirmative protection at the hands of the Commission.

This court cannot and should not attempt to substitute its judgment for that of the Commission. But we must decide whether the Commission has correctly discharged its duties, including the proper fulfillment of its planning function in deciding that the 'licensing of the project would be in the overall public interest. . . .' In addition to the Commission's failure to receive or develop evidence concerning [a] gas turbine alternative, there are other instances where the Commission should have acted affirmatively in order to make a complete record. The Commission neither investigated the use of interconnected power as a possible alternative to the Storm King project, nor required Consolidated Edison to supply such information. . . . There is no evidence in the record to indicate that either the Commission or Consolidated Edison ever seriously considered this alternative. . . . The failure of the Commission to inform itself of these alternatives cannot be reconciled with its planning responsibility under the Federal Power Act.

At the time of its original hearings, there was sufficient evidence before the Commission concerning the danger to fish to warrant further inquiry. . . . On remand, the Commission should take the whole fisheries question into consideration before deciding whether the Storm King project is to be licensed.

[T]he licensing order of March 9 . . . [is] set aside and the case is remanded for further proceedings. ■

QUESTIONS

1. Why do you think the Court determined that the petitioners were "aggrieved parties" under the act?
2. What, according to the Court, should the Commission have done differently before granting the license?

The 1970s was a decade of huge growth in the field of environmental law. The National Environmental Policy Act (NEPA) became effective on January 1, 1970 (see Chapter 3). Those involved in the new environmental activism used NEPA as a tool to litigate environmental issues. Various organizations such as the Friends of the Earth and the Sierra Club sprang up to fight for the protection of the environment. The whole question of who had "standing" to bring an environmental lawsuit was a primary subject of early environmental law litigation. The standard of review of decisions by administrative bodies such as the EPA was another of the issues in the early environmental law cases. Publications such as *The Environmental Law Reporter*® began to follow the exciting new cases capturing the fancy of the country. The body of environmental law decisions expanded, and law schools created separate classes in environmental law.

The 1980s was a decade in which the field of environmental law began to look beyond the mere mechanics of environmental litigation and consider such issues as environmental "elitism" (also called the movement for "environmental justice" or "environmental equity") and environmental "racism." These two doctrines put names to what was perceived as one of the sordid secrets of environmental problems: rich companies ran profitable commercial operations that caused huge environmental damage, but they were able to do so because they located their operations in areas where the inhabitants did not have the monetary resources to fight back or stand up for themselves. The environmental damages at Love Canal and in the Adirondack Mountains

QUESTION
Each decade since the 1970s has shown a different environmental law "personality." What do you think the 2000s will hold for environmental law?

Not-in-My-Back-Yard (NIMBY) This syndrome reflects a common view of citizens living or working near a proposed facility that may pose an environmental threat. The phrase basically means that the citizens don't want such a facility anywhere near where they are. In response to this syndrome, many local governments have begun providing a forum in their facility siting process for citizens to make a public record of their concerns.

environmental justice Ensuring that minority or low-income populations are not unduly exposed to environmental hazards and that such populations are given a forum in which to voice their comments concerning a potential hazard.

environmental racism The practice of locating dangerous environmental activities in areas where minority populations do not have significant resources to speak out on the issue.

environmental elitism The practice of locating dangerous environmental activities in areas of low income or minority populations not having significant resources to speak out on the issue.

raised such issues. Environmental activist groups such as Greenpeace and The Monkey Wrench Gang took strong actions to make their point, including blocking commercial activities such as whale hunting and harvesting of trees. Occasionally, these environmental activists engaged in illegal activities themselves, such as putting sugar in gas tanks and vandalizing equipment and facilities.

The environmental battle of the 1990s has been described as being more political than anything else. Candidates for local, state, and national offices were asked to describe their positions concerning current environmental issues and were held accountable for their votes and decisions. That trend continues to this day, and each president of the United States will be judged by citizens and history partially on the basis of his or her perceived support or lack of support for and protection of the environment.

While it cannot be predicted what direction the environmental movement will take in the twenty-first century, there is no question that the United States will continue to address environmental issues and strive toward protecting the natural world.

ENVIRONMENTAL JUSTICE

Naturally, no one wants an environmentally dangerous manufacturing, processing, or waste disposal site near where they live. This understandable attitude is known as the **NIMBY** syndrome: not in my backyard. No one wants such a facility in *his or her* backyard. The problem is that such facilities have to be sited somewhere, albeit with appropriate environmental protections put in place pursuant to the environmental laws discussed in this text; and large corporations have options as to where they build their facilities.

The concept of **environmental justice** addresses the criteria used to make siting decisions that may be based on factors not related to the operation of the site, but, instead, to the ability of those in the community to influence the siting of such a facility. The concept known as **environmental racism** or **environmental elitism** is based on a perceived problem with the way corporations choose to site their environmentally dangerous operations. Dating back to Love Canal in 1979, it often seems as though dangerous environmental activities are intentionally located in areas near economically challenged residential neighborhoods or neighborhoods comprised mainly of racial minorities.

The cynical interpretation about the choice of siting is that those residents lack the education or financial means to challenge the big corporations in the event there are perceived medical complications suffered by community residents or property values are severely impacted by the presence of such a facility. The movie *Erin Brockovich* is based on the true-life story about just such a situation in California, where residents were suffering a variety of serious or life-threatening illnesses and believed that those illnesses were caused by emissions from a nearby power plant. As the movie depicts, the residents were eventually able to recover some compensation for their damages, but only because a law firm essentially took on the case for free out of a sense that an injustice had been done that needed to be righted.

Another example of such a situation was a Monsanto chemical processing site near Anniston, Alabama. For more than 35 years, Monsanto released polychlorinated biphenyls (PCBs) into the waters and land around its plant. PCBs were banned in 1979 due to their demonstrated link to cancer in humans. Children played in the contaminated drainage ditches near their homes, which would vary in color depending on the pollution released from the plant on a given day. Most residents of this area were economically challenged, and they did not know what was being dumped into the water and land. They ate food grown in the contaminated soil. The per-capita income of families in the area was around $11,371 per year. Eventually, 3,500 plaintiffs sued Monsanto; and in 1992, a jury found Monsanto liable for the health problems and property damage that were linked with the release of the dangerous chemicals. Testimony from Monsanto employees indicated that the company knew of the possible risks of their operations and made a conscious decision to continue operations, thinking the residents would never hold Monsanto liable.

It is situations such as these that have spawned a move toward granting citizens a louder voice in the siting of any potentially hazardous manufacturing, processing, or disposal facility in their vicinity. Such facilities are known as **locally undesirable land uses (LULUs)**. Facilities such as hazardous or nonhazardous waste disposal landfills, nuclear storage facilities, and chemical processing plants fall within this definition. To help with the NIMBY syndrome and other problems associated with operating these types of facilities near residential development, companies wanting to build or operate such facilities have begun offering compensation proposals intended to ease some of the concerns of nearby residents.

ASSIGNMENT

Have you ever found yourself upset or angry about some type of development that was proposed in your neighborhood? Did you want to prevent that development from happening? If so, you have experienced the NIMBY syndrome—not in my backyard. What did you do about your concerns? Often concerned citizens attend public hearings held by their local government concerning a development and express their feelings about the development. Attend a public hearing at your local city or county and see how the governing body reacts to such comments.

ASSIGNMENT

Use the Internet to look up articles about the Love Canal environmental problem in 1979. Analyze the response to that incident and formulate an opinion concerning how well or badly the incident was managed.

locally undesirable land uses (LULUs) Any potentially hazardous manufacturing, processing, or disposal facility in the vicinity of a developed area.

These types of compensation proposals typically fall into these categories: rewards or incentives for a community agreeing to allow a site, mitigation measures designed to lessen any harm to the community, and remedies if the community suffers any harm as a result of the operations at the site. The intention behind such proposals is to reduce community opposition, increase community knowledge concerning the activities at the site, and ensure that a particular community will not have to bear too much of the burden associated with such operations. As part of the local siting process, officials have begun to look at the possible discriminatory aspects of the choice of site. One example of the way in which this increased voice for community residents can work is demonstrated by the ruling in *East Bibb Twiggs Nhd. Assoc. v. Macon-Bibb County Planning Zoning Comm.*[2]

In *East Bibb Twiggs,* area residents brought an action challenging the county's approval of a private landfill. The residents argued that the approval was racially motivated. A majority of residents in the neighborhood where the landfill was approved were black. The plaintiffs had to prove that (1) the siting decision had a disproportionate discriminatory impact and (2) the county acted with the intent to discriminate. There was no evidence that the county's decision was motivated by a discriminatory intent. The court found that there was insufficient evidence to support the residents' contention of discriminatory intent because the only other landfill in the census tract was in an area with a predominantly white population. There was no demonstrated history of discrimination on the part of the county; "[a]t no time does it appear to this court that the [county] abdicated its responsibility either to the public at large, to the particular concerned citizens or to the petitioners. Rather, it appears to this court that the [county] carefully and thoughtfully addressed a serious problem and that it made a decision based upon the merits and not upon any improper racial animus."

Thus, citizens, while not always successful, are seeking better means to get into court and seek justice for what has happened to them as a result of companies conducting environmentally sensitive activities. Constitutional law has been one of the legal sources used in such instances; but the relationship among environmental law, constitutional law, and civil rights has been complicated recently by a couple of court decisions. Previously, it was thought that civil rights claims could be brought through 42 U.S.C. sec. 1983. This Section prohibits citizens from being deprived of rights guaranteed by the U.S.

Constitution or federal law. Naturally, this Section was thought to apply to claims that a party's rights under federal environmental laws had been violated, thus allowing the injured party to bring a claim contending that their constitutional rights had been violated.

The first case that bears on this issue is *Alexander v. Sandoval*.[3] In that case, the U.S. Supreme Court determined there was no private right of action for citizens claiming that they had suffered a violation of their constitutional rights protecting them against discrimination in federally funded programs. In this class action case, plaintiffs sued the Alabama state public safety director, alleging that the administration of driver's license examinations only in English violated federal nondiscrimination laws (Title VI of the Civil Rights Act of 1964). The plaintiffs won in the 11th Circuit Court of Appeals, which affirmed the trial court decision in favor of the plaintiffs. However, the U.S. Supreme Court reversed, holding that Title VI did not provide for a private cause of action to enforce the statute. While sections of the Civil Rights Act of 1964 do permit private suits to enforce the provisions of various statutes, the Supreme Court noted that "private rights of action to enforce federal laws must be created by Congress." The statute in question in this case did not create a private right of action, nor is Congress's intent to create such a cause of action apparent from the language of the statute. "So far as we can tell, this authorizing portion [of the statute] reveals no congressional intent to create a private right of action."

Next, a relatively new case out of the Second Circuit, *Camden Citizens in Action v. New Jersey Dep't of Environ. Protection*,[4] calls into question the ability of citizens to use Section 1983 to bring civil rights claims for violations of federal environmental laws. In that case, the U.S. District Court had granted an injunction to the plaintiffs against the defendant NJDEP. The plaintiffs claimed that NJDEP had violated the Civil Rights Act (42 U.S.C. sec. 1983) by issuing an air permit in violation of Title VI of the act. The basis for this claim was the plaintiffs' contention that the granting of the permit would have an "adverse disparate racial impact" on them by permitting a cement plant to operate near their homes. However, the Court of Appeals reversed the trial court, holding that "inasmuch as [the statute] proscribes only intentional discrimination, the plaintiffs do not have a right enforceable through a 1983 action under the EPA's disparate impact discrimination regulations." The Court of Appeals relied primarily on *Sandoval* in reaching the conclusion that the EPA regulations

REVIEW

The term *police power* in the environmental context represents the ability of state and local governments to make laws protecting the health, safety, and welfare of their citizens.

police power The power of governments to make laws to protect the health, safety, and welfare of citizens.

did not create a private cause of action that plaintiffs could use to enforce the regulation.

The concern is that, taken together, these two decisions will make it more difficult for citizens to bring claims of "environmental racism" or "environmental elitism." In addition to the local land use processes for siting facilities, there is the further layer of state and local law. State and local governments have **police power**, which is defined as "the power to make laws to protect the health, safety, and welfare of citizens." Police power is not limited to the powers given to a law enforcement agency, but is much broader. It includes the power to regulate the use of land and the safety of roadways.

While the federal government has the exclusive authority to pass statutes concerning matters of federal concern (such as interstate commerce), states are often given authority under the federal statutes to enact laws that meet minimum federal requirements. State government then becomes the primary means through which these federal mandates are enforced. To complicate this even further, states are often permitted to enact standards more stringent than the federal standards. This sometimes leads to inconsistent interpretations and applications of federal law in different states. Moreover, states can pass their own statutes governing environmental issues within their boundaries as long as the state statutes are not in conflict with federal laws. These statutes lead to state regulations and to case law interpreting these statutes and regulations. Some local governments (cities or counties) also have passed ordinances or other local laws governing environmental issues of local concern. Examples include local laws limiting or restricting wood burning and requirements that a certain type of vehicle fuel that is friendlier to the environment be used.

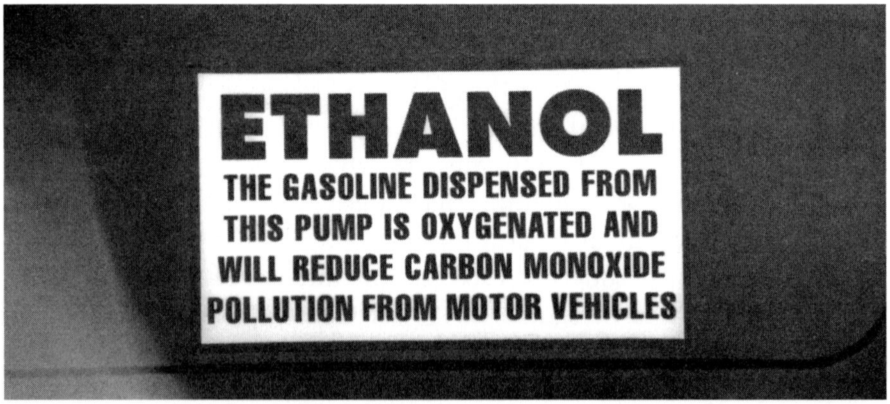

Local governments are taking a more active interest in environmental matters. Many local governments, in addition to allowing increased public input in land use decisions involving LULUs, are evaluating their place in the environmental circle, realizing that environmental issues are important even at the local level. This concept is discussed in the article "Why the Global Environmental Needs Local Government: Lessons from the Johannesburg Summit" by Robert R. M. Verchick (published in *The Urban Lawyer*, Summer 2003, Volume 35, Number 3). In this article, Verchick makes a case for the proposition that responsible development, taking into account environmental issues, is crucial to the success of environmental protection activities worldwide. Consequently, every level of government, from towns and cities to the federal government, has a stake in enacting and enforcing environmental laws to protect human health and the environment.

The scientific study titled "Environmental Regulation and Development: A Cross-Country Empirical Analysis," published in Vol. 29, No. 2, 2001 of the *Oxford Development Studies*, uses indices comparing environmental policies and overall performance of 31 countries. The conclusion of the study is essentially that those countries with strong economic performance show strong environmental performance as well. When a country has a good income per capita, a high degree of urbanization and industrialism, security of property rights, and general administrative efficiency, that country is likely to protect natural resources, regulate water pollution, and impose air pollution controls. Environmental issues touch all levels of government, from nations down to cities; and involvement on all levels is vital to the proper functioning of a global environmental system.

STANDING AND ENVIRONMENTAL LAW

One of the more unique aspects of environmental law is the issue of who, other than the government, may bring suits to enforce environmental laws. Beginning in the late 1960s, organizations began to attempt to enforce legislation concerning the environment by suing in federal courts to force officials of private businesses to comply with environmental provisions. Courts were faced with the problem of deciding when and how these organizations could bring lawsuits in environmental cases.

cases and controversies A phrase describing, collectively, the restraints on federal jurisdiction, such as a prohibition against advisory opinions.

The issue is primarily one raised by the U.S. Constitution. Article III of the Constitution, which creates the federal judicial branch, limits the power of federal courts to decide only **cases and controversies**. The phrase *cases and controversies* has been interpreted by the federal courts to include a number of different restraints on federal jurisdiction. For example, federal courts are prohibited by this provision from issuing advisory opinions; advisory opinions are requests for a court to rule on a legal question without an actual dispute between parties—a kind of "what-if" court ruling. Fedcral courts cannot issue advisory opinions because such situations do not constitute a "case or controversy" as required by Article III of the Constitution.

Another limitation on federal jurisdiction formed by the cases and controversies language is the requirement that plaintiffs in federal court have standing to sue. Parties must have standing to sue in order to bring an action in federal court because judicial power is limited to deciding actual cases and controversies. Standing to sue focuses on whether the plaintiff is the proper party to seek an adjudication of a particular issue in court. Standing means that a plaintiff has a sufficient stake in the case to obtain a sufficient judicial resolution of the controversy.

Some environmental statutes specifically permit an individual citizen to bring a suit to enforce the provisions of the statute. These are sometimes referred to as *private attorney general* provisions because they permit individuals to act as if they were government counsel to enforce the provisions of the statute.

However, many environmental statutes do not contain these private attorney general provisions (including the APA). To be a proper litigant in these situations, a person must have a personal stake in the outcome of the litigation. This personal stake is more than just an interest in the subject matter of the suit. There are three general requirements for standing, as follows:

General Requirements for Standing

1. The plaintiff must have suffered an actual injury or be actually threatened to suffer an injury.
2. The injury must be traceable to the defendant's conduct (the causal connection).
3. The injury must be redressable by a favorable court decision; in other words, the court must be able to prevent or compensate for the injury suffered by the plaintiff.

The standing issue becomes even more complex when the plaintiff is not an individual, but rather an association attempting to sue on behalf of its members. Associational standing requires that the members of the association have standing in their own right; the interests of the members must be those of the association.

The seminal case before the U.S. Supreme Court concerning standing to sue in environmental cases was *Sierra Club v. Morton*.[5]

CASE LAW

SIERRA CLUB V. MORTON, 405 U.S. 727 (1972).

SUMMARY OF CASE: Plaintiff, a conservation organization, sued the Secretary of the Interior, objecting to the defendant's development of national forest into a ski resort. The District Court granted a preliminary injunction; however, the Court of Appeals held that the plaintiff did not have standing to sue and reversed the District Court.

Justice Stewart delivered the opinion of the Court.

The Mineral King Valley is an area of great natural beauty nestled in the Sierra Nevada Mountains in Tulare County, California, adjacent to Sequoia National Park. It has been part of the Sequoia National Forest since 1926, and is designated as a national game refuge by special Act of Congress. Though once the site of extensive mining activity, Mineral King is now used almost exclusively for recreational purposes. Its relative inaccessibility and lack of development have limited the number of visitors each year, and at the same time have preserved the valley's quality as a quasi-wilderness area largely uncluttered by the products of civilization.

The United States Forest Service . . . began in the late 1940s to give consideration to Mineral King as a potential site for recreational development. The proposal of Walt Disney Enterprises, Inc., was chosen from those of six bidders. . . . The final Disney plan, approved by the Forest Service in January 1969, outlines a $35 million complex of motels, restaurants, swimming pools, parking lots, and other structures designed to accommodate 14,000 visitors daily.

Representatives of the Sierra Club, who favor maintaining Mineral King largely in its present state, followed the progress of recreational planning for the valley with close attention and increasing dismay. In June 1969 the Club filed the present suit in the United States District Court for the Northern District of California, seeking a declaratory judgment that various aspects of the proposed development contravene federal laws and regulations governing the preservation of national parks, forests, and game refuges, and also seeking . . . injunctions retraining the federal officials involved from granting their approval or issuing permits in connection with the Mineral King project. . . .

After two days of hearings, the District granted the requested preliminary injunction. . . . The Court of Appeals for the Ninth Circuit reversed . . . [noting] that there was 'no allegation in the complaint that the members of the Sierra Club would be affected by the actions of [the respondents] other than the fact that the actions are personally displeasing or distasteful to them' and concluded that 'we do not believe such club concern without a showing of more direct interest can constitute standing in the legal sense sufficient to challenge the exercise of responsibilities on behalf of all the citizens by two cabinet level officials of the government acting under Congressional and Constitutional authority.' Alternatively, the Court of Appeals held that the Sierra Club had not made an adequate showing of irreparable injury . . . to justify issuance of a preliminary injunction.

The first question presented is whether the Sierra Club has alleged facts that entitle it to obtain judicial review of the challenged action. Whether a party has a sufficient stake in an otherwise justiciable controversy to obtain judicial resolution of that controversy is what has traditionally been referred to as the question of standing to sue. [T]he question of standing depends upon whether the party has alleged such a 'personal stake' in the outcome of the controversy . . . as to ensure that 'the dispute sought to be adjudicated will be presented in an adversary context and in a form historically viewed as capable of judicial resolution.' Where, however, Congress has authorized public officials to perform certain functions according to law . . . the inquiry as to standing must begin with a determination of whether the statute in question authorizes review at the behest of the plaintiff.

Sierra Club relies upon § 10 of the Administrative Procedure Act . . . which provides:

> A person suffering legal wrong because of agency action, or adversely affected or aggrieved by agency action within the meaning of a relevant statute, is entitled to judicial review thereof.

We [have] held . . . that persons had standing to obtain judicial review of federal agency action under § 10 of the APA where they had alleged that the challenged action had caused them 'injury in fact,' and where the alleged injury was to an interest 'arguably within the zone of interests to be protected or regulated' by the statutes that the agencies were claimed to have violated.

[We have not addressed] the question, which has arisen with increasing frequency in federal courts in recent years, as to what must be alleged by persons who claim injury of a noneconomic nature to interests that are widely shared. That question is presented in this case.

The injury alleged by the Sierra Club will be incurred entirely by reason of the change in the uses to which Mineral King will be put, and the attendant change in the aesthetics and ecology of the area. . . . We do not question that this type of harm may amount to an 'injury in fact' sufficient to lay the basis for standing under § 10 of the APA. Aesthetic and environmental well-being, like economic well-being, are important ingredients of the quality of life in our society, and the fact that particular environmental interests are shared by the many rather than the few does not make them less deserving of legal protection through the judicial process. But the 'injury in fact' test requires more than an injury to a cognizable interest. It requires that the party seeking review be himself among the injured.

The impact of the proposed changes in the environment of Mineral King will not fall indiscriminately upon every citizen. The alleged injury will be felt directly only by those who use Mineral King and Sequoia National Park, and for whom the aesthetic and recreational values of the area will be lessened by the highway and ski resort. The Sierra Club failed to allege that it or its members would be affected in any of their activities or pastimes by the Disney development. Nowhere in the pleadings or affidavits did the Club state that its members use Mineral King for any purpose, much less that they use it in any way that would be significantly affected by the proposed actions of the respondents. . . . [T]he Club apparently regarded any allegations of individualized injury as superfluous, on the theory that this was a 'public' action involving questions as to the use of natural resources, and that the Club's longstanding concern with and expertise in such matters were sufficient to give it standing as a 'representative of the public.' This theory reflects a misunderstanding of our cases involving so-called 'public actions' in the area of administrative law.

Some courts have indicated a willingness to [grant standing] by conferring standing upon organizations that have demonstrated 'an organizational interest in the problem' of environmental or consumer protection. . . . It is clear that an organization whose members are injured may represent those members in a proceeding for judicial review . . . but a mere 'interest in a problem,' no matter how longstanding the interest and no matter how qualified the organization is in evaluating the problem, is not sufficient by itself to render the organization 'adversely affected' or 'aggrieved' within the meaning of the APA. . . . [T]he requirement that a party seeking review must allege facts showing that he is himself adversely affected does not insulate executive action from judicial review, nor does it prevent any public interests from being protected through the judicial process. . . . The test of injury in fact goes only to the question of standing to obtain judicial review. Once this standing is established, the party may assert the interests of the general public in support of his claims for equitable relief.

As we conclude that the Court of Appeals was correct in its holding that the Sierra Club lacked standing to maintain this action . . . [t]he judgment is affirmed. ■

QUESTIONS

1. What would the Sierra Club have had to allege in order for the court to find that the club did have standing?
2. Why do you think the Court decided that the Sierra Club did not have standing in this case?

Injury in fact is easy to show when the injury is an economic one; the issue becomes more complex when the injury alleged is to other noneconomic interests. Sierra Club alleged that the injuries to be suffered were changes in the aesthetics and ecology of the park if the ski resort were constructed. In this case, the U.S. Supreme Court acknowledged that potential injuries to aesthetic and environmental well-being were interests that could be protected by the courts.

However, even though the Court determined that environmental interests could be protected, it found that the injury in fact requirement also meant that the party seeking review of the case be himself "among the injured." In this case, the Supreme Court found that the plaintiff, Sierra Club, failed to allege that the club or its members would be affected in any of their activities or pastimes by the development at Mineral King. Sierra Club failed to indicate that any of its members used Mineral King for any purpose. While Sierra Club claimed that its longstanding concern with environmental matters was sufficient to give it standing as a "representative of the public," the Supreme Court rejected this argument; merely being a representative was not sufficient to bring the Sierra Club into the category of someone "affected or aggrieved" by an agency action. The plaintiff "must allege facts showing that he is himself adversely affected"; Sierra Club's failure to do so in this case meant that the organization lacked standing to sue in the Mineral King case. It is interesting to note in this case that the Sierra Club was permitted to amend its complaint to add the required allegations and that the amended complaint was not dismissed on the lack of standing issue. *Sierra Club v. Morton*.[6]

While the U.S. Supreme Court found that the Sierra Club lacked standing in *Sierra Club v. Morton*, the language in this case provided a clear road map for other organizations that wanted to sue to enforce environmental provisions. Later the same year as the *Sierra Club v. Morton* case was announced, a federal District Court in the District of Columbia found that an organization had established standing to sue. In *Students Challenging Regulatory Agency Procedures (SCRAP) v. U.S.*,[7] a group brought a suit under NEPA to prevent the federal Interstate Commerce Commission from imposing a surcharge on interstate shipping of recyclable materials. The organization alleged that its members used these resources, and this allegation was sufficient to give the organization standing to sue under the *Sierra Club* parameters. The *SCRAP* court found that the organization had the right to bring a suit to enforce the rights of its individual members. This case was appealed to the U.S. Supreme Court, where the Court affirmed the ruling that SCRAP had standing to sue.

Other similar rulings followed which granted the Sierra Club standing to sue in environmental cases. In *Sierra Club v. Aluminum Co. of America*,[8] the District Court held that the Sierra Club had standing to sue under the Federal Water Pollution Control Act (FWPCA) where it alleged that the defendant had violated the provisions of its national pollutant discharge elimination system permit. The members, who lived in the area where the water was allegedly being polluted, had a sufficient injury in fact to permit the club standing to sue on their behalf. Similarly, in *Sierra Club v. Block*,[9] the District Court found that the organization had standing to sue federal officials under the Wilderness Act for allegedly failing to claim reserved water rights.

In *Duke Power Co. v. Carolina Environmental Study Group*,[10] the challenge was to place limits on the amount of damages that could be imposed as a result of the operation of nuclear power plants licensed by the Nuclear Regulatory Commission. The U.S. Supreme Court found that the organization had a **personal stake** in the outcome if it could show a "distinct and palpable injury" to the plaintiff and a causal connection between the injury and the challenged conduct.

personal stake A distinct and palpable injury to a plaintiff in a court proceeding and a causal connection between the injury and the challenged conduct.

In *National Wildlife Federation v. Agricultural Stabilization Service,*[11] the Court of Appeals found that an organization had standing to challenge an exemption of 6,500 acres of prairie wetlands in North Dakota. The exemption had been issued under the Food Security Act of 1985, which prohibited federal subsidies for food grown on swampland that had been converted to farmland. The Court found that the organization had established standing due to allegations of injuries to "aesthetic, conservational and recreational values" in the swampland. In *Coalition for the Environment v. Linclay Development Corp.,*[12] a nonprofit environmental organization sued under the APA to force land developers to comply with the NEPA requirements for an environmental impact statement. The Court of Appeals found that the test for standing was twofold: whether the challenged action has caused injury in fact to the plaintiff and whether the injury was to an interest to be protected by the statute allegedly violated.

> 'Injury in fact' is therefore a constitutional limitation on federal jurisdiction and without such injury a case or controversy does not exist . . . . The Supreme Court's opinion in [*Morton*] is unequivocal that those who claim only injury of a non-economic nature may also have standing to challenge governmental action.
>
> *Coalition for the Environment*, p. 165

The Court found that the organization had sufficient interest in these potential noneconomic injuries to grant it standing to sue.

Not all situations where organizations have attempted to sue to enforce environmental statutes have resulted in rulings where the organizations have been determined to have standing to sue. In *Lujan v. Defenders of Wildlife,*[13] the U.S. Supreme Court found that the organization had no standing because it could show only speculation concerning possible future injuries, not injury in fact. Where the organization challenged a requirement under the Endangered Species Act that other agencies consult with the Secretary of the Interior only on federally funded projects, the organization failed to show an imminence of injury. In *Sierra Club v. SCM Corp.,*[14] the Club sued under the Clean Water Act, alleging an excessive discharge of pollutants into a creek. The Court of Appeals found that the organization failed to show "injury in fact" or to identify any member of the organization who had suffered or would suffer such an injury.

A recent case illustrates the variety of standing issues with which courts are tasked in the area of environmental law.

CASE LAW

THE CETACEAN COMMUNITY V. BUSH, 386 F.3D 1169 (9TH CIR. 2004).[15]

SUMMARY OF CASE: A suit was brought against the U.S. government on behalf of the cetacean community of dolphins, whales, and porpoises, alleging that a proposed use of low frequency active sonar (LFAS) violated the Endangered Species Act, NEPA, and the Marine Mammal Protection Act.

Judge Fletcher delivered the opinion of the court.

We are asked to consider whether the world's cetaceans have standing to bring suit in their own name under the Endangered Species Act, the Marine Mammal Protection Act, the National Environmental Protection Act, and the Administrative Procedure Act. We hold that cetaceans do not have standing under these statutes.

The sole plaintiff in this case is the Cetacean Community ("Cetaceans"). The Cetacean Community is the name chosen by the Cetaceans' self-appointed attorney for all of the world's whales, porpoises and dolphins. The Cetaceans challenge the United States Navy's use of Surveillance Towed Array Sensor System Low Frequency Active Sonar ("SURTASS LFAS") during wartime or heightened threat conditions. The Cetaceans allege that the Navy has violated, or will violate, the Endangered Species Act (ESA) . . . the Marine Mammal Protection Act (MMPA) and the National Environmental Protection Act (NEPA). The Navy has developed SURTASS LFAS to assist in detecting quiet submarines at long range. This sonar has both active and passive components. . . . Through their attorney, the Cetaceans contend that SURTASS LFAS harms them by causing tissue damage and other serious injuries, and by disrupting biologically important behaviors including feeding and mating.

The negative effects of underwater noise on marine life are well-recognized. An analysis accompanying the current regulations for the Navy's use of SURTASS LFAS summarizes the harmful effects. . . .

The Cetaceans do not challenge the current regulations. Instead, they seek to compel President Bush and the Secretary of Defense Donald Rumsfeld to undertake regulatory review of use of SURTASS LFAS during threat and wartime conditions. The Navy has specifically excepted such use of SURTASS LFAS from the current regulations. . . . Defendants moved to dismiss the Cetaceans' suit. . . . The court held, *inter alia,* that the Cetaceans lacked standing under the ESA, the MMPA, NEPA and the Administrative Procedure Act (APA).

The Cetaceans contend that an earlier decision of this court requires us to hold that they have standing under the ESA. We first address that decision. In *Palila v. Hawaii Department of Land and Natural Resources,* 857 F.2d 1106

(9th Cir. 1988), a suit to enforce the ESA, we wrote that an endangered member of the honeycreeper family, the Hawaiian Palila bird, "has legal status and wings its way into federal court as a plaintiff in its own right." We wrote, further, that the Palila had "earned the right to be capitalized since it is a party to these proceedings." If these statements . . . constitute a holding that an endangered species has standing to sue to enforce the ESA, they are binding on us in this proceeding.

After due consideration, we agree with the district court that the *Palila* statements are nonbonding dicta. . . . When we decided *Palila*, the case had already been the subject of three published opinions, two by the district court and one by this court. Standing for most of the plaintiffs had always been clear, and standing for the Palila had never been a disputed issue. . . . [W]e noted that "the Sierra Club and others brought an action under the [ESA] on behalf of the Palila."

We have jurisdiction if at least one named plaintiff has standing to sue, even if another named plaintiff to the suit does not. Because the standing of most of the other parties was undisputed in *Palila*, no jurisdictional concerns obliged us to consider whether the Palila had standing. . . . Moreover, we were never asked to decide whether the Palila had standing.

Standing involves two distinct inquiries. First, a . . . federal court must ask whether a plaintiff has suffered sufficient injury to satisfy the "case or controversy" requirement of [the Federal Constitution]. . . . Second, if a plaintiff has suffered sufficient injury . . . a federal court must ask whether a statute has conferred "standing" on that plaintiff.

[The U.S. Constitution] does not compel the conclusion that a statutorily authorized suit in the name of an animal [is] not a "case or controversy." As commentators have observed, nothing in the text of [the Constitution] explicitly limits the ability to bring a claim in federal courts to humans. . . . Animals have many legal rights, protected under both federal and state laws. In some instances, criminal statutes punish those who violate statutory duties that protect animals. . . .

It is obvious that an animal cannot function as a plaintiff in the same manner as a judicially competent human being. But we see no reason why [the Constitution] prevents Congress from authorizing a suit in the name of an animal, any more than it prevents suits brought in the name of artificial persons such as corporations, partnerships or trusts, and even ships, or of judicially incompetent persons such as infants, juveniles and mental incompetents. . . . If [the Constitution] does not prevent Congress from granting standing to an animal by statutorily authorizing a suit in its name, the question becomes whether Congress has passed a statute actually doing so. We therefore turn to whether Congress has granted standing to the Cetaceans under the ESA, the MMPA, NEPA, read either on their own, or through the gloss of . . . the APA. . . .

The ESA contains an explicit provision granting standing to enforce the duties created by the statute. The ESA's citizen-suit provision states that "any person" may "commence a civil suit on his own behalf . . . to enjoin any person, including the United States and any other governmental instrumentality or agency . . . who is alleged to be in violation of any provision of this chapter or regulation." . . . The ESA contains an explicit definition of the "person" who is authorized to enforce the statute. . . . The ESA also contains separate definitions of "species," "endangered species," "threatened species" and "fish and wildlife." . . . It is obvious both from the scheme of the statute, as well as from the statute's explicit definitions of its terms, that animals are the protected rather than the protectors. . . . There is no hint in the definition of "person" . . . that the "person" authorized to bring suit to protect an endangered or threatened species can be an animal that is itself endangered or threatened. . . .

Unlike the ESA, the MMPA contains no explicit provision granting statutory authority to enforce its duties. No court has ever held that an animal—even a marine mammal whose protection is at stake—has standing to sue in its own name to require that party seek a permit or letter of authorization under the MMPA. Absent a clear direction from Congress in either the MMPA or the APA, we hold that animals do not have standing to enforce the permit requirement of the MMPA. . . .

As is true of the MMPA, no provision of NEPA explicitly grants any person or entity standing to enforce the statute, but judicial enforcement of NEPA rights is available through the APA. . . . However, we see nothing in either NEPA or the APA that would permit us to hold that animals who are part of the environment have standing to bring suit on their own behalf.

The Cetaceans argue that even if individual cetaceans do not have standing, their group has standing as an "association" under the APA. . . . We disagree. A generic requirement for associational standing is that an association's "members would otherwise have standing to sue in their own right." As discussed above, individual animals do not have standing to sue under the ESA, the MMPA, NEPA and the APA. . . .

We agree . . . that if Congress and the President intended to take the extraordinary step of authorizing animals as well as people and legal entities to sue, they could, and should, have said so plainly. In the absence of any such statement in the ESA, the MMPA, or NEPA, or the APA, we conclude that the Cetaceans do not have statutory authority to sue.

Affirmed. ■

QUESTIONS

1. Why did the Court determine that the animals did not have the right to sue?
2. Do you think animals should have the right to sue on environmental issues? Why or why not?

The parameters of standing for environmental associations set out in the *Sierra Club v. Morton* case are still in place for organizations seeking to bring suits to enforce environmental statutes. In many cases, organizations can demonstrate that they are representing their members' interest in the noneconomic harm that may be caused by pollution or other ecologically related damage to the environment.

RISK MANAGEMENT AND THE OCCUPATIONAL SAFETY AND HEALTH ACT

risk management An area of management consisting of the evaluation of risks that might affect the successful operation of an entity's activities, attempting to minimize or mitigate those identified risks, and ensuring that sufficient funds or insurance are available to compensate for any losses.

Over the past decade, entities of all sorts have begun using a new concept in risk reduction: **risk management**. Risk management consists of the evaluation of risks that might affect the successful operation of an entity's activities, attempting to minimize or mitigate those identified risks, and ensuring that sufficient funds or insurance are available to compensate for losses, should that become necessary. To the extent risks can be anticipated and dealt with in a thoughtful and effective manner, many environmental losses can be avoided. Loss avoidance is especially important with regard to environmental issues, due to the magnitude of the dollar amounts associated with environmental loss situations.

One of the keys to risk management is to keep damage from increasing incrementally, which can happen when a bad situation is made worse by being handled improperly. An example of this would be when a company or community was to discover that an old, closed landfill had been improperly managed and, as a result, a large volume of soil was contaminated. If the cleanup of the contaminated soil were bungled, the cost and liability to the company or entity would be significantly, and unnecessarily, magnified.

Application of appropriate risk management principles to such a situation is extremely helpful in the successful resolution of an environmental problem. Risk management involves "preventive medicine" as well as assistance in responding to incidents that cannot be prevented. In the "preventive medicine" phase of a facility that implicates environmental law, risk managers can assist by researching the background and environmental history of owners or operators of proposed facilities, can set parameters of a **risk assessment** concerning the facility, and can propose requirements for the operation of the facility that may mitigate any potential risks associated with facility operations. Once a release has occurred or a latent problem has been identified, risk managers can assist by evaluating potential cleanup contractors, identifying applicable insurance or other sources of revenue to pay for the cleanup, and assisting in the filing of forms and reports required as a result of any remediation activities.

risk assessment The process of evaluating risk.

Application of risk management concepts is a relatively new but extremely useful tool in dealing with environmental issues both before and after environmental incidents. All of the environmental laws discussed in this text contain provisions designed to mitigate the risk to human health and the environment from activities that present an environmental risk. However, entities that may be affected by manufacturing, processing, or disposal operations are well served by the use of risk management principles in their assessment of how such facilities might impact their community or how best to remediate an environmental incident.

OCCUPATIONAL SAFETY AND HEALTH ACT (OSH ACT)

One federal agency was created specifically for the purpose of managing risks in the workplace. In 1970, the U.S. Congress enacted the **Occupational Safety and Health Act (OSH Act)**, 29 U.S.C. 651, *et seq.* (1970). Through the OSH Act, Congress also created the

Occupational Safety and Health Act (OSH Act) The federal environmental act enacted to protect the workplace environment.

Occupational Safety & Health Administration (OSHA) The federal agency tasked with the administration and implementation of the Occupational Safety and Health Act (OSH Act).

Occupational Safety & Health Administration (OSHA) as an agency within the Department of Labor (DOL).

Occupational Safety and Health Administration (OSHA)

OSHA has been tasked with ensuring workplace safety. To accomplish its mission, OSHA is required to set limits for employee exposure to toxic substances. The OSH Act requires OSHA to "set the standard which most adequately assures, to the extent feasible, on the basis of the best available evidence, that no employee will suffer material impairment of health or functional capacity even if such employee has regular exposure to the hazard dealt with by such standard for the period of his working life" [29 U.S.C. sec. 655(b)(5)].

National Institute for Occupational Safety and Health (NIOSH) The research institute designed to assist the Occupational Safety & Health Administration (OSHA) set exposure limits for workplace substances.

The OSH Act also established the **National Institute for Occupational Safety and Health (NIOSH)** to assist OSHA in establishing permanent exposure limits. NIOSH is a research agency charged with assisting OSHA by recommending such exposure limits. As a federal regulatory agency, OSHA must comply with the rule-making requirements of the APA in setting exposure limits. As explained in Chapter 1, the APA rule-making process allows for comments from the public and entities that might be affected by the proposed rule. Not all rule-making processes are without controversy, including exposure limits set by OSHA, as is demonstrated by the following case law.

CASE LAW

INDUSTRIAL UNION DEPT., AFL-CIO V. AMERICAN PETROLEUM INSTITUTE, 448 U.S. 607 (1980).[16]

SUMMARY OF CASE: [In October 1976, NIOSH recommended to OSHA that emergency temporary standards (ETS) be adopted for employee exposure to benzene. The NIOSH recommendation was based on studies of workers who had been exposed to benzene and had been diagnosed with an unusually high incidence of leukemia. OSHA adopted an ETS standard for exposure of benzene (one part per million, or ppm), which was invalidated by the Fifth Circuit Court of Appeals. Thereafter, OSHA adopted (through its rule-making procedures) a permissible exposure limit to benzene (also at 1 ppm), which also was invalidated by the Fifth Circuit. In both cases, the federal Court of Appeals held that OSHA had failed to demonstrate that the cost of the standard bore a reasonable relationship to its benefits. OSHA then sought review in the U.S. Supreme Court. After reviewing the scientific studies of exposure to benzene, which the Court criticized as "sketchy at best," the Court took up the matter of the permissible exposure limit.

Justice Stevens delivered the opinion

In the end, OSHA's rationale for lowering the permissible exposure limit to 1 ppm was based, not on any finding that leukemia has ever been caused by exposure to 10 ppm of benzene and that it will *not* be caused at 1 ppm, but rather on a series of assumptions indicating that some leukemias might result from exposure to 10 ppm and that the number of cases might be reduced by reducing the exposure level to 1 ppm. In reaching this result, the Agency first unequivocally concluded that benzene is a human carcinogen. Second, it concluded that industry had failed to prove that there is a safe threshold level of exposure to benzene. [OSHA] determined that 1 ppm was the lowest feasible level of exposure that industry could achieve. Cost estimates for compliance to 1 ppm included $266 million in capital investment, $200 million in start-up costs and $34 million in annual up-keep costs. The OSH Act provides that "occupational safety and health standard" means a standard which requires conditions, or the adoption of use of one or more practices, means, methods, operations or processes, reasonably necessary or appropriate to provide safe or healthful employment and places of employment. The Secretary, in promulgating standards dealing with toxic materials or harmful physical agents under this subsection, shall set the standard which most adequately assures, to the extent feasible, on the basis of the best available evidence, that no employee will suffer material impairment of health or functional capacity even if such employee has regular exposure to the hazard dealt with by such standard for the period of his working life. Development of standards under this subsection shall be based upon research, demonstrations, experiments, and such other information as may be appropriate. In addition, to the attainment of the highest degree of health and safety protection for the employees, other considerations shall be the latest available scientific data in the field, the feasibility of the standards, and experience gained under this and other health and safety laws. [29 U.S.C. sec. 652 (8), 655(b)(5)]

In the Government's view, the definition of the term "standard" has no legal significance. . . . It takes the position that section 655 (b)(5) is controlling and that it requires OSHA to promulgate a standard that either gives an absolute assurance of safety for each and every worker or reduces exposures to the lowest level feasible. The Government interprets "feasible" as meaning technologically achievable at a cost that would not impair the viability of the industries subject to the regulation. The . . . industry representatives, on the other hand, argue that the Court of Appeals was correct in holding that the "reasonably necessary and appropriate language" of [section 652(8)], along with the feasibility requirements . . . requires the Agency to quantify both the

ASSIGNMENT

Does your employer have a risk management program? If so, do you know whether it has successfully reduced or otherwise managed the risk in your organization? If your employer does not have such a program, talk with the appropriate staff person about starting one. You might one day be the beneficiary of such a program.

costs and the benefits of a proposed rule and to conclude that they are roughly commensurate.

. . . We think it is clear that [section 652(8)] does apply to all permanent standards promulgated under the Act and that it requires the Secretary, before issuing any standard, to determine that it is reasonably necessary and appropriate to remedy a significant risk of material health impairment. Only after the Secretary has made the threshold determination that such a risk exists with respect to a toxic substance would it be necessary for him to decide whether [section 655 (b)(5)] requires him to select the most protective standard he can consistent with economic and technological feasibility, or whether, as [the industries] argue, the benefits of the regulation must be commensurate with the costs of its implementation. Because the Secretary did not make the required threshold finding in these cases, we have no occasion to determine whether costs must be weighed against benefits in an appropriate case. . . .

Therefore, before he can promulgate *any* permanent health or safety standard, the Secretary is required to make a threshold finding that a place of employment is unsafe. . . . This requirement applies to permanent standards. . . . For there is no reason why [the definition] of a standard should not be incorporated by reference into [section 655(b)(5)]. . . .

Given the conclusion that the Act empowers the Secretary to promulgate health and safety standards only where a significant risk of harm exists, the critical issue becomes how to define and allocate the burden of proving the significance of the risk in a case such as this, where the scientific knowledge is imperfect and the precise quantification of risk is impossible. The Agency's position is that there is substantial evidence in the record to support its conclusion that there is absolutely no safe level for a carcinogen and that therefore, the burden is properly on industry to prove, apparently beyond a shadow of a doubt, that there *is* a safe level for benzene exposure. . . .

We disagree. As we read the statute, the burden was on the Agency to show, on the basis of substantial evidence, that it is at least more likely than not that long-term exposure to 10 ppm of benzene presents a significant risk of material health impairment. . . .

In this case, OSHA could not even attempt to carry its burden of proof. [The judgment of the Court of Appeals invalidating the regulation was affirmed.] ■

QUESTIONS

1. According to the opinion, how should OSHA have proceeded to promulgate a permanent exposure limit for benzene?

2. Why do you think OSHA argued that industry should bear the burden of proving the "safety" of benzene?

One of the issues for the justices in the Benzene case was whether exposure risks are quantifiable. Ever since the creation of OSHA, various agencies and entities have struggled with the concept of quantifying risks. In 1983, the National Research Council performed a study titled "Risk Assessment in the Federal Government: Managing the Process." This study analyzed the risk assessment process and identified the following four main steps in that process.

Risk Assessment Process

- **Hazard identification:** Is the toxic substance being studied causally linked to particular negative effects to humans or the environment?
- **Dose-response assessment:** How are the exposure levels and the probability of negative effects related?
- **Exposure assessment:** At what level are humans or the environment exposed to the toxic substance?
- **Risk characterization:** How big is the risk?

The study described the elements of risk assessment and risk management through use of a diagram, as shown in Exhibit 2-1.

Another case in which the manner in which OSHA set standards for exposure to toxic substances was *AFL-CIO v. OSHA*.[17] From its creation through 1989, OSHA had promulgated only 24 substance-specific

Elements of Risk Assessment and Risk Management

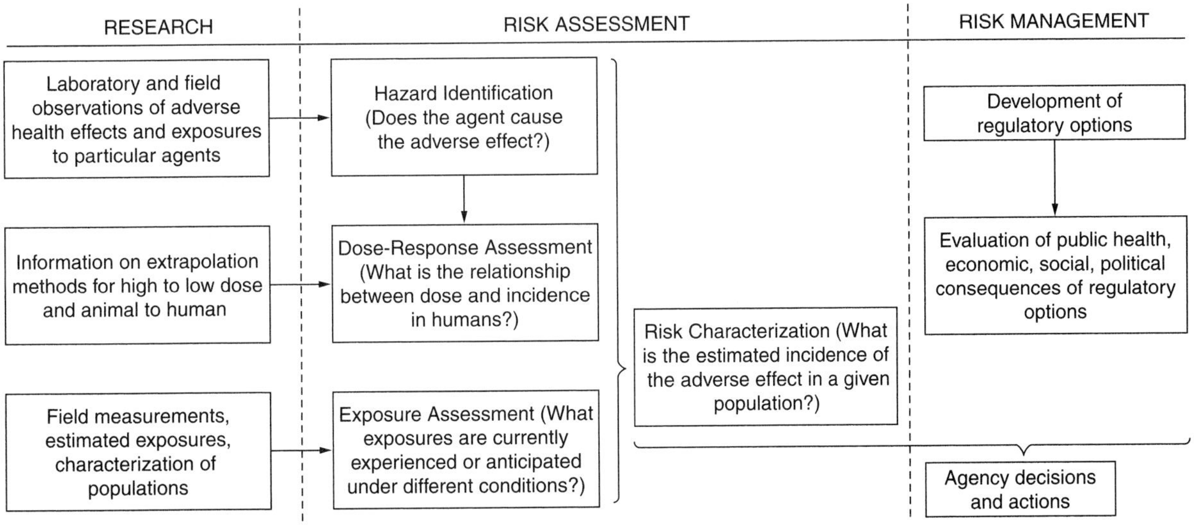
RESEARCH
RISK ASSESSMENT
RISK MANAGEMENT
Laboratory and field observations of adverse health effects and exposures to particular agents
Information on extrapolation methods for high to low dose and animal to human
Field measurements, estimated exposures, characterization of populations
Hazard Identification (Does the agent cause the adverse effect?)
Dose-Response Assessment (What is the relationship between dose and incidence in humans?)
Exposure Assessment (What exposures are currently experienced or anticipated under different conditions?)
Risk Characterization (What is the estimated incidence of the adverse effect in a given population?)
Development of regulatory options
Evaluation of public health, economic, social, political consequences of regulatory options
Agency decisions and actions

EXHIBIT 2-1: RISK ASSESSMENT

health regulations. OSHA's rulemaking was lagging, so OSHA determined to attempt "generic rulemaking" by lumping together many toxic substances in one rulemaking process and allowing limited time for public input. In fact, the rulemaking that was the subject of this litigation involved OSHA promulgating **permissible exposure limits (PELs)** for 428 toxic substances. The allegations made by the industry plaintiffs were that by using this "generic" process, OSHA had failed to create a record sufficient to support its proposed rules concerning the indicated substances. The Court agreed with the industry plaintiffs and found that OSHA was required to quantify, or explain to a reasonable degree, the risk posed by each substance pursuant to the provisions of the OSH Act. The Court indicated that OSHA must make a finding that a significant risk of material health impairment exists for each substance at the current levels of exposure and that a new lower level of exposure is necessary to maintain a safe workplace environment. Thus, OSHA's attempt to "catch up" on setting workplace standards for toxic substances was dealt a blow, and OSHA had to go back and establish the standards for each toxic substance in a reasonable individual manner.

permissible exposure limits (PELs) A standard representing the maximum amount of any substance to which someone may be exposed in the workplace as set by the Occupational & Safety Health Administration (OSHA).

Despite the challenges to its rulemaking, over time, OSHA has successfully enacted many rules to manage the identified risks for the protection of employees. Every workplace in the United States that is subject to OSHA requirements ("covered employers") must post certain posters and signs as part of the OSHA notification and risk management process. To ensure that employees know what protections they have, OSHA has printed a new "Plain Language" poster (OSHA 3165) available in Spanish and English; the poster must be posted in a conspicuous place where employees and applicants for employment can see it. Many individuals are not aware of the protections afforded by more obscure environmental acts, such as the Federal Insecticide, Fungicide, and Rodenticide Act (FIFRA); but they have heard of OSHA and know that it offers protection to the workplace environment.

FEATURE

Sierra Club

Many of the first environmental law court cases were brought by an organization called the Sierra Club. Environmental litigation involving the Sierra Club has contributed to the definition of "standing" in such cases (see "Standing and

Environmental Law" in this chapter), has tested the validity of laws and regulations enacted in the environmental arena, and has educated the courts and the public concerning environmental issues.

What is the Sierra Club? The Sierra Club is a corporation founded in 1892 that had 182 charter members at its inception. In its first year, the Sierra Club successfully campaigned to defeat a proposed reduction in the boundaries of Yosemite National Park. In 1893, then-president of the United States, Benjamin Harrison, established a 13 million-acre Sierra Forest Reserve. These two early projects of the Sierra Club are typical of the types of environmentally related activities in which the organization has become involved since 1892.

THE MISSION STATEMENT OF THE SIERRA CLUB IS TO

1. explore, enjoy, and protect the wild places of the earth.
2. practice and promote the responsible use of the earth's ecosystems and resources.
3. educate and enlist humanity to protect and restore the quality of the natural and human environment.
4. use all lawful means to carry out these objectives.

EARLY INFLUENCES

The mission of the Sierra Club was taken initially from the interests of its first president, John Muir. John Muir was born in Scotland in 1838 and moved with his farming family to Wisconsin in 1849. Mr. Muir loved the outdoors and became a passionate observer of the natural world. To sate this passion, Mr. Muir began to wander the world. He walked 1,000 miles from Indianapolis to California. He visited Cuba and Panama, eventually returning to California, which became his home. He loved the Sierra Nevada region and lived in Yosemite. As a writer, he wrote a series of articles titled "Studies in the Sierra" and a book titled *The Mountains of California*. Eventually, he published more than 300 articles and 10 major books telling stories of his travels. Mr. Muir was deeply involved in lobbying for the creation of Yosemite, Sequoia, Mount Rainier, Petrifed Forest, and Grand Canyon National Parks. As a result, he has been called the "Father of Our National Park System."

A friend suggested to Muir that there should be an association of like-minded people who loved nature and were willing to work to protect it. Mr. Muir once said that the Sierra Club, which became that association, was founded to "do something for wildness and make the mountains glad." The Sierra Club was incorporated in 1892, with its stated purpose "to explore, enjoy, and render accessible the mountain regions of the Pacific Coast; to publish authentic information concerning them; and to enlist the support and cooperation of the people and government in preserving the forests and other natural features of the Sierra Nevada." Mr. Muir was the president of the Sierra Club until he died in 1914. Mr. Muir's legacy and influence is the message of the Sierra Club that nature is to be protected for the enjoyment and use of future generations. In 2005, a new coin was unveiled—a John Muir commemorative quarter. The quarter depicts John Muir standing with a walking stick, looking across at Yosemite Valley, with a California condor soaring in the sky.

Another key contributor to the efforts of the Sierra Club was the photographer Ansel Adams. Mr. Adams was supportive of the work of the Sierra Club for more than 50 years. His black-and-white photographs of nature have inspired many others to become involved in the preservation of wilderness areas.

Fittingly, wilderness areas in California have been named after both John Muir and Ansel Adams.

Sierra Club Activities

Over the years, the Sierra Club has been active in many areas of the environmental movement. From the first efforts to convince the federal government to set aside land for national parks to the present-day efforts to address emerging environmental issues, the Sierra Club has been a major participant in raising the consciousness of citizens to environmental issues.

Since many of the 182 founders of the Sierra Club were scientists, many of the first ventures of the new club involved reporting about excursions, geography, natural history, and forestry.

In the 1930s, the Sierra Club built a series of trails through the Sierra (the main trail would be named after John Muir); and those trails survive to this day. Members of the Sierra Club began to go on expeditions outside California, visiting British Columbia, Alaska, Peru, and even the Himalayas. Through the use of ropes, rock climbing became a favorite pastime of Sierra Club members; and many of the climbs in Yosemite Park were first mapped by Sierra Club aficionados.

Eventually, the major push of the Sierra Club changed from one of encouraging accessibility to natural areas to one of encouraging preservation of natural areas. The outings of the club began to highlight conservation and education along with recreation. Thus began the practice of the Sierra Club to use its outings to educate not only the general public but also government workers, politicians, and corporate officers concerning the need for preservation and conservation of the country's natural resources.

As the Sierra Club grew in scope and influence, it began to hire teams of attorneys to fight in court for the environmental values of club members. The Sierra Club has an Environmental Law Program, with lawyers in California, Colorado, and Washington, D.C. practicing on behalf of the Club. Additionally, outside counsel has often been retained for specific cases. As mentioned earlier, Sierra Club lawsuits were significant in determining who has standing to bring an action related to an environmental issue. Within the past couple of decades, the Sierra Club has taken on many legal cases in support of its causes.

Some of the pending litigation filed by the Sierra Club includes a suit against the Mississippi Department of Environmental Quality for granting permits that would allow expansion of the DuPont DeLisle plant in Mississippi. According to the Sierra Club, this plant discharges almost 14 million pounds of toxic chemicals each year (including about 42 percent of the dioxins released in the entire United States). The plant is located near a low-income, minority community that allegedly has citizens already showing signs of negative health effects from the plant as it presently operates. The lawsuit by the Sierra Club seeks to require DuPont to install appropriate pollution controls to address the expanded production and to make reparations for past pollution violations.

In another lawsuit brought by the Sierra Club, a federal judge in California recently ruled that the Bureau of Reclamation has unlawfully operated the Friant Dam near Fresno, California. The entire flow of the San Joaquin River has been diverted to irrigation canals, drying up a 50-mile stretch of the river. This diversion of water has decimated fisheries and affected spawning salmon. The decision by the judge, after 16 years of litigation, was that the government must take immediate steps to restore the portions of the river system affected by the actions of the Bureau of Reclamation. The restoration will not only impact the wildlife in the area but also will assist in providing reliable drinking water to the San Francisco Bay area and southern California.

Also, in the United States Court of Appeals for the Ninth Circuit, *Natural Resources Defense Council v. United States Forest Service, et al.*, No. 04-35868, D.C. No. CV-03-00029-J-JKS, District of Alaska, Juneau, a federal judge granted the emergency motion of the Natural Resources Defense Council for an injunction to prohibit a timber sale temporarily until it can be determined whether an admitted mistake in the calculation as to the market demand for timber affected a proposed plan to balance the commercial selling of logs with preserving old-growth forests. Such a balance calculation is required by the National Forest Management Act (NFMA) and the land management plan applicable to the area in question.

These are the types of environmental litigation matters with which the Sierra Club concerns itself. All of the efforts of the Sierra Club, from litigation to education to recreation, are intended to support the mission and goals of the organization as indicated earlier. John Muir, in *My First Summer in the Sierra*, expressed the sentiments of members of the Sierra Club when he wrote:

> From meadow to meadow, every one beautiful beyond telling, and from lake to lake through groves and belts of arrowy trees, I held my way northward . . . finding telling beauty everywhere, while the encompassing mountains were calling "Come." I hope I may climb them all. ■

SUMMARY

Environmental law has developed in the United States primarily since the early 1970s. Each decade since the seventies has brought new understandings and new appreciation for the environmental issues society faces. Even local governments have begun to address environmental issues within their borders. Newer concepts, such as environmental justice and LULUs, have a role in the study and practice of environmental law. Older concepts, such as the concept of standing to bring a lawsuit, have been reexplored as part of the evolution of environmental law. Risk assessment and risk management are factors in the workplace environment through the OSH Act and the efforts of OSHA.

KEY TERMS

- Cases and controversies
- Environmental elitism
- Environmental justice
- Environmental racism
- Locally undesirable land uses (LULUs)
- National Institute for Occupational Safety and Health (NIOSH)
- Not-in-My-Back-Yard (NIMBY)
- Occupational Safety and Health Act (OSH Act)

- Occupational Safety & Health Administration (OSHA)
- Permissible exposure limits (PELs)
- Personal stake
- Police power
- Risk assessment
- Risk management

REVIEW QUESTIONS AND HANDS-ON ACTIVITIES

1. What was the first major environmental law? When was it passed?
2. Environmental laws have been in place in the United States for only about 30 years. Do you think that environmental laws affect citizens on a daily basis? Explain your answer.
3. In your local newspaper, find an article about a controversial development in your community. Follow the story and see how the community reacts to the issues and how long the issues are newsworthy.
4. Review the ordinances or resolutions of your nearest metropolitan area. What processes are in effect for the public to comment on or contribute to decisions related to LULUs?
5. Evaluate the cases in this chapter related to the section "Standing and Environmental Law." Has the concept of standing evolved sufficiently to address the standing issues that are unique to environmental law, such as whether whales have standing to bring a lawsuit?
6. How have the standing criteria changed over the past 30 years for environmental law? Do you see any continuing trend related to standing criteria?
7. What is risk management, and how is it linked to environmental law?
8. Do you think that OSHA accomplishes the purposes for which it was intended?
9. OSHA contends that it has reduced workplace fatalities by more than 60 percent and workplace illnesses and injuries by 40 percent

even though employment in the United States has doubled from 58 million workers at 3.5 million worksites to 115 million workers at 7.2 million worksites. (Source: OSHA website) Do you believe that working conditions in the United States have improved to the point where OSHA is no longer needed? Why or why not?

HELPFUL WEBSITES

http://www.cdc.gov/niosh (NIOSH)

http://www.epa.gov./compliance (EPA, Compliance and Enforcement)

http://www.ejrc.cau.edu (Environmental Justice Resource Center at Clark Atlanta University)

http://www.epa.gov/compliance/environmentaljustice/index.html (EPA, Environmental Justice)

http://www.epa.gov/compliance/environmentaljustice/interagency/index.html (EPA, Environmental Justice, Interagency Working Group)

http://www.epa.gov/ocr (EPA, Civil Rights)

http://www.eli.org (Environmental Law Institute)

http://www.lawvianet.com (Environmental LawNet)

http://www.osha.gov (OSHA)

ENDNOTES

1. *Scenic Hudson Preservation Conference v. Federal Power Commission*, 354 F.2d 608 (2d Cir. 1965).
2. *East Bibb Twiggs Nhd. Assoc. v. Macon-Bibb County Planning Zoning Comm.*, 706 F. Supp. 880 (M.D.Ga. 1989), aff'd, 888 F.2d 1573 (11th Cir. 1989).
3. *Alexander v. Sandoval*, 532 U.S. 275 (2001).
4. *Camden Citizens in Action v. New Jersey Dep't of Environ. Protection*, 274 F.3d 771 (2d Cir. 2001), cert. den., 536 U.S. 939 (2002).
5. *Sierra Club v. Morton*, 405 U.S. 727 (1972).

6. *Sierra Club v. Morton*, 348 F. Supp. 219 (N.D. Cal. 1972).
7. *Students Challenging Regulatory Agency Procedures (SCRAP) v. U.S.*, 346 F. Supp. 189 (D.C. DC 1972), aff'd sub. nom., *United States v. Students Challenging Regulatory Agency Procedures*, 412 U.S. 669 (1973).
8. *Sierra Club v. Aluminum Co. of America*, 585 F. Supp. 842 (D.C. NY 1984).
9. *Sierra Club v. Block*, 622 F. Supp. 842 (D. Colo. 1985).
10. *Duke Power Co. v. Carolina Environmental Study Group*, 438 U.S. 59 (1978).
11. *National Wildlife Federation v. Agricultural Stabilization Service*, 901 F.2d 673 (8th Cir. 1980).
12. *Coalition for the Environment v. Linclay Development Corp.*, 504 F.2d 156 (8th Cir. 1974).
13. *Lujan v. Defenders of Wildlife*, 504 U.S. 555 (1992).
14. *Sierra Club v. SCM Corp.*, 747 F.2d 99 (8th Cir. 1984).
15. *The Cetacean Community v. Bush*, 386 F.3d 1169 (9th Cir. 2004).
16. *Industrial Union Dept., AFL-CIO v. American Petroleum Institute*, 448 U.S. 607 (1980).
17. *AFL-CIO v. OSHA*, 965 F.2d 962 (11th Cir. 1992).

CHAPTER 3

NATIONAL ENVIRONMENTAL POLICY ACT (NEPA)

TITLE: The National Environmental Policy Act (NEPA)

CITATION: 42 U.S.C. Sections 4321-4370c (1969)

REGULATIONS: 40 C.F.R. 1500.1 *et. seq.*

PURPOSE: To create a national environmental policy and allow public input into the process of formulating a national response to environmental issues. To require federal agencies to consider environmental issues as they implement projects.

HISTORY: Employment Act of 1946
Resources and Conservation Act of 1960

LEARNING OBJECTIVES

After studying this chapter, the reader should be able to

- describe the differences between this environmental law and other environmental laws.
- explain NEPA's nature as a procedural, rather than substantive, law.
- explain the definitions and functions of an EA and an EIS.
- describe what the "hard look" doctrine is and how it applies to environmental activities.

NATIONAL ENVIRONMENTAL POLICY ACT

The National Environmental Policy Act (NEPA) may well be the most innovative environmental law yet enacted in the United States. Before NEPA was passed, lawmakers heard from citizens who were increasingly concerned about the deteriorating condition of the environment in the United States and the possible consequences as a result of that situation.

While there had been an early attempt through the Resources and Conservation Act of 1960 to create a national council of environmental advisers, that act was not successful in creating a national environmental policy. Thus, NEPA took effect on January 1, 1970, as an attempt to establish a system for the formulation of a national environmental policy.

ELEMENTS OF NEPA

NEPA's three most important elements are as follows:

ELEMENTS OF NEPA

1. A declaration of national environmental policies and goals
2. Establishment of "action-forcing" provisions, ensuring compliance with those policies and goals
3. Establishment of a Council on Environmental Quality (CEQ) in the Office of the President of the United States

Council on Environmental Quality (CEQ) Three individuals appointed by the president of the United States and confirmed by the Senate. Their job is to assist the president in assessing the quality of the environment, determining whether federal agencies are complying with the requirements of the National Environmental Policy Act (NEPA), and suggesting new national policies to preserve and improve the environment.

QUESTION

Had you ever heard of the CEQ before reading about it in this text? Find out who the current appointees are to the CEQ. Do the three people appointed to the CEQ have too much influence on national environmental policy? Explain.

The environmental policies and goals set forth in NEPA are general and broad in nature. They highlight the impact of human activity on the environment, emphasize the need to create a healthy human environment, and recognize the need to preserve and enhance the environment.

NEPA forces federal agencies to give environmental issues due consideration in their decision making as they begin projects. NEPA also creates the **Council on Environmental Quality (CEQ)**. The three individuals appointed to the CEQ by the president of the United States (and confirmed by the U.S. Senate) are tasked by NEPA to assist the president with assessing the quality of the environment, determining whether federal agencies are complying with NEPA's requirements, and suggesting new national policies to preserve and improve the environment. President Clinton created the Office of Environmental Policy and announced that in 1994, it would be merged with the CEQ. The combination of these two offices strengthened the CEQ, which had been operating with limited staff and resources for several years prior to President Clinton's actions.

CEQ regulations require federal agencies to incorporate NEPA requirements into their plans in the early stages. NEPA requires agencies to use a "systematic, interdisciplinary approach" and to creatively conceive of alternatives as the agencies begin the planning process. The provisions of NEPA make these requirements mandatory for all federal agencies. Interestingly, the only federal agency to which courts have given some limited exemption from having to follow the requirements of NEPA is the EPA. NEPA does not give the EPA any exemption (although subsequent acts such as the Energy Supply and Environmental Coordination Act of 1974, the Clean Air Act (CAA), and the Clean Water Act (CWA) provide some relief for the EPA), but the EPA has successfully argued that since its job is the protection of the environment, it naturally is presumed to take environmental issues into account when performing its duties under the law.

REVIEW
NEPA is a procedural act, rather than a substantive act.

The difference between NEPA and other federal environmental acts is that the requirements of NEPA are "procedural" rather than substantive. NEPA has no set scientific standards to be applied with respect to the subject matters it covers; rather, it requires that federal agencies follow certain procedures during the decision-making process prior to the implementation of particular types of federal projects. This focus on procedural matters and national policy, rather than scientific standards and treatment methodologies, is part of what makes NEPA unique among federal environmental acts.

The mandates of NEPA were succinctly stated by the U.S. District Court in *Calvert Cliffs' Coordinating Comm. Inc. v. United States Atomic Energy Comm'n.*[1]

CASE LAW

CALVERT CLIFFS' COORDINATING COMM. INC. V. UNITED STATES ATOMIC ENERGY COMM'N, 449 F.2D 1109 (D.C. CIR. 1971).

SUMMARY OF CASE: Petitioners in three different cases (consolidated for this appeal) argued that the Atomic Energy Commission's regulations did not require an exercise of discretion that would protect the environment "to the fullest extent possible," as required by NEPA.

Circuit Judge Wright delivered the opinion of the court.

These cases are only the beginning of what promises to become a flood of new litigation—litigation seeking judicial assistance in protecting our natural environment. Several recently enacted statutes attest to the commitment of the Government to control, at long last, the destructive engine of material "progress."

But it remains to be seen whether the promise of this legislation will become a reality. Therein likes the judicial role. In these cases, we must for the first time interpret the broadest and perhaps the most important of the recent statutes: the National Environmental Policy Act of 1969 (NEPA). We must assess claims that one of the agencies charged with its administration has failed to live up to the congressional mandate. Our duty, in short, is to see that important legislative purposes, heralded in the halls of Congress, are not lost or misdirected in the vast hallways of the federal bureaucracy.

NEPA, like so many other reform legislations of the past 40 years, is cast in terms of a general mandate and broad delegation of authority to new and old administrative agencies. It takes the major step of requiring all federal agencies to consider values of environmental preservation in their spheres of activity and it prescribes certain procedural measures to ensure that those values are in fact fully respected. Petitioners argue that rules recently adopted by the Atomic Energy Commission [AEC] to govern consideration of environmental matters fail to satisfy the rigor demanded by NEPA. The Commission, on the other hand, contends that the vagueness of the NEPA mandate and delegation leaves much room for discretion and that the rules challenged by petitioners fall well within the broad scope of the Act. We find the policies embodied in NEPA to be a good deal clearer and more demanding than does the Commission. We conclude that the Commission's procedural rules do not comply with the congressional policy. Hence we remand these cases for further rule making.

We begin our analysis with an examination of NEPA's structure and approach. . . . The relevant portion of NEPA . . . sets forth the Act's basic substantive policy: that the federal government "use all practicable means and measures" to protect environmental values. Congress did not establish environmental protection as an exclusive goal; rather, it desired a reordering of priorities, so that environmental costs and benefit will assume their proper place along with other considerations. . . . [T]he Act provides that "it is the continuing responsibility of the Federal government to use all practicable means, consistent with other essential considerations of national policy," to avoid environmental degradation, preserve "historic, cultural, and natural" resources, and promote "the widest range of beneficial uses of the environment without undesirable and unintended consequences."

Thus the general policy of the Act is a flexible one. It leaves room for a responsible exercise of discretion and may not require particular substantive results in particular problematic instances. However, the Act also contains very important "procedural" provisions—provisions which are designed to see that all federal agencies do in fact exercise the substantive discretion given them.

These provisions are not highly flexible. Indeed, they establish a strict standard of compliance.

NEPA, first of all, makes environmental protection a part of the mandate of every federal agency and department. The [AEC], for example, had continually asserted, prior to NEPA, that it had no statutory authority to concern itself with the adverse environmental effects of its actions. Now, however, its hands are no longer tied. It is not only permitted, but compelled, to take environmental values into account. Perhaps the greatest importance of NEPA is to require the [AEC] and other agencies to *consider* environmental issues just as they consider other matters within their mandates.

The sort of environmental values which NEPA compels is clarified. . . . In general, all agencies must use a "systematic, interdisciplinary approach" to environmental planning and evaluation "in decisionmaking which may have an impact on man's environment." In order to include all possible methods and procedures . . . which will "insure that presently unquantified environmental amenities and values may be given appropriate consideration in decisionmaking along with economic and technical considerations." "Environmental amenities" will often be in conflict with "economic and technical considerations." To "consider" the former "along with" the latter must involve a balancing process. In some instances environmental costs may outweigh economic and technical benefits and in other instances they may not. But NEPA mandates a rather finely tuned and "systematic" balancing analysis in each instance.

To ensure that the balancing analysis is carried out and given full effect, [NEPA] requires that responsible officials of all agencies prepare a "detailed statement" covering the impact of particular actions on the environment, the environmental costs which might be avoided, and alternative measures which might alter the costbenefit equation. . . . [B]y compelling a formal 'detailed statement' and a description of alternatives, NEPA provides evidence that the mandated decision making process has in fact taken place and, most importantly, allows those removed from the initial process to evaluate and balance the factors on their own.

Of course, all of these . . . duties are qualified by the phrase "to the fullest extent possible." We must stress as forcefully as possible that this language does not provide an escape hatch for footdragging agencies; it does not make NEPA's procedural requirements somehow "discretionary." Congress did not intend the Act to be such a paper tiger. Indeed, the requirement of environmental consideration "to the fullest extent possible" sets a high standard for the agencies, a standard which must be rigorously enforced by the reviewing courts.

We conclude, then that . . . NEPA mandates a particular sort of careful and informed decision making process and creates judicially enforceable duties. The reviewing courts probably cannot reverse a substantive decision on its merits . . . unless it be shown that the actual balance of costs and benefits that was struck was arbitrary or clearly gave insufficient weight to environmental values. But if the decision was reached procedurally without individualized consideration and balancing of environmental factors—conducted fully and in good faith—it is the responsibility of the courts to reverse.

In the cases before us now, we do not have to review a particular decision by the [AEC] granting a construction permit or an operating license. Rather, we must review the [AEC]'s recently promulgated rules which govern consideration of environmental values in all such individual decisions. The rules were devised strictly in order to comply with the NEPA procedural requirements—but petitioners argue that they fall far short of the congressional mandate.

. . . The [AEC] regulations provide that in an uncontested proceeding the hearing board shall on its own "determine whether the application and the record . . . contain sufficient information . . . to support affirmative findings" on various nonenvironmental factors. NEPA requires at least as much automatic consideration of environmental factors. In uncontested hearings, the board need not necessarily go over the same ground covered in the "detailed statement." But it must at least examine the statement carefully to determine whether "the review by the [AEC] regulatory staff has been adequate." And it must independently consider the final balance among conflicting factors that is struck in the staff's recommendation.

The rationale of the Commission's limitation of environmental issues to hearings in which parties affirmatively raise those issues may have been one of economy. . . . But all of the NEPA procedures take time. Such . . . costs are not enough to undercut the Act's requirement that environmental protection be considered "to the fullest extent possible."

. . . We hold that . . . the [AEC] must revise its rules governing consideration of environmental issues. We do not impose a harsh burden on the Commission. For we require only an exercise of substantive discretion which will protect the environment "to the fullest extent possible." No less is required if the grand congressional purposes underlying NEPA are to become a reality.

Remanded for proceedings consistent with this opinion. ■

QUESTIONS

1. What does the court say is the underlying purpose of NEPA?

2. How does the court say that the Commission failed to meet the requirements of NEPA?

APPLICABILITY OF NEPA

What types of actions invoke the requirements of NEPA? NEPA's requirements apply only to certain types of actions by federal agencies. If a proposed federal action docs not "individually or cumulatively have a significant effect on the human environment" (as determined by examining the proposed action itself and by examining the results of similar actions), the action is considered a "non-major action" and is categorically excluded from the requirements of NEPA. 40 C.F.R. Section 1508.4 (1991). Also, actions that have only "minor" federal involvement may be exempted from NEPA. A case in which the parameters of NEPA were considered is *Norton v. Southern Utah Wilderness Alliance.*[2]

CASE LAW

NORTON V. SOUTHERN UTAH WILDERNESS ALLIANCE, 542 U.S. 55 (2004).

SUMMARY OF CASE: Environmental organizations sued the Bureau of Land Management (BLM) seeking declaratory and injunctive relief for BLM's failure to act to protect public lands from damage caused by off-road vehicle (ORV) use. The Tenth Circuit Court of Appeals held that BLM could be required under the APA to comply with its nonimpairment obligation.

Justice Scalia delivered the opinion of the Court.

In this case, we must decide whether the authority of a federal court under the Administrative Procedure Act (APA) to "compel agency action unlawfully withheld or unreasonably delayed" . . . extends to the review of the [BLM]'s stewardship of public lands under certain statutory provisions and its own planning documents.

Almost half the State of Utah, about 23 million acres, is federally administered by the Bureau of Land Management (BLM), an agency within the Department of the Interior. For nearly 30 years, BLM's management of public lands has been governed by the Federal Land Policy and Management Act of 1976 (FLMPA) . . . which "established a policy in favor of retaining public lands for multiple use management."

Of course, not all uses are compatible. Congress made the judgment that some lands should be set aside as wilderness at the expense of commercial and recreational uses. . . . The designation of a wilderness area can only be made by an Act of Congress.

In 1991 . . . 2 million [acres] were recommended as suitable for wilderness designation. This recommendation was forwarded to Congress, which has not yet acted upon it. Until Congress acts one way or the other, FLPMA provides that "the Secretary shall continue to manage such lands . . . in a manner so as not to impair the suitability of such areas for preservation as wilderness."

Protection of wilderness has come into increasing conflict with another element of multiple use, recreational use of so-called off-road vehicles (ORVs), which include vehicles primarily designed for off-road use, such as sport utility vehicles. . . . [T]he use of ORVs on federal land has negative environmental consequences, including soil disruption and compaction, harassment of animals, and annoyance of wilderness lovers. . . . The BLM faces a classic land use dilemma of sharply inconsistent uses, in a context of scarce resources and congressional silence with respect to wilderness designation.

In 1999, respondents . . . filed this action . . . against BLM . . . [and] sought declaratory and injunctive relief for BLM's failure to act to protect public lands in Utah from damage caused by ORV use . . . [claiming]that BLM had failed to take a "hard look" at whether, pursuant to the National Environmental Policy Act of 1969 (NEPA) . . . it should undertake supplemental environmental analyses for areas in which ORV use had increased.

The District Court entered a dismissal . . . [and] the Tenth Circuit reversed. The majority acknowledged that [under the APA] "federal courts may order agencies to act only where the agency fails to carry out a mandatory, nondiscretionary duty." It concluded, however, that BLM's nonimpairment obligation was just such a duty, and therefore BLM could be compelled to comply. . . .

The APA authorizes suit by "[a] person suffering legal wrong because of agency action, or adversely affected or aggrieved by agency action within the meaning of a relevant statute." . . . Thus a claim . . . can only proceed where a plaintiff asserts that an agency failed to take a *discrete* agency action that it is *required to take*. . . . [T]he limitation to *required* agency action rules out judicial direction of even discrete agency action that is not demanded by law. . . . [T]hus when an agency is compelled by law to act within a certain time period, but the manner of its action is left to the agency's discretion, a court can compel the agency to act, but has no power to specify what the action must be. . . .

With these principles in mind, we turn to [the] claim that by permitting ORV use in certain [areas], BLM violated its mandate to "continue to manage . . . in a manner so as not to impair the suitability of such areas for preservation as wilderness." . . . [The statute] is mandatory as to the object to be achieved, but it leaves BLM a great deal of discretion in deciding how to achieve it. It assuredly does not mandate, with the clarity necessary to support judicial action . . . , the total exclusion of ORV use.

Finally, we turn to [the claim] that BLM failed to fulfill certain obligations under NEPA. . . . NEPA requires a federal agency to prepare an environmental impact statement (EIS) as part of any "proposals for legislation and other major Federal actions significantly affecting the quality of the human environment." Often an initial EIS is sufficient, but in certain circumstances an EIS must be supplemented. [W]e interpreted [NEPA] . . . to require an agency to take a "hard look" at the new information to assess whether supplementation might be necessary.

[Plaintiff] argues that evidence of increased ORV use is "significant new circumstances or information" that requires a "hard look." We disagree. As we noted . . . supplementation is necessary only if "there remains 'major Federal action[n]' to occur. . . . " Here . . . [t]here is no ongoing "major Federal action" that could require supplementation.

The judgment of the Court of Appeals is reversed. . . . ■

QUESTIONS

1. Why did the Court find that there was no "major Federal action" in this case?
2. Do you agree that there was no "major Federal action"? Why or why not?

Another such case is *Department of Transportation v. Public Citizen.*[3] In that case, Public Citizen and other organizations sued the Department of Transportation (DOT) for alleged violations of NEPA and the CAA. The petitioners claimed that DOT issued rules for the regulation of Mexican motor carriers without considering any environmental impact that Mexican trucks could cause within the United States. The trucks were to enter the United States after the president lifted a moratorium on Mexican trucks because the moratorium was in violation of the North American Free Trade Agreement (NAFTA).

The rules adopted by DOT were not accompanied by an EIS, as required by NEPA. The petitioners claimed that the presence of Mexican motor carriers in the United States would likely have an impact on the environment (increased emissions, noise, etc.) and that, therefore, an EIS was required. DOT issued a Finding of No Significant Impact (FONSI), which the petitioners claimed was "arbitrary and capricious" since it failed to take these environmental impacts into consideration.

The Supreme Court found that DOT had no ability to countermand the president's decision to lift the moratorium on Mexican motor carriers. Because DOT had no discretion but to regulate and inspect the motor carriers, an EIS would serve no purpose and, therefore, was not required under NEPA. The connection between DOT's regulation of the Mexican motor carriers and the entry of the trucks is insufficient to make DOT responsible under NEPA. Since DOT would be unable to act on an EIS, if prepared, it made no sense to require an EIS. Therefore,

> . . . where an agency has no ability to prevent a certain effect due to its limited statutory authority over the relevant actions, the agency cannot be considered a legally relevant 'cause' of the effect. Hence, under NEPA . . . the agency need not consider these effects in its [EIA] when determining whether its action is a "major Federal action."
>
> p. 2217

These cases have been helpful in understanding when the requirements of NEPA apply to the actions of federal agencies.

environmental assessment (EA) The beginning of the process found in the National Environmental Policy Act (NEPA) to determine the impact of certain proposed federal actions.

environmental impact statement (EIS) A detailed analysis of the environmental impact of a proposed federal action. Follows the environmental assessment (EA) as part of the NEPA process.

Finding of No Significant Impact (FONSI) A FONSI finding is a conclusion by a federal agency that a proposed action will not have a significant impact on the environment. Such a finding is one of the possible conclusions reached as part of the evaluation process set forth in the National Environmental Policy Act (NEPA). The NEPA process includes the completion of an environmental assessment (EA), which can be used to make a FONSI determination.

ENVIRONMENTAL ASSESSMENTS

What are NEPA's procedural requirements? First, it is necessary for any federal agency with a proposed project to do an **environmental assessment (EA)**. An EA is a preliminary way of screening a project to determine if the agency will have to prepare a full-blown **environmental impact statement (EIS)**. The EA includes a discussion of the need for the project, a list of alternatives for implementing the project, the anticipated environmental impacts of the listed alternatives, and a review of the agencies and people who were consulted in the drafting of the EA. At this stage of the process, there is no requirement of public input; but agencies have found that it is helpful to include public input in their EA considerations at this early stage to ensure that all potential environmental ramifications of the project are being considered and to help complete the record for the NEPA process.

Sometimes a review of the EA indicates that the proposed project will have little impact on the human environment. When this is the case, the agency prepares a **Finding of No Significant Impact (FONSI)**. The FONSI uses the EA to explain why the project should not require a complete EIS due to its minimal environmental impact.

An EA is not nearly as complete as an EIS, but the EA is a good indication of the degree of environmental impact a proposed project will have; it also is good preparation for an EIS, should one be necessary.

REVIEW

Fonzie was a character on the television sitcom *Happy Days;* but in environmental law, a FONSI is a Finding of No Significant Impact reached at the end of an EA.

ENVIRONMENTAL IMPACT STATEMENTS

Unless a proposed federal project is categorically excluded by its nature from having to comply with other requirements of NEPA or when the EA results in a FONSI, the agency must complete a full EIS. An EIS is designed to assist public officials in making decisions about projects. An EIS is based on information concerning the potential environmental effects of the proposed project analyzed in light of each alternative way to complete the project.

As part of the EIS process, a "lead agency" must be designated. That agency is responsible for completing the EIS. Other involved agencies are designated as "cooperating agencies." Due to the sheer magnitude of the production of an EIS (paperwork associated with an EIS can fill up an entire room from floor to ceiling), the lead agency frequently hires outside consultants to assist with preparation. Even if a consultant is hired, the lead agency must remain actively involved in the preparation of the EIS. Any consultants hired must remain under the control of the lead agency, which is ultimately responsible for the work product associated with the EIS, including its scope and content. Further, no outside consultant can have a conflict of interest in the project (no financial interest in the project other than the fees received for assisting with the EIS).

The lead agency begins the EIS process by determining the scope of the proposed action. This **scoping** requirement is one of the keys to NEPA since it requires an agency to figure out the parameters of its proposed project. At this stage of the process, the public is usually involved for the first time. Among other things, scoping identifies issues significant enough to be addressed in depth during the EIS process and sets a timetable for the EIS process up to and including the final determination concerning the proposed action.

scoping This portion of the environmental impact statement (EIS) process includes identifying and addressing significant issues related to a proposed action, including the range of possible actions, alternatives, and possible environmental impacts related to the alternatives.

Once a project has been sufficiently scoped, the meat of the EIS process begins. During the early stages of this process, the lead agency begins to gather environmental data related to each of the alternatives identified for the project. The EA is often used as a starting point for this process.

An EIS must include the following:

COMPONENTS OF AN ENVIRONMENTAL IMPACT STATEMENT

- The expected environmental impacts of the proposed project
- Any unavoidable adverse environmental impacts connected with the project's implementation
- Any reasonable alternatives to the proposed project
- A discussion concerning the balance between the intended temporary use of the human environment as part of the proposed project and the expected long-term use of that environment
- Any commitment of resources involved in the proposed project that are irreversible or irretrievable if the project is implemented

CEQ regulations addressing the content of an EIS place special emphasis on an evaluation of the possible alternatives involved with the project. The CEQ requires for each alternative, among other things, an analysis of its direct effects, indirect effects (including any effects on the economic growth of the area), and compatibility with plans of other governmental entities (land use plans and other regulations). A determination of whether potential alternatives have been adequately explored is often made on a case-by-case basis.

CASE LAW

NATURAL RESOURCES DEFENSE COUNCIL, INC. V. MORTON, 458 F.2D 827 (D.C. CIR.1972).[4]

SUMMARY OF CASE: Conservation groups sued the Secretary of the Interior to prevent the sale of oil and gas leases on the Outer Continental Shelf off eastern Louisiana. The District Court granted a preliminary injunction to prevent the sale of the leases, and the Secretary appealed to the Court of Appeals for the District of Columbia.

Judge Leventhal delivered the opinion of the Court.

This appeal raises a question as to the scope of the requirement of the National Environmental Policy Act (NEPA) that environmental impact statements contain a discussion of alternatives. Before us is the Environmental Impact Statement [Statement] . . . filed by the Department of the Interior with respect to its proposal . . . for the oil and gas general lease sale, of leases to some 80 tracts of submerged lands, primarily off eastern Louisiana. . . . [T]hree conservation groups brought this action . . . to enjoin the proposed sale. . . . [T]he District Court held a hearing and granted a preliminary injunction enjoining the sale of these leases pending compliance with NEPA. The Government appealed. . . .

On June 15, 1971, Secretary of Interior Rogers Morton . . . announced that a general oil and gas lease sale of tracts on the Outer Continental Shelf (OCS) off eastern Louisiana would take place in December, 1971. . . . On October 28, 1971, [the Secretary] promulgated the "final Environmental Impact Statement" (hereafter Statement). . . .

While the Statement presents questions . . . this document is not challenged on the ground of failure to disclose the problems of environmental impact of the proposed sale. On the contrary, these problems are set forth in considerable range and detail. . . .

Adjacent to the proposed lease area is the greatest estuarine coastal marsh complex in the United States, some 7.9 million acres, providing food, nursery habitat and spawning ground vital to fish, shellfish and wildlife, as well as food and shelter for migratory waterfowl, wading birds and fur-bearing animals. . . .

The coastal areas of Louisiana and Mississippi contain millions of acres suitable for outdoor recreation, with a number of state and federal recreation areas, and extensive beach shorelines. . . .

As to the probable impact of issuance of leases on the environment the Statement did not anticipate continuation of debris from drilling operations, in view of recent regulations prohibiting dumping of debris on the OCS. The Statement acknowledged some impact from construction of platforms, pipelines and other structures. A concluding section . . . particularly noted the destruction of marsh and of marine species and plants from dredging incident to pipeline installation, and the effect of pipeline canals in e.g., increasing ratio of water to wetlands and increasing saltwater intrusion.

Oil pollution is the problem most extensively discussed in the Statement. . . . The statement acknowledges that both short- and long-term effects on the environment can be expected from spillage, including in that term major spills . . . , minor spills from operations and unidentified sources, and discharge of waste water contaminated with oil. . . .

The District Court recognized both that there is a profound national energy crisis and that the Outer Continental Shelf has been a prolific source of oil and gas. . . . The court found that the Statement failed to provide the "detailed statement" required by NEPA of environmental impact and alternatives. . . .

We reject the implication of . . . the Government's submission which began by stating that while the Act requires a detailed statement of alternatives, it "does not require a discussion of the environmental consequences of the suggested alternative." A sound construction of NEPA . . . requires a presentation of the environmental risks incident of reasonable alternative courses of action. The agency may limit its discussion of environmental impact to a brief statement, when that is the case, that the alternative course involves no effect on the environment, or that their effect, briefly described, is simply not significant. A rule of reason is implicit in this aspect of the law as it is in the requirement that the agency provide a statement concerning those opposing views that are responsible. . . .

While the consideration of pertinent alternatives requires a weighing of numerous factors, such as economics, foreign relations, national security, the fact remains that, as to the ingredient of possible adverse environmental impact, it is the essence and thrust of NEPA that the pertinent Statement serve to gather in one place a discussion of the relative environmental impact of alternatives.

The Government contends that the only discussion of "alternatives" required for discussion under NEPA are those which can be adopted and put into effect by the official or agency issuing the Statement. . . . [W]e do not agree that this requires a limitation to measures the agency or official can adopt. . . . When a proposed action is an integral part of a coordinated plan to deal with a broad problem, the range of alternatives that must be evaluated is broadened. . . . The impact statement is not only for the exposition of the thinking of the agency, but also for the guidance of these ultimate decision-makers [the president and Congress], and must provide them with the environmental effects of both the proposal and the alternatives, for their consideration along with the various other elements of the public interest. . . .

What NEPA infused into the decision-making process in 1969 was a directive as to the environmental impact statements that was meant to implement the Congressional objectives of Government coordination, a comprehensive approach to environmental management, and a determination to fact problems of pollution "while they are still of manageable proportions and while alternative solutions are still available" rather than persist in environmental decision-making wherein "policy is established by default and inaction" and environmental decisions "continue to be made in small but steady increments" that perpetuate the mistakes of the past without being dealt with until "they reach crisis proportions."

We reiterate that the discussion of environmental effects of alternatives need not be exhaustive. What is required is information sufficient to permit a reasoned choice of alternatives so far as environmental aspects are concerned. As to alternatives not within the scope of authority of the responsible official, reference may of course be made to studies of other agencies—including other impact statements. Nor is it appropriate, as the Government argues, to disregard alternatives merely because they do not offer a complete solution to the problem.

[T]he requirement in NEPA of discussion as to reasonable alternatives does not require "crystal ball" inquiry. Mere administrative difficulty does not interpose such flexibility into the requirements of NEPA as to undercut the duty of compliance "to the fullest extent possible." But if this requirement is not rubber, neither is it iron. The statute must be construed in the light of reason if it is not to demand what is, fairly speaking, not meaningfully possible, given the obvious, that the resources of energy and research—and time—available to meet the Nation's needs are not infinite. . . .

In the last analysis, the requirement as to alternatives is subject to a construction of reasonableness, and we say this with full awareness that this approach necessarily has both strengths and weaknesses. Where the environmental aspects of alternatives are readily identifiable by the agency, it is reasonable to state them—for ready reference by those concerned with the consequences of the decision and its alternatives.

[The Government's] Motion [is] denied. ■

QUESTION

1. What does the court say is the purpose of the requirement for discussion of alternatives?

Finally, CEQ regulations require an EIS to evaluate the cumulative effects of a proposed project, including an analysis of past, present, and future activities within the area. If any of these effects can be mitigated, the EIS must identify the appropriate mitigation measures. See *Methow Valley Citizens Coun. v. Regional Forester*.[5]

While NEPA requires an EIS to be "clear and concise," the EIS for any significant federal project will involve the identification and evaluation of many alternatives, resulting in a comprehensive—and voluminous—product. Appendix B of this text contains an example of a summary of an EIS. It is an Executive Summary of the EIS for King Range National Conservation Area in California. Even the Executive Summary, let alone the text of the EIS, is difficult to follow in places and might not be termed "clear and concise."

CASE LAW

MINNESOTA PUBLIC INTEREST RESEARCH GROUP V. BUTZ, 498 F.2D 1314 (8TH CIR. 1974).[6]

SUMMARY OF CASE: A nonprofit corporation sought an injunction against logging in the Boundary Waters Canoe Area until the Secretary of Agriculture complied with NEPA. The District Court held that an EIS was required by NEPA and issued the injunction.

Judge Gibson delivered the opinion of the Court.

The plaintiff . . . filed a complaint asking for declaratory and injunctive relief against further logging the in the Boundary Waters Canoe Area (BWCA). . . . The District Court, after a hearing on the merits, enjoined the defendants from logging 'in those areas of the active timber sales on the BWCA which are contiguous with the main virgin forest areas of the BWCA pending the Forest Service's completion of its new BWCA Management Plan and accompanying impact statement.'

Crucial to our determination of the issue raised is whether or not the modification of existing [contracts] for cutting of virgin timber, the extension of some of these contracts, and the supervision of the day-to-day activities in the operation of the timber cutting contracts in the BWCA area constitute major federal action significantly affecting the quality of the human environment within the purview of [NEPA].

The BWAC, located in northern Minnesota, is a unique natural resource with some 1,060,000 acres of lakes, streams, and timber which . . . forms the only canoe wilderness area in the world. . . . It is also highly regarded by others . . . who value the thousands of acres of marketable timber it contains.

[The Secretary] assert[s] that there has been no major federal action since the effective date of NEPA (January 1, 1970). . . . These appeals present a question of the applicability of NEPA to private logging operations carried out pursuant to pre-NEPA Forest Service timber sales within the BWCA. Specifically in question is § 102(2)(c) of NEPA that requires the preparation of an EIS for 'major Federal actions significantly affecting the quality of the human environment.' Should this court affirm the District Court's determination that the Forest Service's actions regarding these timber sales after January 1, 1970, constitute major federal action significantly affecting the quality of the human environment[?]. . . .

Timber harvesting has been a source of public controversy surrounding the BWCA. In November, 1971, soon after its formation [plaintiff] requested the Forest Service to prepare an EIS considering the effects of logging in the BWCA and to halt all logging in the BWCA until the statement was completed. . . .

No environmental impact statements have been prepared for any of the sales. . . . The position of the Forest Services . . . is that there has been no major federal action since the effective date of NEPA. The District Court held otherwise and enjoined timber cutting. . . .

Does the Forest Service's involvement in these timber sales constitute major federal action significantly affecting the quality of the human environment? [NEPA] requires preparation of an EIS for "every recommendation or report on proposals for legislation and other major federal action significantly affecting the quality of the human environment." What constitutes other major federal action is not defined in the Act.

[NEPA] contains a Congressional direction that environmental factors be considered 'to the fullest extent possible.' An initial decision not to prepare an EIS precludes the full consideration directed by Congress. In view of the concern for environmental disclosure present in NEPA, the agency's discretion as to whether an impact statement is required is properly exercised only within narrow bounds. Action which could have a significant effect on the environment should be covered by an impact statement. We think that the threshold decision as to whether or not to prepare an EIS should be reviewed . . . on the grounds of its reasonableness. The lead agency should prepare an EIS if it is reasonable to anticipate a cumulatively significant impact on the environment from federal action.

An agency decision concerning NEPA requirements is not one committed to the agency's discretion by law within the meaning of the APA. . . . The Congressional command that agencies cooperate in attaining the goals of NEPA 'to the fullest extent possible' requires the courts to look at the good faith efforts of the agency to comply. To upset an agency determination not to prepare an impact statement, it still must be shown that the agency's determination was not reasonable under the circumstances. This will require a showing that the project could significantly affect the quality of the human environment. . . .

Looking now to the timber sales in question, it was established in the District Court that there is a significant effect on the BWCA from these logging operations. However, defendants contend that any adverse effect on the BWCA does not 'significantly affect the quality of the human environment' as there is no evidence showing that the human users of BWCA have ever seen a timber sale. . . . We think NEPA is concerned with indirect effects as well as direct effects. There has been increasing recognition that man and all other life on earth may be significantly affected by actions which on the surface appear insignificant. . . . We agree with the District Court that there is 'major Federal action significantly affecting the quality of the human environment' and an impact statement is required.

The judgment of the District Court . . . is affirmed. ■

QUESTIONS

1. Why did the court determine that there was a "major Federal action" in this case?

2. Do you agree that there was a "major Federal action"? Why or why not?

Record of Decision (ROD) This document must be prepared whenever an agency makes a decision or recommendation concerning an action proposed pursuant to the National Environmental Policy Act (NEPA).

hard look A term used by the U.S. Supreme Court to describe the type of analysis that should be given not only to the evaluation of a National Environmental Policy Act (NEPA) matter but also to any court review of an environmental issue.

Once an EIS has been drafted, it is subjected to a rigorous approval process that includes a large dose of public input. Copies of the EIS are made available to the public, the CEQ, and the president of the United States. Everyone is invited to make written comments concerning the project, which are submitted as part of the approval process. This opportunity for comment from the public on the draft EIS is in addition to the opportunity provided during the scoping process and, eventually, during the process of finalizing the EIS and adopting the **Record of Decision (ROD)**, which constitutes the final agency action related to an EIS.

While judicial review of a ROD is not specifically provided for in NEPA, the courts have found that their review is implied in the act. Judicial review is typically limited to a determination as to whether an agency's compliance with NEPA has been "adequate." In *Citizens to Preserve Overton Park v. Volpe*,[7] which was not a NEPA case, the Supreme Court determined that courts should ensure that agencies have taken a **hard look** at the issues intended to be addressed by the procedural requirements of NEPA. The "hard look" doctrine has been applied not only to NEPA cases but to all court review in all environmental law matters. A court is not permitted to substitute its own judgment for the agency, but decide only whether the agency's factual determination was "arbitrary, capricious, an abuse of discretion, or otherwise not in accordance with law." This standard of review, which is the predominant standard in environmental law, makes it extremely difficult for any party challenging an agency decision to win its challenge. If, on the other hand, there is a challenge to the manner in which an agency interpreted or applied the law (other than its own law; if, for example, the EPA were interpreting its own regulations), the court has an opportunity to make a broader and more substantive review of the agency action. As always, a party seeking court relief from an agency action must have standing by demonstrating that he or she will incur a "significant injury" from the proposed project and that he or she is within the "zone of interest" sought to be protected by the legislative enactment.

SPECIAL ETHICAL CONCERNS FOR PARALEGALS

Paralegals can have substantial responsibilities in dealing with administrative agencies, such as the EPA. Paralegals working with administrative agencies should keep the following issues in mind:

1. Most federal agencies are subject to the APA. (Most states have a state version of the APA as well.) This legislation governs how agencies make rules and how agencies make decisions in individual cases as well (such as licensing or permitting actions).
2. Virtually all administrative agencies have specific rules or internal procedures governing time limits, forms, and similar bureaucratic issues. Attorneys often rely on paralegals to determine the intricacies of agency procedures.
3. Dealing with large agencies, such as the EPA, can be confusing. An organization chart of the agency, if available, can be a tremendous help in sorting out the various departments, subdivisions, and individuals associated with a specific agency.

ENVIRONMENTAL LAW PROFESSIONAL PROFILE

Edith R. Mayfield

What is the most challenging part of your job?

The challenging aspects of my job include keeping up with technology and automation, utilizing my skills to provide essential support to six attorneys, and being alert to situations that might have an environmental impact on my community.

What advice do you have for paralegal students interested in environmental law?

Think "green" and realize that environmental law cuts across other areas of the law such as corporate and real estate law. Get involved with the environmental issues in your community. I work for the Hugh L. Carey Battery Park Authority (<http://www.batteryparkcity.org>), which is a New York State public benefit corporation whose mission is to plan, create, coordinate, and maintain a balanced community of commercial, residential, retail, and park space within its designated 92-acre site on the lower west side of Manhattan. Since the creation of the Authority's Residential Environmental Guidelines in the year 2000 and the Governor's Green Building Tax Credit, "green" buildings have been springing up all over Battery Park City, including an environmentally friendly high-rise residential building that received honorable recognition from the United States

(*continued*)

Environmental Protection Agency (EPA). Students should also get involved with a firm or company whose mission continues and whose vision expands.

What special skills are needed to do your work?

Having the ability to multitask, to work independently and with others; having excellent writing, organizational, and computer skills; and having the ability to stay up to date on changes in applicable laws and regulations.

Do you have any words of wisdom for paralegal students?

After becoming a paralegal, uphold the profession and produce quality work. Discover your talent. Be ambitious and take initiative. Read trade publications. Get exposure to other areas of the law through volunteerism. If possible, during employment, take advantage of company-sponsored training opportunities. And remember: if you're not being challenged, you're not growing—so move on, if necessary.

Edith R. Mayfield is a Legal Coordinator and Assistant Corporate Secretary for the Battery Park City Authority in New York City. She received her Paralegal Certificate from Adelphi University in 1991, her AAS degree in General Business/Management from New York University in 1994, her BS degree in Business from Marymount College of Fordham University in 1996, and her Certificate in U.S. Law and Methodologies from New York University in 2004. She is the author of an article entitled "Environmental Justice" in the February/March 2002, National Paralegal Reporter.

SUMMARY

The purpose of NEPA is to create a national environmental policy and to allow public input into the process of formulating a national response to environmental issues. One of the unique characteristics of NEPA when compared with other federal environmental acts is that NEPA is a purely procedural act. It does not contain any of the substantive, scientific, pollutant-specific information that other acts contain. NEPA requires federal agencies to consider environmental issues as they implement projects. The president of the United States appoints three members to the CEQ, and these three individuals determine the course of environmental policy during their term of appointment. The provisions of NEPA apply only to "major federal actions." The first step in determining the extent to which the federal government must incorporate environmental principles into a project is the EA. Unless there is a FONSI at the end of the EA, the government will be required to provide an EIS. The process of completing an EIS is lengthy, paper-intensive, and complex. NEPA requires the EIS to explore many environmental aspects of a project and, as part of the scoping process, to solicit public input. Most citizens have heard of an EIS, but they may not know how significant it is to the state of the environment that the federal government must provide such information prior to beginning a major project.

KEY TERMS

- Council on Environmental Quality (CEQ)
- Environmental Assessment (EA)
- Environmental Impact Statement (EIS)
- Finding of No Significant Impact (FONSI)
- Hard look
- Record of Decision (ROD)
- Scoping

REVIEW QUESTIONS AND HANDS-ON ACTIVITIES

1. Who appoints the CEQ?
2. What information is obtained through an EA?
3. What is the process for approval of an EIS?
4. What is the relationship between an EA and an EIS?
5. How important is the scoping portion of the EIS process?
6. Even proposed federal legislation can trigger the requirement that an EIS be completed (for a legislative EIS, scoping is not required and a draft may be sufficient) if the potential environmental effects of the legislation are significant enough. Identify a proposed piece of federal legislation that required an EIS and analyze the effect of the EIS on the ultimate fate of the legislation.
7. Read the excellent discussion of the nature of the requirement that an EIS include possible mitigation measures in the following cases cited in this chapter: *Methow Valley Citizens Coun. v. Regional Forester*, 833 F.2d 810 (9th Cir. 1987), rev'd sub nom, *Robertson v. Methow Valley Citizens*, 490 U.S. 332 (1989). Write one paragraph summarizing the analysis and findings of those two cases.

8. NEPA does not clearly state whether its provisions apply to federal projects outside the boundaries of the United States. Clearly, Section 102 (2)(f) of NEPA requires all federal agencies to recognize the "worldwide and long-range character of environmental problems." President Carter's Executive Order No. 12114 emphasized that federal agencies should consider the effects of projects outside the United States. Neither NEPA nor President Carter's Executive Order *require* agencies to comply with NEPA for projects outside the United States. Should NEPA be amended to include such projects? Why or why not?
9. In recent years, NEPA's provisions have been used to address such environmental problems as global warming, biodiversity, pollution prevention, ozone depletion, and sustainable growth. Pick one of those topics and learn how NEPA has been used to move toward a solution of the problems associated with the issue.
10. Do NEPA's procedural provisions accomplish the goal for which they were enacted? Why or why not?

HELPFUL WEBSITES

http://www.eh.doe.gov/nepa (Department of Energy, Office of NEPA Policy and Compliance)

http://www.epa.gov/compliance/nepa/index.html (EPA, NEPA)

http://www.epa.gov/seahome/eacase.html (EPA, Environmental Assessment Case Study)

http://www.NAEP.org (National Association of Environmental Professionals™)

http://www.iaia.org (International Association for Impact Assessment)

http://www.lcv.org (League of Conservation Voters)

http://www.ncsl.org (National Conference of State Legislatures)

http://www.nrdc.org (National Resources Defense Council)

ENDNOTES

1. *Calvert Cliffs' Coordinating Comm. Inc. v. United States Atomic Energy Comm'n*, 449 F.2d 1109 (D.C. Cir. 1971).
2. *Norton v. Southern Utah Wilderness Alliance*, 542 U.S. 55 (2004).
3. *Department of Transportation v. Public Citizen*, 541 U.S. 752 (1978).
4. *Natural Resources Defense Council, Inc. v. Morton*, 458 F.2d 827 (D.C. Cir. 1972).
5. *Methow Valley Citizens Coun. v. Regional Forester*, 833 F.2d 810 (9th Cir. 1987), rev'd sub nom, *Robertson v. Methow Valley Citizens*, 490 U.S. 332 (1989).
6. *Minnesota Public Interest Research Group v. Butz*, 498 F.2d 1314 (8th Cir. 1974).
7. *Citizens to Preserve Overton Park v. Volpe*, 401 U.S. 402 (1971).

CHAPTER 4

CLEAN WATER ACT (CWA)

TITLE: The Clean Water Act (CWA)

CITATION: 33 U.S.C. secs. 1251-1376 (1991)

REGULATIONS: 40 C.F.R. secs. 100 to 149 (1997)

PURPOSE: To "restore and maintain the chemical, physical and biological integrity" of the "waters of the United States."

HISTORY: Rivers and Harbors Act of 1899 (Refuse Act)
Federal Water Pollution Control Act of 1948
Federal Water Pollution Control Act Amendments of 1972 (FWPCA or CWA)
Water Quality Act of 1987 (WQA)

LEARNING OBJECTIVES

After studying this chapter, the reader should be able to

- describe which waters are covered by the Act.
- define *pollutant.*
- explain the CWA permit system.
- describe what the National Pollutant Discharge Elimination System (NPDES) requires.
- explain technology-based standards.
- describe the major provisions of the Oil Pollution Act (OPA) and the Safe Drinking Water Act (SDWA).

The most recent version of the federal statutes designed to keep the waters of the United States clean and safe is called the Clean Water Act, or CWA. This chapter not only will discuss the main provisions of the CWA but also will include discussions concerning key subparts of the CWA, such as the Oil Pollution Act (OPA), and related acts such as the Safe Drinking Water Act (SDWA).

WATERS OF THE UNITED STATES

waters of the United States All waters in which the United States has an interest, including navigable waters of the United States, interstate waters and their tributaries, and waters that may be used in commerce.

The CWA addresses the cleanliness and safety of only the **waters of the United States**. Exactly which waters fall within the definition of "waters of the United States" has been the subject of much litigation under the CWA. The definition in the act reads as follows: "all waters of the United States including the territorial seas." This general definition has been further defined to describe more specifically what is included. Basically, any surface water (groundwaters are not covered by the CWA unless they connect hydrologically with waters of the United States) in which the United States does or might have an interest, that can or could be used for navigation, that connects or could connect with an interstate waterway, or that is or could be used for interstate commerce will be considered a water of the United States. Surprisingly, this definition has even been interpreted to include an arroyo ("a watercourse in an arid region"), which is usually dry, but through which water could flow and end up in a public body of water. *United States v. Phelps Dodge Corp.*[1] Waters of the United States have been held to include wetlands (such as marshes and bogs), artificially created canals, and even mangrove swamps. *United States v. Huebner;*[2] *Weiszmann v. District Engineer;*[3] *P.F.Z. Properties Inc. v. Train.*[4] See also, 160 A.L.R. Fed. 585.

CASE LAW

UNITED STATES V. RIVERSIDE BAYVIEW HOMES, INC., 474 U.S. 121 (1985).[5]

SUMMARY OF CASE: The Army Corps of Engineers brought a suit against a land developer to prevent the developer from filling in low-lying wetlands without a permit under the CWA. The district court granted the Corps' request, the developer appealed, and the Court of Appeals reversed the district court.

Justice White delivered the opinion of the Court.

This case presents the question whether under the Clean Water Act (CWA), 33 U.S.C. 1251 *et. seq.*, together with certain regulations promulgated under its authority by the Army Corps of Engineers, authorizes the Corps to require landowners to obtain permits from the Corps before discharging fill material into wetlands adjacent to navigable bodies of water and their tributaries.

The relevant portions of the Clean Water Act . . . have remained essentially unchanged [since the enactment]. Under [the CWA], any discharge of dredged or fill materials into the "navigable waters"—defined as the "waters of the United States"—is forbidden unless authorized by a permit issued by the Corps of Engineers. . . . After initially construing the Act to cover only waters navigable in fact, in 1975 the Corps issued interim final regulations redefining "the waters of the United States" to include not only actually navigable waters but also tributaries of such waters, interstate waters and their tributaries, and nonnavigable intrastate waters whose use or misuse could affect interstate commerce. . . . More importantly for present purposes, the Corps construed the Act to cover all "freshwater wetlands" that were adjacent to other covered waters. A "freshwater wetland" was defined as an area that is "periodically inundated" and is "normally characterized by the prevalence of vegetation that requires saturated soil conditions for growth and reproduction. . . ."

Respondent Riverside Bayview Homes, Inc. (hereafter respondent) owns 80 acres of low-lying marshy land near the shores of Lake St. Clair in Macomb County, Michigan. In 1976, respondent began to place fill materials on its property as part of its preparations for construction of a housing development. The Corps of Engineers, believing that the property was an "adjacent wetland" under the . . . regulation defining "waters of the United States," filed suit in the United States District Court for the Eastern District of Michigan, seeking to enjoin respondent from filling the property without the permission of the Corps.

The District Court held that the portion of respondent's property lying below 575.5 feet above sea level was a covered wetland and enjoined respondent from filling it without a permit. Respondent appealed . . . and the Sixth Circuit reversed. The court construed the Corps' regulation to exclude from the category of adjacent wetlands . . . wetlands that were not subject to flooding by adjacent navigable waters at a frequency sufficient to support the growth of aquatic vegetation. . . . Under the court's reading of the regulation, respondent's property was not within the Corps' jurisdiction, because its semiaquatic characteristics were not the result of frequent flooding by the nearby navigable waters. Respondent was therefore free to fill the property without obtaining a permit.

The question whether the Corps of Engineers may demand that respondent obtain a permit before placing fill material on its property is primarily one of regulatory and statutory interpretation: we must determine whether respondent's property is an "adjacent wetland" within the meaning of the applicable regulation, and, if so, whether the Corps' jurisdiction over "navigable waters" gives it statutory authority to regulate discharges of fill material into such a wetland. . . .

The regulation extends the Corps'authority . . . to all wetlands adjacent to navigable or interstate waters and their tributaries. Wetlands, in turn, are defined as lands that are "inundated *or saturated* by surface or *ground water* at a frequency and duration sufficient to support, and that under normal circumstances do support, a prevalence of vegetation typically adapted for life in saturated soil conditions." The plain language of the regulation refutes the Court of Appeals' conclusion that inundation or "frequent flooding" by the adjacent body of water is a *sine qua non* of a wetland under the regulation. Indeed, the regulation could hardly state more clearly that saturation by either surface or ground water is sufficient to bring an area within the category of wetlands, provided that the saturation is sufficient to and does support wetland vegetation.

The history of the regulation underscores the absence of any requirement of inundation. . . . Without the nonexistent requirement of frequent flooding, the regulatory definition of adjacent wetlands covers the property here. T[he district] court found that the wetland located on respondent's property was adjacent to a body of navigable water, since the area characterized by saturated soil conditions and wetland vegetation extended beyond the boundary of respondent's property to Black Creek, a navigable waterway. . . . [I]f the regulation itself is valid as a construction of the term "waters of the United States" as used in the Clean Water Act, a question which we now address, the property falls within the scope of the Corps' jurisdiction over "navigable waters" under . . . the Act.

An agency's construction of a statute it is charged with enforcing is entitled to deference if it is reasonable and not in conflict with the expressed intent of Congress. . . . Accordingly, our review is limited to the question whether it is reasonable, in light of the language, policies, and legislative history of the Act for the Corps to exercise jurisdiction over wetlands adjacent to but not regularly flooded by rivers, streams, and other hydrographic features more conventionally identifiable as "waters."

On a purely linguistic level, it may appear unreasonable to classify "lands" wet or otherwise, as "waters." Such a simplistic response, however, does justice neither to the problem faced by the Corps in defining the scope of its authority . . . nor to the realities of the problem of water pollution that the Clean Water Act was intended to combat. In determining the limits of its power to regulate discharges under the Act, the corps must necessarily choose some point at which water ends and land begins. Our common experience tells us that this is often no easy task: the transition from water to solid ground is not necessarily . . . an abrupt one. Rather, between open waters and dry land may lie shallows, marshes, mudflats, swamps, bogs. . . . Where on this continuum to find the limit of "waters" is far from obvious. . . .

We cannot say that the Corps' conclusion that adjacent wetlands are inseparably bound up with the "waters" of the United States—based as it is on the

Corps' and the EPA's technical expertise—is unreasonable. In view of the breadth of federal regulatory authority contemplated by the Act itself and the inherent difficulties of defining precise bounds to regulable waters, the Corps' ecological judgment about the relationship between the waters and their adjacent wetlands provides an adequate basis for a legal judgment that adjacent wetlands may be defined as waters under the Act. . . . Because respondent's property is part of a wetland that actually abuts on a navigable waterway, respondent was required to have a permit in this case. . . .

Accordingly, the judgment of the Court of Appeals is reversed. ■

QUESTION

1. Do you agree with the Supreme Court's reasoning in interpreting the phrase *waters of the United States*? Why or why not?

One term used in the definition of waters of the United States is **navigable**. This term means "deep and wide enough to afford passage for ships." A recent U.S. Supreme Court case, *Solid Waste Agency of Northern Cook County v. United States Army Corps of Engineers*,[6] clarified whether the definition of "waters of the United States" includes gravel pit ponds, which are described as "nonnavigable, isolated, intrastate waters . . . subject to protection as habitats for migratory birds."

navigable A term used in the definition of waters of the United States to mean "deep and wide enough to afford passage for ships."

CASE LAW

SOLID WASTE AGENCY OF NORTHERN COOK COUNTY V. U.S. ARMY CORPS OF ENGINEERS, 531 U.S. 159 (2001).

SUMMARY OF CASE: The agency sued because the Corps of Engineers (Corps) denied its request for a waste disposal permit. The U.S. Court of Appeals for the Seventh Circuit upheld the denial, holding that the Corps' jurisdiction under the CWA extended to an abandoned gravel pit.

Chief Justice Rehnquist delivered the opinion of the Court.

[T]he Clean Water Act . . . regulates the discharge of dredged or fill material into "navigable waters." The [Corps] has interpreted [the Act] to confer federal authority over an abandoned sand and gravel pit in northern Illinois which provides habitat for migratory birds. We are asked to decide whether the provisions of [the Act] may be fairly extended to these waters. . . . We answer [this] question in the negative.

Petitioner . . . [sought] to locate and develop a disposal site for baled non-hazardous solid waste. The Chicago Gravel Company informed [the petitioner] of the availability of a 533-acre parcel . . . which had been the site of a sand and gravel pit mining operation for three decades up until about 1960. Long since abandoned, the old mining site eventually gave way to a successional stage forest, with its remnant excavation trenches evolving into a scattering of permanent and seasonal ponds of varying size . . . and depth.

The [petitioner] decided to purchase the site for disposal of [its] baled non-hazardous solid waste. [The petitioner] contacted . . . the Corps to determine if a federal landfill permit was required under [the Clean Water Act].

[The CWA] grants the Corps authority to issue permits "for the discharge of dredged or fill material into the navigable waters at specified disposal sites." The term "navigable waters" is defined under the Act as "the waters of the United States, including the territorial seas." . . . In 1986, in an attempt to "clarify" its jurisdiction, the Corps stated that [the Act] extends to intrastate waters, [including waters] which are or would be used as habitat by birds protected by Migratory Bird Treaties; or which are or would be used as habitat by other migratory birds which cross state lines. . . . This last promulgation has been dubbed the "Migratory Bird Rule."

The Corps originally concluded that it had no jurisdiction over the site because it contained no "wetlands," or areas which support "vegetation typically adapted for life in saturated soil conditions." However, after the Illinois Nature Preserves Commission informed the Corps that a number of migratory bird species had been observed at the site, the Corps reconsidered and ultimately asserted jurisdiction over the balefill site pursuant to the . . . "Migratory Bird Rule."

During the application process, [the petitioner] made several proposals to mitigate the likely displacement of the migratory birds and to preserve a great blue heron rookery located on the site. Its balefill project ultimately received local and state approval. . . . Despite [the petitioner's] securing the required water quality certification from the Illinois Environmental Protection Agency, the Corps refused to issue a [CWA] permit.

Petitioner filed suit under the [APA] . . . challenging both the Corps' jurisdiction over the site and the merits of its denial of the . . . permit. The District Court granted summary judgment to the respondents . . . and petitioner renewed its attack on respondents' use of the "Migratory Bird Rule" to assert jurisdiction over the site. Petitioner argued that [the Corps] exceeded their statutory authority in interpreting the CWA to cover nonnavigable, isolated, intrastate waters based on the presence of migratory birds. . . .

Congress passed the CWA for the stated purpose of "restoring and maintaining the chemical, physical and biological integrity of the Nation's waters." . . . Relevant here, [the CWA] authorizes respondents to regulate the discharge of fill material into "navigable waters." Respondents have interpreted these words to cover the abandoned gravel pit at issue here because it is used as habitat for migratory birds. We conclude that the "Migratory Bird Rule" is not fairly supported by the CWA. . . .

Where an administrative interpretation of a statute invokes the outer limits of Congress' power, we expect a clear indication that Congress intended that result. . . . Respondents argue that the "Migratory Bird Rule" falls within Congress' power to regulate intrastate activities that "substantially affect" interstate commerce. They note that the protection of migratory birds is a "national interest of very the first magnitude.". . . But this is a far cry, indeed, from the "navigable waters" and "waters of the United States" to which the statute by its terms extends.

[W]e find nothing approaching a clear statement from Congress that it intended [the CWA] to reach an abandoned sand and gravel pit such as we have here. Permitting respondents to claim federal jurisdiction over ponds and mudflats falling within the "Migratory Bird Rule" would result in a significant impingement of the States' traditional and primary power over land and water use. Rather than expressing a desire to readjust the federal-state balance in this manner, Congress chose to "recognize, preserve, and protect the primary responsibilities and rights of States . . . to plan the development and use . . . of land and water resources."

We hold that . . . the "Migratory Bird Rule" exceeds the authority granted to respondents under . . . the CWA. The judgment of the Court of Appeals for the Seventh Circuit is therefore reversed.

Dissent by Justice Stevens, with whom Justice Souter, Justice Ginsburg and Justice Breyer join.

Today . . . the Court takes an unfortunate step that needlessly weakens our principal safeguard against toxic water. It is fair to characterize the Clean Water Act as "watershed" legislation. The statute endorsed fundamental changes in both the purpose and the scope of federal regulation of the Nation's waters. . . .

The Court has previously held that the Corps' broadened jurisdiction under the CWA properly included . . . low-lying marshy land that was not itself navigable. . . . In its decision today, the Court draws a new jurisdictional line, one that invalidates the 1986 Migratory bird regulation as well as the Corps' assertion of jurisdiction over all waters except for actually navigable waters, their tributaries, and wetlands adjacent to each. . . .

The shift in focus of federal water regulation from protecting navigability toward environmental protection reached a dramatic climax in 1972, with the passage of the CWA. The Act . . . was universally described by its supporters as the first truly comprehensive federal water pollution legislation. . . . [The CWA] was principally intended as a pollution control measure. . . . Because of the statute's ambitious and comprehensive goals, it was, of course, necessary to expand its jurisdictional scope. Thus, although Congress opted to carry over the traditional jurisdictional term "navigable waters" [from other acts] . . . it broadened the *definition* of that term to encompass all "waters of the United States.". . . Viewed in light of the history of federal water regulation [and] the broad definition . . . it is clear that the term "navigable waters" operates in the statute as a shorthand for "waters over which federal authority may properly be asserted." . . . The Corps' interpretation of the statute as extending beyond navigable waters, tributaries of navigable waters, and wetlands adjacent to each is manifestly reasonable therefore entitled to deference. . . . ■

QUESTIONS

1. Why did the court determine that the "Migratory Bird Rule" was invalid?
2. Do you agree with the majority decision or the dissent? Why?

The U.S. Supreme Court weighed in again concerning the definition of "waters of the United States" in *Rapanos v. United States*.[7]

CASE LAW

RAPANOS V. UNITED STATES, ___ U.S. ___, 126 S. CT. 2208, 165 L.ED. 2D 159 (2006).

Justice Scalia delivered the opinion of the Court.

In April 1989, petitioner John A. Rapanos backfilled wetlands on a parcel of land in Michigan that he owned and sought to develop. This parcel included 54 acres of land with sometimes saturated soil conditions. The nearest body of navigable water was 11 to 20 miles away. Regulators had informed Mr. Rapanos that his saturated fields were "waters of the United States" . . . that could not be filled without a permit. Twelve years of criminal and civil litigation ensued.

The burden of federal regulation on those who would deposit fill material in locations denominated "waters of the United States" is not trivial. In deciding whether to grant or deny a permit, the U.S. Army Corps of Engineers (Corps) exercises the discretion of an enlightened despot, relying on such factors of "economics," "aesthetics," "recreation," and "in general, the needs and welfare of the people.". . . The average applicant for an individual permit spends 788 days and $271,596 in completing the process, and the average applicant for a nationwide permit spends 313 days and $28,915—not counting costs of mitigation or design changes. . . . "Over $1.7 billion is spent each year by the private and public sectors obtaining wetlands permits." These costs cannot be avoided because the Clean Water Act "imposes criminal liability" as well as steep civil fines. . . . In this litigation, for example, Mr. Rapanos faced 63 months in prison and hundreds of thousands of dollars in criminal and civil fines. . . .

The enforcement proceedings against Mr. Rapanos are a small part of the immense expansion of federal regulation of land use that has occurred under the Clean Water Act—without any change in the statute—during the past five Presidential administrations. In the last three decades, the Corps and . . . EPA have interpreted their jurisdiction over the "waters of the United States" to cover 270 to 300 million acres of swampy lands in the United States. . . .

We first interpreted the proper interpretation of . . . [the] phrase "the waters of the United States" in *United States v. Riverside Bayview Homes, Inc.* . . . [W]e upheld the Corps' interpretation of the "waters of the United States" to include wetlands that "actually abutted on" traditional navigable waters.

Following our decision in *Riverside Bayview*, the Corps adopted increasingly broad interpretations of its own regulations under the Act. . . . [These] interpretations extended the "waters of the United States" to virtually any land feature over which rainwater or drainage passes and leaves a visible mark. . . .

. . . Rapanos . . . deposited fill material without a permit into wetlands on three sites near Midland, Michigan. . . . The United States brought civil enforcement proceedings against . . . Rapanos. . . . The District Court found that the described wetlands were "within federal jurisdiction" because they were "adjacent to other waters of the United States," and held [Rapanos] liable for violations of the CWA. . . . On appeal, the United States Court of Appeals for the Sixth Circuit affirmed, holding that there was federal jurisdiction over the wetlands at all three sites. . . .

We need not decide the precise extent to which the qualifiers "navigable" and "of the United States" restrict the coverage of the Act. Whatever the scope of the qualifiers, the CWA authorizes federal jurisdiction only over the "waters." . . . The only natural definition of the term "waters," our prior and subsequent judicial constructions of it, clear evidence from other provisions of the statute, and this Court's canons of construction all confirm that "the waters of the United States" . . . cannot bear the expansive meaning that the Corps would give it.

The Corps' expansive approach might be arguable if the [Act] defined "navigable waters" as "water of the United States." But the "waters of the United States" is something else. The use of the definite article ("the") and the plural number ("waters") show strongly that [the Act] does not refer to water in general. In this form, "the waters" refers more narrowly to water "[a]s found in streams and bodies forming geographical features such as oceans, rivers [and] lakes." . . . On this definition, "the waters of the United States" include only the relatively permanent, standing or flowing bodies of water. . . . None of these terms encompasses transitory puddles or ephemeral flows of water. . . .

Most significant of all, the CWA itself categorizes the channels and conduits that typically carry intermittent flows of water separately from "navigable waters" by including them in the definition of "point source." The Act defines "point source" [in a way that] conceive[s] . . . "point sources" and "navigable waters" as separate and distinct categories. The definition[s] would make little sense if the two categories were significantly overlapping. . . .

Therefore, *only* those wetlands with a continuous surface connection to bodies that are "waters of the United States" in their own right, so that there is no clear demarcation between "waters" and wetlands, are "adjacent to" such waters and covered by the Act. Wetlands with only an intermittent, physically remote hydrologic connection to "waters of the United States" . . . lack the necessary connection to covered waters. . . . Thus establishing that wetlands such as those at the Rapanos site . . . are covered by the Act requires two findings: First, that the adjacent channel contains a "water of the United States" . . . ; and second, that the wetland has a continuous surface connection with that water, making it difficult to determine where the "water" ends and the "wetland" begins. . . .

Because the Sixth Circuit applied the wrong standard to determine if these wetlands are covered "waters of the United States," and because of the paucity of the record . . . the lower courts should determine, in the first instances whether the ditches or drains near each wetland are "waters" in the ordinary sense of containing a relatively permanent flow; and (if they are), whether the wetlands in question are "adjacent" to these "waters" in the sense of possessing a continuous surface connection that creates the boundary-drawing problem [of establishing where the water ends and wetland begins]. . . . We vacate the judgments of the Sixth Circuit and remand . . . for further proceedings. ■

QUESTION

1. How does this opinion impact the effectiveness of the Clean Water Act?

It is too early to tell whether the findings of the Supreme Court in *Rapanos* will clarify the reach of the CWA or whether they will, as one analyst indicated, further "muddy the waters."

POLLUTANTS

The next definition important to understanding the CWA is that of a **pollutant**. This term includes any

> Dredged spoil, solid waste, incinerator residue, sewage, garbage, sewage sludge, munitions, chemical wastes, biological materials, radioactive materials, heat, wrecked or discarded equipment, rock, sand, cellar dirt and industrial, municipal and agricultural waste.
>
> [33 U.S.C. 1362 (6)]

pollutant Dredged spoil; solid waste; incinerator residue; sewage; garbage; sewage sludge; munitions; chemical wastes; biological materials; radioactive materials; heat; wrecked or discarded equipment; rock; sand; cellar dirt; and industrial, municipal, and agricultural waste.

As you can see, this definition is broad and renders almost any substance a pollutant. The fact that "heat" is considered a pollutant is something that might not be expected, unless one considers the effect of temperature changes on fish and other water life. Even small changes in temperature can be deadly to many types of fish and plant life. Although most ocean waters are not considered "waters of the United States" and, therefore, are not covered by the CAA, the changes in ocean currents during the past decade, bringing with them changes (primarily increases in water temperature) to the water environment, have resulted in the destruction of many water habitats and the population of living creatures in the oceans. Organisms that are extremely susceptible to temperature changes, such as corals in the ocean, have been wiped out by increases in ocean temperatures. The same is true in inland waters, although the diversity of life is not typically as broad.

PERMIT SYSTEMS

Having defined which waters are governed by the CWA, it is appropriate to determine how the Act is administered. Like most federal acts, the CWA utilizes a permit system to accomplish its goals. The permit system used in the CWA is the **National Pollutant Discharge Elimination System (NPDES)**, which is designed to keep track of the substances being put in the water and the concentration levels of those substances. Several key definitions are associated with the NPDES permit program. The CWA prevents the discharge of a pollutant into

National Pollutant Discharge Elimination System (NPDES) Pursuant to the Clean Water Act (CWA), this system determines, through the permitting process, the types and amounts of pollutants discharged into waters and streams. The process includes the following: the filing of an application, certification by the state, Fact Sheet or Statement of Basis, opportunity for the public to provide comment, and issuance or denial of a permit.

point source As defined in the Clean Water Act (CWA), any discernible, confined, and discrete conveyance, including but not limited to any pipe, ditch, channel, tunnel, conduit, well, discrete fissure, container, rolling stock, concentrated animal feeding operation [such as a feed lot], or vessel or other floating craft, from which pollutants are or may be discharged.

the waters of the United States from a **point source**. A point source is defined as follows:

POINT SOURCE

. . . any discernable, confined and discrete conveyance, including but not limited to any pipe, ditch, channel, tunnel, conduit, well, discrete fissure, container, rolling stock, concentrated animal feeding operation, or vessel or other floating craft, from which pollutants are or may be discharged. This term does not include agricultural stormwater discharges and return flows from irrigated agriculture.

[33 U.S.C. Section 1362 (14)]

Fittingly, this inclusive definition has been interpreted broadly by courts. See, e.g., *Sierra Club v. Abston Construction Company*[8]; *United States v. Earth Sciences, Inc.*[9]; *Appalachian Power Co. v. Train.*[10] *Point source* has been held to include ships, airplanes, and even the offshore nets of a salmon farm. *Barcelo v. Brown*[11]; *U.S. Public Interest Research Group v. Atlantic Salmon of Maine, L.L.C.*[12] See also, 52 A.L.R. Fed. 885.

Another case in which the definition of *point source* is addressed is *South Florida Water Management District v. Miccosukee Tribe of Indians.*[13]

CASE LAW

SOUTH FLORIDA WATER MANAGEMENT DISTRICT V. MICCOSUKEE TRIBE OF INDIANS, 541 U.S. 95 (2004).

SUMMARY OF CASE: Indian Tribe sued the South Florida Water Management District (District) under the Clean Water Act, contending that a pumping facility operated by the District was required to obtain a discharge permit. The District Court granted summary judgment for the Tribe, and the U.S. Court of Appeals for the Seventh Circuit affirmed.

Justice O'Connor delivered the opinion of the Court.

Petitioner [District] operates a pumping facility that transfers water from a canal into a reservoir a short distance away. Respondent [Tribe] brought a . . . suit under the Clean Water Act contending that the pumping facility is required to obtain a discharge permit under the National Pollutant Discharge Elimination System (NPDES). The District Court agreed and granted summary judgment to [the Tribe]. The . . . United States Circuit Court of Appeals for the Eleventh Circuit affirmed. Both the District Court and the Eleventh Circuit rested their holdings on the predicate determination that the canal and reservoir are two distinct water bodies. For the reasons explained below, we vacate and remand for further development of the factual record as to the accuracy of that determination.

The Central and South Florida Flood Control Project (Project) consists of a vast array of levees, canals, pumps and water impoundment areas. . . . Historically, [the] land was itself part of the Everglades. . . . Starting in the early 1900s . . . the State began to build canals to drain the wetlands and make them suitable for cultivation. These canals proved to be a source of trouble; they lowered the water table, allowing salt water to intrude upon coastal wells, and they proved incapable of controlling flooding. Congress established the Project in 1948 to address these problems. . . . The local sponsor and day-to-day operator of the Project is the . . . District. . . . The Project has wrought large-scale hydrologic and environmental change in South Florida, some deliberate and some accidental.

Rain on the western side of the . . . levees falls into the wetland ecosystem. . . . Rain on the eastern side of the levees, on the other hand, falls on agricultural, urban and residential land. Before it enters the . . . canal, whether directly as surface runoff or indirectly as groundwater, that rainwater absorbs contaminants produced by human activities. The water [on one side] therefore differs chemically from that [on the other side]. Of particular interest here, the [western side] water contains elevated levels of phosphorous, which is found in fertilizers used by farmers in the western basin. When water . . . is pumped cross the levees, the phosphorous it contains alters the balance of the [eastern] ecosystem (which is naturally low in phosphorous) and stimulates the growth of algae and plants foreign to the Everglades ecosystem. The phosphorous-related impacts of the Project are well known and have received a great deal of attention from state and federal authorities for more than 20 years. A number of initiatives are currently under way to reduce these impacts and thereby restore the ecological integrity of the Everglades. [The] . . . Tribe, impatient with the pace of this progress, brought this Clean Water Act suit. . . . [The Tribe] sought . . . to enjoin the operation [of the pumping station].

Congress enacted the Clean Water Act [Act] in 1972. Its stated objective was "to restore and maintain the chemical, physical, and biological integrity of the Nation's waters." To serve those ends, the Act prohibits "the discharge of any pollutant by any person" unless done in compliance with some provision of the Act. The provision relevant to this case . . . establishes the . . . NPDES. Generally speaking, the NPDES requires dischargers to obtain permits that place limits on the type and quantity of pollutants that can be released into the Nation's waters. The act defines the phrase "discharge of a pollutant" to mean "any addition of any pollutant to navigable waters from any point source." A "point source," in turn is defined as "any discernable, confined and discrete conveyance," such as a pipe, ditch channel or tunnel "from which pollutants are or may be discharged."

According to the Tribe, the District cannot operate [the pumping station] because the pump station moves phosphorous-laden water [from one side to the other]. The District does not dispute that phosphorous is a pollutant, or that [the canals] are navigable waters within the meaning of the Act. The question, it contends, is whether the operation of the . . . pump constitutes the "discharge of [a] pollutant" within the meaning of the Act.

Because it believed that water in the [western] canal would not flow into [the eastern canal] without the operation of the . . . pump station, the Court of Appeals concluded that [the pump station] was the cause-in-fact of the addition of pollutants to [the eastern canal] . . . and held that the . . . pump station requires a NPDES permit. . . .

In the courts below, as here, the District contended that the [canals] are not distinct water bodies at all, but instead are two hydrologically indistinguishable parts of a single water body. . . . The Tribe does not dispute that if [the canals] are simply two parts of the same water body, pumping water from one into the other cannot constitute an "addition" of pollutants. . . .What the Tribe disputes is the accuracy of the District's factual premise; according to the Tribe, [the two canals] are two [bodies of water], not one. . . .

Summary judgment is appropriate only where there is no genuine issue of material fact. The record before us leads us to believe that some factual issues remain unresolved. . . .

We find that further development of the record is necessary to resolve the dispute over the validity of the distinction between [the two canals]. . . . Accordingly, the judgment of the United States of Appeals for the eleventh Circuit is vacated, and the case is remanded for further proceedings consistent with this opinion. ■

QUESTION

1. What was the most important "material fact" that the court believed needed to be determined in this case?

NPDES PERMIT PROCESS

The NPDES program prohibits the discharge of any pollutant from any point source into a water of the United States without a permit. NPDES permits are issued by the EPA unless a state has a NPDES program approved by the EPA, in which case the state may issue the permit. Since most states have approved NPDES permit programs, NPDES permits are typically issued by states. State requirements must, in all areas, be at least as restrictive as federal requirements and are frequently more restrictive.

The permit process has seven stages, regulated pursuant to 40 C.F.R. Part 124 (1997). First, *application for a NPDES permit* is made on an approved form and must be signed by a "responsible corporate officer." This officer signs a certification, under penalty of law, that he or she is aware of the facts contained in the application and that the information provided is true, accurate, and complete. Given this requirement, the signing officer often chooses to call together those within the company who have actual knowledge concerning the operation of the facility to confirm the accuracy of the information in the application before he or she signs. This is the way the officer protects himself or herself from inadvertently providing false or misleading information and suffering serious personal penalties. If the owner and operator of a point source facility are two separate entities, the operator is the person who applies for and receives the permit. The application form requires specific and significant information about the facility and the nature of the proposed discharges from the facility. The application must be made at least 180 days prior to when the applicant intends to begin the proposed discharge or 180 days before an existing permit is scheduled to expire. (If a timely application is made for a new permit, the existing permit will, if necessary, be "continued" beyond 180 days while the new permit is being processed.) It is important to note that a new permit is required not only when a facility intends to begin discharging for the first time but also when a facility that is already discharging wants to significantly change the quantity or type of its discharge.

The second stage of the process involves *certification by the state* that the proposed permit conditions will comply with all applicable federal (EPA) permit requirements, including effluent limitations and water quality standards. This certification by the state can be waived directly; or it can be waived by a state electing not to certify the draft permit within 60 days, in which case the state is deemed to have waived its certification.

In the third stage of the NPDES permit process, documents are prepared by the approving entity for release to the public so that the public is provided adequate notice concerning the specifics of the request. These documents include a *Fact Sheet* or *Statement of Basis* for the requested permit and either a draft permit or an intent to deny. The Fact Sheet or Statement of Basis explains the way the application was analyzed and the bases for the permit terms and conditions.

The fourth stage provides the *opportunity for the public to provide comment* concerning the proposed permit or denial of the permit. After a period of at least 30 days, during which the public may provide written comment, an informal public hearing may be held to allow the public an opportunity to provide further input. This stage is the manifestation of the administrative law requirement that regulatory activities include a mechanism through which the public has the opportunity to participate in the process, as further described in Chapter 1 of this text.

Stage 5 is the *issuance or denial of a permit*. If a permit is issued, it is typically effective 30 days after issuance and is usually valid for five years. The permit issued at this stage is called a final permit.

Following the issuance of a final permit, any person may request an evidentiary hearing before an administrative law judge (ALJ). This constitutes the sixth stage of the permit process. The person requesting such a hearing must do so in writing within 30 days of the issuance of a final permit and must provide all legal and factual issues to be raised in the appeal. The request for such a hearing must be granted or denied within 30 days of the request. If a hearing is held at this stage, it is a formal hearing, much like a trial, and a record is kept of the proceedings. This type of hearing also is presided over by an ALJ. The decision of the ALJ may be appealed within 30 days of the initial decision to the EPA Environmental Appeals Board (part of the office of the EPA Administrator). The result of this appeal is considered a "final agency action" that may then be appealed to the courts, which is the seventh, and final, stage in the permit process.

When the final agency action is taken by the EPA, the decision is appealed to the federal Court of Appeals. When a state agency takes the final agency action, the appeal is to the appropriate state court. The standard of review by the courts is a very difficult standard to meet: a court will overturn the decision of the administrative agency only when the decision was "arbitrary and capricious," an "abuse of discretion," "contrary to a constitutional right," or otherwise legally inappropriate. Basically, these high appellate standards mean that if there is any competent evidence in the record of the administrative process to support the decision of the administrative body, the administrative decision will be allowed to stand.

REVIEW

NPDES Permit Process

Stage 1: Application

Stage 2: Certification by the state

Stage 3: Documents released to the public, including a Fact Sheet or Statement of Basis

Stage 4: Opportunity for public comment

Stage 5: Issuance or denial of the permit

NPDES PERMIT CONDITIONS

A NPDES permit is designed to establish effluent limitations that are appropriate to the activity being proposed and that are enforceable by the applicable regulatory agency.

TECHNOLOGY-BASED STANDARDS

The EPA, through rulemakings, determines "effluent guidelines" that are applicable nationally. The guidelines are specific to various industrial categories and types of dischargers within each industrial category. The effluent guidelines include the following:

Best Practicable Technology (BPT) The minimum level of required treatment for pollutants.

Best Conventional Technology (BCT) A technology level applicable to the discharge of conventional pollutants.

Best Available Technology (BAT) A technology level applicable to the discharge of toxic and nonconventional pollutants.

Best Available Demonstrated Technology (BADT) A demonstrated technology level applicable to the discharge of toxic and nonconventional pollutants.

EFFLUENT GUIDELINES

- **Best Practicable Technology (BPT)**
  Refers to the minimum level of required treatment for pollutants
- **Best Conventional Technology (BCT)**
  Applies to discharges of conventional pollutants
- **Best Available Technology (BAT)**
  Applies to discharges of toxic and nonconventional pollutants
- **Best Available Demonstrated Technology (BADT)**
  Applies a demonstrated technology level to the discharge of toxic and nonconventional pollutants

Best Professional Judgment (BPJ) The use of scientific analysis of the type, amount, location, and other relevant conditions connected with a proposed discharge.

New Source Performance Standards (NSPS) Standards applicable to new source discharges.

fundamentally different factor (FDF) A type of variance given under the Clean Water Act (CWA) when a discharger can demonstrate that factors applied to determining the technology-based standards for its facility are fundamentally different from the factors considered when the Environmental Protection Agency (EPA) developed the effluent limitations guidelines for the type of facility the discharger is operating.

If the discharger is in an industrial category for which guidelines have not been established or if the proposed discharge does not have established guidelines, the EPA will use the **Best Professional Judgment (BPJ)** principle to determine the appropriate permit limitations for the proposed discharge. The application of BPJ will involve a scientific analysis of the type, amount, location, and other relevant conditions connected with the proposed discharge.

In 1972, the CWA was amended to add requirements that industrial dischargers meet scientific standards applicable to their discharges. For nonconventional pollutants, dischargers were required to achieve BPT by July 1, 1977, and BAT by July 1, 1983. For conventional pollutants such as biological oxygen demand, total suspended solids, fecal coliform, pH, and oil and grease, the standard set in 1977 was BCT. This is a more lenient standard than BPT and BAT.

None of these standards applies to new source discharges, for which the appropriately designated **New Source Performance Standards (NSPS)** of "best available demonstrated control technology" (similar to BAT standards, but often more stringent) is applied. Since the standards for new source discharges are higher than for other types of discharges, dischargers frequently challenge their designation as a new source discharger, hoping to be restricted, instead, by the less-stringent standards applied to existing discharges.

Statutes providing for the imposition of technology-based standards also provide an opportunity for a discharger to receive, under certain circumstances, a "variance," or reprieve, from technology-based standards applicable to a particular discharge. Variances are typically and appropriately difficult to obtain since the standards are imposed to prevent water pollution and any variation from the standards carries with it a potential increased risk of such pollution. Although several types of variances are available under the CWA, the most common type of variance obtained is a **fundamentally different factor (FDF)** variance. This variance may be obtained when a discharger can demonstrate that factors applied to determining the technology-based standards for its facility are fundamentally different than the factors considered when the EPA developed the effluent limitations guidelines for the type of facility the discharger is operating. A determination as to whether a discharger is entitled to a FDF variance is based on an evaluation of factors such as the following:

FACTORS INFLUENCING A DETERMINATION AS TO WHETHER AN FDF VARIANCE IS WARRANTED

- The type of pollutants in the discharge
- The volume of the discharge
- Environmental impacts of the discharge not related to water quality
- Energy requirements of the proposed treatment technology
- An evaluation of the discharger's facility, equipment, and processing practices, including the age, size, and location of the facility

A FDF variance will not be granted merely because it would be too expensive for the discharger to comply with applicable technology-based standards.

Chapter 1 of this text noted that science plays a large role in environmental law. This is demonstrated by the proliferation of technology-based scientific standards that are part of the CWA.

WATER QUALITY STANDARDS

In addition to the technology-based limitations determined by the EPA, states are allowed to establish **water quality standards** for waters within their jurisdiction. Each state establishes water quality standards consisting of two elements: (1) *use classifications* and (2) *water quality criteria*.

water quality standards
Standards established by states for waters within their jurisdiction. The standards consist of two elements: use classifications and water quality criteria.

Use classifications involve states classifying waters based on their intended use. Waters may be classified as public drinking water supplies; waters for the propagation of fish and wildlife; waters to be used for recreational purposes; and waters intended for industrial, agricultural, or other uses.

After classifying waters by intended use, each state sets water quality standards. In accordance with the Water Quality Act of 1987, these standards must be numerical and incorporate the physical, chemical, and biological characteristics of water suitable for each of the identified intended uses. States typically base their standards on the federal water quality standards.

As indicated, the standards establish a maximum numerical level of a given pollutant in water used for a particular purpose. The standards

total maximum daily load (TMDL) The amount of pollutants a certain body of water can tolerate without exceeding applicable water quality standards.

individual control strategies (ICSs) Standards set for bodies of water that, even with the application of technology-based limitations, will not meet the state's water quality standards.

are established by the application of scientific formulas, taking into account, among other things, the flow of the water into which a pollutant will be discharged, the rate of mixture with the water, and the **total maximum daily load (TMDL)** of pollutants a certain body of water can tolerate without exceeding applicable water quality standards.

Another requirement of the Water Quality Act of 1987 is that states establish a list of "impaired" waters within their jurisdiction. Waters included on this list are those waters that will not meet the state's water quality standards even after technology-based limitations are imposed. For these waters, **individual control strategies (ICSs)** are determined and typically made part of NPDES permit restrictions.

TOXICITY TESTING

As an additional protection against water pollution not prevented by technology-based limitations or water quality limitations, NPDES permits contain requirements that dischargers conduct toxicity testing. Toxicity testing requirements are individually created for a particular NPDES permit and address such criteria as frequency of testing, types of testing needed, and use of the testing results.

STORM WATER DISCHARGES

The Water Quality Act of 1987 included a requirement that the EPA establish regulations and issue permits for storm water discharges. These requirements are applicable to industrial activity and discharges from municipal storm sewer systems serving in excess of 100,000 people. The Water Quality Act sets forth the application procedure for NPDES storm water permits and provides for individual, group, or general (multiple industrial segments in many areas) permits.

SEA AND OCEAN DISCHARGES

There are two ways in which water pollution into seas, oceans, or contiguous zones is regulated. First, a NPDES permit may be issued for a discharge into such waters if the discharge will not result in an "unreasonable degradation of the marine environment." [40 C.F.R. sec. 125.121 (e)]

Second, dumping of pollutants into the marine environment is governed under the MPRSA. (33 U.S.C. sec. 1401-14) As a practical matter, the only material that may be dumped into oceans is dredged soil; and even the disposal of this material is carefully regulated as to designated locations and type and amount of material to be dumped.

NONPOINT SOURCE DISCHARGES

The definition of a point source was provided earlier in this chapter. A **nonpoint source** is any source of water pollution that does not fit within the definition of a point source. Pursuant to the Water Quality Act of 1987, states are primarily responsible for control of nonpoint sources of water pollution. The states are required to submit to the EPA state management programs designed to reduce pollution from nonpoint discharges. The state programs are required to include a plan for achieving the reduction goals and a timetable for implementation of the reduction measures. Agricultural runoff is one example of a nonpoint source discharge and is the main type of water pollution from such sources.

nonpoint source A source of pollutant that is not quantifiable or not easily quantified. Examples include runoff from a farm or a city street.

SPILLS

How does the CWA address the reality that, despite all of the efforts to prevent unapproved discharges, they are bound to happen? The CWA has requirements dealing with preventing, reporting, and responding to spills.

Many facilities are required to develop **spill prevention control and countermeasure (SPCC) plans**. These plans require facilities to be prepared for the worst-case spill. The plans must be reviewed and certified by a registered professional engineer, must be updated periodically, and must be approved by the EPA. Some of the items addressed in a SPCC plan include providing information about the person in charge of a facility, training plans, equipment testing, and types of storage containers.

spill prevention control and countermeasure plans (SPCC) Plans that require facilities to be prepared for the worst-case spill.

In addition to these prevention measures, the CWA contains requirements about the reporting of spills. Facilities must immediately report certain types of spills to the National Response Center. Any discharge of a harmful quantity of oil or a hazardous substance to navigable waters or to a shoreline requires an immediate report. Discharges that are identified or anticipated or that are in compliance with a NPDES permit are excluded from the discharge notification requirement.

ENFORCEMENT

Many environmental acts, including the CWA, have severe civil and criminal penalties for violations of the act. The federal government (through the EPA) and each state having an authorized permit program may bring an enforcement action under the CWA. The enforcement options available under this act include the following:

CWA Enforcement Options

- An administrative order
  - may require compliance with the act and/or a permit.
  - may assess an administrative penalty such as
    - loss of permit.
    - fines.
- A civil action
  - may assess fines.
  - may impose an injunction.
- A criminal action
  - may assess fines.
  - may impose imprisonment.

Typically, criminal actions will be brought when there has been a knowing or negligent violation of an environmental law. Typical of these types of penalties, owners and operators of facilities from which discharges occur are strictly liable for the cleanup costs of the spill and any damage caused by the spill. Penalties for discharges, in addition to the costs just enumerated, include fines of up to $25,000 per day (which may be tripled under certain circumstances) and can even include criminal penalties. Other fines for violations of the act can reach $250,000 per day.

In addition to suits brought by governmental entities, citizens are permitted to file lawsuits against any person for violating the CWA or against the EPA for failing to enforce the act where it is required to do so. A citizen suit may be brought only when neither a state nor the EPA is diligently prosecuting a violation. These suits may be filed only for a continuing violation or for one that occurs on an off-and-on basis. Suits for past violations that have already been addressed are not allowed.

OIL POLLUTION ACT (OPA)

In 1990, the *Oil Pollution Act (OPA)* was enacted. Some environmental acts or amendments to existing acts come about in response to particular environmental events. In the case of OPA, the event

Reprint by permission. Universal Press Syndicate

that prompted its enactment was the *Exxon Valdez* spill in Alaska in 1989.

Among other things, OPA gives the federal government primary authority in the event of an oil spill (although it does not preempt state law), requires vessels carrying oil to meet stringent construction requirements, sets specific manning standards for piloting oil tankers, and increases the severity and scope of liability for oil spills. OPA requires vessels and facilities to have response plans in the event of a spill and requires a National Contingency Plan addressing the assignment of duties and responsibilities among federal, state, and local agencies responding to a spill.

There are few defenses to violations of OPA since it is also a strict liability law. So unless there was an act of God, an act of war, or an act or omission by a third party, any party responsible for an oil spill will incur significant damages. A key type of damage for which there is liability under OPA is damage to natural resources. As with other environmental acts, OPA carries serious civil and criminal penalties for the violation of its provisions.

SAFE DRINKING WATER ACT (SDWA)

The **Safe Drinking Water Act (SDWA)** was enacted in 1974 and represents federal controls on the water used in municipal water systems. SDWA's restrictions apply to water in public drinking water

Safe Drinking Water Act (SDWA) Enacted in 1974, this act represents federal controls on the water used in municipal water systems. The act's provisions apply to water in public drinking water systems, underground hazardous waste injection wells, and some aquifers.

primary standards A category of standards under the Safe Drinking Water Act (SDWA). These standards relate to contaminants that might cause adverse effects on people's health.

secondary standards A category of standards under the Safe Drinking Water Act (SDWA). These standards relate to contaminants that might affect the appearance or odor of the water.

recommended maximum contaminant level (RMCL) The standard renamed the maximum contaminant level goal. This standard represents the level of a contaminant at which no known or anticipated adverse effects on the health of persons occur and that allows an adequate margin of safety.

maximum contaminant level (MCL) The maximum level of a drinking water contaminant under the Safe Drinking Water Act (SDWA).

systems, underground hazardous waste injection wells, and some aquifers.

SDWA created two sets of standards for regulating contaminants in drinking water: **primary standards** and **secondary standards**. Primary standards are those designed to regulate contaminants that might cause adverse effects on people's health, and secondary standards are those that might affect the appearance or odor of the water. The secondary standards are not federally enforceable. The creation of these secondary standards makes SDWA different from every other environmental act discussed in this text because it is the only federal act that contains this type of "aesthetic" standard. Most people prefer their drinking water to look clean and drinkable, not clouded, brown, or silty; and SDWA includes standards designed to meet this preference.

For the purposes of SDWA requirements, *contaminant* is defined broadly as "any physical, chemical, biological, or radiological substance or matter in water." [42 U.S.C. sec. 300f(6)] Pursuant to its authority under SDWA, the EPA initially established a **recommended maximum contaminant level (RMCL)**. Next, the EPA was required to establish a final primary drinking water standard. This final standard would be either a **maximum contaminant level (MCL)** or a water treatment technique that would presumably cause the treated water to meet the desired standards.

In 1986, SDWA was amended to address several issues. Congress was concerned about how long it was taking the EPA to establish final standards, was worried about the fact that many municipal water systems lacked the resources to comply with SDWA, and was disturbed by the lack of flexibility built into SDWA to allow states to address regional needs. The 1986 amendments addressed all of those issues. For example, the amendments established certain types of acceptable treatment and simplified the process whereby the EPA enacted regulations.

SDWA applies to **public drinking water systems (PDWSs)**, which are defined in the Act as follows:

> . . . a system for the provision to the public of piped water for human consumption, if such system has at least fifteen service connections or regularly services at least twenty-five individuals. Such term includes (A) any collection, treatment, storage, and distribution facilities under control of the operator of such system, and (B) any collection or pretreatment storage facilities not under such control which are used primarily in connection with such system.

[42 U.S.C. sec. 300f (3)]

Pursuant to the 1986 amendments, the previously stated RMCL standard was redesignated the **maximum contaminant level goal (MCLG)**. An MCLG is supposed to be set ". . . at the level at which no known or anticipated adverse effects on the health of persons occur and which allows an adequate margin of safety." [42 U.S.C. sec. 300f (3)] Both acute and chronic health risks are considered when the list of contaminants is created. Based on scientific research establishing at which concentration levels contaminants can become dangerous to humans, the EPA sets the appropriate levels for each contaminant. The EPA has determined that there is no safe level of exposure for carcinogens (substances that have been determined to cause cancer), so public drinking water can contain no known carcinogens at all. Once an MCLG is set by the EPA, the EPA must then set a MCL as close as feasible to the MCLG. *Feasibility* is defined as follows:

> . . . feasible with the use of the best technology, treatment techniques and other means which the [EPA] Administrator finds, after examination for efficacy under field conditions and not solely under laboratory conditions, are available (taking cost into consideration). . . .

[SDWA sec. 1412, 42 U.S.C. sec. 300g-1(b)(5)]

public drinking water system (PDWS) A system for the provision to the public of piped water for human consumption if such system has at least 15 service connections or regularly services at least 25 individuals. It also includes any collection, treatment, storage, and distribution facilities under the control of the operator of such a system and any collection or pretreatment storage facilities not under such control that are used primarily in connection with such a system.

maximum contaminant level goal (MCLG) As part of the 1986 amendments to the Safe Drinking Water Act (SDWA), the standard previously known as the recommended maximum contaminant level was redesigned as the maximum contaminant level goal and represents the level of a contaminant at which no known or anticipated adverse effects on the health of persons occur and that allows an adequate margin of safety.

This definition clearly indicates that the EPA must use "field tests" to determine the appropriate MCL for a contaminant and not rely on mere laboratory tests. If a particular system cannot meet a MCL due to the condition of its raw water, even using the best technology, treatment techniques, or other means identified by the EPA, with costs taken into consideration, a variance may be granted to the system for that contaminant, allowing a higher level than the MCL, but still protecting the health of the consumers using the system. If an MCL cannot be met for reasons other than the quality of the raw water, an exemption can be granted for a period of three years for certain water systems, as long as there will be no danger to the health of the system users.

As previously stated in this chapter, these primary standards are mandatory, but the secondary standards under SDWA, those that address how public drinking water looks and smells, cannot be enforced by the EPA. By making the health-based standards mandatory, SDWA accomplishes its purpose, which is to protect the public from contaminated water. This goal is not always reached, but SDWA has been successful in greatly reducing the amount of dangerous water the public has consumed from public systems.

FEATURE

THE *EXXON VALDEZ* OIL SPILL

It was just after midnight on March 24, 1989, when the oil tanker *Exxon Valdez* struck a reef in Prince William Sound, Alaska. Prince William Sound is a water passage 70 miles long; and while it contains hazards such as the Bligh Reef, which the *Exxon Valdez* struck, the hazards are known and can be avoided by ships with a crew that knows the area and is attentive to its duty. For a variety of reasons, the crew of the *Exxon Valdez* failed to exercise the care necessary to navigate the passage safely and thus had an accident that spilled nearly 11 million gallons of oil on the placid waters of the Sound.

The captain of the *Exxon Valdez* was Joseph Hazelwood. On March 23, 1989, while oil was being loaded onto the ship at the Alyeska Terminal in Valdez, Alaska, for its trip through the Sound, Captain Hazelwood and some of the other ship's officers visited at least two bars in Valdez. The captain had several alcoholic beverages during the afternoon and evening before returning to the ship. Testimony was given during the court proceedings from the cab driver who drove the party back to the ship, as well as the security guard at the terminal gate, that none of the officers appeared intoxicated, although various members of the ship's crew reported that they smelled alcohol on Captain Hazelwood's breath and that his eyes were "watery." At a later trial, Captain Hazelwood was found not guilty of operating a vessel while intoxicated. In any event, subsequent analysis of the causes of the accident indicate that while the captain's activities may have contributed to the accident, other lapses also played a major role in the grounding of the ship.

By 9:21 p.m. on the evening of March 23, 1989, the *Exxon Valdez* had cleared the dock at the Alyeska terminal and had begun its journey. Pilot William Murphy, who had piloted the ship into the dock the previous evening, also piloted the ship out into the Valdez Narrows. The ship was accompanied by a tugboat for this portion of the trip. Exxon company policy requires that two ship's officers be present on the bridge during transit of the Narrows, but Captain Hazelwood left the bridge at 9:35 p.m. and did not return to the bridge until after the ship had left the Narrows. The ship cleared the Narrows at 10:49 p.m. Captain Hazelwood was called to the bridge at 11:05 because Pilot Murphy was going to disembark from the ship. Pilot Murphy disembarked at 11:24 p.m. During the disembarkation process, Captain Hazelwood was the only officer on the deck. Applicable regulations of the National Transportation Safety Bureau require that there be a lookout on the bridge; but during the time of the disembarkation, there was no lookout on the bridge of the *Exxon Valdez*.

By 11:25 p.m., Captain Hazelwood had increased the speed of the ship to sea speed and got approval from the Vessel Traffic Center to use a particular sea lane in the Sound. The captain had apparently asked to use the "inbound" land rather than the "outbound" lane to avoid small icebergs. At some point, without permission, the ship moved even further east out of the inbound lane. Even though the captain told the traffic center that he was changing his heading and reducing speed to "wind my way through the ice," the ship continued to accelerate. Again without permission, the captain changed his heading. After engaging in discussions about using a computer to power the ship up to "sea speed full ahead," the captain left the bridge at approximately 11:53 p.m.

Third Mate Gregory Cousins, who had been on duty for six hours and was scheduled to be relieved, did not wake his relief for the midnight to 4 a.m. watch, electing to stay on duty himself. He was the only officer on the deck, which, as was previously noted, is against Exxon rules. Having a second officer on the bridge, especially in light of the fatigued condition of Third Mate Cousins, might have prevented the accident. Someone who was more alert might have noted the ship's dangerous position, the failure of its efforts to turn, the status of the autopilot steering, and the continuing threat of ice.

At some point just after midnight, Third Mate Cousins plotted a course that would have moved the ship back toward the traffic lanes. The sighting of the Bligh Reef light in a place where it should not have been indicated that the ship was seriously off course and going too fast for its location. The order was given to change course. Cousins called Captain Hazelwood in his cabin and told him that the ship was heading back toward the traffic lanes and would likely encounter some ice. The ship turned sluggishly, and Cousins' instructions got increasingly urgent. As Cousins called the captain to tell him the ship was in serious danger, there was a jolt. It was 12:04 a.m., and the *Exxon Valdez* had just run aground on Bligh Reef.

The *Exxon Valdez* was carrying approximately 53 million gallons of oil in 11 cargo tanks. Eight of the tanks were punctured by the Reef; and within three and a quarter hours, at least 5.8 million gallons had been spilled into the Sound. Captain Hazelwood rushed to the bridge and tried desperately to get the ship off the Reef; but finally, at 12:19 a.m., the captain ordered that the ship's engines be reduced to idle. At 12:26 a.m., the captain radioed the ship's status to the traffic center. During the next hour, despite warnings from his crew concerning the stability of the ship, the captain again tried to power the ship off the reef. It was not until 1:41 a.m. that the captain abandoned his efforts to free the ship from the reef.

In the days and years since that night, there have been many responses to the *Exxon Valdez* incident. First, there was the response to the spill itself, followed by an attempt to determine the causes of the incident and enact laws to prevent such incidents in the future. Looking at the initial response to the environmental problems caused by the spill, there was a need for swift action in an attempt to mitigate damage to wildlife, the economy, and the environmental habitat of Prince William Sound.

The spill extended 460 miles to a tiny village on the Alaskan Peninsula. Amazingly, as of 2004, this spill is no longer in the top 50 spills internationally in terms of size. In terms of damage to the environment, however, many consider the *Exxon Valdez* accident to be the worst ever. The spill affected fish and wildlife in the spill area, including fowl, sea otters, harbor porpoises, sea lions, and whales. The damage caused to the fish population of the Sound adversely affected the commercial fishing industry, which makes up a large part of the economy in the area.

The initial response was handled by the On-Scene Coordinator of the U.S. Coast Guard since the accident happened in open navigable waters. The first action taken was to close the Port of Valdez to water traffic. As reported by the EPA, by noon the day after the spill, the Alaska Regional Response Team was active; and the National Response Team became involved a short time later. An organization called Alyeska, representing several oil companies operating in the region, including Exxon, took initial charge of the cleanup operation in accordance with the contingency plan for that area.

The initial cleanup operation consisted of three primary methods as follows:

- Burning
- Mechanical clean-up
- Chemical dispersants

The burning operation was accomplished by towing a fire-resistant boom between two ships until the boom was soaked with oil. The boom was then moved away from the spill and the oil set on fire. The efforts to reduce the spill by further burning were hampered by the weather, so this method did not have a meaningful effect on the cleanup effort.

A mechanical cleanup using booms and skimmers (a specially rigged mechanism attached to a ship and designed to literally skim the oil off the water) was attempted; but that effort, too, was hampered by problems. The skimmers kept getting clogged with oil and kelp, and the repairs to the damaged skimmers took a long time. Also, it was difficult to transfer the oil that had been skimmed from the ships into more permanent containers. The efforts to use mechanical means to remediate the situation were only slightly more successful than the attempts to use burning.

While chemical dispersants were available, Alyeska did not have the equipment necessary to apply them; so private companies did. However, the Sound was so calm that there was not enough wave action to mix the dispersants with the oil; so the technique did not work well enough to warrant its use.

While these efforts to remove the oil from the Sound were in process, other efforts were being made to save as much of the fish and wildlife as possible. Centers were devoted to cleaning waterfowl and sea otters that had become contaminated with oil. In addition, locations where seal pups were born and locations set aside for fish hatcheries were identified and special cleanup operations were begun to minimize the damage to those populations. Despite the efforts of all involved, many fish, fowl, and mammals could not be saved.

The eventual success of the efforts to clean up the environment and protect the living creatures in the area of Prince William Sound will be addressed later in this feature, but it is important to the study of environmental law to learn what the legal ramifications of this incident were to Exxon and the crew of the *Exxon Valdez.* As previously discussed in this text, violations of environmental laws can result in civil and criminal penalties. In 1991, two years after the spill, a settlement was reached between the State of Alaska, the U.S. government, and Exxon. The settlement resolved both the civil and criminal charges against Exxon.

For criminal violations of the environmental laws, Exxon was fined $150 million—the largest fine ever assessed for an environmental crime. The U.S. District Court forgave $125 million in recognition of Exxon's cleanup efforts. The remaining $25 million was divided between the North American Wetlands Conservation fund and the national Victims of Crime fund. As restitution for the damage to the fish, wildlife, and lands caused by the spill, Exxon agreed to pay $100 million, which was divided equally between the federal and state governments.

The civil penalties paid by Exxon included $900 million over a 10-year period. If the U.S. government had identified any further damages before September 1, 2006, fines up to an additional $100 million would have been assessed.

Captain Hazelwood was found not guilty of operating a vessel under the influence of alcohol; but he was found guilty of a misdemeanor criminal offense called negligent discharge of oil, for which he was fined $50,000 and given 1,000 hours of community service in Alaska (a sentence he served and completed prior to the deadline the court gave him).

The dollar amounts of the criminal and civil penalties that Exxon paid may seem staggering; but given the fact that, to this day, remediation efforts are still being undertaken in Prince William Sound, one can only imagine the costs of the cleanup since March 1989.

It has been more than 10 years since the *Exxon Valdez* spill; and during that time, there have been continuing efforts to address the environmental problems caused by the accident. Studies show that the concentrations of oil at the sites with the worst oil pollution have greatly decreased. In addition, some of the species groups affected by the spill, including harbor seals, pink salmon, and many seabirds, have not suffered any significant impact from the incident. Many of the species that suffered initial trauma from the spill show definite signs of recovery.

How has the money from the settlement been spent by the Oil Spill Trustee Council, which is the entity that was entrusted with the use of the funds toward the recovery effort? Much of the money has been spent for habitat restoration and protection. More than $400 million dollars of the settlement has been used to purchase habitat for the species affected by the incident. The legal mechanisms used to acquire the use of the land include conservation easements, timber easements, and fee simple land acquisitions. Both large and small land parcels have been purchased.

One of the species that has benefited from this type of property acquisition is the water bird the marbled murrelet. This bird needed to have its upland terrestrial nesting habitat protected; so as part of the recovery effort, land was purchased throughout the area of the spill to give the marbled murrelet and other species unpolluted locations in which to nest.

An additional portion of the settlement moneys, $285 million, has been dedicated to a scientific program designed to better understand the marine ecosystem in Alaska. Studies have been conducted to try to determine the reasons behind recurring disease in the Pacific herring population. Studies have shown that the prey available to some of the major species in the area has shifted, which has affected the harbor seal population.

One odd finding from these scientific studies is that killer whales that pass through the spill area (transient whales) have contaminant levels more than 10 times that of whales that stay in the area (resident whales). The theory is that the transient whales eat mostly marine mammals while passing through, to fuel their travel, whereas the resident killer whales, not needing as much immediate energy, eat mostly fish. Apparently, due to their longer lives and size, the marine mammals in the area contain more contamination than do the fish. Therefore, the transient whales eating the more contaminated mammals have a higher level of contamination in their blubber than the resident whales.

Settlement moneys also have been spent on bricks and mortar. To reduce pollutants entering Prince William Sound, several new "environmental operating stations" are in place. Facilities and services at these stations are intended to dispose of used oil, household hazardous waste, and scrap metals. In addition, in 1996, the Alaska SeaLife Center opened. The center provides education to the public about the marine environment, houses an advanced marine research facility, and provides animal rehabilitation for injured marine mammals and seabirds. More than $26 million was provided by the Trustee Council for the research function of the facility.

In addition to the significant recovery efforts that have come about as a result of the spill, much has been done in the areas of spill prevention and response. It became clear almost immediately after the spill that the prevention and response capability of the area around Prince William Sound was inadequate, especially in light of the volume of oil shipments that pass through the Sound. In light of this realization, many improvements have been made to the prevention and response capability of the area. Improvements include satellite monitoring of oil tankers by the U.S. Coast Guard, the use of escort vehicles, utilization of specially trained pilots with local experience, new legislation concerning the configuration of oil tankers, contingency planning for the area, additional skimming equipment, containment booms, and dispersants.

Perhaps the most important result of the spill is the enactment of the OPA, designed to increase spill prevention and response capability not only in Prince William Sound but in all waters of the United States (see additional information in this text).

Thus, while the wreck of the *Exxon Valdez* was, and remains, an environmental tragedy, from an environmental law standpoint, it has sparked many positive changes to the manner in which environmental incidents are prevented, anticipated, and responded to. As a postscript, the ship once named the *Exxon Valdez* has since been renamed the *Sea River Mediterranean* and is prohibited from ever returning to Prince William Sound. ■

SUMMARY

The CWA was enacted to restore and maintain the chemical, physical, and biological integrity of the waters of the United States. "Waters of the United States" has been very broadly and, some would say, uncertainly defined by the courts. What is considered "navigable" is part of the CWA analysis. The CWA requires identification of pollutants and contains a comprehensive permit system. One of the key requirements of the CWA is the NPDES. Point sources and nonpoint sources are identified and addressed. Both technology-based standards and water quality standards are utilized to ensure the quality of water. Water is tested for its toxicity. The CWA addresses storm water discharges and ocean discharges. Following the *Exxon Valdez* oil spill, the OPA was passed in an attempt to reduce the risk that such a disaster would happen again. Another part of the CWA, the SDWA, has been largely effective in improving the quality of water consumed from public water systems, using both primary and secondary standards. Water is second only to air in its immediacy to the continuation of life. The CWA covers many water-related subjects in an attempt to ensure that the water that you drink; the water that you use in daily living; the water that is the source of your food; and the water in which you recreate is safe, clean, and protected.

KEY TERMS

- Best Available Demonstrated Technology (BADT)
- Best Available Technology (BAT)
- Best Conventional Technology (BCT)
- Best Practicable Technology (BPT)
- Best Professional Judgment (BPJ)
- Fundamentally different factor (FDF)
- Individual control strategies (ICSs)
- Maximum contaminant level (MCL)
- Maximum contaminant level goal (MCLG)
- National Pollutant Discharge Elimination System (NPDES)
- Navigable
- New Source Performance Standards (NSPS)
- Nonpoint source
- Point source
- Pollutant
- Primary standards
- Public drinking water systems (PDWSs)
- Recommended maximum contaminant level (RMCL)
- Safe Drinking Water Act (SDWA)
- Secondary standards
- Spill prevention control and countermeasure (SPCC) plans
- Total maximum daily load (TMDL)
- Water quality standards
- Waters of the United States

REVIEW QUESTIONS AND HANDS-ON ACTIVITIES

1. Define *waters of the United States.*
2. What types of waterways have been found to be "navigable"?
3. What is the purpose of the NPDES?
4. Describe the difference between a point source and a nonpoint source.
5. What event triggered the enactment of the OPA?
6. Define primary and secondary standards under the SDWA.

7. Water is one of the essentials of human life, so it is understandable why many requirements exist concerning water quality. Are the requirements of the provisions of the CWA sufficient to ensure that water will serve the needs of humanity for years to come? If not, what is missing?
8. Review the decision of the U.S. Supreme Court in *Solid Waste Agency of Northern Cook County v. United States Army Corps of Engineers*, 531 U.S. 159 (2001). This decision focused on an evaluation of what constitutes a "navigable waterway" for purposes of applying the provisions of the CWA. Write a one-paragraph summary of the finding of this case.
9. The OPA is one of the environmental acts passed in direct response to a particular incident: the *Exxon Valdez* oil spill. Is it appropriate to respond to particular environmental incidents with legislation? Why or why not?
10. The SDWA contains nonmandatory standards concerning the appearance and smell of municipal drinking water. Should these standards be made mandatory? Why or why not?

HELPFUL WEBSITES

http://www.epa.gov/ow (EPA, Water)

http://www.cleanwaternetwork.org (Clean Water Network)

http://www.epa.gov/owm (EPA, Wastewater Management)

http://www.epa.gov/adopt (EPA, Adopt Your Watershed)

ENDNOTES

1. *United States v. Phelps Dodge Corp.*, 391 F. Supp. 1181 (D. Ariz. 1975).
2. *United States v. Huebner*, 752 F.2d 1235 (7th Cir. 1984).
3. *Weiszmann v. District Engineer*, 526 F.2d 1302 (5th Cir. 1976).
4. *P.F.Z. Properties Inc. v. Train*, 393 F. Supp. 1370 (D.D.C. 1975).
5. *United States v. Riverside Bayview Homes, Inc.*, 474 U.S. 121 (1985).

6. *Solid Waste Agency of Northern Cook County v. United States Army Corps of Engineers*, 531 U.S. 159 (2001).
7. *Rapanos v. United States*, ___ U.S. ___, 126 S. Ct. 2208, 165 L.Ed. 2d 159 (2006).
8. *Sierra Club v. Abston Construction Company*, 620 F.2d 41 (5th Cir. 1980).
9. *United States v. Earth Sciences, Inc.*, 599 F.2d 368 (10th Cir. 1979).
10. *Appalachian Power Co. v. Train*, 545 F.2d 1351 (4th Cir. 1976).
11. *Barcelo v. Brown*, 478 F. Supp. 646 (D.C. P.R. 1979).
12. *U.S. Public Interest Research Group v. Atlantic Salmon of Maine, L.L.C.*, 215 F. Supp. 2d 239 (D. Me. 2002).
13. *South Florida Water Management District v. Miccosukee Tribe of Indians*, 541 U.S. 95 (2004).

CHAPTER 5

CLEAN AIR ACT (CAA)

TITLE: The Clean Air Act (CAA)

CITATION: 42 U.S.C. secs. 7401-7671(q) (1991)

REGULATIONS: 40 C.F.R. secs. 50-97 (1997)

PURPOSE: To protect human health and the quality of the environment by requiring that the air meet specific standards concerning identified pollutants.

HISTORY: Clean Air Act of 1963
Motor Vehicle Air Pollution Control Act of 1965
Air Quality Act of 1967
Amended 1970, 1977, 1990, 1991

LEARNING OBJECTIVES

After studying this chapter, the reader should be able to

- describe the technology standards applicable to the CAA.
- explain National Ambient Air Quality Standards (NAAQS) and State Implementation Plans (SIPs).
- describe attainment and nonattainment areas.
- define a new source.
- describe a PSD permit program and an operating permit program.
- define an allowance.

Air is the external ingredient most immediately needed to sustain human life. Consequently, having good air quality is a high priority for everyone. Visible air pollution has been called many things, including "brown cloud" and "dirty haze," but some of the most dangerous air pollution is invisible to the human eye. As the United States has become more industrialized and factories and processing plants release new and more harmful pollutants into the air, federal law has been modified frequently in an attempt to ensure that the health of humans and the environment is preserved.

Best Available Control Technology (BACT) The maximum degree of reduction in pollutants achievable in light of economic, energy, and environmental factors.

Generally Available Control Technology (GACT) The technology generally available to reduce air emissions at a facility.

Maximum Achievable Control Technology (MACT) Standards based on existing technology as well as the level of control achieved by sources in each source category demonstrating the best results in eliminating pollutants.

Reasonably Available Control Technology (RACT) A technology standard pursuant to the Clean Air Act (CAA) requiring facilities to use air cleaning technology reasonably available to facilities of that type and with the same type of emissions.

TECHNOLOGY STANDARDS

The *Clean Air Act (CAA)* contains two types of standards: *technology standards* and *emission standards*. Through use of these standards, the CAA seeks to establish generally applicable air quality and control technology requirements. The technology standards used in the CAA provide many similar acronyms. **BACT (Best Available Control Technology)**, **GACT (Generally Available Control Technology)**, **MACT (Maximum Achievable Control Technology)**, and **RACT (Reasonably Available Control Technology)** are all CAA technology acronyms. Technology standards usually require the use of particular equipment that, in the opinion of the EPA, is appropriate for the applicable technology standard.

EMISSION STANDARDS

Emission standards in the CAA do not require use of a particular level of technology; instead, they focus on the levels of pollutants allowed from emissions. For example, a source using a fossil fuel boiler may be limited to emissions containing no more than 1 pound for every BTU (British thermal unit) of energy produced.

Both types of standards (technology and emissions) demonstrate that the success of the CAA is highly dependent on scientists and experts in various technological fields to establish and continually revise particular scientific standards.

The question of when the CAA standards apply to supersede other clean air standards was addressed in *Engine Manufacturers Ass'n v. South Coast Air Quality Management District.*[1] In that case, the district passed rules that prohibited the purchase or lease by various fleet operators of vehicles that did not comply with stringent emission standards. The engine manufacturers sued, claiming that the rules were invalid because they were preempted by the CAA.

ASSIGNMENT

Practice using the acronyms for the CAA technology standards—BACT, GACT, MACT, and RACT—making sure you know what the letters in each acronym stand for. At least all of the CAA technology standard acronyms rhyme!

The trial court and the Ninth Circuit Court of Appeals upheld the validity of the rules, and the manufacturers appealed to the U.S. Supreme Court.

The Supreme Court vacated the lower court's decision, holding that certain rules passed by the district were preempted by the CAA. Specifically, the Supreme Court found that the CAA prohibited states (or their districts) from enacting rules to enforce "any standard" relating to the control of emissions from new motor vehicles or their engines. (42 U.S.C. § 7543) The district claimed that the rules were not preempted because the rules applied only to purchase of vehicles, not to their manufacture or sale. The rules adopted by the district required operators to buy or lease vehicles that complied with strict emission reduction standards. The district claimed that "standard" meant only regulations that compel manufacturers to meet specified emission limits; this interpretation would mean that restrictions concerning purchase of vehicles were preempted by the CAA, but that sale restrictions were not preempted.

However, the Supreme Court found that the term *any standard* in the CAA refers not just to methods of enforcement. The CAA does not treat sales restrictions and purchase restrictions differently; and "a command, accompanied by sanctions, that certain purchasers may buy only vehicles with particular emission characteristics is as much an 'attempt to enforce' a 'standard' as a command, accompanied by sanctions, that a certain percentage of a manufacturer's sales volume must consist of such vehicles." (At p. 1763) To the extent that the rules attempted to enforce "any standard" relating to the control of emissions, the rules were preempted by the CAA. Thus, it appears that any emissions standards are to be controlled by the CAA standards and the authority to set those standards may not be usurped by the states.

NATIONAL AMBIENT AIR QUALITY STANDARDS (NAAQS)

The CAA is designed to set maximum levels of pollutants in "outside air" for areas typically accessible to the public. A key term used in the CAA is *ambient air*. Ambient air is "outside air" outside the boundaries of one's fence line. These maximum levels of pollutants are called the **National Ambient Air Quality Standards (NAAQS)**.

National Ambient Air Quality Standards (NAAQS) The maximum levels of pollutants allowed in the ambient air (air outside the boundaries of one's fence line).

The NAAQS program is one of the key elements of the CAA. NAAQS have been determined for the following six pollutants, which are called the criteria pollutants:

CRITERIA POLLUTANTS

- Carbon monoxide (CO)
- Lead (Pb)
- Nitrogen dioxide (NO_2)
- Ozone (O_3)
- Particulate matter with an aerodynamic diameter of less than 10 microns (PM10)
- Sulfur dioxide (SO_2)

For each of these pollutants, there are *primary NAAQS* (designed to protect human health) and *secondary NAAQS* (designed to promote public welfare). Pursuant to the CAA, NAAQS are supposed to be reviewed every five years; but the EPA has not always met this requirement. These NAAQ requirements are source-specific, meaning that each source of air pollutants is required to comply with specific standards.

The EPA's ability to set NAAQS has been challenged in court.

CASE LAW

WHITMAN V. AMERICAN TRUCKING ASSOC., 531 U.S. 457 (2001).[2]

SUMMARY OF CASE: When the EPA revised NAAQS for particulate matter and ozone, a number of suits were brought to address the issues of whether the EPA could consider costs in setting NAAQS and whether the CAA permitted revision of the ozone standards.

Justice Scalia delivered the opinion of the Court.

These cases present the following questions: (1) Whether . . . the Clean Air Act (CAA) delegates legislative power to the Administrator of the Environmental Protection Agency (EPA). (2) Whether the Administrator may consider the costs of implementation in setting national ambient air quality standards [NAAQS) under the CAA. (3) Whether the Court of Appeals had jurisdiction to review the EPA's interpretation of Part D . . . of the CAA . . . with respect to implementing the revised ozone NAAQS. If so, whether the EPA's interpretation of that part was permissible.

[T]he CAA . . . requires the . . . EPA to promulgate NAAQS for each air pollutant for which "air quality criteria" have been issued under [the Act]. Once a NAAQS has been promulgated, the Administrator must review the standard (and the criteria on which it is based) "at five-year intervals" and make "such revisions . . . as may be appropriate." These cases arose when, on July 18, 1997, the Administrator revised the NAAQS for particulate matter (PM) and ozone. . . . American Trucking Associations [and others] challenged the new standards in the Court of Appeals for the District of Columbia. . . .

The Court of Appeals accepted some challenges and rejected others. It agreed . . . that [the CAA] delegated legislative power to the Administrator in contravention of the United States Constitution . . . because it found that the EPA had interpreted the statute to provide no "intelligible principle" to guide the agency's exercise of authority. . . . On the second issue that the Court of Appeals addressed, it unanimously rejected the . . . argument that the court should depart from the rule . . . that the EPA may not consider the cost of implementing a NAAQS in setting the initial standard. It also rejected [the] argument that the implementation provisions for ozone found in Part D . . . of the CAA were so tied to the existing ozone standard that the EPA lacked the power to revise the standard. . . .

[It has previously been] held that "economic considerations [may] play no part in the promulgation of ambient air quality standards under . . . the CAA." [ATA] argue[s] that [this] decision is incorrect. We disagree. . . .

[The CAA] instructs the EPA to set primary ambient air quality standards "the attainment and maintenance of which . . . are requisite to protect the public health" with "an adequate margin of safety." . . . [We think] it fairly clear that this text does not permit the EPA to consider costs in setting the standards. The language, one scholar has noted, "is absolute." The EPA, "based on" the information about health effects contained in the technical "criteria" documents . . . is to identify the maximum airborne concentration of a pollutant that the public health can tolerate, decrease the concentration to provide an "adequate" margin of safety, and set the standard at that level. Nowhere are the costs of achieving such a standard made part of that initial calculation. . . .

Even so, [ATA] argue[s], many more factors than air pollution affect public health. In particular, the economic cost of implementing a very stringent standard might produce health losses sufficient to offset the health gains achieved in cleaning the air—for example, by closing down whole industries and thereby impoverishing the workers and consumers dependent upon those industries.

That is unquestionably true, and Congress was unquestionably aware of it. . . . [The] CWA permitted the Administrator to waive the compliance deadline for stationary sources [of air pollution] if . . . sufficient control measures were simply unavailable and "the continued operation of such sources is *essential . . . to the public health* or welfare." . . . We have therefore refused to find implicit in ambiguous sections of the CAA an authorization to consider costs that has elsewhere, and so often, been expressly granted. . . .

[The] CAA instructs the EPA to set "ambient air quality standards the attainment and maintenance of which is, in the judgment of the Administrator, based on [the] criteria and allowing an adequate margin of safety, are requisite to protect the public health." The Court of Appeals held that this section as interpreted by the Administrator did not provide an "intelligible principle" to guide the EPA's exercise of authority in setting NAAQS. . . . The court hence found that the EPA's interpretation (but not the statute itself) violated the nondelegation doctrine. . . . We disagree.

In a delegation challenge, the constitutional question is whether the statute has delegated legislative power to the agency. [T]he Constitution vests "all legislative Powers herein granted . . . in a Congress of the United States." This text permits no delegation of those powers . . . and so we repeatedly have said that when Congress confers decision making authority upon agencies *Congress* must "lay down by legislative act an intelligible principle to which the person or body authorized to [act] is directed to conform." We have never suggested that an agency can cure an unlawful delegation of legislative power by adopting in its discretion a limiting construction of the statute. . . . Whether the statute delegates legislative power is a question for the courts, and an agency's voluntary self-denial has no bearing upon the answer.

We agree that . . . the CAA at a minimum requires that "for a discrete set of pollutants and based on published air quality criteria that reflect the latest scientific knowledge, [the] EPA must establish uniform national standards at a level that is requisite to protect public health from the adverse effects of the pollutant in the ambient air." These limits are strikingly similar to . . . ones we [have] approved. . . . [The] CAA [mandate] to set air quality standards at the level that is "requisite" . . . to protect the public health with an adequate margin of safety, fits comfortably within the scope of discretion permitted by our precedent.

The final two issues . . . concern the EPA's authority to implement the revised ozone NAAQS in areas whose ozone levels currently exceed the maximum level permitted by that standard. The CAA designates such areas "nonattainment," and . . . it exposes them to additional restrictions over and above the implementation requirements imposed generally by . . . the CAA. These additional restrictions are found in . . . Part D. . . .

The Administrator first urges . . . that we vacate the judgment of the Court of Appeals on this issue because it lacked jurisdiction to review the EPA's implementation policy. . . . [T]he EPA argues that its implementation policy was not agency "action," was not "final" action, and is not ripe for review. We reject each of these contentions.

We have little trouble concluding that this constitutes final agency action subject to review. The bite in the phrase "final action" . . . is . . . in the word "final," which requires that the action under review "mark the consummation of the agency's decisionmaking process." Only if the "EPA has rendered its last word on the matter" in question . . . is its action "final" and thus reviewable. That standard is satisfied here. . . .

The decision is also ripe for our review. Ripeness "requires us to evaluate both the fitness of the issues for judicial decision and the hardship to the parties of withholding court consideration." . . . The question before us here is purely one of statutory interpretation that would not "benefit from further factual development of the issues presented." Nor will our review "inappropriately interfere with further administrative action," . . . since the EPA has concluded its consideration of the implementation issue. Finally, as for the hardship to the parties: The respondent States must—on pain of forfeiting to the EPA control over implementation of the NAAQS—promptly undertake the lengthy and expensive task of developing state implementation plans (SIPs) that will attain the new, more stringent standard within five years. . . . Such statutes . . . "permit judicial review directly, even before the concrete effects normally required for . . . review are felt." . . . The EPA may not construe the statute in a way that completely nullifies textually applicable provisions meant to limit its discretion. . . . An interpretation . . . at odds with [the statute's] structure and manifest purpose cannot be sustained. We therefore find that the EPA's [nonattainment] implementation policy to be unlawful. . . .

To summarize our holdings in these unusually complex cases: (1) The EPA may not consider implementation costs in setting primary and secondary NAAQS under . . . the CAA. (2) [The CAA] does not delegate legislative power to the EPA in contravention of the . . . Constitution. (3) The Court of Appeals had jurisdiction to review the EPA's interpretation of . . . the CAA, relating to the implementation of the revised ozone NAAQS. (4) The EPA's interpretation of that Part is unreasonable.

The judgment of the Court of Appeals is affirmed in part and reversed in part, and the cases remanded for proceedings consistent with this opinion. ■

QUESTIONS

1. Do you think the EPA should consider the cost of attaining a specific air quality standard? Why or why not?
2. Why did the Court determine that the EPA's interpretation of the rule in this case was "unreasonable"?

In another recent U.S. Supreme Court case, the issue presented was whether the EPA had the obligation to regulate carbon dioxide emissions under the CAA to address the issue of global warming.

CASE LAW

MASSACHUSETTS V. EPA, ___U.S. ___, 127 S. CT. 1438 (2007).

SUMMARY OF CASE: Several states and associations brought a suit against the EPA to force the agency to regulate carbon dioxide and other emissions because of the allegation that these emissions were causing climatological and environmental changes. The lower courts ruled that the EPA administrator could exercise his discretion in refusing to enact the rules requested.

Justice Stevens delivered the opinion of the Court.

A well-documented rise in global temperatures has coincided with a significant increase in the concentration of carbon dioxide in the atmosphere. Respected scientists believe the two trends are related. For when carbon dioxide is released into the atmosphere, it acts like the ceiling of a greenhouse, trapping solar energy and retarding the escape of reflected heat. It is therefore a species—the most important species—of a "greenhouse gas."

Calling global warming "the most pressing environmental challenge of our time," a group of States, local governments, and private organizations, alleged in a petition for certiorari that the Environmental Protection Agency (EPA) has abdicated its responsibility under the Clean Air act to regulate the emissions of four greenhouse gases, including carbon dioxide. Specifically, petitioners asked us to answer two questions concerning the meaning of . . . the Act: whether EPA has the statutory authority to regulate greenhouse gas emissions from new motor vehicles; and if so, whether its stated reasons for refusing to do so are consistent with the statute. . . .

[The CAA] provides: "The EPA Administrator shall by regulation prescribe (and from time to time revise) in accordance with the provisions of this section, standards applicable to the emission of any air pollutant from any class or classes of new motor vehicles or new motor vehicle engines, which in his judgment cause, or contribute to, air pollution which may reasonably be anticipated to endanger public health or welfare. . . ."

The Act defines "air pollutant" to include "any air pollution agent or combination of such agents, including any physical, chemical, biological, radioactive . . . substance or matter which is emitted into or otherwise enters the ambient air." "Welfare" is also defined broadly: among other things, it includes "effects on . . . weather . . . and climate."

When Congress enacted these provisions, the study of climate change was in its infancy. . . . [T]he scientific understanding of climate change [has] progressed. In 1990, the Intergovernmental Panel on Climate Change (IPCC) . . . published its first comprehensive report on the topic. Drawing on expert opinions from across the globe, the IPCC concluded that "emissions resulting from human activities are substantially increasing the atmospheric concentrations of greenhouse gases [which] will enhance the greenhouse effect, resulting on average in an additional warming of the Earth's surface. . . ."

On October 20, 1999, a group of 19 private organizations filed a rulemaking petition asking EPA to regulate "greenhouse gas emissions from new motor vehicles under . . . the Clean Air Act." . . . On September 8, 2003, EPA entered an order denying the rulemaking petition. The agency gave two reasons for its decision: (1) that contrary to the opinions of its former general counsels, the Clean Air Act does not authorize EPA to issue mandatory regulations to address global climate change . . . and (2) that even if the agency had the authority to set greenhouse gas emission standards, it would be unwise to do so at this time. . . . In essence, EPA concluded that climate change was so important that unless Congress spoke with exacting specificity, it could not have meant the agency to address it. Having reached that conclusion, EPA believed it followed that greenhouse gases cannot be "air pollutants" within the meaning of the Act. . . . Given [the] residual uncertainty [concerning the causal link between carbon dioxide emissions and the rise in global surface air temperatures], EPA concluded that regulating greenhouse gas emissions would be unwise.

The agency furthermore characterized any EPA regulations of motor-vehicle emissions as a "piecemeal approach" to climate change. . . . According to EPA, unilateral EPA regulation of motor-vehicle greenhouse gas emissions might also hamper the President's ability to persuade key developing countries to reduce greenhouse gas emissions. . . .

The scope of our review of the merits of the statutory issues is narrow. As we have repeated time and again, an agency has broad discretion to choose how best to marshal its limited delegated responsibilities. . . . We . . . "may reverse any action found to...arbitrary, capricious, an abuse of discretion, or otherwise not in accordance with law."

On the merits, the first question is whether . . . the Clean Air Act authorizes EPA to regulate greenhouse gas emissions from new motor vehicles in the event that it forms a "judgment" that such emissions contribute to climate change. We have little trouble concluding that it does. . . . On the face of [the statute], the definition [of air pollutant] embraces all airborne compounds of whatever stripe, and underscores that intent through the repeated use of the word "any" [air pollutant]. . . . The statute is unambiguous. . . .

EPA finally argues that it cannot regulate carbon dioxide emissions from motor vehicles because doing so would require it to tighten mileage standards, a job (according to EPA) that Congress has assigned to DOT [Department of Transportation]. But that DOT sets mileage standards in no way licenses EPA to shirk its environmental responsibilities. EPA has been charged with protecting the public's "health" and "welfare" . . . a statutory obligation wholly independent of DOT's mandate to promote energy efficiency. . . . The two obligations may overlap, but there is no reason to think the two agencies cannot both administer their obligations and yet avoid inconsistency. . . .

While the [CAA] does condition the exercise of EPA's authority on its formation of a "judgment" . . . that judgment must relate to whether an air pollutant "cause[s] or contribute[s] to, air pollution which may reasonably be anticipated to endanger public health or welfare." . . . If EPA makes a finding of endangerment, the Clean Air Act requires the agency to regulate emissions of the deleterious pollutant from new motor vehicles. . . . Under the clear terms of the Clean Air Act, EPA can avoid taking further action only if it determines that greenhouse gases do not contribute to climate change or if it provides some reasonable explanation as to why it cannot or will not exercise its discretion to determine whether they do. . . . EPA has refused to comply with this clear statutory command.

In short, EPA has offered no reasoned explanation for its refusal to decide whether greenhouse gases cause or contribute to climate change. Its action was therefore "arbitrary, capricious, . . . or otherwise not in accordance with law." . . .

The judgment of the Court of Appeals is reversed, and the case is remanded for further proceedings consistent with this opinion. ■

QUESTIONS

1. Why do you believe the EPA refused to regulate carbon dioxide emissions under the CAA?

2. Why did the Court determine that the EPA's refusal to regulate greenhouse gases was "arbitrary and capricious"?

STATE IMPLEMENTATION PLANS (SIPs)

How are NAAQS implemented? Each state is required to enact a **State Implementation Plan (SIP)**. The CAA sets minimum standards for the state SIPs. If a state fails to attain the NAAQ goals, the minimum requirements for its SIP will be more stringent than if the state had attained the NAAQ goals. The enactment of state SIPs is accomplished through the usual federal procedural requirements involving notice and an opportunity for the public to comment.

State Implementation Plan (SIP) Enacted by each state based on standards set by the Clean Air Act (CAA). Requirements vary depending on whether the state has met the National Ambient Air Quality Standards (NAAQS).

SIP Requirements

- Adequate personnel funding/authority:
  Each state must demonstrate that it has allocated adequate personnel and monetary resources to implement its SIP.
- Air quality data:
  Provisions must be made for collecting such data and transmitting it to the EPA.
- Air quality modeling:
  Technology must be sufficient to be able to "model" or project the effect of emissions.
- Contingency plans:
  States must have sufficient emergency powers to address emissions that present an imminent and substantial danger to the public.
- Enforceable emission limitations:
  This element includes appropriate limitations, control measures, economic incentives, and timetables for the emission requirements.
- Enforcement:
  A SIP must establish an enforcement program, which will be supplemented by the operating permit program established in the CAA.
- Interstate air pollution:
  States must prevent emissions in their state that negatively affect air quality requirements in other states.
- Local consultation:
  States must provide for consultation with counties, cities, and other political subdivisions and allow their participation in the enactment and implementation of the SIP.
- Monitoring and emission data:
  SIPs require adequate monitoring and reporting of data by certain emission sources.
- "Part D requirements":
  For areas that do not attain the NAAQS, a SIP must provide for compliance with special requirements found in Part D of the CAA for those types of areas.
- Permit fees:
  The owner or operator of certain emissions sources must pay, as part of the permit fees, an amount sufficient to cover the state costs associated with the granting, monitoring, and enforcement of the permit.
- Preconstruction review and notification:
  Part C of the CAA requires that new "major" sources of air pollution comply with pre-construction requirements related to the prevention of significant deterioration. "Minor" sources of air pollution also have preconstruction requirements that must be met.
- Revision:
  The SIP must provide for its own revision as federal requirement, technology, or conditions change.

Federal Implementation Plan (FIP) If the Environmental Protection Agency (EPA) is not satisfied that a state has successfully enacted a State Implementation Plan (SIP) for the preservation of air quality in that state, the federal government may enact its own plan (FIP) for that state.

attainment states States that are in compliance with (having attained) the National Ambient Air Quality Standards (NAAQS).

As just indicated in the "revision" discussion, a SIP must change as federal requirements, technology, or conditions within a state change. Once approved by the EPA, a SIP may be enforced through state or federal law. The EPA may require a state to revise its SIP if the EPA deems the SIP deficient in any way. While states have primary responsibility for protecting air quality through the SIPs, if the EPA is not satisfied that a state's SIP is adequate, the EPA may promulgate a **Federal Implementation Plan (FIP)**.

States which have attained the NAAQS are called **attainment states.** In addition to the basic requirements for a SIP, additional SIP requirements are imposed on states that have not attained the NAAQS. Such states are called **nonattainment states**. For these states, the SIP must be expanded to include the following:

Additional SIP Requirements for Nonattainment States

- Annual incremental reductions in nonattainment pollutants
- Automatic contingency measures to be implemented if the area does not make significant progress or obtain the NAAQS by the appropriate deadline
- Identification and quantification of new emissions and a documentation that new emissions will not interfere with eventual attainment of the NAAQS
- If permitted, the revised SIP may provide substitute equivalent techniques for modeling, inventory, and planning as long as the substituted techniques are at least as effective as the EPA's suggested methods
- Inventory of current emissions from all sources of the nonattainment pollutants
- Permit requirements for any new or modified "major" or "minor" new sources
- Provisions requiring that all existing sources and major sources (as soon as possible) comply with RACT technology

nonattainment states States that do not meet the National Ambient Air Quality Standards (NAAQS).

For specific pollutants in nonattainment areas, the 1990 Amendments to the CAA added significant requirements. These requirements include the following:

- Carbon monoxide (CO)
  Nonattainment areas for carbon monoxide are classified as moderate or serious. All such areas were to have come into compliance by the end of 2000. Many carbon monoxide nonattainment areas will have to comply with RACT standards.
- Ozone (O_3)
  If required ozone levels are not attained, the nonattainment areas are classified as marginal, moderate, serious, severe, or extreme

depending on how serious the problem is; and the areas are given various periods of time to come into compliance, with the most seriously affected areas being given the longest amount of time. For example, southern California was given 20 years beginning in 1990 to come into compliance. Existing sources and stationary sources not governed by another control technique will have to achieve RACT standards.

- Particulate matter with an aerodynamic diameter of less than 10 microns (PM10)
  Initially, all PM10 nonattainment areas were classified as moderate; but if they had not come into compliance by the end of 1994, they were reclassified depending on the severity of the noncompliance. All PM10 nonattainment areas were to have come into compliance no later than the end of 2001, although that did not happen. Most of the PM10 nonattainment areas were required to use RACT standards.

QUESTION
The SIP requirements are quite extensive. Can you think of any other requirements that could be added to this list? Are there requirements that you believe could be deleted because they are unnecessary?

NEW SOURCES

The CAA makes distinctions between the technological standards mandated for minor retrofitting of existing sources and the standards for new sources. New sources are required to meet more stringent standards than the standards required for minor retrofitting of existing sources. The new source standards are, in most cases, more expensive to implement and achieve than standards required for minor modifications to existing sources. Theoretically, new sources possess the ability to design and finance their facilities to meet evolving technological standards, while requiring existing sources making only minor modifications to "catch up" technologically would be prohibitively expensive and would prevent the existing sources from being competitive. Thus, the CAA is one of the environmental acts that acknowledges the fiscal impacts of regulations; and when concessions can be made without compromising the intended effect of the act, the CAA provides for differences in technological standards to address fiscal issues.

Despite provisions that assist existing sources in maintaining fiduciary viability, the CAA does distinguish between minor modifications to existing sources and reconstructions of or significant modifications to those sources. Existing sources intending to make major modifications must typically meet the same standards as new sources. If a "reconstruction" of an existing facility is so extensive that it is basically the same as replacing the facility "at the end of its useful life," the new source standards will apply.

NEW SOURCE PERFORMANCE STANDARDS (NSPS)

The technological standards required of new sources are called New Source Performance Standards (NSPS). These standards, set by the EPA, often consist of numerical emissions limitations based on scientific studies determining "adequately demonstrated" "best technology" to achieve a particular "degree of emission reduction." (CAA Section 111) In some cases, however, it is not feasible to set such standards, so the EPA uses a different method to define its requirements. Where numerical emissions standards cannot reasonably be imposed, the EPA may require standards for design, equipment, or operations. NSPS represent the minimum standards required at new or significantly modified existing sources.

Interestingly, while the provisions of the CAA dictate that NSPS are supposed to be reviewed and modified every eight years, the EPA has not kept up with this timetable. In response to this lax compliance with the CAA, the 1990 Amendments to the CAA required the EPA administrator to make revisions to particular standards.

PRECONSTRUCTION PERMITTING

To ensure that the NSPS are achieved, the CAA requires preconstruction review and permitting. Permit requirements are determined based on whether the new source is located in an attainment or nonattainment area for the particular pollutant or pollutants expected to be emitted by the new source. New sources located in attainment areas must comply with a permit program designed for **prevention of significant deterioration (PSD)**. New sources located in nonattainment areas must comply with a nonattainment permit program.

prevention of significant deterioration (PSD) PSD is a standard for new sources of air pollution located in attainment areas. The new sources must comply with a permit program designed to maintain the air quality at approximately the same level as before the new source was added.

PSD PERMIT PROGRAM

Again, the PSD permit program applies to new sources or to significant modifications to existing sources in an attainment area. PSD permits require an owner or operator of a facility to demonstrate that the source will:

- comply with ambient air quality levels intended to prevent deterioration of air quality (PSD levels).
- use BACT for each pollutant to be emitted in significant amounts.

BACT is just one of the many technology-based acronyms found in the CAA, most of which rhyme. (RACT and MACT are two others.) As noted previously, BACT is the acronym for Best Available Control Technology. The CAA defines BACT as "the maximum degree of reduction . . . achievable" in light of economic, energy, and environmental factors.

BACT requirements have typically been left up to states; but in 1987, the EPA issued a guidance document known as the top-down guidance, which strengthens the role of the EPA in setting BACT standards and restricts the role of the states. In essence, the provisions of this procedure do what the name implies: ensure that the setting of BACT standards comes from the top down—from the EPA to the states to the owners and operators. The EPA's authority to set BACT standards was challenged by the state of Alaska.

In *Alaska Department of Environmental Conservation v. Environmental Protection Agency*,[3] Alaska sued the EPA because the EPA prevented Alaska from issuing a permit for PSD to permit a zinc mine expansion under the CAA. Alaska planned to issue the permit based on its determination that the mine's BACT was sufficient. The EPA claimed that Alaska's BACT determination was unreasonable because the BACT was insufficient; Alaska claimed that the EPA's authority under CAA was limited to ensuring that the PSD permit contained a BACT determination.

The CAA prohibits any major air pollutant facility from construction unless it is equipped with the "best available control technology." The EPA is authorized under the CAA to issue orders to states that are not complying with the provisions of the CAA. Alaska had initially required the mine operator to use an emission control technology known as selective catalytic reduction (SCR), which reduces nitrogen oxide emissions by 90 percent. However, the mine operators proposed a cheaper alternative technology, known as Low Nox, which would reduce nitrogen oxide emissions by 30 percent; and Alaska accepted this alternative as the BACT.

> Centrally at issue in this case is the question whether EPA's oversight role, described by Congress in CAA . . . extends to ensuring that a state permitting authority's BACT determination is reasonable in light of the statutory guidelines. . . . [Alaska] argues that the statutory definition of BACT . . . unambiguously assigns to the [state] alone the determination of the control technology qualifying as 'best available.' EPA claims no prerogative to designate the

> correct BACT; the Agency asserts only the authority to guard against unreasonable designations.
> *Alaska Department of Environmental Conservation*, at pp. 993, 1002

The Supreme Court held that the EPA had supervisory authority over the reasonableness of the state's BACT determination; the EPA properly determined that the Alaska's BACT determination in this case lacked sufficient evidentiary support. The CAA grants to the EPA oversight authority when the local agency's BACT determination is not "faithful to the statute's definition." This case clarifies the authority of the EPA to set BACT standards.

To what types of emissions do the BACT requirements apply? BACT applies to any regulated pollutant a source has the potential to emit in a significant amount. An exception to this category is that as part of the 1990 Amendments to the CAA, substances listed as part of the air toxics program are not required to be regulated by the PSD program. (The definition and applicability of air toxics is discussed later in this chapter.) Keep in mind that just because the federal regulations do not require air toxics to be regulated under the PSD program does not mean that states will not impose such a requirement. States may impose more strict requirements than those imposed under federal environmental programs, but states cannot impose less restrictive regulations.

criteria pollutants Carbon monoxide (CO), sulfur dioxide (SO_2), nitrogen dioxide (NO_2), ozone (O_3), lead (Pb), and particulate matter (PM10).

air toxics Hazardous organic materials, metals, and other substances on a list of regulated substances kept pursuant to the Clean Air Act (CAA).

BACT permit review has usually addressed both **criteria pollutants** and **air toxics**. Criteria pollutants, identified earlier in this chapter, include pollutants such as carbon monoxide, lead, and ozone. Air toxics are hazardous organic materials, metals, and other substances as added by the list of regulated substances. As of 2006, 188 substances were regulated as air toxics, including nonmethane hydrocarbons, oxides of nitrogen, and carbon dioxide (42 U.S.C. sec. 7521).

Air toxics are regulated pursuant to Section 112 of the CAA. In 1990, the regulation of air toxics changed from being health-based to technology-based. All major sources (defined by quantities of emissions of listed substances) must comply with the appropriately named "major source" program, and other sources may be required to comply with an "area" program. Major source categories include facilities such as oil refineries and chemical plants.

ASSIGNMENT

Find out how many substances are presently regulated as air toxics.

The EPA has worked on standards for more than 50 categories of sources. The standards for each category must require technology that achieves MACT. To set appropriate standards, the EPA must study existing technology as well as the level of control achieved by sources in each category demonstrating the best results.

The first set of MACT standards established by the EPA were called the **Hazardous Organic NESHAP (HON)**. They covered emissions of 112 air toxics relating to nearly 370 organic chemical manufacturers using more than 940 chemical manufacturing processes.

Hazardous Organic NESHAP (HON) The first set of technology standards meeting the Maximum Achievable Control Technology (MACT) standards under the Clean Air Act (CAA).

Procedures established in the 1990 Amendments to the CAA were designed to protect public health with an "ample margin of safety." These procedures were believed to be necessary since MACT standards are technology-based rather than health-based. The health-based standards in the 1990 Amendments calls for an analysis of health risks no more than eight years after the MACT standard is implemented. If the MACT standard does not reduce lifetime risk for known or suspected carcinogens to the most exposed individual to less than one in a million, additional controls will be required.

In addition to the PSD requirements already discussed, the CAA PSD permitting program may require sources located near national parks or other sensitive areas to show that their emissions will not affect other standards related to air quality, such as visibility.

NONATTAINMENT AREA PERMIT PROGRAM

To review, a nonattainment area is an area that has not attained the NAAQS for a particular pollutant, new major stationary sources, or significant modifications of existing major sources. For purposes of this permit program, a major source is generally described as a source having the potential to emit a nonattainment pollutant in amounts in excess of a particular technology-based standard.

Unlike the PSD permit programs for attainment areas, which are implemented primarily by the EPA, states are responsible for implementing the nonattainment permit programs. Facilities subject to these permit programs are required to ensure that they can reach the **Lowest Achievable Emission Rate (LAER)**. LAERs are based on the most stringent limitations contained in a state's SIP or the most stringent limitations achieved in practice for a similarly situated facility, whichever is more stringent.

Lowest Achievable Emission Rate (LAER) A standard based on the most stringent limitations contained in a state's State Implementation Plan (SIP) or the most stringent limitation achieved in practice for a similarly situated facility, whichever is more stringent.

Additionally, the states' nonattainment permit programs require new facilities and existing facilities intending to make major modifications to figure out a way to ensure an "offset" of pollutant emissions. For every proposed emission of a pollutant, facilities must arrange for nearby facilities to reduce their emissions. The more serious the nonattainment problem in a particular area, the more strict the offset requirements will be for a new facility or an existing one seeking major modifications. The necessary offset is described as a ratio. For example, the ratio for one nonattainment area might be 1.2 to 1, while the ratio in another nonattainment area might be 1.5 to 1.

Facilities seeking nonattainment permits must demonstrate that any other sources it owns or operates is in compliance with applicable regulations or has a plan to come into compliance.

Lastly, facilities must demonstrate that the benefits of the proposed source (or the modifications to an existing source) outweigh the environmental and social detriments associated with the facility.

If "reconstruction" of an existing facility is so extensive that the reconstruction is basically the same as replacing the facility "at the end of its useful life," the new source standards may apply to the extent that the NSPS program must be followed. A reconstruction meeting this definition does not, in any event, trigger the PSD or nonattainment permit programs. Typically, reconstruction involving 50 percent or more of a facility will be deemed a reconstruction and require the facility, barring exceptions, to comply with NSPS. Even though a facility may be proposing a reconstruction that meets the previous definition, the NSPS does not apply when a finding is made that the NSPS is technologically or economically infeasible or where cost considerations, remaining useful life, and potential emissions reductions make application of the NSPS inappropriate.

The rules regarding modification of facilities are slightly different from the rules regarding reconstruction of facilities.

FOR PURPOSES OF THIS PORTION OF THE CAA, A MODIFICATION IS DEFINED AS A CHANGE THAT

- is physical or operational.
- will result in an increase in emissions of a regulated pollutant.
- does not constitute an activity such as routine repair, replacement, or maintenance.

The EPA interpreted the modification rule very broadly, interpreting the rule to mean that virtually any modification that did not constitute routine repair, replacement, or maintenance invoked the application of the rule. Due to this inclusive interpretation by the EPA, the modification rule was analyzed by the U.S. Court of Appeals for the Seventh Circuit in a case entitled *Wisconsin Electric Power Company* ["WEPCo"] *v. Reilly*.[1]

In *WEPCo*, the EPA determined that certain proposed renovations to be made to WEPCo's Port Washington power plant (on Lake Michigan) would subject the plant to pollution control provisions of the CAA. WEPCo appealed this determination, claiming that the modifications were included in the exceptions under the CAA for minor changes that would not trigger the pollution control provisions of the act. WEPCo argued that changing out rear steam drums and more than 40 air heaters over a period of four years was simply equipment replacement and was not the kind of change that should trigger the operation of CAA since the act exempted "routine maintenance" from the pollution control requirements. However, the court found that the changes were replacements of "major generating station systems" and were modifications of sufficient scope to trigger the pollution control requirements of CAA. It is significant that WEPCo was unable to identify any other power plant that had undergone such extensive replacements, leading the court to conclude that the changes were anything but "routine."

The 1990 CAA Amendments did not include language that required the EPA to modify its interpretation of the modification rule, but rules promulgated in 1992 by the EPA did provide some clarification. In 1992, the EPA held a New Source Review Workshop to address not only the modification rule but also the entire preconstruction permitting program. A rule promulgated by the EPA in 1994 effectively reversed the *WEPCo* decision and demonstrated that the EPA continues to flex its muscles in this area of CAA enforcement.

If a new source or an existing source seeking to make significant modifications is located in an area that is an attainment area for some pollutants and a nonattainment area for other pollutants, the facility may be required to meet the standards for both a PSD permit program and a nonattainment permit program.

OPERATING PERMIT PROGRAM

The two preconstruction permitting programs just outlined (for attainment and nonattainment areas) address issues associated with facilities that have not yet begun operating. The operating permit program, as evidenced by its name, controls activities at facilities that are already operating.

The operating permit program was introduced to the CAA in the 1990 Amendments. Prior to that time, there were no source-specific permits for operating facilities, and SIPs controlled operations at those facilities. Pursuant to the 1990 Amendments (Title V), each state is required to create and implement source-specific permit requirements for existing facilities. Theoretically, such a permit program would incorporate all state and federal requirements for most pollutants, thus simplifying the regulatory process for these facilities. Each state must have its permit program approved by the EPA; and to receive approval, the state programs must meet at least minimum EPA standards. Once approved, the permit programs are administered by the states, but the EPA retains the right to monitor and enforce the program requirements. Further, the EPA retains the right to review individual permit applications submitted by facilities.

The permit regulations found in Section 70.3 of Title V of the 1990 CAA Amendments require each state program to include regulation of the following sources:

Sources Regulated by State CAA Programs

- Any major source as defined by the CAA
- Any source subject to a standard, a limitation, or another requirement under Section 111 of the CAA
- Any source subject to a standard or requirement under Section 112 of the CAA (with the exception that being subject to the accidental release provision alone will not trigger the larger permitting requirement)
- Any affected source under Title IV of the CAA
- Any source in a source category designated by the EPA

A state may defer regulation of non-major sources by up to five years. Also, if a state determines that particular types of sources are not significant risks due to their size, emission levels, or production rate, a state may develop exemptions to regulation for those facilities so long as the exemptions do not violate any EPA mandatory requirements. A state program must include standard application forms.

APPROVAL OF A PERMIT PROGRAM

A state's permit program becomes effective upon approval by the EPA. The EPA can grant full approval, partial approval, or interim approval. Interim approval is the least favorable approval because it means that a state has quite a bit of work to do to achieve final and full approval. Interim approval is for a limited period of time and allows for limited permitting only. Partial approval means that a state has final approval of a portion of its plan but still has work to do to get full final approval. Full approval, as the name implies, is full and final approval by the EPA that allows a state to implement its permitting program in its entirety. If a state fails to implement a permit program on its own, the EPA may develop a federal operating permit program. (40 C.F.R. Part 71)

PERMIT PROCESS

The procedures for obtaining a permit for an existing source are similar to other permitting processes found in environmental law. A source must submit a fully completed application. A state has up to 60 days to determine if an application is complete, or the application will automatically be deemed complete.

The application must describe a compliance plan that ensures that the facility will comply with existing laws and regulations. The compliance plan must be capable of implementation within one year of the effective date of a permit.

APPLICATION CRITERIA

An application must list

- all major emissions of pollutants.
- all emissions of "regulated air pollutants."
- identification of all emissions points.
- rates of emissions in tons per year and in other compliance increments.
- identification of all air pollution control requirements.

Once a source has submitted a timely and complete application, the source is permitted to operate until the application is processed. Ordinarily, it is a violation of the CAA to operate without an approved permit; but once a timely and completed application has been filed, a source is given a permit shield, allowing the source to operate without penalty.

PERMIT ISSUANCE

Within 18 months of receiving a complete application, the permitting entity (the applicable state or the EPA in a state that does not have an approved program) must take final action on an application.

Permit Provisions

A permit is issued for a fixed term that cannot exceed five years. The permit includes

- applicable emissions limitations and standards.
- certification, testing, monitoring, record keeping, and reporting requirements related to compliance with the standards imposed.
- permit conditions prohibiting sulfur dioxide emissions exceeding applicable allowances.
- a severability clause, which ensures the integrity of the remaining permit provisions should one part of the permit be challenged and declared invalid.
- a statement that the permit may be revoked, modified, reopened, reissued, or terminated for cause.
- a provision to ensure that the source pays all applicable application fees.
- provisions allowing inspection and entry by the permitting authority.
- a schedule of compliance, including regular progress reports.

Often, to allow carefully limited operational flexibility, permits are issued based on several different operational options. If a facility were to change its operations but stay within one of the permitted options, no permit revision would be required as a result of the change.

Permit requirements imposed by a state only (not federal requirements) are not federally enforceable. Any terms that are not specifically identified as being not federally enforceable may be enforced by the EPA.

Before a permit can be issued, the CAA requires that the public be given an opportunity to read and comment on the proposed permit. When public notice is given, the public has at least 30 days to comment.

If there are a sufficient number of requests from the public, a public hearing will be held.

If a state is the permitting entity, the state must submit a copy of each permit application, draft permit, and final permit to the EPA for review. If the EPA objects to the permit within 45 days, the state may not issue the permit. The EPA must object to any permit that does not meet the applicable requirements of the CAA. The state has 90 days to revise and resubmit a permit to the EPA. If it does not do so, the EPA has final authority to issue or deny the permit under conditions of the EPA's choosing.

After the EPA's 45-day review period, any person can petition the EPA to object to issuance of a particular permit. The objection must be based on objections raised during the public comment period unless the objections could not be raised during that time because it was not practicable to raise the objection then or because the basis for the objection arose after the comment period.

Before issuance of a permit, the permitting entity also must provide notice of each draft permit to every "affected state" during the public comment period. To be considered an "affected state," a state must be a state whose air quality may be affected and that is contiguous to the state in which the source is located or must be within 50 miles of the source.

CHANGES TO A PERMIT

Over time, any existing facility will need to modify its operational procedures. These operational changes may trigger a need to modify a permit issued under the CAA. Facilities have traditionally had some flexibility concerning the need to apply for changes to a CAA permit. (40 C.F.R. Part 70) A facility must make a change to its permit only when the facility cannot operate under the new procedures without violating its existing permit or when the change triggers a requirement not triggered by the previous mode of operation.

TYPES OF CHANGES TO CAA PERMITS

There are basically four types of changes to a CAA permit:

- Administrative amendment
- *De Minimus* revision
- Minor revision
- Significant revision

Administrative Amendment

Typically, an administrative amendment is a simple revision correcting very minor mistakes or changes in information submitted as part of a permit, such as a typographical error, a change in business name, or some similar factual information not specifically related to the substance of the operations of the facility. No public notice is required for this type of permit change.

REVIEW
The term *de minimus* as used in the law refers to something that is very minor or minimal in scope. Something considered *de minimus* is typically even less substantial than something that is "minor."

De Minimus Revision

The term *de minimus* refers to something that is very minor or minimal in scope. For a change that is more than just technical, as with an administrative amendment, but not significant in the overall operation of a facility, this type of revision may be available. Public notice is provided for this revision, but only after the revision has been made, at which time the public can request that a state disapprove or revoke the revision.

Minor Revision

To be eligible for this type of revision, the facility seeking the change must be in compliance with its existing permit and the requested change cannot put the facility in violation of any requirement applicable to that facility. This type of revision is necessary when there is a substantive change in operations categorized as greater than *de minimus* and less than significant. Public notice and opportunity to object are a part of this process, and the facility must wait either 21 or 28 days before implementing the change to allow for public input and a possible citizen suit objecting to the proposed change.

Significant Revision

Unlike the more streamlined procedures for the three categories just outlined, the procedures necessary for a significant change are not meaningfully different from those necessary to obtain a permit in the first instance. Notice of the proposed change must be given to the public, affected states, and the EPA.

TRADING

The CAA does allow facilities/sources to trade emissions limits as long as all of the facilities in the area stay within the applicable emissions caps for pollutants as set by the EPA. In other words, as a region, the operating facilities may not produce emissions that exceed the EPA cap for any given pollutant for the area in question.

ACCIDENTAL RELEASES

All environmental regulatory laws contain provisions addressing the possibility that the systems designed for a particular facility will not operate as expected and that unintended, unexpected release may occur. The CAA is no exception to this rule and includes provisions designed to control and prevent accidental releases of regulated hazardous pollutants or other extremely hazardous substances. [CAA Section 112 (r)]. The 1990 Amendments to the CAA require owners and operators of facilities who have such hazardous substances present in more than threshold quantities to prepare risk management plans to address accidental releases. Additional controls against accidental releases include annual audits and safety inspections.

ACID RAIN

Acid rain is rain that contains high quantities of two substances: sulfur dioxide (SO_2) and nitrogen oxides (NOx). The 1990 Amendments to the CAA regulate emissions of these substances. Title IV of the Amendments creates a program for limiting sulfur dioxide emissions and addresses the tracking, trading, monitoring, excess emission penalties, and offset plans. (40 C.F.R. Parts 72, 73, 75, 77 and 78)

acid rain Rain that contains high quantities of sulfur dioxide and nitrogen oxides.

ASSIGNMENT

Acid rain has been a controversial subject for many years. Find a recent article addressing the topic and determine whether it appears that the problem has been solved.

ALLOWANCES

A sulfur dioxide allowance is an authorization to emit 1 ton of sulfur dioxide. A facility will be given an allowance that cannot be exceeded during a calendar year. Failure to stay within the allowed emission level results in penalties that are designed to be so costly that it is more cost-effective to comply with the emissions levels than to pay the penalties. The 1990 Amendments described the legal characteristics of an allowance and specified that allowances are not a property right and can be limited, revoked, or modified. As part of its permit, a facility must say whether it can operate within its own allowance limitations or whether it intends to obtain allowances from other sources to meet its operational needs.

QUESTION

You may have received an allowance from your parents when you were a child. How, if at all, does the concept of allowances in the CAA differ from the allowance you received when you were younger?

Best Available Retrofit Technology (BART) Pursuant to the Clean Air Act (CAA), states are required to use this level of technology to eliminate certain visible air pollution.

plume blight Impairment of visibility as a result of plumes, which are identifiable columns obscuring visibility.

regional haze The technical term for what is more commonly known as smog. A general film impairing visibility over a large area.

ASSIGNMENT

Does the municipality in which you live have a smog problem? If it does, some type of CAA program is undoubtedly in place to address the issue. Find out what restrictions or limitations your municipality must live with to ensure cleaner air.

The concept of allowances brings some unique situations to environmental law. Every year an auction is held at which allowances can be purchased by any entity having a permit providing for the holding of allowances. The auction is to ensure fair and orderly transfer of allowances and preserve competition in the electric power industry (which is the major industry involved in the emission of sulfur dioxides). In addition, the CAA provides for a reserve of allowances owned by the EPA, which can be purchased from the EPA if a new utility cannot purchase its allowances any other way.

VISIBILITY STANDARDS

Since the 1977 CAA Amendments, there have been visibility standards applicable to the states. The goal of these standards is to eliminate any human-made impairments to clear visibility.

Through their SIPs, states are to develop the **Best Available Retrofit Technology (BART)** in an effort to eliminate **plume blight** (impairment of visibility as a result of plumes) in certain environmentally sensitive areas (large parks and wilderness areas). Another type of visible air pollution is **regional haze**. *Regional haze* is the technical term for what most people call smog. Where a plume is an identifiable column obscuring visibility, regional haze is more of a general film impairing visibility over a much larger area.

Visibility issues also are a part of the PSD permitting program, which requires a new or modified source to evaluate whether its emissions will adversely affect air quality, including visibility.

ENFORCEMENT

Like the other federal environmental acts, the CAA provides for a variety of enforcement mechanisms. The CAA contains an *administrative enforcement* provision, which allows the EPA administrator to bring an enforcement action directly against a violator rather than go through the courts. This provision is modeled after a similar provision in the CWA and allows the administrator to seek civil penalties up to $200,000 or more. The administrator gives notice to the alleged violator, which is then given 30 days to request an adjudicatory hearing.

The administrator also may issue field citations (similar to tickets) for minor violations.

A case in which the EPA exercised this authority is *Tennessee Valley Authority v. Whitman*.[5] The Tennessee Valley Authority (TVA) refused to comply with an administrative compliance order (ACO) issued by the EPA. The TVA had undertaken rehabilitation projects at several power plants without CAA permits. The U.S. Court of Appeals for the Eleventh Circuit found that the EPA's authority to issue ACOs, which had civil and criminal penalties, was unconstitutional. The U.S. Supreme Court refused to grant certiorari, permitting the decision of the Eleventh Circuit to stand.

> Although the CAA empowers the EPA to issue ACOs that have the status of law, we believe that the statutory scheme is unconstitutional to the extent that severe civil and criminal penalties can be imposed for noncompliance with the terms of an ACO. Accordingly, ACOs are legally inconsequential and do not constitute final agency action. . . . The EPA must prove the existence of a CAA violation in district court; until then, TVA is free to ignore the ACO without risking the imposition of penalties for noncompliance with its terms.
> *Tennessee Valley Authority*, at page 1239

To the extent that ACOs were authorized by the CAA with the force of law (subjecting violators to monetary penalties and imprisonment), the CAA is unconstitutional. Such orders cannot be enforced because they delegate power to the EPA that is beyond the constitutional scope of an executive branch agency. Thus, the EPA's authority to enter ACOs is limited to some degree.

The CAA also allows the EPA to enter into *consent agreements*, although the EPA's authority in this regard has been challenged. One case in which a challenge was made is *Sierra Club v. Browner*.[6] In the trial court memorandum opinion in this case, the plaintiffs brought an action to compel the EPA administrator to promulgate regulations under the CAA Amendments of 1990. In these amendments, Congress required the EPA to list hazardous air pollutants and directed the EPA to publish categories of major sources of the listed pollutants. The EPA had entered into a consent agreement with a pipeline company, but the new regulations changed the agreement. The issue before the court was whether the court had jurisdiction to order the EPA to promulgate the regulations. (The agreement specified that the EPA would promulgate the regulations.) The court determined that it did have jurisdiction in this case and that the EPA properly used its discretion in issuing the regulations. The regulations were not in conflict with the provisions of the CAA.

The CAA further allows *private citizens* to bring suit for civil penalties for a failure to abide by the provisions of the CAA. In one such suit, *Tanner v. Armco Steel Corp.*,[7] the plaintiffs sued to recover for injuries they allegedly sustained as a result of their exposure to air pollutants emitted by the defendants' petroleum refineries and plants along the Houston Ship Channel. The plaintiffs based their complaint on the alleged "constitutional right" to "a healthy and clean environment." The plaintiffs asserted that the body of state and municipal regulations concerning clean air constituted "state action" sufficient to trigger liability under the Civil Rights Act (42 U.S.C. § 1983), which provides that no citizen may be deprived of any constitutional right by anyone acting "under color of state law."

However, the court ruled that there was no "constitutional right to a healthy and clean environment." While there may be a state tort suit, this federal court found that there was no federal constitutional violation. Thus, even though citizens may bring actions alleging a failure to follow the requirements of the CAA, such suits are not founded in constitutional principles, but in tort principles.

The CAA additionally provides for the imposition of criminal felony penalties against "any person" (a definition that includes individual, corporations, and partnerships) who knowingly violates the CAA. Some of these criminal penalties apply only to "senior management personnel" or "corporate officers," but many penalties can be enforced against anyone involved in the violation.

Knowingly making false statements to the EPA, failing to keep required records, or failing to pay a fee owed to the government under the CAA (such as a permit fee) are among the offenses that can bring fines up to $100,000 and a year in jail for individuals and up to $500,000 for corporations. Fines are doubled for repeat offenders.

Even more severe standards for criminal penalties under the CAA relate to the release of toxics that place another person in "imminent danger of death or serious bodily injury." To "knowingly" make such a release brings penalties of up to $250,000 and 15 years in jail.

To "negligently" make such a release brings a fine of up to $100,000 and a year in jail. By criminalizing negligent behavior, the CAA strives to avoid the defense by corporate officials that they did not know what was going on in their facilities. The theory is that such officials should have known and to not know is negligent.

Because of these strict criminal penalties, many companies have devised systems of internal compliance audits in which they attempt to identify and solve problems before the violations are discovered and before serious penalties accrue. The CAA regulations encourage self-audits, and companies that have an effective self-audit program are given leniency in criminal proceedings. Companies are required to report violations that they discover, but self-reported violations are dealt with differently than those discovered by other enforcement mechanisms. When a company has an internal audit program, makes timely and voluntary disclosure of violations, makes good faith efforts to remedy any violations, appropriately disciplines its employees, and makes good faith efforts to reach resolution concerning compliance issues with the enforcement agencies, criminal prosecution can usually be avoided.

POLITICS AND ENVIRONMENTAL LAW

Laws, including environmental laws, are made by legislators elected by their constituents. By definition, then, those legislators are politicians. Whether they are the product of party politics or are backed by some other interest group, politicians must take stands on various issues facing their constituency. Environmental laws are no exception. The positions politicians take on environmental issues are the subject of praise and criticism by various factions within the press and public. One of the environmental topics for which politicians are held accountable is air quality. Air quality is, understandably, a political issue; and the views and actions of politicians on the subject have often been a source of fodder for political cartoonists, as demonstrated by the following panel. The cartoon was selected not because its content represents the views of the author, but because it is a good example of how politicians are treated and because it pokes fun at the sitting president. Regardless of party affiliation or stance on environmental issues, no president is immune from such attacks.

(*continued*)

Courtesy of Joe Heller, Green Bay Press Gazette

The public will continue to voice its opinion about the views and actions of lawmakers concerning every issue, but especially those issues that touch close to home, such as environmental issues.

ENVIRONMENTAL LAW PARALEGAL PROFILE

Derek Kirchmeier

What is your favorite part of your job?

Fortunately, I have been a paralegal who has been treated like an attorney over my 12 years of working in a law firm setting. This means I have been involved in settlement negotiations, all aspects of discovery, pretrial motions, trial, and post-trial work and have felt that my opinion meant something when asked about the most salient points in a case. I love the adventure of the legal environment and not knowing what is going to happen from one day to the next. I have been fortunate enough to work with individuals who never placed labels on their staff, and so I was not limited in what my role was or what my contributions would be.

Describe the duties you perform in a typical day.

There really is no "typical" day. I presently am responsible for developing cases for the attorneys from start to finish. This currently involves identifying discovery issues; staying on top of deadlines; analyzing cases for potential problem areas; addressing the need for experts; identifying and organizing the best way to handle thousands of pages of documents; keeping track of hundreds of witnesses, deposition prep, witness interviews, medical summaries, witness chronologies, legal research, and general research; meeting with and updating the attorneys on the status of cases; drafting settlement statements; and drafting trial testimony. Those are a few of the things that come to mind and may need to be done in a given day. This is on top of maintaining filing to some extent and addressing various billing issues.

What is the most challenging part of your job?

The most challenging part of my job is to remember hundreds of names for up to 10 cases, as well as keeping track of the hundreds, if not thousands, of facts for each case. It is also a challenge many times to find an expert in a particular field. To ultimately take those facts and piece them together to see the whole picture is the most rewarding aspect of the work of a paralegal.

What advice do you have for paralegal students interested in working on environmental law issues?

Environmental law is beyond challenging. It will push your mind at times to the very brink. You will be required to work very long hours for a fantastic cause. You can burn out quickly if you are not prepared to work many 16-hour days for weeks in a row. Because the environmental laws are constantly changing (or even more challenging, the fact that they have changed so much over just a few years), different standards apply for different time periods. You have got to be prepared, again, to leave no stone unturned; review documents from every agency, third-party, or person you can think of; and not take no for an answer.

Do you have any tips for success?

To be successful as a paralegal, never think you know it all and never assume you do know something. If you are not 100 percent sure, ask an experienced lawyer, or someone who does know, for advice. Do not try to solve all of the world's problems in a case that you become so enthralled with that the rest of the world, including your family and friends, gets lost in the shuffle. Stay level-headed. Be prepared for anything by leaving no stone unturned, no witness silent. Regardless of whether you are a plaintiff or a defendant, a lawsuit is a stressful time for all of the parties involved. And if you try to remember that the other side is human, you will find that negotiations are more successful; and it is more likely you will be able to resolve the case.

Are special skills required for your job?

Patience, awareness, thinking outside the box, leaving no stone unturned, perseverance, a knack for learning, and admitting when you are wrong are some of the biggest assets you can have for becoming a successful paralegal.

(continued)

Do you have other information or thoughts to share with paralegal students interested in environmental law?

With environmental law, I find one's satisfaction level depends on the case—on what you want. I worked for a very small firm and worked with a lawyer who took on Fortune 500 companies. It was truly a David versus Goliath endeavor several times over. If you are truly interested in environmental litigation, you need to tighten your bootstraps and plan for a long haul. Of course, there are other aspects of environmental litigation that will not require the sacrifice that litigation does, but you should truly know what it is in the environmental arena you want to pursue before just diving in.

Derek Kirchmeier is a paralegal with Godin & Baity, LLC, in Denver, Colorado. He previously worked more than 10 years as a senior litigation paralegal with The Hannon Law Firm, LLC, also in Denver. In the absence of the firm's office administrator, Mr. Kirchmeier provided that service. Mr. Kirchmeier is actively involved in raising his daughters with his wife, running, and collecting baseball cards.

SUMMARY

The purpose of the CAA is to protect human health and the quality of the environment by requiring that specific air standards be met concerning identified pollutants. Technology plays a major part in the effectiveness of the CAA. CAA technology standards are identified by acronyms, including BACT, GACT, MACT, and RACT. In addition to technology standards, the CAA has emissions standards that must be met. To regulate the quality of ambient air, the CAA provides for the setting of NAAQS, both primary and secondary. NSPS are included in the CAA. For attainments areas, a PSD program makes sure the air quality does not deteriorate. As part of the BACT review, criteria pollutants and air toxics are addressed. The CAA provides for operating plan programs, which may result in the issuance of a permit. While the CAA regulations are complex and seemingly endless, they are appropriate to protect that substance most critical to life—air.

KEY TERMS

- Acid rain
- Air toxics

- Attainment state
- Best Available Control Technology (BACT)
- Best Available Retrofit Technology (BART)
- Criteria pollutants
- Emission standards
- Federal Implementation Plan (FIP)
- Generally Available Control Technology (GACT)
- Hazardous Organic NESHAP (HON)
- Lowest Achievable Emission Rate (LAER)
- Maximum Achievable Control Technology (MACT)
- National Ambient Air Quality Standards (NAAQS)
- Nonattainment state
- Plume blight
- Prevention of Significant Deterioration (PSD)
- Primary NAAQS
- Reasonably Available Control Technology (RACT)
- Regional haze
- Secondary NAAQS
- State Implementation Plan (SIP)
- Technology standards

REVIEW QUESTIONS AND HANDS-ON ACTIVITIES

1. What is a technology-based standard? Name three found in the CAA.
2. Describe the differences between primary and secondary NAAQS.
3. What is a SIP?
4. What is the difference between an attainment and nonattainment state?
5. Define *new source*.
6. What is the purpose of the PSD permitting program?
7. What do you think about the number of different technology standards used in the CAA? Are there too many? Create a CAA technology standard (and appropriate acronym) that might

serve more than one purpose, thus eliminating the need for so many acronyms.

8. What nearby major metropolitan area has an air pollution problem? Find out what steps that city has taken to reduce its air pollution and whether it is presently an attainment or nonattainment area.

9. What do you think about the concepts of trading the right to emit a certain pollutant or the concept of allowances? Explain why these concepts enhance or detract from the intentions behind the CAA.

10. As mentioned in the chapter, air pollution is a very political topic. Read the article entitled "Changing the Rules—How the Bush Administration Quietly—and Radically—Transformed the Nation's Clean Air Policy" by Bruce Barcott. What is your evaluation of the author's analysis?

HELPFUL WEBSITES

http://www.epa.gov/oar (EPA, Office of Air and Radiation)

http://www.epa.gov/air/oaqps/peg_caa/pegcaain.html (EPA, Plain English Guide to the Clean Air Act)

http://www.airnow.gov (AIRNow)

http://www.savethecleanairact.org (SaveTheCleanAirAct.org)

http://www.cleanairworld.org (Clean Air World)

http://www.cleanairtrust.org/cleanairact.html (the Clean Air Trust)

ENDNOTES

1. *Engine Manufacturers Ass'n v. South Coast Air Quality Management District*, 540 U.S. 1087 (2004).
2. *Whitman v. American Trucking Assoc.*, 531 U.S. 457 (2001).
3. *Alaska Department of Environmental Conservation v. Environmental Protection Agency*, 540 U.S. 461 (2004).

4. *Wisconsin Electric Power Company* ["WEPCo"] *v. Reilly*, 893 F.2d 901 (7th Cir. 1990).
5. *Tennessee Valley Authority v. Whitman*, 336 F.3d 1236 (11th Cir. 2003), cert. den. sub nom. *Leavitt v. Tennessee Valley Authority*, 541 U.S. 1030 (2004).
6. *Sierra Club v. Browner*, docket no. 93–124 (September 20, 1994).
7. *Tanner v. Armco Steel Corp.*, 340 F. Supp 532 (S.D. Tex. 1972).

CHAPTER 6

RESOURCE CONSERVATION AND RECOVERY ACT (RCRA)

TITLE: The Resource Conservation and Recovery Act (RCRA)

CITATION: 42 U.S.C. secs. 6901, *et seq.* (1976)

REGULATIONS: 40 C.F.R. secs. 261, *et seq.*

PURPOSE: To minimize the present and future threat to human health and the environment by regulating the handling of hazardous waste.

HISTORY: Hazardous and Solid Waste Amendments (HSWA) (1984)

LEARNING OBJECTIVES

After studying this chapter, the reader should be able to

- describe the meaning of cradle-to-grave.
- define the terms *solid waste* and *hazardous waste.*
- describe the four characteristics of hazardous waste.
- define generators, transporters, and Treatment, Storage, and Disposal (TSD) facilities and the requirements imposed on them.

One would think it is self-evident that anything called ***hazardous waste*** *should be carefully monitored and regulated. Until the Resource Conservation and Recovery Act (RCRA) was promulgated in 1976, however, hazardous waste was something that most people seemed to prefer to ignore, pretending that it did not exist or, if it did exist, hoping it would magically vanish without harming them. Hazardous waste has been dumped in ditches, left in barrels, sunk in oceans, and burned in attempts to dispose of it. Unfortunately, these methods of disposal did nothing to erase the danger to humans and the environment caused by such substances. Each year in the United States, more than 300 tons of hazardous waste must be dealt with. The proper care and handling of hazardous waste is a problem that cannot be ignored.*

hazardous waste As defined in the Resource Conservation and Recovery Act (RCRA), hazardous waste is a solid waste, or combination of solid wastes, which, because of its quantity, concentration, or physical, chemical, or infectious characteristics may: (1) cause, or significantly contribute to, an increase in mortality or an increase in serious, irreversible, or incapacitating reversible, illness; or (2) pose a substantial threat or potential hazard to human health or the environment when improperly transported, treated, stored or disposed of, or otherwise managed.

cradle-to-grave A term used to describe the intent of the RCRA to control hazardous wastes from their creation (cradle) to their disposal (grave).

solid waste As defined in the RCRA, a solid waste is broadly defined as any garbage, refuse, sludge from a waste treatment plant, water supply treatment plant or air pollution control facility and other discarded material, including solid, liquid, semisolid, or contained gaseous materials resulting from industrial, commercial, mining and agricultural activities, and from community activities. The definition does not include solid or dissolved material in domestic sewage or solid or dissolved material in irrigation return flows or industrial discharges that are point sources subject to permitting requirements pursuant to the Clean Water Act (CWA).

CRADLE-TO-GRAVE

The RCRA contains a program designed to minimize the creation of hazardous waste and ensure its safe transport, treatment, and disposal. You have heard the expression **cradle-to-grave**. It is a term used to describe the intent of the RCRA to control hazardous wastes from their creation (cradle) to their disposal (grave). To accomplish this mission, the RCRA contains regulations applicable to generators and transporters of hazardous waste, as well to those who treat, store, and dispose of such waste.

HAZARDOUS WASTE

What is hazardous waste? To understand what constitutes hazardous waste, you must identify what is meant by the term **solid waste** because all hazardous waste is first described as solid waste.

SOLID WASTE IS BROADLY DEFINED IN SECTION 1004 OF THE RCRA AS FOLLOWS:

The term "solid waste" means any garbage, refuse, sludge from a waste treatment plant, water supply treatment plant or air pollution control facility and other discarded material, including solid, liquid, semisolid, or contained gaseous materials resulting from industrial, commercial, mining and agricultural activities, and from community activities but does not include solid or dissolved materials in irrigation return flows or industrial discharges which are point sources subject to permits under section 402 of the Federal Water Pollution Control Act, as amended, or source, special nuclear, or by-product material as defined by the Atomic Energy Act of 1954, as amended. (68 Stat. 923)

Thus, solid waste includes waste that is solid, liquid, semisolid, and even gaseous. Further, the definition is so broad that it encompasses almost every kind of substance generated by the activities of urban areas.

In its regulatory definitions, the EPA has amplified the definition of solid waste. First, the EPA defines *discarded material*, one of the terms in the statutory definition of solid waste, as any material that is abandoned or recycled or that is "inherently waste-like." A material is considered abandoned when it is disposed of; burned; or accumulated, stored, or treated prior to or in lieu of abandonment. The EPA also has chosen to broadly define *inherently waste-like* through its regulations.

QUESTION

Does it seem logical that the term *solid waste* includes semisolid and gaseous waste? Think of a term that better describes those substances presently included in solid waste.

Even materials that are reclaimed or recycled can be defined as solid wastes pursuant to EPA regulations.

Hazardous waste is defined in Section 1004 of the RCRA as follows:

HAZARDOUS WASTE

. . . a solid waste, or combination of solid wastes, which because of its quantity, concentration, or physical, chemical or infectious characteristics may:

A. Cause, or significantly contribute to an increase in mortality or an increase in serious irreversible, or incapacitating reversible illness; or

B. Pose a substantial present or potential hazard to human health or the environment when improperly treated, stored, transported, or disposed of, or otherwise managed.

For the most part, a solid waste also is considered a hazardous waste unless it falls within one of the regulatory exemptions established by the EPA. The EPA has exempted, among other materials

- household waste.
- agricultural wastes returned to the soil as fertilizer.
- mining overburden returned to the mine site.
- utility wastes from coal combustion.
- oil and natural gas exploration drilling waste.
- wastes from the extraction, beneficiation, and processing of ores and minerals, including coal.
- cement kiln dust wastes.
- arsenic-treated wood wastes generated by end users of such wood.
- some chromium-bearing wastes.

LISTS

As part of its categorization of wastes into those that are considered hazardous and those that are not, the EPA has developed lists of hazardous waste. These **EPA lists** of hazardous waste are found at 40 C.F.R. Part 261. To facilitate identification and monitoring, each hazardous

EPA lists Lists of hazardous wastes developed by the EPA assigning a number to various types of specific hazardous wastes.

ASSIGNMENT
Find a way to memorize the types of lists used by the EPA to categorize waste and the kinds of waste included in those lists.

waste on each list is assigned a number, not by batch, but by the type of hazardous waste. For example, toluene, a specific hazardous waste, is assigned its own number; and every time toluene is one of the wastes handled, the manifest will show, among other things, the number reflecting the presence of toluene.

The first EPA list, the *F list*, contains hazardous wastes from nonspecific sources. A nonspecific source is a source not particular to a specific industry or manufacturing process.

The second EPA list, the *K list*, contains hazardous wastes from specific sources. A specific source is a particular type of industry or manufacturing process.

The third list has two designation letters, P and U, assigned to two groups of commercial chemical products that, when discarded, are deemed hazardous. The wastes with a P designation are those deemed acutely hazardous when discarded. The wastes with a U designation are those that are toxic and, therefore, hazardous when discarded. The wastes on the P list are more strictly regulated due to their nature as being "acutely" hazardous when discarded.

EPA regulations allow a company to ask that wastes generated at its facility be removed from the hazardous waste lists. This process is known as **delisting**. A company must file a petition with the EPA requesting delisting, and the petition must show any of the hazardous constituents that caused the waste to be put on the list in the first place or any other characteristics that would cause the waste to be hazardous.

delisting When the waste generated by the treatment of a hazardous waste does not exhibit any of the characteristics for which the untreated waste was deemed hazardous, the residue waste may be delisted by the EPA. The effect of delisting is to remove many of the requirements placed on the generation, transportation, treatment, storage, or disposal of the delisted waste.

CHARACTERISTICS OF HAZARDOUS WASTE

Even if a waste is not on any of the EPA's hazardous waste lists, it may still be subject to regulation under the RCRA if it possesses any of the characteristics of hazardous waste. Hazardous waste has the following four characteristics:

CHARACTERISTICS OF HAZARDOUS WASTE

- **Ignitability**
- **Corrosivity**
- **Reactivity**
- **Toxicity**

Ignitability

A solid waste is considered ignitable when it is "capable during handling of starting a fire or exacerbating a fire once started." (40 C.F.R. 261.21) To determine whether a waste meets this standard, depending

ignitability A characteristic of hazardous waste that is capable during handling of starting a fire or exacerbating a fire once started.

upon its state (solid, liquid, or gaseous), the waste can undergo a particular scientific test. If a waste is a liquid, the flash point by temperature will determine whether the waste is subject to RCRA requirements. If a waste is a nonliquid and can cause a fire through friction, absorption of moisture, or spontaneous chemical changes and it burns so vigorously when ignited that it creates a hazard, the waste will be regulated. The test for gases and oxidizers is determined by regulations of the DOT. Any ignitable waste will have an EPA number of D001.

Corrosivity

The EPA made corrosivity a characteristic of a regulated waste due to the organization's concern that if a substance could corrode a container, the waste might escape the container, the integrity of the handling process would be breached, and other wastes might be released. Scientific research has concluded that wastes at either the high or low end of the pH scale (high on the acid scale or high on the base scale) can be harmful to human health; so corrosives are something that should not be released into the environment. Wastes exhibiting corrosive characteristics sufficient to be regulated under the RCRA are given an EPA number of D002.

corrosivity A characteristic of hazardous waste that involves wastes at either the high or low end of the pH scale.

Reactivity

If a waste shows signs of being extremely unstable and having the characteristic of reacting violently or exploding during handling or management, it will be controlled as a reactive waste. Wastes are tested for their reactivity by determining how they react when mixed with water and when heated and by testing their reaction to other situations in which they might commonly be found during handling or management. As of yet, there are no exacting numeric standards for reactivity sufficient to be regulated under the RCRA, as there are for ignitability and corrosivity. Consequently, in making a designation, the EPA uses a description of the characteristics to be looked for. Reactive wastes have a number of D003.

reactivity A characteristic of hazardous waste that has the characteristic of reacting violently or exploding during handling or management.

Toxicity

A waste is toxic enough to be regulated under the RCRA when, under mismanagement conditions, it is likely to leach hazardous concentrations of certain toxic constituents into groundwater. To test whether a waste qualifies, the EPA has created tests designed to simulate the conditions of a landfill. The test developed by the EPA to determine

toxicity A characteristic of hazardous waste that is likely to leach hazardous concentrations of certain toxic constituents into groundwater under mismanagement conditions.

Toxicity Characteristic Leaching Procedure (TCLP) The method by which the toxicity of a material is analyzed. In a laboratory, the material being tested is mixed with an acetic acid solution for a specific period of time. The acetic solution is then checked for certain heavy metals and organic compounds. If the compounds or heavy metals are detected in the solution in quantities greater than the limits prescribed in the RCRA, the material will be considered a hazardous waste due to its toxicity.

mixture rule A rule holding that any nonhazardous waste that is mixed with a hazardous waste becomes a part of the hazardous waste due to the fact that such mixing has occurred.

derived-from rule A rule providing that residue from the treatment of *listed* hazardous wastes is considered hazardous waste regardless of whether the resulting residue is, in fact, hazardous. The residue from *characteristic* hazardous wastes is considered hazardous only when the residue exhibits a hazardous waste characteristic.

whether a waste contains contaminants at the levels of concern to the EPA is called the **Toxicity Characteristic Leaching Procedure (TCLP)**. The TCLP tests for specific organic chemicals, inorganics, and insecticides/herbicides. Toxic wastes are assigned an EPA number of D004–D043 depending on which contaminant(s) cause the waste to be deemed hazardous.

MIXTURE RULE

The **mixture rule** is a rule promulgated by the EPA to address a situation where a hazardous waste and a solid waste are mixed together. Whenever this happens, the mixture is deemed to be a hazardous waste unless it is given an exemption. Exemptions are granted if

- a mixture of hazardous and solid waste does not exhibit the same hazardous waste characteristic as the portion of the waste mixture deemed "hazardous" due to its exhibiting that characteristic.
- a mixture contains wastewater and its hazardous constituents are regulated under the CWA.
- a mixture consists of some discarded chemical product resulting from extremely minor losses during manufacturing operations.

The exemptions to the mixture rule apply only when the mixture in question results from the usual waste management process or production. When the mixture of wastes results from intentional dilution, the mixing may constitute treatment and may not qualify for an exemption.

DERIVED-FROM RULE

A waste that is generated from (derived from) the treatment, storage, or disposal of a hazardous waste also is considered a hazardous waste unless it is otherwise exempted. This is the aptly-stated **derived-from rule**. There are exemptions to this rule. If a waste derived from a listed hazardous waste does not exhibit the hazardous waste characteristic of the hazardous waste from which it was derived, it will not be subject to RCRA regulation as a hazardous waste.

CONTAINED-IN RULE

The **contained-in rule** embodies the idea that material that is contaminated with hazardous waste (the hazardous waste is contained in the material) also should be regulated as hazardous waste pursuant to the applicable provisions of the RCRA. The types of material that often fall into this rule (because they end up containing hazardous waste) include water, soil, and debris.

contained-in rule The rule stating that material that is contaminated with hazardous waste also is regulated as hazardous waste.

RECYCLING AND RECLAMATION

As noted previously, both the statutory and regulatory definitions of solid waste are very broad. The EPA has chosen to use this broad definition as a means of regulating certain types of recycling and reclamation activities as well as certain types of materials used in recycling or reclamation. (40 C.F.R. sec. 261)

Types of Recycling and Reclamation Activities Regulated by the RCRA

For the purposes of RCRA regulation, recycling or reclamation activities include the following:

- Recycling that constitutes land disposal
- Burning (incineration) to recover energy
- Reclamation
- Speculative accumulation

Also, for the purposes of RCRA regulation, materials that are considered solid wastes when they are recycled (with a couple of exceptions) include the following:

- Spent materials
- Listed and characteristic sludges
- Listed and characteristic by-products
- Commercial chemical products
- Scrap metal

The goal of the EPA has been to avoid the application of RCRA regulations to production activities and to confine such application to waste management activities.

owner The person who owns a facility, either in whole or in part. The broad definition of *person* in federal environmental law leads to the term owner also being defined broadly.

operator The person responsible for overall operation of a facility. Pursuant to federal environmental laws, the definition of *person*, and consequently the definition of *operator*, is quite broad.

treatment, storage, and disposal (TSD) facility Pursuant to the RCRA, such hazardous waste facilities are strictly regulated in areas such as design, construction, operation, and closure.

WASTE MANAGEMENT ACTIVITIES

Pursuant to Section 3010(a) of the RCRA, any person who manages hazardous waste must let the EPA know it is managing a hazardous waste within 90 days of the waste being identified as hazardous. As noted previously, a "person" for purposes of environmental law may be an individual, a partnership, a corporation, or any other legal entity. A hazardous waste "manager" is a generator, transporter, or **owner** or **operator** of a **treatment, storage, and disposal (TSD) facility**.

As part of this notification process, the manager of hazardous waste must provide its name, its location, and the EPA number(s) for the listed and characteristic hazardous waste(s) it manages. Every management site the entity runs must be identified separately to the EPA. A failure to notify the EPA of waste management activities as required by the RCRA renders any regulated activity unlawful, including the generation, transportation, treatment, storage, or disposal of hazardous waste.

GENERATORS

generator Any person whose act or process produces hazardous waste or whose act first causes a hazardous waste to become subject to regulation. All generators must acquire a generator identification number from the EPA and comply with regulations governing their activities found in the RCRA.

manifest A document used to keep track of hazardous waste shipments. Consisting of six parts, a manifest is created by a hazardous waste generator and must follow each load of hazardous waste from the generator through transportation to its ultimate disposal destination.

Generators of hazardous waste are those who generate or produce the wastes. In other words, a generator is the person who "creates" the waste. Hazardous waste is not produced as a product by itself. It is waste produced as a by-product of some manufacturing activity. The RCRA requires generators to handle waste in accordance with standards set for that activity and to prepare **manifests** used to track the waste from the time of its creation to the time of its disposal. Generators are regulated under Section 3002 of the RCRA.

Generators are the people responsible for initiating the entire RCRA regulatory scheme for the management of hazardous waste. The safety and security of the system depends on generators following the applicable procedures for each tiny bit of hazardous waste so it can be followed and monitored from "cradle-to-grave."

GENERATOR

EPA regulations define a *generator* as

> . . . any person, by site, whose act or process produces hazardous waste identified or listed [in RCRA regulations] or whose act first causes hazardous waste to become subject to regulation. [40 C.F.R. Section 260.10(a)(26)]

This definition confirms that every generator is regulated site by site where the waste is generated. If a corporation has several plants or facilities whose manufacturing or production activities result in the generation of hazardous waste, it is required to separately identify and submit each facility to regulation.

Uniform Hazardous Waste Manifest

The first record of the "life" of hazardous waste is the **Uniform Hazardous Waste Manifest**. This document accompanies hazardous waste at all times. The manifest acts as a control measure, ensuring that hazardous waste can be identified and monitored through its ultimate disposal. The manifest will include at least the following:

Uniform Hazardous Waste Manifest A document that accompanies hazardous waste at all times from its generation through its disposal.

- The appropriate description of the waste so that it can be transported in compliance with DOT regulations. This description will include the EPA Identification Number of the waste.
- The EPA Identification Number of each transporter of the waste. (As will be discussed in more detail later in this chapter, everyone who handles hazardous waste must have its own EPA Identification Number.)
- The EPA Identification Number of the TSD facility or another facility that will receive the waste from the transporter.
- A certification that the waste has been appropriately packaged and labeled. This certification must be made by hand on each manifest so the signer can be identified and the signature verified if such verification later becomes necessary as part of some enforcement activity.

Another required certification on a manifest is a consequence of the RCRA requirements that generators attempt, through their management practices, to reduce the quantity and toxicity of wastes. The certification language connected with this requirement is as follows:

> I have a program in place to reduce the volume and toxicity of waste generated to the degree I have determined to be economically practicable and I have selected the method of treatment, storage, or disposal currently available to me which minimizes the present and future threat to human health and the environment.

Separate copies of the fully completed manifest must be made for every handler of the waste through its disposal. Each handler of the waste completes the next section of the manifest before the waste is transferred to the care and control of the subsequent handler. Thus, the generator hands off the manifest to the transporter, who completes a section and hands off the manifest to the TSD facility. After the waste is finally disposed of, the facility disposing of the waste (usually a TSD facility) sends a copy of the manifest back to the generator so the circle of record keeping is complete. If the generator does not receive the manifest in a timely manner (within 45 days) or the manifest was not properly completed, the generator must file an "exception report" with either the state or the EPA. The generator also must contact all those entities in the chain of custody of the waste to determine which entity failed to complete the manifest properly. The exception report will include a copy of the applicable manifest and a letter that describes the efforts of the generator to locate the waste and the manifest. The report also must relate the results of the generator's search efforts.

As previously noted, generators must prepare hazardous waste for transportation off the production site. Proper packaging, labeling, marking, and placarding must be used.

Exhibit 6-1 includes examples of placards used in the transportation of materials covered by the RCRA.

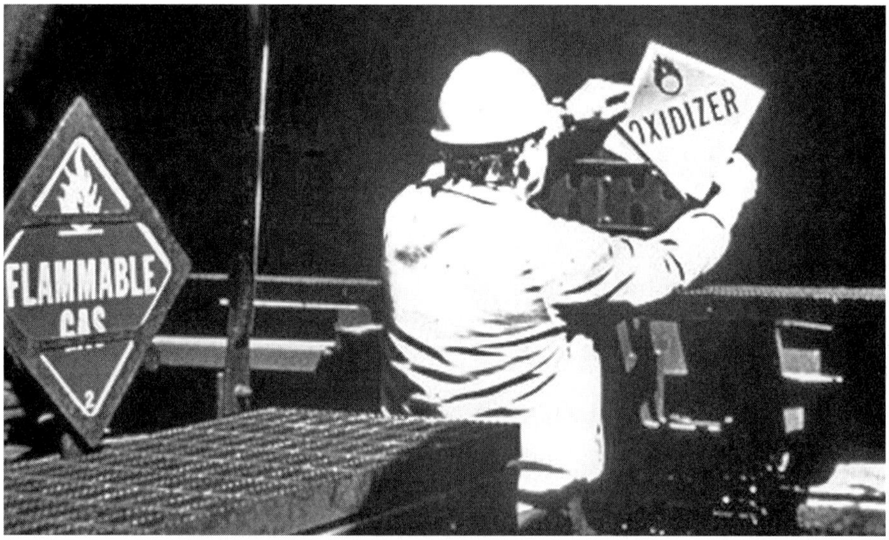

EXHIBIT 6-1 PLACARDING INFORMATION

Any container of 110 gallons or less must exhibit the name and address of the generator, as well as the manifest number and the following statement:

> Hazardous Waste: Federal law prohibits improper disposal. If found, contact the nearest police or public safety authority or the United States Environmental Protection Agency.

Illegal Dumping

The intensity and care with which waste is tracked through the manifest system is a direct result of the danger to human health and the environment that the handling of hazardous waste poses. RCRA statutory and regulatory provisions are designed in light of this danger and are intended to decrease, as much as possible, the possibility that hazardous waste will just disappear from the tracking system. Every attempt is made to avoid such waste being illegally dumped or otherwise disposed of, as was often the case prior to the promulgation of the RCRA and its tracking requirements. Illegal dumping sites are still found, usually in desolate rural areas or in bodies of water. Waste is found buried in barrels in landfills not intended for the disposal of hazardous waste and other locations where a transporter is not likely to be observed. Most illegal dumping is done at night to avoid detection.

The reasons behind illegal dumping of hazardous waste boil down to one thing: money. It is very expensive to follow RCRA regulations.

TIGER **BY BUD BLAKE**

Those who generate hazardous waste are the ones who arrange for illegal dumping with the cooperation of unscrupulous transporters. If a generator or transporter is involved in illegal dumping, it typically will not have an EPA Identification Number; so it does not appear on the EPA's "radar screen." Sophisticated illegal generators and transporters often have forged manifests or attempt to disguise their load.

In recent years, it has become more difficult for generators and transporters to avoid detection and succeed in their illegal dumping activities. Suspected dumping routes and means of conveyance are monitored—with vehicles and trains experiencing unannounced inspections, especially suspicious vehicles on lightly traveled roadways at night.

SPECIAL ETHICAL CONSIDERATIONS FOR PARALEGALS

Because paralegals often have first contact with clients, paralegals may be faced with the difficult situation of receiving information about an illegal dump or a release of hazardous materials. Clients may seek legal advice concerning their responsibilities for reporting, cleanup, or other issues. It is imperative that, despite the client's frequent perception of this situation as an emergency, the paralegal refrain from giving any advice to the client. Although it may be tempting to confirm what the client already knows, the paralegal must refer the client to the attorney in all situations.

Waste Minimization

Each generator files biennial reports with either the EPA or the state, listing the EPA numbers of all those involved in the handling of waste generated by that entity. Additionally, the types and volumes of wastes generated must be specified. The reports also outline the efforts made by generators to comply with the **waste minimization** requirements of the RCRA. Generators must retain a manifest for three years, but they typically maintain them much longer than that.

waste minimization A requirement of generators pursuant to the RCRA that efforts be made to reduce the volume and risk associated with hazardous materials.

Generators are allowed to export hazardous waste to foreign countries; but they must follow strict procedures concerning such export, including notifying the EPA at least four weeks in advance of the first shipment in each calendar year. Whoever receives the waste in the foreign country must provide confirmation of receipt and complete the appropriate documentation, including the manifest. Anyone wanting to import hazardous waste into the United States is considered a generator and must follow all regulations applicable to generators prior to transporting the waste to the United States.

Small Quantity Generators (SQGs)

The EPA has developed special rules for generators who generate waste in quantities smaller than a certain amount each month. These generators are known, appropriately, as **small quantity generators (SQGs)**. SQGs are allowed to store small amounts of waste on their sites for a short period of time without a permit. SQGs still must use the uniform manifest system and ensure that the waste they generate is properly transported, treated, stored, and disposed of.

small quantity generator (SQG) As defined in the RCRA, a small quantity generator is one that generates more than a certain minimum quantity of hazardous waste but less than a certain maximum quantity of hazardous waste. SQGs have slightly relaxed regulatory storage and transportation time limits compared to larger generators.

TRANSPORTERS

A **transporter** is anyone who moves hazardous waste from one place to another off a given site. For example, if hazardous waste is moved from the facility where it was generated to a facility where it can be treated, the entity moving the waste from the first facility to the second is a transporter. Transportation of hazardous waste can be via any form of transportation, including air, rail, land, or water; but such wastes are typically transported by trucks or railcars. Transporters are required to use particular containers, labels, and placards on their mode of transportation to ensure that the waste is moved safely and that the public and first responders, such as police or fire departments, are placed on notice concerning the hazardous nature of the load. In addition, transporters are required to carry the manifests initiated by the generators so that every bit of the waste can be tracked. Transporters are regulated pursuant to Section 3003 of the RCRA.

transporter A person engaged in the off-site transportation of hazardous waste by air, rail, roadway, or water.

The RCRA transportation requirements apply not only to interstate movement but also to intrastate movement. The only movement of hazardous wastes that is not covered by the RCRA transportation requirements is movement within the same production or manufacturing site. Use of a public road invokes the transportation requirements.

The RCRA transportation standards applicable to the movement of hazardous waste are closely tied with standards promulgated by the DOT pursuant to the Hazardous Materials Transportation Act. Both sets of regulations address labeling, marking, placarding, and use of containers. Transporters also are required to have a plan to respond to spills, must have an EPA Identification Number, and cannot accept hazardous waste for transport without a proper manifest completed by the generator. Both the EPA and the DOT can enforce regulations against transporters.

As outlined previously, the transporter must keep the manifest with the waste at all times and must sign off on the manifest before taking the waste from the generator and when delivering the waste to the TSD facility. For at least three years, transporters keep copies of the manifests reflecting the hazardous waste they have transported. Under the RCRA, waste may be stored by a transporter at a transfer facility for up to 10 days without the need for a storage permit. A transfer facility is a place where waste is typically stored as a normal part of the transportation process. Such facilities usually have a loading dock and a storage area as well as a large yard where the transportation vehicles can maneuver to load and unload wastes.

Transporters can become generators if they manipulate the wastes that come into their possession in certain ways. If, for example, a transporter were to mix hazardous wastes from different manifests or mix hazardous wastes so they require different EPA Identification Numbers, the transporter will be deemed to have generated new hazardous waste and must follow all of the regulations applicable to generators. Importing hazardous waste from a foreign country also subjects a transporter to certain regulations applicable to generators.

TREATMENT, STORAGE, AND DISPOSAL (TSD) FACILITIES

Facilities that receive hazardous waste for any one of three purposes (treatment, storage, or disposal) are required to comply with strict performance standards under the RCRA. Under the RCRA, the definition of *facility* includes the contiguous land (land lying next to the buildings, ponds, landfills, or other operational features of a hazardous waste operation), structures, other appurtenances, and improvements on the land. The facilities performance standards include specifications as to use of technology, monitoring, staffing, training, and many other activities. TSD activities are regulated pursuant to Section 3004 of the RCRA, and the facilities themselves are permitted under Section 3005 of the RCRA.

treatment facility A facility that qualifies for purposes of the RCRA if its operator uses any method, technique, or process, including neutralization, designed to change the physical, chemical, or biological character or composition of any hazardous waste so as to neutralize such waste or so as to recover energy or materials resources from the waste or so as to render such waste nonhazardous or less hazardous; safer to transport, store, or dispose of; or amenable for recovery, amenable for storage, or reduced in volume.

Treatment Facility

A facility will qualify as a **treatment facility** for purposes of the RCRA if its operator uses any method, technique, or process intended to change the physical, chemical, or biological character or composition of a hazardous waste so as to neutralize the waste or to recover energy or material resources from the waste or to render the waste nonhazardous or less hazardous; safer to transport, store, or dispose of; or amenable for recovery, amenable for storage, or reduced in volume. In other words, there is little a facility can do to a hazardous waste that will not fall within this broad definition of what constitutes treatment.

Storage Facility

The RCRA defines a **storage facility** as one that holds hazardous waste for a temporary period, at the end of which period the waste is treated, disposed of, or moved elsewhere for additional storage.

storage facility A facility that holds hazardous waste for a temporary period, at the end of which period the waste is treated, disposed of, or moved elsewhere for additional storage.

Disposal Facility

A **disposal facility** under the RCRA is a facility where hazardous waste is intentionally placed into or on land or water and at which waste will remain after the facility is closed.

disposal facility A facility where hazardous waste is intentionally placed into or on land or water and where waste will remain after the facility is closed.

PERMITTING OF FACILITIES

Every owner and operator of a TSD facility must obtain a *RCRA operating permit* prior to beginning construction of the facility. (Section 3005) A permit is individual to a facility, so corporations with operations at multiple locations must permit each location separately.

The permit application consists of two parts: **Part A** and **Part B**. Part A of the application requires basic information related to the application: the name of the applicant, the location of the facility, the nature of the business, regulated activities to be conducted at the facility, and a topographic map of the proposed site. A Part B application is more detailed and substantial because it must demonstrate compliance with all applicable technical standards for the type of facility proposed. The provisions of the final permit as granted will govern the operations of a particular facility. Proposed facilities must submit both parts of the application at the same time. In a state where the EPA has given the state permission to administer its own RCRA program, the state will be the entity to review the permit. Otherwise, the EPA will review the permit.

Part A and Part B permit application Two parts or types of an application required in certain circumstances pursuant to the RCRA. Upon passage of the RCRA, existing treatment, storage, and disposal (TSDs) facilities (also known as interim status facilities) were required to file this application with the EPA for a permit to continue to do business until they received their full operating permit.

Once an application is filed, there are specific procedures for processing the application and, if appropriate, issuing the permit (see 40 C.F.R. Part 124). As with most regulatory processes, the basic outline of the procedure consists of an application, a review, issuance of draft permits, public comment, and issuance of a final permit. Pursuant to the

Hazardous and Solid Waste Amendments (HSWA) of 1984, most permits cannot be granted for a period longer than 10 years. Permits for land disposal facilities must be reviewed every five years, although any permit may be reviewed and modified at any time during its term. Whenever a permit is reviewed, the standards will be analyzed to ensure that the facility continues to meet the applicable regulations.

CORRECTIVE ACTION FOLLOWING RELEASES

The RCRA requirement for corrective action applies to all hazardous waste releases at a unit within a TSD facility regardless of when the waste was placed in the unit or even whether the unit or the facility is still in operation. A unit within a TSD facility can be a tank, a lagoon, a waste pile, or any other location where hazardous waste has been placed. Once a release has occurred, the facility must take corrective action within the time frames and in the manner specified in its permit. Occasionally, if a release has migrated beyond the boundaries of a facility, the facility may have to take remedial action outside its property limits.

INSPECTION

Any EPA or state representative may inspect the buildings, vehicles, equipment, grounds, and records of any person who handles hazardous waste, including generators, transporters, or owners or operators of TSD facilities. (Section 3007) This inspection authority also extends to sites where hazardous waste has, at any time, been handled, even if the waste is no longer handled at the facility or the facility is closed. The inspectors are authorized to copy records, take samples of waste, and visually inspect any portion of a facility they so choose. Pursuant to the HSWA, inspections must be performed at privately owned TSD facilities every two years. Facilities operated by any level of government (federal, state, or local) must be inspected every year.

Inspections pursuant to the RCRA are subject to the protections against unreasonable search and seizure provided by the Fourth Amendment to the U.S. Constitution (see Chapter 1). The Fourth Amendment protections typically require that a warrant be obtained prior to an inspection by an administrative agency (see *Marshall v. Barlow's Inc.*[1]). In practice, however, it is rare for a facility to require the

EPA or a state to obtain a search warrant before an inspection is allowed. The reasoning behind this effective waiver of Fourth Amendment protection is that if an inspector without a warrant is turned away, facilities believe the inspector will think the facility is worried about a possible violation and wants time to remedy the problem. So when the inspector comes back, he or she will have a warrant and a very critical eye.

FACILITY STANDARDS

Due to the complexity of operations at TSD facilities, together with the significant risks posed if operations are not performed correctly, specific standards have been set for all functions of a TSD facility.

GENERAL CATEGORIES OF TSD FACILITY STANDARDS

Certain general categories of standards apply to TSD facilities. These standards include the following:

- Personnel training
- Security
- Financial responsibility
- Specific design and operating standards depending on the type of facility and whether it contains
  - storage tanks.
  - landfills.
  - incinerators.

All operators of TSD facilities must obtain an EPA Identification Number. It is expected that the operator will know in advance and plan for particular types of hazardous waste that the facility will handle. Consequently, the operator is required to contract for or perform a detailed chemical and physical analysis of a representative sample of the expected hazardous waste before it is handled at the TSD facility. This analysis requirement ensures that the operator is capable of planning, designing, building, and operating the facility so that the waste expected at the facility will be managed properly.

REVIEW
Operators of TSD facilities must obtain an EPA Identification Number.

Design, Construction, and Operation Standards

Again, due to the requiremens and risks posed by operation of TSDs, RCRA has imposed specific design, construction, and operation standards for facilities.

TSD Facility Design Standards

For each type of facility regulated under the RCRA, specific design standards relate to the following:

- **Containers**
  - A container is any portable device for storing or handling hazardous waste; containers include drums, pails, and boxes.
  - Containers must be kept closed except when waste is being added.
  - Container storage areas must be inspected at least once a week; and the tanks must be inspected daily to identify leaks, corrosion, or other structural problems.
  - Storage areas must have secondary containment systems.
- **Tanks**
  - Tanks are stationary devices made primarily of nonearthen materials that provide structural support and ancillary devices.
  - Tanks must be constructed of appropriate materials (determined by the type of waste being handled).
  - Tanks must be operated using procedures to control overflows and spills.
  - Tanks must be maintained in good condition and must be handled to avoid leaks or ruptures.
  - Storage areas must have secondary containment systems.
- **Surface impoundments**
  - A surface impoundment is any natural or human-made excavation or diked area designed to hold hazardous wastes containing or consisting of free liquids. Pits, ponds, and lagoons are types of surface impoundments.
- **Waste piles**
  - A waste pile is any noncontainerized accumulation of nonflowing hazardous waste.
  - Waste piles must have a liner on a supporting base, a leachate (a liquid, originally rain or groundwater, that has passed through a landfill mass and therefore contains soluble materials from that mass) collection and removal system above the liner, and surface water controls.
- **Landfills**
  - A landfill is a disposal facility where hazardous waste is placed in or on the land.
  - All new, replacement, and expansion units at surface impoundments and landfills are required to have double liners, leachate collection systems, leak detection, and groundwater monitoring systems.
- **Incinerators**
  - An incinerator is controlled flame combustion used to destroy hazardous waste.
  - This method often is used to produce energy from the destruction of waste.
  - Incineration must achieve a destruction and removal efficiency (DRE) of at least 99.9 percent for the main hazardous constituents of each incinerated load.
  - Incineration must meet applicable air emissions standards.
- Land treatment units
- Thermal treatment units
- Chemical, physical, and biological treatment units
- Underground injection wells
- Containment buildings
- Miscellaneous units

(40 C.F.R. secs. 264 and 265)

Facility Security

Operators of TSD facilities must install a security system. That system has to prevent unknowing entry and minimize the possible unauthorized entry onto the active portion of the facility of people or livestock. (TSD facilities are typically located in rural areas, and livestock often is on the adjacent properties.) Security systems typically include a 24-hour surveillance system, physical barriers such as fences or walls, a single entry gate, and signs posted around the perimeter warning of "Danger" on the premises.

Personnel Training

Personnel hired to work at TSD facilities are required to be rigorously trained for whatever job tasks they are expected to complete. Due to the danger posed by the characteristics of the material being handled (ignitability, reactivity, corrosivity, or toxicity), it is critical that TSD facilities reduce the possibility of an accident. In addition, staff members at TSD facilities must be adequately trained to assist with attempts to reduce the risk that human error will contribute to an accident. Workers must receive their training in classrooms or on the job within six months of being hired and receive annual evaluations to ensure their continued competence. Among the subjects covered in the training are emergency preparedness and response procedures.

Emergency Response Preparedness

The types of accidents that are most likely to occur at a facility include a spill, an explosion, or a fire. Typically, facilities must have certain equipment to detect and respond to an accident, such as

- a system for raising an internal alarm.
- a device capable of summoning external help, such as fire, law enforcement, and medical assistance.
- equipment to control spills and fires.
- equipment capable of decontaminating people who have been exposed to hazardous waste without proper protection.

All equipment intended for response to an accident must be regularly maintained and inspected. The physical layout of a facility must be designed to allow appropriate access by emergency equipment. A close relationship must be maintained between the operator of a facility and

container Defined in the RCRA as any portable device for storing or handling hazardous waste.

tanks Stationary devices made primarily of nonearthen materials that provide structural support, typically for the storage of liquids.

surface impoundments Any natural or human-made excavation or diked area designed to hold hazardous wastes containing or consisting of free liquids. Pits, ponds, and lagoons are types of surface impoundments.

waste pile Any noncontainerized accumulation of nonflowing hazardous waste.

landfill A disposal facility where hazardous waste is placed in or on the land.

incinerator A regulated facility for disposing of hazardous waste by burning it at an extremely high temperature.

the emergency response personnel who would come to the facility in the event of an accident. Emergency response units usually conduct practice exercises at a facility and have maps of the facility layout with them at all times. Areas surrounding a TSD facility will know what types of waste are handled at the facility and how to control spills or fires involving that waste, as well as how to treat anyone exposed to that type of waste. The financial responsibility for a TSD facility includes the requirement that sufficient insurance be maintained to address claims of personal injury or property damage.

Record Keeping

A considerable amount of paperwork is associated with the operation of a TSD facility, including managing the all-important manifests that accompany the waste when it arrives at a facility. When waste and its accompanying manifest arrives at a facility, the manifest must be signed and dated and a copy given to the transporter. Within 30 days, an operator must return a fully executed copy of the manifest to the generator who initiated it. All manifests must be kept at the TSD facility at least three years. Other record keeping requirements include a need to maintain records of the type and quantity of all waste received at the facility; the method and date of its treatment, storage, or disposal; the location of each amount of waste at the facility; the results of waste analyses; and records of all tests and inspections. Specific reports that must be kept include a biennial report detailing waste management activities for the previous year, reports regarding **unmanifested waste** (waste accepted at the facility without a manifest), and reports related to accidents at the facility.

REVIEW

When a TSD facility closes, there is a post-closure period of 30 years, during which time the facility is inspected and monitored to ensure that all hazards are addressed.

unmanifested waste Waste accepted at a treatment, storage, and disposal (TSD) facility without a manifest.

Closure Requirements

Once a TSD facility is no longer accepting wastes, the facility is said to be in its **closure** phase. Many regulatory requirements are applicable to this phase of a facility's operational life, during which time the facility must complete all TSD operations. Additionally, there is a post-closure period of 30 years. Both closure phases are heavily regulated.

closure The ceasing of operations at a facility pursuant to an approved closure plan and in compliance with all applicable regulatory requirements.

All facilities must have a detailed closure plan, which is approved by the applicable regulating entity (the EPA or the state). The financial responsibility requirements in the permitting process ensure that there is adequate funding to implement the closure and post-closure phases of the facility's operations.

STATE-REGULATED HAZARDOUS WASTE PROGRAMS

The RCRA allows states to create and administer their own hazardous waste programs in lieu of administration by the EPA as long as the state-administered program is consistent with the federal program and ensures adequate compliance with RCRA provisions. States are permitted to enact RCRA laws that are no less strict than the federal RCRA provisions. Because the RCRA specifically prohibits state and local governments from adopting regulations less strict than RCRA requirements, it impliedly permits state and local governments from adopting regulations *more* strict than the RCRA. Occasionally, this dual administration of the RCRA results in joint permitting. The EPA ends up enforcing the HSWA provisions, and states enforce the remainder of the RCRA provisions.

CASE LAW

BLUE CIRCLE CEMENT, INC. V. BOARD OF COUNTY COMMISSIONERS, 27 F.3D 1499 (10TH CIR. 1994).[2]

SUMMARY OF CASE: Manufacturing plant challenged the county board's hazardous waste zoning ordinances. The District Court granted summary judgment for the board, and the manufacturer appealed.

Circuit Judge Ebel delivered the opinion of the Court.

Blue Circle, an Alabama corporation with its principal place of business in Georgia, operates a quarry and cement manufacturing plan in Rogers County, Oklahoma. Since opening this facility in 1960, Blue Circle has used coal and natural gas as fuel in its cement kilns. To reduce the cost of heating its kilns, Blue Circle sought to convert to Hazardous Waste Fuels ("HWFs"), which are derived from the blending of various industrial wastes and possess high British Thermal Unit ("BTU") value. The Board's regulatory actions in direct response to Blue Circle's proposed fuel conversion project gave rise to this dispute. . . .

Initially, Blue Circle concluded that the Board's approval to use HWFs was unnecessary. The zoning ordinance in effect when Blue circle commenced its fuel conversion project in the early 1980s required industrial operators to obtain a conditional use permit to establish an "industrial waste disposal" site. Blue Circle contended that burning HWFs . . . constituted "recycling" or "burning for energy recovery," not disposal. . . .

However, the Board disagreed with Blue Circle's interpretation of the Ordinance and informed company officials that burning HWFs in the cement kilns required a conditional use permit. . . . [R]ather than apply for a conditional use permit to burn HWFs at its cement plant, Blue Circle filed suit in the United States District Court for the Northern District of Oklahoma, seeking declaratory judgment . . . that the use of HWFs did not constitute industrial "disposal." . . . While the suit was pending, the Board . . . [amended] the Ordinance to include "recycling" and "treatment" sites among those facilities for which the Ordinance requires a conditional use permit. By this express language, the Board unequivocally subjected hazardous waste recycling and treatment to the same regulatory and permit scheme that was applicable to industrial waste disposal.

Blue Circle then filed an amended complaint alleging that the Ordinance as amended was preempted by RCRA. . . . The [trial] court held that. . . . RCRA did not preempt the Board's zoning Ordinance. . . .

In our review of the merits of Blue Circle's challenge to the Rogers County Ordinance, we first discuss whether RCRA preempts the Ordinance's restrictions on hazardous waste and recycling within the County. This inquiry requires us to consider RCRA's division of hazardous waste regulatory authority between the federal government, on the one hand, and States and their political subdivisions, on the other.

Absent explicit preemptive language, we have recognized at least two types of implied preemption: field preemption, where the scheme of federal regulation is "so pervasive as to make reasonable the inference that Congress left no room for the States to supplement it". . . and conflict preemption, where "compliance with both federal and state regulations is a physical impossibility." . . .

Here, although there may very well be both express and implied preemption by RCRA of more permissive state and local regulations pertaining to hazardous wastes, it is clear that we have neither express preemption nor implied field preemption of state and local hazardous waste regulations that are more restrictive than RCRA. Under . . . RCRA, Congress expressly empowers state and local governments to adopt sold and hazardous waste management regulations that are "more stringent" than those imposed on the federal level by the . . . EPA pursuant to RCRA.

Accordingly, Congress explicitly intended not to foreclose state and local oversight of hazardous waste management more strict than federal requirements. . . . Thus, if the Board's ordinance were to run afoul of the Supremacy Clause, it would only be because of the implied preemption that precludes a state or local regulation from frustrating the full accomplishment of congressional purposes embodied in a federal statute—in this case, RCRA.

In order to determine whether this Ordinance frustrates the purposes of RCRA, we must consider "whether [the local] regulation is consistent with the structure and purpose of the [federal] statute as a whole." . . . RCRA is the comprehensive federal hazardous waste management statute governing the treatment, storage, transportation, and disposal of hazardous wastes which have adverse effects on health and the environment. . . . One of RCRA's stated purposes is to assist states and localities in the development of improved solid waste management techniques to facilitate resource recovery and conservation. . . . The Hazardous and Solid Waste Amendments of 1984 increased RCRA's emphasis on recovery and recycling of hazardous wastes. . . . RCRA enlists the states and municipalities to participate in a "cooperative effort" with the federal government to develop waste management practices that facilitate the recovery of "valuable materials and energy from solid waste." . . . At the heart of this federal-state cooperation in hazardous waste regulatory enforcement is . . . the so-called savings clause. That section bars states and municipalities from imposing requirements "less stringent" than the federal provisions, but permits states to adopt "more stringent" provisions. . . . [However, a] state or local zoning ordinance affecting hazardous waste disposal, treatment, and recycling cannot imperil the federal goals under RCRA. . . . If a more stringent hazardous waste regulatory measure is hostile to the federal policy of encouraging hazardous waste treatment, recycling, and materials recovery in place of land disposal, some kind of analysis must take place to determine how severely such an ordinance actually interferes with the federal policy and to evaluate the importance of the local interests that the ordinance purportedly serves. . . .

[F]or instance, the Eighth Circuit held that . . . RCRA preempted a county ordinance that imposed an outright ban on the storage, treatment, or disposal of "acute hazardous waste." . . . Similarly, the Supreme Court of Louisiana held that RCRA preempted a parish ordinance's flat ban on hazardous waste disposal because "spotty . . . parochial control" in the nature of a "stifling prohibition" would undermine RCRA's hazardous waste management goals. . . .

First, ordinances that amount to an explicit or de facto total ban of an activity that is otherwise encouraged by RCRA will ordinarily be preempted by RCRA. Second, an ordinance that falls short of imposing a total ban on encouraged activity will ordinarily be upheld, so long as it is supported by a record establishing that it is a reasonable response to a legitimate local concern for safety or welfare. Significant latitude should be allowed to the state or local authority. However, if the ordinance is not addressed to a legitimate local concern, or if it is not reasonably related to that concern, then it may be regarded as a sham and nothing more than a naked attempt to sabotage federal RCRA policy of encouraging the sale and efficient disposition of hazardous waste materials.

Consequently, some review of local ordinance is required. . . . Guided by . . . our understanding of RCRA's overall legislative scheme, we turn to the language of the Rogers County Ordinance. . . . Blue Circle contends that [the] Ordinance frustrates RCRA's objective to encourage resource recovery and recycling because no landowner within the Commission's geographical jurisdiction can satisfy all the site location requirements. Blue Circle notes that [as required in the ordinance], there are no 160-acre parcels in the county, situated in an industrially-zoned region, whose boundaries are at least one mile from any platted residential area. . . . There is a serious dispute over whether this ordinance imposes a de facto ban on the burning of HWFs in Rogers County. . . . This . . . merely serves to highlight how inappropriate summary judgment was on this record. . . . [T]here is nothing in the record identifying what specific safety or health hazards the Board believes would be presented if Blue Circle were to burn HWFs at its cement facility. . . .

In conclusion, this record is quite inadequate to support summary judgment for the Board on the preemption question. There is a genuine dispute concerning whether this Ordinance is a reasonable response to protect a legitimate local concern or whether it is really a sham, with the purpose and effect simply of frustrating the policy of RCRA to encourage the recycling of hazardous waste and the safe use of HWFs. On remand, the parties must be permitted to develop a factual record addressing these issues. . . .

We reverse the district court's order of summary judgment regarding Blue Circle's federal preemption . . . challenges to the Rogers County Ordinance and remand for consideration. ■

QUESTION

1. Do you think the RCRA should or should not preempt local ordinances? Why?

ENFORCEMENT

The typical enforcement mechanisms are available to the EPA under the RCRA, including administrative actions, civil actions, and criminal prosecutions. The EPA may seek injunctive relief to motivate immediate action in the event of a violation or may give a facility a time limit within which to come into compliance or face further legal action.

In *Leland v. Moran*,[3] the plaintiffs, residents near an illegal solid waste dump site, sued under the Civil Rights Act (42 U.S.C. § 1983) to enforce the provisions of the RCRA. The trial court held that because the RCRA had specific statutory provisions related to enforcement of its provisions, section 1983 was not available to enforce the provisions of the RCRA. The plaintiffs were found not to have a constitutionally protected interest that could be protected outside the provisions of the RCRA.

Violations can be anything from failing to keep a report properly, to transporting hazardous waste without a proper permit, to knowingly disposing of hazardous waste in an improper manner.

Civil actions for violations can result in penalties of up to $25,000 per day of violation, regardless of whether the violator has taken action to correct the violation. In addition, a permit can be suspended or revoked if a violation is proven.

The RCRA also provides for criminal penalties in the event there is a "knowing" violation of RCRA requirements. Criminal penalties include fines of up to $50,000 and up to two years in prison. The criminal portion of the RCRA also describes the crime of "knowing endangerment," described as a situation where a person violates the RCRA and "knows at that time that he thereby places another person in imminent danger of death or serious bodily injury." (Section 3008) This violation brings with it more substantial penalties, including fines of up to $250,000 and a possibility of up to 15 years in prison. An "organizational defendant" (a corporation, a partnership, or another business organization) may be fined up to $1 million.

As was discussed previously, many federal environmental acts provide citizens with the opportunity to bring suit against a violator of federal statutes or against the EPA for failing to enforce federal environmental provisions. The RCRA is no exception to this trend. If a citizen substantially prevails in such litigation, he or she may recover attorneys' fees. The HSWA of 1984 allow citizens to bring suit where management (past or present) of a waste management facility has placed citizens in imminent or substantial endangerment.

The RCRA does not allow citizen suits against the EPA relating to the siting or permitting of a hazardous waste facility, among other reasons, for situations where the EPA is already pursuing a RCRA action or where the offending party is taking remedial action pursuant to an administrative order obtained by the EPA.

RESEARCH AND DEVELOPMENT

The RCRA requires the EPA to engage in research and development activities in cooperation with other federal, state, local, and private entities. The EPA is supposed to conduct, encourage, and promote research, investigations, experiments, training, demonstrations, surveys, and public education. The efforts can pertain to protecting human health or the environment, developing new technology or methods of waste handling, reducing the volume of wastes generated, and instituting remediation methods. Unfortunately, many in the environmental field are of the opinion that the EPA has not substantially complied with this RCRA requirement and has not made research and development a high priority, preferring to spend its resources on permitting and enforcing waste management activities.

FEATURE

Yucca Mountain Repository

What is it?

In Nye County, Nevada, on federal land located about 100 miles northwest of Las Vegas, the U.S. Department of Energy (DOE) has created a site intended to be a repository for approximately 70,000 metric tons of waste consisting mostly of spent nuclear fuel and high-level radioactive material. The site is known as Yucca Mountain.

How was this site chosen?

Yucca Mountain is a mountain located in the Mojave Desert. This particular desert location was selected because of its geological characteristics and arid climate. The area of the Mojave Desert in which the site is located gets only 7 inches of rain per year, which helps alleviate concerns about runoff from the site. In addition, the site has a very low water table. Yucca Mountain sits over a deep aquifer (a layer of underground sand, gravel, or spongy rock in which water collects) that is used for drinking water and irrigation, but is far enough below the disposal site that it should not be impacted by the facility. The nearby area is sparsely populated.

How will the repository work?

Presently, the material to be placed in Yucca Mountain is stored at sites in 43 states. Special transportation casks have been developed and manufactured in which to transport and store this very dangerous waste material. The casks will be transported to the site by truck and rail. The plan is to place the radioactive waste inside the mountain approximately 1,000 feet below the surface of the land. Given the low water table, the waste will still be 1,000 feet above where the nearest water is located. The DOE expects that the low rainfall, lack of permeability (ability to be penetrated) of the rock making up the mountain, and the composition of the casks will prevent the material from ever reaching groundwater, air, soil, or any other medium through which it could pose a threat to human life.

How long will the stored material be dangerous?

The EPA has adopted a 10,000-year compliance period for this facility (see 40 C.F.R. Part 197). In keeping with that time frame, the DOE is following protection standards designed to keep humans safe for up to 10,000 years after the facility closes. Protection standards include an individual protection standard, a human intrusion standard, and a groundwater protection standard. Discussions have even evaluated the potential effects for up to 1 million years, although it is virtually impossible to determine what the effects might be that far in the future. The nuclear industry, several environmental and public interest groups, and the state of Nevada challenged the standards set by the EPA and the DOE. In 2004, the U.S Court of Appeals for the District of Columbia Circuit upheld all of the standards except the 10,000-year time frame covered by the standards.

QUESTION

Ten thousand years is a long time by anyone's standards! Imagine what the world will be like 10,000 years from now, when, if all goes as planned, Yucca Mountain will once again be safe for humans. What do you think about the concept of disposing of spent nuclear fuel and high-level radioactive waste in a manner that requires a 10,000-year waiting period before they are safe? Do you think the plan will be implemented? Will future generations find a better way to dispose of these materials and "clean up" Yucca Mountain?

When will the facility start receiving waste?

At this time, the DOE hopes to begin receiving material in 2017. Much has been done to prepare for the opening of this facility, but much work yet remains. Before the facility can open

- the DOE must submit an application to the Nuclear Regulatory Commission (NRC) for a license to build the Yucca Mountain Repository. As of November 2006, the DOE expected to submit its license application to the NRC by June 30, 2008.
- tthe EPA must issue its final amended public health and environmental protection standards.

REVIEW
For updates concerning the progress of the plan to deposit spent nuclear fuel and high-level radioactive waste in Yucca Mountain in the Nevada desert, visit the DOE Web site at http://www.ocrwm.doe.gov.

- the NRC must revise the licensing requirements (see 10 C.F.R. Part 63) so they are consistent with the EPA's amended standards.
- if the NRC approves the license application of the DOE, the repository must be constructed and an application for a license to receive radioactive waste must be submitted to the NRC.
- the NRC must approve the license after determining that the site meets the EPA's public health and environmental protection standards.

If all of these conditions are successfully met, nearly all of the radioactive and spent nuclear fuel waste in the United States will be deposited in the middle of a mountain in the Nevada desert and left there essentially in perpetuity. ■

SUMMARY

The purpose of the RCRA is to minimize the present and future threat to human health and the environment by regulating the handling of hazardous waste. The RCRA is designed to control hazardous waste from "cradle-to-grave." To be regulated by the RCRA, a substance must be classified as a solid waste and must meet the criteria to be classified as a hazardous waste. The EPA uses four lists (F, K, P, and U) to classify hazardous waste. Hazardous waste has four characteristics: ignitability, corrosivity, reactivity, and toxicity. The provisions of the RCRA are inclusive enough to regulate certain recycling and reclamation activities. The RCRA imposes many requirements on generators and transporters of hazardous waste and on those who operate hazardous waste TSD facilities. All TSD facilities are required to meet strict design, operation, and construction standards and must obtain a RCRA operating permit. In addition, TSD facilities are required to have a closure and post-closure plan to ensure the continued safety of the facility. The strictness of RCRA regulations reflect the seriousness of the substances with which the act is concerned and provide as much comfort as possible concerning the safety of all phases of the handling of hazardous wastes.

KEY TERMS

- Closure
- Contained-in rule
- Containers
- Corrosivity

- Cradle-to-grave
- Delisting
- Derived-from rule
- Disposal facility
- EPA "lists"
- Generators
- Hazardous waste
- Ignitability
- Incinerators
- Landfills
- Manifest
- Mixture rule
- Operator
- Owner
- Part A and Part B Permit Application
- Reactivity
- Small quantity generators (SQGs)
- Solid waste
- Storage facility
- Surface impoundments
- Tanks
- Toxicity
- Toxicity Characteristic Leaching Procedure (TCLP)
- Transporter
- Treatment facility
- Treatment, storage, and disposal (TSD) facility
- Uniform Hazardous Waste Manifest
- Unmanifested waste
- Waste minimization
- Waste piles

REVIEW QUESTIONS AND HANDS-ON ACTIVITIES

1. Define the terms *solid waste* and *hazardous waste.*
2. How does the term *cradle-to-grave* describe the RCRA process?
3. Name the four characteristics of hazardous waste.
4. Define the terms *generators*, *transporters*, and *owners and operators.*
5. What is a TSD facility?

6. Describe some of the information included in a RCRA operating permit.
7. Create your own phrase replacing *cradle-to-grave* to describe the handling of hazardous waste pursuant to the RCRA. Is this degree of regulation needed in light of the type of materials regulated pursuant to the RCRA? Why or why not?
8. Does it seem appropriate that the definition of solid waste includes both liquids and gases? Is the inclusive definition of solid waste needed to serve the purposes of the RCRA?
9. Find an article on the Internet explaining the types of situations in which hazardous materials are incinerated and the various results and purposes of that method of processing.
10. Learn more about your community. Visit a landfill or a hazardous waste TSD facility in your county. What operations that you observed were required by the RCRA?

HELPFUL WEBSITES

http://www.epa.gov/rcraonline (EPA, Welcome to RCRA Online)

http://www.epa.gov/oswer (EPA, Office of Solid Waste and Emergency Response (OSWER))

http://www.epa.gov/epaoswer/hazwaste/data (EPA, Hazardous Waste Data)

http://www.dec.ny.gov (New York State Department of Environmental Conservation)

ENDNOTES

1. *Marshall v. Barlow's Inc.*, 436 U.S. 307 (1978).
2. *Blue Circle Cement, Inc. v. Board of County Commissioners*, 27 F.3d 1499 (10th Cir. 1994).
3. *Leland v. Moran*, 235 F. Supp. 2d 153 (N.D. NY 2002).

CHAPTER 7

COMPREHENSIVE ENVIRONMENTAL RESPONSE, COMPENSATION, AND LIABILITY ACT (CERCLA)

TITLE: The Comprehensive Environmental Response, Compensation, and Liability Act (CERCLA)

CITATION: 42 U.S.C. secs. 9601, *et seq.* (1980)

REGULATIONS: 40 C.F.R. secs. 33.001, *et seq.*

PURPOSE: To address the hazards to human health and the environment presented by inactive or closed hazardous waste sites.

HISTORY: National Contingency Plan (NCP) (1973)
Superfund Amendments and Reauthorization Act (SARA) (1986)

LEARNING OBJECTIVES

After studying this chapter, the reader should be able to

- describe the *Superfund.*
- define *hazardous substances, pollutants,* and *contaminants.*
- describe a release.
- explain remediation.
- describe the National Contingency Plan (NCP).
- define the acronyms RI/RA, ARARs, and ROD.
- explain what potentially responsible parties (PRPs) are and how they are identified.
- explain how cost recovery actions are handled.

REVIEW
CERCLA is also known as the Superfund.

Superfund The name given to the Comprehensive Environmental Response, Compensation, and Liability Act (CERCLA) and to the fund originally designated by that act to assist with the cleanup of contaminated sites.

SUPERFUND

The *Comprehensive Environmental Response, Compensation, and Liability Act (CERCLA)* is one of the best-known environmental acts. Also described as **Superfund** due to one of its provisions, this act was promulgated to address problems caused by inactive, closed,

release Any spilling, leaking, pumping, pouring, emitting, emptying, discharging, injecting, escaping, leaching, dumping, abandoning, or disposing of any hazardous chemical, extremely hazardous substance, or other hazardous substance into the environment.

hazardous substance A material listed in the CERCLA that invokes the need for a facility to comply with certain release notification requirements.

contaminant Any substance that will cause or may reasonably be anticipated to cause harmful health effects.

facility All buildings, equipment, structures, and other stationary items located on a single site or on contiguous or adjacent sites owned, operated, or controlled by the same person or entity. For some reporting purposes in environmental law, the term also includes motor vehicles; rolling stock; aircraft; and any land, structures, or appurtenances or improvements used for the treatment, storage, or disposal of waste.

vessel Any craft used as a means of transportation on water.

environment Air, land, water, and all living things on Earth.

Reportable Quantity (RQ) The amount of hazardous substance which triggers a reporting requirement under CERCLA.

or abandoned hazardous waste sites. Essentially, CERCLA picks up where the RCRA leaves off. Once a hazardous waste site is closed, if problems arise, such as when a release occurs, CERCLA takes over to regulate the cleanup of the facility.

CERCLA has been a controversial act. Many have criticized its provisions requiring any person who has been involved in the history of a site to be part of the remediation process, regardless of how long that person was involved with the site or how little that person actually contributed to the eventual problem. These provisions arguably have a chilling effect on industry by making involvement with such a site virtually economically infeasible if a post-active environmental problem ever were to occur.

SCOPE OF CERCLA

CERCLA's provisions are triggered by a **release** of a **hazardous substance**, pollutant, or **contaminant** from a **facility** or **vessel** into the **environment**. The definition of each of those key terms is outlined next.

Hazardous Substances

CERCLA addresses problems associated only with hazardous substances. For purposes of CERCLA, hazardous substances are defined as "substances that are listed or designated for regulation under other environmental acts." For example, any substance described as a **listed hazardous waste** or *characteristic hazardous waste* under the RCRA, a hazardous substance or **toxic pollutant** under the CWA, a *listed hazardous pollutant* under the CAA, or an **imminently hazardous chemical substance or mixture** under the Toxic Substances Control Act (TSCA) falls within the definition of a hazardous substance under CERCLA. CERCLA regulations contain a list of such hazardous substances. (Section 40 C.F.R. Part 302)

If a substance qualifies as a hazardous substance under CERCLA, regulations apply to any releases related to that substance, regardless of the amount or volume of the substance at issue. In other words, the release of any quantity of a hazardous substance establishes liability. CERCLA does contain quantity-based reporting requirements, but that **Reportable Quantity (RQ)** does not affect liability under the act.

One of the key exclusions from the CERCLA definition of hazardous substance is petroleum. Aptly named the "petroleum exclusion," this exclusion affects many of the CERCLA sites. If a company's only contribution to a CERCLA site is related to petroleum contamination, that company will not have CERCLA liability. The company will not get off free under environmental law, however, since RCRA provisions may implicate that company for its contamination. Many closed gasoline service stations avoid CERCLA regulation but may incur liability pursuant to the RCRA. Although petroleum may contain other hazardous substances (such as benzene, toluene, and xylene—known as the BTX compounds), if the quantity and existence of those substances is typical for refined petroleum, the presence of those substances will not cause the petroleum to lose its exemption. On the other hand, if there are contaminants added to petroleum during its use, those contaminants will be considered hazardous substances and will be regulated under CERCLA.

listed hazardous waste A hazardous waste determined by the EPA to meet one or more factors such as toxicity, persistence, degradability, potential for accumulation in tissue, flammability, corrosivity, or another hazardous characteristic. Wastes are listed in four groups designated as F wastes, K wastes, P wastes, and U wastes.

toxic pollutant Any pollutant as defined by the Clean Water Act (CWA) deemed toxic to human health or the environment.

imminently hazardous chemical substance or mixture A chemical substance or mixture that poses an immediate potential threat to human health or the environment.

POLLUTANTS AND CONTAMINANTS

In addition to addressing releases of hazardous substances, CERCLA also permits the EPA to address releases of pollutants and contaminants. CERCLA's definition of pollutants and contaminants is extremely broad and covers almost any substance as long as that substance "will or may reasonably be anticipated to cause" specified harmful health effects. [42 U.S.C. sec. 9601 (33)] The EPA does not have the same enforcement options with respect to pollutants and contaminants as it does with respect to hazardous substances, having greater options to recover cleanup costs for releases of hazardous substances than for pollutants or contaminants.

Release

A release of a hazardous substance, pollutant, or contaminant triggers the ability of the EPA to respond. As with many critical terms under CERCLA, the term *release* is broadly defined as follows:

RELEASE

". . . any spilling, leaking, pumping, pouring, emitting, emptying, discharging, injecting, escaping, leaching, dumping or disposing into the environment. . . ." [42 U.S.C. sec. 9601(22)]

The list of releases that are excluded from this definition includes emissions from motor vehicle exhaust, aircraft, vessels, certain nuclear releases, and normal fertilizer application. While at first it may seem too lenient to exclude these emissions from the definition of release, such exclusions become more understandable with the realization that these types of emissions are covered under the provisions of other environmental acts. The emissions are regulated, just not under CERCLA.

The EPA is entitled to respond to both releases and *threats of releases*. Like the definition of *release*, the definition of *threat of release* is broad and is described more by subjective determinations of what may be a threat rather than specific scientific criteria. If a hazardous substance is located where it might migrate or otherwise find itself in an unprotected part of the environment, the situation will be deemed to present a threat of release. Corroding or abandoned tanks also pose such a threat.

Facilities and Vessels

To invoke CERCLA's cost recovery and abatement provisions, there must be a release from a facility or a vessel. This is an oddly exclusionary requirement for cost recovery and abatement situations, since there is no similar requirement for response-only situations. In practice, however, this does not cause a practical problem since CERCLA's definition of *facility* is so broad that the EPA is not hindered in its cost recovery and abatement actions. A facility as defined in CERCLA includes a building, a structure, an installation, equipment, a pipe, a pipeline, or a well. Even more broadly, a facility is defined as ". . . any site or area where a hazardous waste has . . . come to be located." [42 U.S.C. sec. 9601(9)] *Vessels* are defined simply as any craft used as a means of transportation on water.

REVIEW
Many of the definitions in CERCLA are very broad. One example is the definition of *facility*, which is defined, in essence, as anywhere hazardous substances may be found.

Environment

The last important term necessary for understanding the scope of CERCLA is what constitutes the environment, since CERCLA is triggered by releases into the environment. Not surprisingly, this term also is defined broadly and includes surface water, groundwater, drinking water supplies, land surface, subsurface strata, and ambient air.

CERCLA REMEDIATION

Suppose that a release of a hazardous substance has occurred in a manner sufficient to trigger an EPA response under CERCLA. The EPA now has a couple of options as to how to proceed to remedy the problem. Both response options result in the successful cleanup or remediation of the problem, but the EPA's degree of involvement varies with each option. The EPA's first option is to do the cleanup itself and then seek recovery of the cleanup costs. The second option is for the EPA to identify **potentially responsible parties (PRPs)** and have those persons pay for and effect the cleanup.

potentially responsible parties (PRPs) Parties identified by the EPA as potentially responsible for the cleanup of hazardous substances pursuant to CERCLA.

WHEN IS THE EPA AUTHORIZED TO RESPOND?

Under CERCLA, the EPA is authorized to respond if

- there is a release or substantial threat of a release into the environment of a hazardous substance.
- there is a release or substantial threat of a release into the environment of a pollutant or contaminant that may present an imminent and substantial danger to the public health or welfare.

NATIONAL CONTINGENCY PLAN

Regardless of how the EPA responds to a release or threatened release, the EPA must comply with the provisions of the **National Contingency Plan (NCP)**. (40 C.F.R. Part 300) The NCP was first promulgated in connection with the FWPCA. (33 U.S.C. secs. 1251, *et seq.*) The initial focus of the NCP in its role as part of the FWPCA was to address responses to releases of hazardous substances. When CERCLA was passed in 1980, the role of the NCP was increased, but its emphasis stayed the same—responses to releases of hazardous substances.

National Contingency Plan (NCP) A plan designed to address responses to releases of hazardous substances.

The NCP outlines the roles of various groups, including National Response Teams, Regional Response Teams, On-Scene Coordinators, and Remedial Project Managers. All of those organizations play a part in responding to releases. The NCP designates a hierarchy within

ASSIGNMENT

Find the current NPL. Are there sites high on the list within 100 miles of where you live?

National Priorities List (NPL) A list prioritizing the releases or threats of release of hazardous materials in the United States for the purpose of allocating financial and administrative assistance. This list is compiled by the EPA pursuant to CERCLA. The list is comprised of uncontrolled hazardous substance releases that are priorities for long-term remedial evaluation and response.

removal An action in response to an environmental emergency. A removal is intended to contain the problem and reduce the immediate risk to human health and the environment.

remediation A lengthy response following the initial response action related to the cleanup of a hazardous materials release. The intent of remediation is to effect a permanent cleanup of the contaminated site.

those groups, addresses the methods for determining an appropriate response, outlines procedures for removals or remedial actions, and sets forth the format for the EPA's administrative record in support of its action.

One component of the NCP is the **National Priorities List (NPL)**. This list, updated annually, requires the EPA to determine which releases or threats of release in the United States should be given financial and administrative priority. In setting these priorities, the EPA is to take into consideration risks to the health and welfare of the public and possible damage to the environment. The EPA looks at threats to drinking water and air quality in making this determination. A decision by the EPA to place a site on the NPL is significant enough to be considered an action sufficient to trigger the provisions of the APA (see Chapter 1). APA procedures include notice and an opportunity for the public to comment prior to a final decision being made. From a financial perspective, the NPL is an important list because Superfund moneys are available only for long-term remediation of sites on the NPL.

TYPES OF RESPONSES

CERCLA provides for two basic types of EPA responses: **removal** and **remediation**. Removal actions address environmental emergencies. Since the key to a response to an emergency is to contain the problem and reduce the immediate risk, removal actions include such activities as fencing a release site or immediately cleaning up a spill. Removal actions are available for all situations involving the release of hazardous substances, pollutants, or contaminants. A site need not be on the NPL for removal actions to occur. Often a removal action is merely the first step or first phase in a longer response process at a badly contaminated site. Typically, a response action is one that can be completed within two years and costs no more than $2 million. There are exceptions to these limitations, including situations where the emergency requires a more protracted response, the danger to public health or the environment is immediate and serious, or the removal action is just the first phase of a longer and bigger response.

A remedial action is the longer, bigger response that follows a response action. A remedial action is intended to effect a permanent cleanup of a contaminated CERCLA site and may take years or even decades to complete. Remedial actions may include excavation and the construction of dikes, trenches, or clay covers, as well as activities designed to permanently destroy or neutralize the contaminants found at the site.

The length and complexity of remedial actions makes them very costly enterprises, so those who are responsible financially for that cost—the PRPs—will get involved in the remedial process as early and meaningfully as possible to try to minimize their expenditures for the cleanup.

How does a site come to the attention of the EPA and require remedial action? If a release has happened at a site, the release has been properly reported, and removal has been or is being accomplished, the EPA may take note of the site at that point. Citizens can report a site to the EPA. Also, routine or nonroutine investigations by the federal or state government may reveal a significant problem.

THE REMEDIAL PROCESS

Once a site has come to the attention of the EPA, such as a site where a release has occurred or where a release is threatened, the site is placed on the *Comprehensive Environmental Response, Compensation, and Liability Information System (CERCLIS)*. CERCLIS is the official list of CERCLA sites.

QUESTION

How does CERCLIS differ from the NPL?

Once a site has been placed on CERCLIS, the EPA will conduct a **Preliminary Assessment (PA)**. This initial assessment of a CERCLIS site is intended to determine whether the site is truly a risk for the release of hazardous substances. The PA typically involves the review of reports related to the site, as well as a site inspection.

Preliminary Assessment (PA) Part of the process established pursuant to the National Environmental Policy Act (NEPA), this initial assessment assists in determining whether a proposed action may require further investigation to learn whether the action poses an environmental risk.

Following the PA, the EPA will assess the results to determine whether a site presents a significant enough risk that it "scores" high enough on the hazardous ranking system to be placed on the NPL (see the discussion earlier in this chapter). If the EPA is sufficiently interested in the site, the EPA will conduct a further investigation to delve into the specifics of the situation at the site, including what particular hazardous substances are at the site, where any release might go, and what humans or environmental concerns are in the way of such a release. The information from the PA and the information from this subsequent investigation will be used to "score" the site and determine whether the site will be placed on the NPL. Obtaining a certain score is necessary for a site to be placed on the NPL. [40 C.F.R. Part 300 (Appendix A)]

The permanent cleanup plan is customized for each CERCLA site. Therefore, the nature of the cleanup process varies from site to site and consequently will affect the length of the remedial process. The EPA drafts a document each year called the Superfund Comprehensive Accomplishments Plan (SCAP). This document lists each Superfund site the EPA expects to work on during the fiscal year and gives an outline of what the EPA intends to accomplish at the site during each quarter of that year.

Remedial Investigation/ Feasibility Study (RI/FS) A two-part process designed to ensure that there is enough information to analyze the possible remediation alternatives for a site containing hazardous substances so a permanent cleanup plan can be finalized.

How does the EPA decide what the remedial action plan will be for a particular site? The first step is to conduct a **Remedial Investigation/ Feasibility Study (RI/FS)**. This two-part process is designed to ensure that there is enough information to analyze the possible remediation alternatives for a site so a permanent cleanup plan can be finalized. Although a RI/FS study has two parts, the two phases often interrelate and/or overlap.

The first part of the study is the Remedial Investigation (RI) [see, generally, 40 C.F.R. sec. 300.430 (d)]. Given the complexity of scientifically and physically assessing the nature of sites containing hazardous substances, it is not surprising that a RI often takes years to complete. The scientific and physical assessment during a RI typically includes testing of the air, soil, and water at the site, then using that information to determine the nature of any risk to humans and the environment from the site's present condition and from any future release of contaminants.

At the conclusion of the RI, the EPA drafts a Feasibility Study (FS). The FS outlines possible remediation alternatives for the site based on the results of the RI. If the site or the problem is extensive, the cleanup plan suggested in the FS usually will include "phasing" of the cleanup process by breaking the site down into operable units. The cleanup of each operable unit will be done sequentially, making the cleanup process longer, but more easily managed.

How clean is clean? That question has been debated for years in the environmental community. The goal of a remediation action is to "clean up" a contaminated hazardous substances site, but the degree to which a site must be remediated to be considered "clean" is the subject of debate at nearly every site. As indicated previously, each site presents different cleanup problems depending on the nature of the contamination, the physical properties of the site, and the type of development surrounding the site. Must a site be cleaned up to where it was prior to any disposal or release? Must a site be cleaned up until it is no longer a danger to humans and the environment? Typically, some level of contamination will always be present at the site, even after remediation; but the goal is to reduce the level of contamination and danger from release to the point where the site is no longer dangerous to humans or the environment. The 1986 SARA Amendments (see previous discussion) contain stricter requirements for remediation of these types of sites than predecessor statutes. Consequently, the complexity and intensity of cleanup efforts has increased in the past couple of decades. Some have argued that the EPA requires such strict remediation actions that sites end up being "cleaner" than contiguous sites where no contamination occurred except through normal urban pollution and the accumulation of debris. In any case, the EPA will make a determination as to what is "clean enough" for a given site; and that site will be remediated accordingly.

On many urban street corners, cleanup operations have taken place on a small scale where a site was once operated as a gas station and contaminants leaked from underground storage tanks. These sites are usually remediated by the removal of contaminated soil out to a specified radius and the replacement of that soil with "clean" fill dirt. Groundwater in the vicinity is monitored to ensure that the contamination has not reached sources or levels that would be dangerous to humans. The sites are then left to sit, during which time they are monitored in an effort to determine whether the cleanup was adequate. Eventually, if a site has been properly remediated, new development will be allowed to occur.

If that type of remediation is necessary for a very small site such as a former gas station, imagine the type and extent of remediation required at larger, more contaminated sites! As noted previously, the cost of a remedial action is directly proportional to the length and complexity of the cleanup required. So those paying for the cleanup will take an active role in working with the EPA to determine the scope and nature of the remediation action needed.

Section 121 of CERCLA contains required cleanup standards. Remedial actions must meet the goals of CERCLA and, to the extent possible, the NCP. Less importantly, remediation actions are to be as cost-effective as possible and still meet the substantive goals of CERCLA. This goal of selecting cost-effective remedies is somewhat contradicted by the NCP, which provides that the cost effectiveness of a remedy is a minor consideration to be used only when several similarly effective remedies are identified for a site.

Pursuant to Section 121, the ideal remediation action is one that involves a permanent treatment of hazardous substances, resulting in a reduction of their volume, toxicity, or mobility. [42 U.S.C. sec. 963 (b)] Consequently, any treatment that permanently destroys hazardous substances is a preferred solution. Solutions involving merely the containment of hazardous substances with the goal of never letting them "escape" into the environment are not favored solutions. Another solution that is disfavored is moving the hazardous substances to another location where they become a problem for someone else.

In support of its preference for permanent treatment solutions over solutions that involve merely babysitting hazardous substances until a better solution is found, CERCLA requires that remediation actions achieve all **Applicable or Relevant and Appropriate Requirements (ARARs)** if substances are left on-site. ARARs are defined as follows:

- Any standard, requirement, criteria, or limitation under any federal environmental law

- Any promulgated standard, requirement, criteria, or limitation under a state environmental or facility siting law that is more stringent than the federal standard

Thus, compliance with ARARs means that a site's remediation plan must meet the highest cleanup requirements found in federal or state statutes and regulations. Since all sites are unique, the applicable stringent requirements will vary from site to site. Consideration and recommendation of applicable ARARs typically will occur during the RI/FS process as the EPA considers alternative remedies.

Nine criteria divided into three categories are identified in the NCP for evaluating remedies under CERCLA. If a remedy fails to meet the two **threshold criteria**, no further analysis is required and the remedy will not be considered as an alternative. If a remedy meets the threshold criteria, the analysis will move to application of the five **primary balancing criteria**. Lastly, the two **modifying criteria** are considered part of the evaluation process.

Applicable or Relevant and Appropriate Requirement (ARAR) If, to be lawful and effective, a CERCLA remedial action requires compliance with a provision of another environmental law, that requirement is called an ARAR.

threshold criteria The overall protection of human health and the environment and compliance with Applicable or Relevant and Appropriate Requirements (ARARs).

primary balancing criteria Long-term effectiveness, reduction, short-term effectiveness, implementability and cost are criteria to be considered once threshold criteria are met.

modifying criteria State acceptance and community acceptance of a remedy pursuant to CERCLA.

Nine Criteria for Evaluating Remedies

- Threshold Criteria
  - Overall protection of human health and the environment
  - Compliance with ARARs
- Primary Balancing Criteria
  - Long-term effectiveness, including permanence
  - Reduction of volume, toxicity, or mobility through treatment
  - Short-term effectiveness
  - Implementability
  - Cost
- Modifying Criteria
  - State acceptance
  - Community acceptance

As noted, compliance with the threshold criteria is mandatory before a potential remedy will even be considered part of a remediation plan. Any remedy meeting those criteria faces application of the primary balancing criteria; then the modifying criteria are *considered*, but not mandated, as part of the evaluation of a possible remedy. If a potential remedy has "passed the test" of the threshold and primary balancing criteria, only a very strong outcry from a state or community will cause that remedy to be dropped from the list of solutions for a site.

One of the threshold criteria is "compliance with ARARs." Consequently, identification of the proper ARARs for a site becomes one of the primary tasks in evaluating a potential CERCLA remedy. As defined, ARARs requires consideration of "applicable" and "relevant and appropriate" statutes or other requirements. The NCP defines *applicable* in this context as an ARAR ("requirement") that "specifically addresses a hazardous substance, pollutant, contaminant, remedial action, location, or other circumstance found at a CERCLA site." [40 C.F.R. sec. 300.400 (g)(1)] Applying those criteria to a site requires an analysis concerning where a release from a site might migrate. For example, if a release at a site causes the surrounding air, water, or soil to become contaminated, those federal or state laws or regulations concerning contamination of air, water, or soil would be examined to determine what appropriate remedy would ensure that the standards contained in those federal or state laws or regulations would be met. If, on the other hand, a release from a site involves only contamination of soil, only those laws or regulations addressing such contamination would be applicable.

The NCP's definition of what constitutes a "relevant and appropriate" ARAR ("requirement") is more subjective than the NCP's definition of what constitutes an "applicable" requirement and, therefore, is more difficult to apply in any given site analysis. Factors to be considered in this portion of the analysis of a particular requirement include the following:

Factors in the Analysis of "Relevant and Appropriate" Requirement

- The purpose of the requirement being considered
- The purpose of the CERCLA action being proposed
- The medium regulated or affected by the requirement and the medium contaminated at the site (*medium* means air, water, soil, etc.)
- The substances regulated by the requirement
- The substances at the site
- The activities regulated by the requirement
- The remedial action being considered
- Any variances, waivers, or exemptions of the requirement and their availability given the circumstances present at the site
- The type of site regulated by the requirement
- The type of site affected by the release or CERCLA action
- The type and size of the structure or facility regulated by the requirement
- The type and size of any structure affected by the release or being considered as part of the CERCLA action
- Any consideration of use or potential use of the resources affected by the requirement and the use or potential use of the affected resources at the site

If, following the analysis of what is "applicable" and "relevant and appropriate," an ARAR is determined to meet those standards, the ARAR must be used as part of the remedy for a site unless a waiver is granted by the EPA.

Even if a remedy does not, in and of itself, meet appropriate ARARs, the EPA may use it as a remedy at a CERCLA site if

- it is only part of a total remedy that will meet the ARAR.
- compliance with the ARAR will pose a greater risk to human health or the environment than the proposed remedy.
- compliance is impracticable from an engineering technological standpoint.
- the remedy will serve the same purpose as the ARAR by meeting the same standard of performance.

- a state has not consistently applied the ARAR under similar circumstances.
- a remedy is being financed by the Superfund and not applying the ARAR to protect human health and the environment will leave money in the Superfund better used for remedial actions at other sites.

RECORD OF DECISION (ROD)

Once an RI/FS has been completed, a Record of Decision (ROD) will be issued by the EPA. The ROD becomes part of the administrative record of the case. This document details all facts gleaned by the EPA in its evaluation and investigation of a site and explains how those facts were applied to the law to reach the remedies selected. The ROD describes the remedies selected for the site and explains how the EPA reached its decision concerning those remedies. Specifically, the ROD must explain how the CERCLA requirements will be met by the proposed remedies, including a finding that the remedies selected will protect human health and the environment. The ROD must outline the applicable ARARs and explain how they will be met by the proposed remedies. Consistent with other CERCLA goals, the ROD describes the cost effectiveness of the proposed remediation plan and explains how the plan incorporates the most permanent solutions to any hazardous substances found at the site.

As part of the administrative process associated with all such environmental actions, the public is given an opportunity to comment concerning the proposed remedies. If public comments concerning the RI/FS or the remedies selected by the EPA are received, the ROD must address those concerns. Thus, these public comments as addressed in the ROD become part of the administrative record of the case and may be examined should there be an appeal.

In addition to addressing comments from the public, the EPA must consult with any states affected by the site and its proposed cleanup. [42 U.S.C. sec. 9604(c)(2)] The EPA will not be allowed to access Superfund moneys to assist with the cleanup unless the affected state or states enter into an agreement with the EPA documenting a willingness to provide future maintenance of the remedial action selected, ensure the availability of an off-site location for necessary off-site disposal, and pay 10 percent of the cost of the remedial action. If the affected state or states are not able to enter into such an agreement, the EPA's funding source for the cleanup will be seriously compromised.

THE CLEANUP PROCESS

Remedial Design (RD) *See* Remedial Action (RA).

Remedial Action (RA) Part of the remedial action process described in CERCLA. This portion of the remedial process involves the design of the remedial action and the implementation of that design.

Having issued a ROD, the EPA will turn to implementation of the cleanup process. The first step in this process is for the EPA to complete a **Remedial Design (RD)**. The RD is a detailed document, comparable to the construction drawings an engineer or an architect might draft. (In fact, most RDs include engineering drawings.) The drawings should be sufficiently detailed to allow the cleanup action to proceed.

Upon completion of the RD, the EPA will take **Remedial Action (RA)**. As the term implies, this action is the actual implementation of the cleanup process. As you can imagine from the preceding discussion, the remediation of a CERCLA site is long and costly. Costs are typically in the millions or tens of millions of dollars. Ideally, remediation is accomplished using Superfund moneys; however, the Superfund will not prevent PRPs from the liability and cost associated with their share of the remediation action.

LIABILITY UNDER CERCLA

Who is liable?

CERCLA LIABILITY

The following parties may be held liable for most CERCLA costs and damages:

- Current owners and operators
- Former owners and operators of a facility who were involved with a facility during the time any hazardous substance was disposed of at the facility
- Persons who arranged for the disposal or treatment of hazardous substances that they owned or possessed at a facility
- Person who transported hazardous substances to disposal or treatment facilities that were selected by the transporter [42 U.S.C. sec. 9607(a)(1)-(a)(4)]

In short, any person who was involved with the creation, handling, or disposal of hazardous materials at a site will be held liable pursuant to Section 107(a) of CERCLA. Often these potentially liable persons are categorized as (1) current owners and operators, (2) former owners and operators, (3) generators or arrangers, and (4) transporters.

Owners and Operators Generally

CERCLA provisions hold any owner or operator of a CERCLA site liable. The definition of this term in CERCLA has been held by courts to hold any person who participates in management or owns an interest in a business liable for a company's waste disposal efforts (see *United States v. NEPACCO*[1]). CERCLA secs. 101(20)(a) and 107 (a)(3) form the basis of what is known as the **control test** pursuant to which corporate officers or parent corporations may be liable under CERCLA. This test provides that "[a]ny person who . . . arranged for disposal . . . of hazardous substances owned or possessed by such person . . ." is liable. In other words, a person or corporation will be deemed to meet the control test if he, she, or it actually made decisions affecting the handling of hazardous waste at a particular site. This control does not need to be specific control of the waste handling part of an operation as long as there is general control over business operations (see *United States v. NEPACCO*).

control test Any person who arranged for disposal of hazardous substances owned or possessed by such person is deemed to have sufficient control to be considered an owner or operator pursuant to CERCLA.

No corporate officer or person will be able to dodge CERCLA liability by insulating himself or herself from the day-to-day activities at a site. If that person had the *right to control* specific activities, even if that right is not exercised, CERCLA liability will accrue (see *United States v. Fleet Factors Corp.*[2]).

CASE LAW

UNITED STATES V. FLEET FACTORS CORP., 901 F.2D 1550 (11TH CIR. 1990), CERT. DEN., 498 U.S. 1046 (1991).

SUMMARY OF CASE: Fleet Factors was sued by the U.S. government to recover the costs of hazardous waste removal under CERCLA.

Judge Kravitch delivered the opinion of the Court.

In 1976, Swainsboro Print Works (SPW), a cloth printing facility, entered into a "factoring" agreement with Fleet in which Fleet agreed to advance funds against the assignment of SPW's accounts receivable. . . . In August 1979, SPW filed for bankruptcy under Chapter 11. The factoring agreement . . . continued with court approval. . . . On February 27, 1981, SPW ceased operations and began to liquidate its inventory. Fleet continued to collect on the accounts receivable assigned to it under the Chapter 11 factoring agreement. In December 1981, SPW was adjudicated a bankrupt under Chapter 7 and a trustee assumed title and control of the facility.

In May 1982, Fleet foreclosed on its security interest in some of SPW's inventory and equipment, and contracted with . . . Baldwin to conduct an auction of the collateral. . . . On August 31, 1982, Fleet allegedly contracted with . . . Nix to remove the unsold equipment in consideration for leaving the premises "broom clean." Nix left the facility by the end of December 1983.

On January 20, 1984, the . . . EPA inspected the facility and found 700 fifty-five gallon drums containing toxic chemicals and forty-four truckloads of material containing asbestos. The EPA incurred costs of nearly $400,000 in responding to the environmental threat at SPW. . . .

The government sued . . . SPW and Fleet to recover the cost of cleaning up the hazardous waste. Fleet's motion for summary judgment was denied. . . . Fleet subsequently brought this appeal challenging the court's denial of its motion for summary judgment. . . .

[CERCLA] was enacted by Congress in response to the environmental and public health hazards caused by the improper disposal of hazardous wastes. The essential policy underlying CERCLA is to place the ultimate responsibility for cleaning up hazardous waste on "those responsible for problems caused by the disposal of chemical poison." . . .

. . . Accordingly, CERCLA authorizes the federal government to clean up hazardous waste dump sites and recover the cost of the effort from certain categories of responsible parties.

The parties responsible for costs incurred by the government in responding to an environmental hazard are: 1) the present owners and operators of a facility where hazardous wastes were released or are in danger of being released; 2) the owners or operators of a facility at the time the hazardous wastes were disposed; 3) the person or entity that arranged for the treatment or disposal of substances at the facility; and 4) the person or entity that transported the substances to the facility. The government contends that Fleet is liable for the response costs associated with the waste at the SPW facility as either a present owner and operator of the facility, or the owner or operator of the facility at the time the wastes were disposed. . . .

CERCLA holds the owner or operator of a facility containing hazardous waste strictly liable to the United States for expenses incurred in responding to the environmental and health hazards posed by the waste in that facility. . . . It is undisputed that from December 1981, when SPW was adjudicated a bankrupt, until the July 1987 foreclosure sale [to the county for unpaid taxes], the bankrupt estate and trustee were owners of the facility. Similarly, the evidence is clear that neither Fleet nor any of its putative agents had anything to do with the facility after December 1983. . . .

CERCLA also imposes liability on "any person who at the time of the disposal of any hazardous substance owned or operated any . . . facility at which such hazardous substances were disposed of. . . . " CERCLA excludes from the definition of "owner or operator" any "person who, without participating in the management of a . . . facility, holds indicia of ownership primarily to protect his security interest in the . . . facility." Fleet has the burden of establishing its entitlement to this exemption. . . . There is no dispute that Fleet held an "indicia of ownership" in the facility . . . and that this interest was held primarily to protect its security interest in the facility. The critical issue is whether Fleet participated in management sufficiently to incur liability under the statute.

The construction of the secured creditor exemption is an issue of first impression in the federal appellate courts. . . . The trial judge concluded that from the inception of Fleet's relationship with SPW in 1976 to June 22, 1982, when Baldwin entered the facility, Fleet's activity did not rise to the level of participation in management sufficient to impose CERCLA liability. The court, however, determined that the facts alleged by the government with respect to Fleet's involvement after Baldwin entered the facility were sufficient to preclude the granting of summary judgment in favor of Fleet on this issue.

[T]he statutory language chosen by Congress explicitly holds secured creditors liable if they participate in the management of the facility. . . . Under the standard we adopt today, a secured creditor may incur [CERCLA] liability, without being an operator, by participating in the financial management of a facility to a degree indicating a capacity to influence the corporation's treatment of hazardous wastes. It is not necessary for the secured creditor actually to involve itself in the day-to-day operations of the facility to be liable . . . [n]or is it necessary for the secured creditor to participate in management decisions relating to hazardous waste. Rather, a secured creditor will be liable if its involvement with the management of the facility is sufficiently broad to support the inference that it could affect hazardous waste disposal decisions if it so chose. . . .

Our ruling today should encourage potential creditors to investigate thoroughly the waste treatment systems and policies of potential debtors. If the treatment systems seem inadequate, the risk of CERCLA liability will be weighed into the terms of the loan agreement. Creditors, therefore, will incur no greater risk than they bargained for and debtors, aware that inadequate hazardous waste treatment will have a significant adverse impact on their loan terms, will have powerful incentives to improve their handling of hazardous wastes. . . .

We agree with the court below that the government has alleged sufficient facts to hold Fleet liable under [CERCLA]. From 1976 until SPW ceased printing operations on February 27, 1981, Fleet's involvement with the facility was within the parameters of the secured creditor exemptions to liability. During this period, Fleet regularly advanced funds to SPW against the assignment of SPW's accounts receivable. . . . Fleet's involvement with SPW . . . increased substantially after SPW ceased printing operations at the . . . plant on February 27, 1981, and began to wind down its affairs. . . . Fleet was also involved in operational management of the facility. . . . These facts, if proven, are sufficient to remove Fleet from the protection of the secured creditor exemption. . . .

Because there remain disputed issues of material fact, the case is remanded for further proceedings consistent with this opinion. ■

QUESTIONS

1. Why did the Court find that Fleet should be liable for cleanup costs under CERCLA?

2. Why do you think CERCLA has a strict liability standard?

This broad, inclusory definition of who may be liable under CERCLA better serves one of the purposes of CERCLA, which is finding as many people as possible to be PRPs so there will be a larger pool of money from which the costs of cleanup may be taken and better remediation may be effected.

CURRENT OWNERS AND OPERATORS

It makes logical sense that those who own or operate a facility at the time it becomes subject to the provisions of CERCLA should be considered liable parties. With few exceptions, the current owner and operator of a facility will be liable regardless of whether it had any involvement in the handling, disposal, or treatment at the facility or whether hazardous substances were disposed of at the facility during that owner or operator's particular tenure with the facility. Given this broad definition, a situation could occur where a company took over ownership or control of a facility after all essential operations at the facility had been completed and still be liable for problems at the facility not of the company's causing. In an effort to avoid what would be considered an unfair result in a situation such as this, a provision in the 1986 SARA Amendments created the **innocent purchaser defense**. If a current owner or operator can demonstrate that it did not know and had no reason to know at the time of purchase that hazardous

innocent purchaser defense A defense available to a current owner or operator of a facility who can demonstrate that, at the time of purchase, it did not know and had no reason to know that hazardous materials had been handled at a site.

materials had been handled at the site, that owner or operator may be exempt. To claim this defense, the entity must further demonstrate that it conducted a due diligence investigation (made such inquiries concerning the status of the facility as a reasonable purchaser in the industry would make) prior to purchasing the property in order to claim this exemption.

QUESTION
Is the innocent purchaser defense appropriate given the nature of CERCLA sites? How much due diligence must a current owner or operator perform in order to claim this defense?

If an entity acquires an interest in a facility merely to protect its financial exposure with respect to the facility (such as a bank holding a note on such property), that entity will be exempt from liability. Similarly, a governmental entity that acquires a property through a tax sale or another legal mechanism not evidencing overt intent to own the property will be exempt from liability.

Even lessees can be liable as owners (see *United States v. Monsanto Co*[3]). However, even though the courts have been generously inclusive in their interpretation of who is considered an owner, entities that hold mere easement in a property, without further active involvement in the site, will not be considered owners (see *Long Beach Unified Sch. Dist. V. Dorothy B. Goodwin Living Trust*[4]).

FORMER OWNERS AND OPERATORS

CERCLA provisions related to former owners and operators are intended to hold liable only those former owners or operators who were involved in a facility during the time when the disposal of hazardous substances occurred. If entities owned or operated a site at a time other than when disposal occurred, courts have found that they are not liable under CERCLA (see *New York v. Shore Realty Corp.*[5]).

While at first the courts' interpretation may seem less inclusive than other interpretations leading to liability under CERCLA, courts have broadly defined what is considered disposal for purposes of determining whether a former owner or operator may be liable. Disposal under CERCLA has been held to include those definitions of that term contained in the RCRA, which defines the term as "the discharge, deposit, injection, dumping, spilling, leaking or placing any of any solid waste or hazardous waste into or on any land or water . . . ." [42 U.S.C. sec. 6903(3)] So in addition to the commonly understood definition of what constitutes disposal, some courts have determined that movement of waste after disposal also is considered disposal under

CERCLA (see *United States v. Waste Indus.*[6]). Other courts have not been as inclusive (see *Ecodyne Corp. v. Shah*[7]).

PERSONS ARRANGING FOR DISPOSAL OR TREATMENT

Liable parties falling within this category include "any person who by contract, agreement, or otherwise arranged for disposal or treatment . . . of hazardous substances owned or possessed by such person . . . ." [42 U.S.C. sec. 9607(a)(3)] Breaking this definition down, liability attaches when an entity (1) arranges for disposal and (2) has ownership or possession of hazardous substances.

Almost any connection between two entities resulting in the disposal of hazardous substances will meet the definition of being an entity that "arranges for disposal" of such materials. In fact, one court found that knowledge that the disposal of hazardous substances will result from an arrangement is not even necessary for an entity to be deemed to have arranged for disposal (see *Florida Power & Light v. Allis Chalmers Corp.*[8]). However, other courts have found that the term *arranges for* implies some intent that the materials be disposed of (see *Amcast Indus. Corp. v. Detrex Corp.*[9] and *United States v. Cello-Foil Prods., Inc.*[10]).

The part of the definition requiring that the entity have "owned or possessed" the hazardous substances has not been given as much weight in the determination of liability. The legal doctrine of constructive possession has been applied to this situation. Constructive possession is found when an entity has the right to control the substance even when there is no legal ownership or possession of the substance (see *United States v. Bliss*[11]).

One last hurdle that might limit the number of entities in this category found liable under CERCLA has been jumped by the courts not requiring scientific proof matching waste found at the site with waste arranged for disposal by an entity. If the site contains waste "like" that of the waste arranged to be disposed, the courts will impose liability (see *United States v. Wade*[12]).

TRANSPORTERS

CERCLA imposes liability on a transporter "who accepts or accepted any hazardous substances for transport to disposal or treatment facilities or sites selected by such person from which there is a release or a threatened release." [42. U.S.C. sec. 9607(a)(4)] Under this Section, only a transporter who made the decision as to where the substances would be disposed (in other words, "selected" the disposal site) will be held liable. Courts must hear factual evidence concerning how the disposal site was selected to determine whether a transporter will be deemed liable under CERCLA.

ASSESSMENT OF LIABILITY

In light of the potential dangers to human health and the environment associated with sites that are subject to CERCLA actions, the act appropriately provides several types of mechanisms whereby the EPA can identify and assess liability related to those sites. The two general liability provisions in CERCLA are as follows:

- 42 U.S.C. sec. 9606 provides that the EPA may seek a judicial order requiring a liable party to abate any danger to public health or the environment.
- 42 U.S.C. sec. 9607 provides that the EPA and private parties may recover their cleanup costs.

Further, CERCLA contains provisions allowing *citizen suits* brought by private parties to enforce the act's provisions, permits the EPA to compel private citizens to protect human health and the environment, and grants authority to natural resources trustees to bring actions when natural resources are damaged.

These liability provisions are broad and provide the EPA with strong legal backing to enforce the provisions of CERCLA. On top of the strength of the provisions noted, courts have applied the most stringent liability theories available in the law: strict, joint and several, and retroactive liability. As discussed in Chapter 1, with strict liability, the person engaging in a hazardous activity is strictly liable for the damages he or she caused. The theory behind this type of liability is that persons who are performing especially dangerous activities should be liable for any damage caused by their actions whether or not they were exercising reasonable care (so, without regard to the principles of negligence) and no matter what they intended to happen. The courts have supported the use of strict liability in CERCLA actions (see, e.g., *Levin Metals Corp. v. Parr-Richmond Terminal Co.*[13] and *United States v. Northeastern Pharmaceutical & Chem. Co.*[14]).

CASE LAW

UNITED STATES V. NORTHEASTERN PHARMACEUTICAL & CHEM. CO., 810 F.2D 726 (8TH CIR. 1986), CERT. DEN., 484 U.S. 848 (1987).

SUMMARY OF CASE: Northeastern Pharmaceutical & Chemical Co. (NEPACCO) appealed a judgment of the U.S. District Court, which found it liable for response costs incurred by the U.S. government related to cleanup of a hazardous waste site pursuant to CERCLA.

Judge McMillan delivered the opinion of the Court.

NEPACCO . . . appeal[s] from a final judgment entered in the district court for the Western District of Missouri finding them . . . liable for response costs incurred by the government after December 11, 1980, and all future response costs relative to the cleanup of the Denney farm site that are not inconsistent with the national contingency plan (NCP) pursuant to . . . the Comprehensive Environmental Response, Compensation, and Liability Act of 1980 (CERCLA). . . .

The United States cross-appeals from that part of the district court judgment denying recovery of response costs incurred before December 11, 1980. . . .

From April 1970 to January 1972 NEPACCO manufactured the disinfectant hexachlorophene at its . . . plant. NEPACCO leased the plant. . . . The manufacturing process produced various hazardous and toxic by-products. . . . The waste by-products were pumped into a holding tank which was periodically emptied by waste haulers. Occasionally, however, excess waste by-products were sealed in 55-gallon drums and then stored at the plant.

In July 1971 . . . NEPACCO [was] approached . . . with a proposal to dispose of the waste-filled 55-gallon drums on a farm . . . about seven miles south of [the plant]. In mid-July 1971 . . . approximately 85 of the 55-gallon drums [were dumped] into a large trench on the . . . farm. [The trench was then filled in.] Only NEPACCO drums were disposed of at the . . . farm site.

In October 1979 the Environmental Protection Agency (EPA) received an anonymous tip that hazardous wastes had been disposed of at the . . . farm. Subsequent EPA investigation confirmed that hazardous wastes had in fact been disposed of at the . . . farm and that the site was not geologically suitable for the disposal of hazardous wastes. . . . During April 1980 the EPA conducted an on-site investigation, exposed and sampled 13 of the 55-gallon drums, which were found to be badly deteriorated, and took water and soil samples. The samples were found to contain "alarmingly high" concentrations of [hazardous wastes].

In July 1980, the EPA installed a temporary cap over the trench to prevent the entry and run-off of surface water and to minimize contamination of the surrounding soil and groundwater. . . . In August 1980, the government filed its initial complaint against NEPACCO. . . . In June 1981 . . . excavation of the trench [began]. In November 1981 the site was closed. The 55-gallon drums are now stored in a specially constructed concrete bunker on the . . . farm. The drums as stored do not present an imminent and substantial endangerment to health or the environment; however, no plan for permanent disposal has been developed, and the site will continue to require testing and monitoring in the future.

In August 1982 the government filed an amended complaint adding counts for relief pursuant to CERCLA. CERCLA was enacted after the filing of the initial complaint. . . .

The district court found that [the chemicals found at the farm] were "hazardous substances" within the meaning of RCRA. . . . The district court held that RCRA requires a finding of negligence in order to hold past off-site generators and transporters liable for response costs . . . and thus RCRA did not apply to past non-negligent off-site generators and transporters of hazardous substances. . . .

CERCLA . . . authorizes the EPA to take direct "response" actions, which can include either short-term "removal" actions or long-term "remedial" actions, or both, pursuant to the NCP, with funds from the "Superfund," and to seek recovery of response costs from responsible parties . . . in order to replenish the Superfund. The EPA can also use CERCLA to seek injunctions to compel responsible parties to clean up hazardous waste sites. . . .

The district court applied CERCLA retroactively . . . , but held government could not recover response costs incurred before the effective date of CERCLA, December 11, 1980. The district court also held CERCLA imposes a standard of strict liability. . . . The district court correctly found Congress intended CERCLA to apply retroactively. We acknowledge there is a presumption against retroactive application of statutes. . . . We hold, however, that CERCLA . . . is "merely a standard 'effective date' provision that indicates the date when an action can first be brought and when the time begins to run for issuing regulations and doing other future acts mandated by the statute." . . .

. . . Although CERCLA does not expressly provide for retroactivity, it is manifestly clear that Congress intended CERCLA to have retroactive effect. The language used in the key liability provision . . . refers to actions and conditions in the past tense: "any person who at the time of disposal of any hazardous substances owned or operated. . . ."

Further, the statutory scheme itself is overwhelmingly remedial and retroactive. CERCLA authorizes the EPA to force responsible parties to clean up inactive or abandoned hazardous substance sites . . . and authorizes federal, state and local governments and private parties to clean up such sites and then seek recovery of their response costs from responsible parties. . . . Cleaning up inactive and abandoned hazardous waste disposal sites is a legitimate legislative purpose, and Congress acted in a rational manner in imposing liability for the cost of cleaning up such sites upon those parties who created and profited from the sites and upon the chemical industry as a whole. . . .

[We also] address the question whether the government can recover response costs incurred prior to CERCLA's effective date. . . . In fact, . . . Congress intended to permit recovery of pre-CERCLA response costs [based on] . . . the legislative history. . . . In summary, we hold the district court erred in finding that CERCLA does not authorize recovery of pre-enactment response costs. . . .

The district court . . . held that under RCRA . . . proof of fault or negligence was required in order to impost liability upon past off-site generators and transporters. Because the government did not allege or prove negligence, the district court found no liability under RCRA. . . . The government argues that the standard of liability under RCRA . . . is strict liability, not negligence, and that liability under RCRA can be imposed even though the acts of disposal occurred before RCRA became effective in 1976. We agree. . . .

As amended, RCRA specifically applies to past generators and transporters [of hazardous wastes]. . . . From the legislative history . . . , it is clear that Congress intended RCRA . . . to impose liability without fault or negligence and to apply to the present conditions resulting from past activities. In other words, RCRA . . . applies to past non-negligent off-site generators like NEPACCO and to non-negligent past transporters. . . . We reverse that part of the district court judgment holding that RCRA does not apply to past non-negligent off-site generators and transporters.

In conclusion, we hold (1) that CERCLA applies retroactively, (2) the government can recover its pre-enactment response costs under CERCLA, [and] (3) RCRA imposes strict liability upon past off-site generators and transporters of hazardous waste. . . .

Accordingly, the judgment of the district court is affirmed in part, reversed in part, and remanded for further proceedings consistent with this opinion. . . . ■

QUESTIONS

1. Why did the Court decide that CERCLA should apply retroactively?
2. Why did the Court decide that CERCLA permitted the government to recover costs of cleanup before CERCLA was enacted?

In addition to strict liability, courts also have imposed "joint and several" liability, a principle that holds all those contributing to the damage equally liable for that damage, regardless of their percentage of contribution to the situation. Courts have imposed this type of liability in CERCLA cases where more than one party contributed to the damages involved. This situation typifies nearly every CERCLA case, so this type of liability is nearly always imposed by the courts.

Lastly, CERCLA imposes "retroactive" liability that allows the EPA and courts to reach back into time and impose CERCLA's requirements on parties whose actions contributed to damages at a CERCLA site *prior* to the enactment of CERCLA (see *Kelly v. Thomas Solvent Co.*[15]).

Tort theory usually requires that for liability to be imposed, a person must have taken an action that caused damage. CERCLA typically has been enforced by courts in a manner that seems to ignore the "causation" portion of this requirement. If a person acts at a CERCLA site and damages are incurred at that site, the person will be held liable in some amount regardless of whether it is proven in court how much of the damages were caused by the person or even if the person's actions actually caused any of the damage (see *United States v. Monsanto Co.*[16]).

ACTIONS TO RECOVER DAMAGES TO NATURAL RESOURCES

While most actions brought by the EPA pursuant to the provisions of CERCLA involve the recovery of costs as outlined next, the EPA is increasing its activities with respect to recovering for damages caused to natural resources. Pursuant to Section 107(a)(4)(C) of CERCLA, parties may be held liable for "damages for injury to, destruction of, or loss of natural resources, including the reasonable costs of assessing such injury, destruction or loss resulting from such a release."

The scope of this provision might be thought of as less broad at first because the definition of "natural resources" applicable to this Section includes those natural resources commonly associated with that term, such as land, wildlife, fish, and other living things; but the provision limits recovery to loss or damage of only those resources owned, held in trust, or otherwise controlled by a state, the federal government, or an Indian tribe. In other words, damages to privately owned property may not be recovered.

Any damages recovered through actions brought under this Section are intended to be used to restore or replace the resource or for acquisition of an equivalent resource. [42 U.S.C. sec. 9607(f)(1)]

Ordinary citizens are not authorized to bring an action to recover for damage to natural resources. Only federal or state "trustees" may bring such actions. These designated trustees have been trained to assess damages to natural resources and to bring actions to recover the costs of such damages. Section 111 of CERCLA contains direction concerning how to assess costs for damage or loss of natural resources.

Actions to recover these costs and damages are brought primarily against individuals since the Superfund may be used to assist with this effort only where ". . . the President determines that the claimant has exhausted all administrative and judicial remedies to recover the amount of such claim from the person who may be liable under section 107." [42 U.S.C. sec. 9611(b)(2)(A)]

The provisions related to actions brought to recover for damage or loss to natural resources provide that the standard of proof on such claims is a mere preponderance of evidence. A trustee must demonstrate that the defendant's release of a hazardous substance was the "sole or substantially contributing cause of each alleged injury to natural resources" (see *United States v. Montrose Chem. Corp. of California*[17]).

The trustee also must show the following:

- What resource was damaged
- Specifically where the damaged resource was located
- When the resource was damaged
- Which hazardous substance release caused the damage
- How the resource was exposed to the substance

As public sentiment grows toward the preservation of natural resources, so will the EPA's use of this CERCLA provision to restore and replace natural resources damaged or lost through improper management of hazardous substances.

COST RECOVERY ACTIONS

What costs can be recovered in a CERCLA Section 107 action?

In a Section 107 cost recovery action, the following criteria must be met:

- Liable parties must be identified.
- There must be a release or a threatened release.
- A hazardous substance has been released.
- The release must be from a vessel or facility.
- The release has resulted in response costs.

response An action resulting in removal or remediation pursuant to CERCLA.

What are response costs? A **response** is defined as an action resulting in removal or remediation. [42 U.S.C. sec. 9601(25)] Before there can be removal or remediation, many activities must occur; and the costs of most of these activities may be included in the recovery action, as well as the costs of the removal or remediation itself. Costs or activities that may be included in the cost recovery action include but are not limited to the following:

- Sampling or monitoring to assess the scope of a release or threatened release (see *Cadillac Fairview/California, Inc. v. Dow Chem. Co.*[18]).
- Detecting, identifying, controlling, and disposing of hazardous substances (see *NL Indus. v. Kaplan*[19]).
- Investigating the danger to human health or the environment (see *Brewer v. Ravan*[20]).
- Covering EPA's administrative and overhead costs (see *United States v. Hardage*[21]).
- Covering attorneys' fees (for example, Department of Justice (DOJ) and EPA attorneys' fees associated with a CERCLA enforcement action). On the other hand, private parties may recover attorneys' fees only for work "closely tied with an actual clean-up" (see *Key Tronic Corp. v. United States*[22]).

The courts have found that certain costs are *not* recoverable as response costs. Examples of these costs include lost profits, general damages, medical monitoring costs, and installation of monitoring wells associated with another event.

For any costs to be recovered under CERCLA, the party recovering costs must demonstrate compliance with other CERCLA requirements.

First, the costs must be "necessary" to the response action. [42 U.S.C. sec. 9607(a)(4)(B)] If they are not, the costs will not be recovered.

Another requirement that must be met before costs can be recovered is compliance with the provisions of the NCP. To meet this standard, the EPA has a lesser burden than a private entity seeking to recover costs. The EPA needs to show only that its costs are "not inconsistent" with the NCP (and the burden is on the defendant to show that the EPA's costs are inconsistent with the NCP), whereas the burden is on private entities to demonstrate that their costs are "consistent" with the NCP. Some courts have found that private entities must comply with the NCP strictly in order to recover costs (see *Amland Prop. Corp. v. ALCOA*[23]). Other courts have found that "substantial compliance" is sufficient (see *Wickland Oil Terminals v. ASARCO, Inc.*[24]).

The cost recovery actions just described result in the recovery of appropriate costs by the EPA and private parties utilizing the Superfund. Another mechanism present in CERCLA permits the recovery of cleanup moneys from liable parties rather than the Superfund. This other procedure is called an **abatement action**.

abatement action A judicial proceeding wherein the EPA asks the court to require a Potentially Responsible Party (PRP) to abate an imminent and substantial endangerment to the public health or the environment.

Abatement Actions

CERCLA Section 106 permits the EPA (no private actions are allowed) to ask a court to require a PRP to abate an imminent and substantial endangerment to the public health or welfare or to the environment because of an actual or threatened release of a hazardous substance from a facility. As noted previously, the costs of this abatement are paid by the liable parties rather than the Superfund.

A Section 106 action, unlike a Section 107 action previously described, allows the EPA to seek abatement not only when there is an existing imminent and substantial risk but also when there *may be* an imminent and substantial risk if some action is not taken. Typically, courts have used the same standards for liable parties under Section 106 as they have for Section 107 actions. Since courts have construed the definitions of *imminent* and *endangerment* so broadly, it is not difficult to find that there *may be* a threat and that there *is* an existing threat. Therefore, many EPA actions include claims under Section 106 and Section 107.

These two sections do have differences, however. An equitable remedy is one which permits the court to fashion a remedy other than just money damages in an attempt to remedy a situation. Equity essentially means "fairness." Section 106 allows a court to "grant such relief as the public interest and the equities of the case may require." The language of Section 107 does not contain similar language. Consequently, defendants in Section 106 actions have been found by some courts to have the ability to assert equitable defenses to the EPA's allegations.

Another difference between the sections is that while a Section 106 action allows a court to order an "abatement" of a threat to the public health or the environment and the payment of related costs, Section 107 allows the recovery of costs for actions up to and including full site remediation. Since it may not be necessary to effect a full remediation in order to "abate" a release or a threatened release, a court's options are more limited with respect to the nature of the remedy ordered.

ASSIGNMENT
Describe the differences between Section 106 and Section 107 cost recoveries.

Section 106 not only authorizes the EPA to seek judicial relief but also allows the EPA to avoid the court system (unless there is an appeal) by unilaterally issuing an administrative order.

ADMINISTRATIVE ORDERS

In recent years, the enforcement mechanism of choice for the EPA under CERCLA has been the issuance of administrative orders. Before the EPA can exercise this very powerful tool, there must be

- the existence of
  - an actual or threatened release.
  - a hazardous substance.
  - a release of a hazardous substance from a facility.
- an administrative finding that there is or may be an imminent or substantial endangerment.
- relief that "may be necessary" to abate the danger.

The reason this tool is so powerful is that PRPs do not have much recourse to contest the EPA's finding that such conditions exist until after the action has been taken and the EPA is seeking further enforcement or recovery of its costs. Unlike most EPA determinations, there is no provision for the solicitation of public comment concerning the

EPA's findings that sufficient grounds exist to issue an administrative order and require RA.

The subject of an EPA administrative order may have a conference with the EPA concerning the EPA's determinations, but the scope of the conference is limited to a discussion about whether the EPA's decision is based on sufficient or accurate information. The subject of the order cannot challenge the substance of the order (the remedy ordered) at this point in the proceedings.

If a judicial review of the RAs ordered is later sought by the subject of the order, the court will review the record to determine whether the EPA acted in an arbitrary or capricious manner in accordance with the law. Unless a court can make any of those findings, the court will affirm the remediation ordered by the EPA. If liability is questioned, a court may consider that portion of the proceedings in a ***de novo* trial** (a "new" trial not based on the administrative record).

***de novo* trial** A "new" trial not based on the record from a lower tribunal.

As noted previously, a party who is issued an administrative order must, under most circumstances, pay for the costs of the RA ordered. The exception to that general rule is when the party can demonstrate that he or she complied with a cleanup order but is not liable or that the EPA's action was arbitrary, capricious, or not in accordance with law. To prove that either of those situations exists is a difficult task, and most parties are not able to meet their burden of proof. Consequently, very few administrative orders are successfully challenged in court.

The fact that there is very little chance at a successful judicial challenge to an administrative order issued by the EPA means that a liable party is left with little choice but to try to settle with the EPA. Most EPA actions result in settlements due to the fact that settlements decrease the ultimate costs to all parties and shorten the length of time the process takes.

CONSENT DECREE/ORDER

Settlements are beneficial not only to liable parties but also to the EPA. Through settlements, the EPA is able to conserve Superfund resources as well as its own resources. Liable parties find settlements beneficial because they have more input into the RAs ordered, can avoid litigation costs, and often can minimize their cleanup costs.

While liable parties may find the EPA more flexible in settlement discussions than in litigation, there are still constraints on EPA's ability to enter into a settlement agreement. The EPA has "model" settlement agreements and typically does not vary from those documents. The 1986 SARA Amendments, in Section 122 of CERCLA, sets forth the limits of the EPA's authority to settle CERCLA enforcement actions. This Section details both procedural and substantive requirements on the EPA.

What do settlements with the EPA typically cover? With any CERCLA site, waste was contributed by parties that are either defunct or bankrupt at the time of an enforcement action. The waste share of these parties is known as the **orphan share**. Consequently, a settlement agreement for a specific site will address less than the total volume of waste at that site. Often liable parties will ask the EPA to contribute funds for the portion of the costs attributable to this orphan share. When this occurs, the dollars contributed to the settlement are known as mixed funding because the funding is mixed between the liable parties and the EPA. Those settling with the EPA also will ask the EPA to carve out a portion of the RA or costs and attempt to impose that liability on those PRPs who are not part of the settlement.

orphan share Waste contributed by parties that are either defunct or bankrupt at the time of a CERCLA enforcement action.

Section 122 of CERCLA suggests that the EPA determine whether any party is a minor, or *de minimus*, contributor to site problems and settle with that party with real finality. Real finality means that the EPA will agree not to sue the party again for a particular site unless the facts the EPA used to determine that the party was not a significant contributor turn out to be erroneous.

QUESTION

Does the term *orphan share* accurately describe the allocation of waste to which it refers?

Most parties are not able to get such a final settlement with the EPA because the EPA will not know for sure that the remediatation agreed to in a settlement will successfully address the threat until the remediation is complete. The EPA does have the authority to include a covenant not to sue in settlement agreements, but those covenants typically contain so many conditions that the covenant is not comforting to its beneficiaries.

EPA settlements are categorized as a **consent decree** or a **consent order**. A consent decree is filed with and signed by a federal court, while a consent order does not result from any type of judicial action. This distinction is counterintuitive since you think of an order as being something a judge would issue; but in this case, a judge issues a decree.

consent decree An order entered by a federal court. This term is part of CERCLA.

consent order An agreement outside of a court proceeding. This term is part of CERCLA.

There are penalties for failure to abide by a consent decree or a consent order. The decree or order may contain stipulated damages for failure to comply, or a court may assess appropriate penalties later.

FAILURE TO COMPLY WITH EPA ENFORCEMENT ORDERS

It is undeniable that the EPA controls enforcement proceedings and that parties who have no legitimate argument concerning liability or the propriety of the EPA's action are best served by completing the RA as quickly and cost effectively as possible. There are severe penalties under CERCLA for failure to comply with a Section 106 cleanup order. First, monetary penalties of up to $25,000 per day of a violation may accrue. If a court were to find that a party was unjustified in its failure or refusal to comply with such an order, the court also could order punitive damages (damages designed to "punish" the party against whom they are ordered).

A party subject to a Section 106 order does have the ability to raise substantive defenses to explain its noncompliance. These defenses include the following:

- That it was not liable under CERCLA or had a defense to such liability
- That it was a *de minimus* (minor) contributor to the release or threatened release
- That the order was legally invalid
- That it could not comply with the order due to a financial, technical, or other cause
- The action was not cost-effective as required by CERCLA or is otherwise inconsistent with the NCP

These defenses were summarized in *Solid State Circuits v. United States Envtl. Protection Agency*,[25] where the court found that to prevail, "a party must show that the applicable provisions of CERCLA, EPA regulations and policy statements, and any formal or informal hearings or guidance the EPA may provide, give rise to an objectively reasonable belief in the invalidity or inapplicability of the cleanup order." This is a stringent, but not impossible, standard to achieve.

One of the defenses noted previously is that an entity may argue that it is not liable under CERCLA. The only affirmative defenses specifically available pursuant to Section 107 are that a release or threatened release is caused, *in its entirety*, by

- an act of God.
- an act of war.
- an act or omission of a third party as long as the defendant did his or her best to avoid the foreseeable acts of that third party.

While those defenses are the only specified defenses in Section 107, courts have allowed parties to raise equitable defenses in such proceedings (see *United States v. Hardage*).[21] Some of these equitable defenses include an argument that the defendant exercised due care, that the defendant complied with existing standards, that the doctrine of laches prevents EPA success, that the EPA has unclean hands, and that the EPA is estopped from pursuing its claims.

While defendants have had moderate success asserting statutory and equitable defenses in CERCLA cases, the courts have not been receptive to arguments that the EPA did not comply with procedural requirements, such as failure to provide a private party with the opportunity to clean up a site, failure to notify PRPs, or failure to list a site on the NPL (see, e.g., *New York v. Shore Realty Corp.*).[5]

STATUTES OF LIMITATIONS

With the 1986 SARA Amendments, CERCLA obtained provisions setting forth the statutes of limitations for various CERCLA proceedings [see Section 113(g)]. Cost recovery actions for removals must be brought within three years of completion of the removal. Cost recovery actions for remediations must be brought within six years "after initiation of physical on-site construction of the remedial action." If a cost recovery action is brought within three years of the completion of a removal action, the EPA is allowed to "tack on" the removal costs to the remediation costs.

Claims for damage to natural resources must be brought within three years of the date of the discovery of the loss and its connection with the release or the date of promulgation of natural resource damage assessment regulations. [42 U.S.C. sec. 9613(g)(1)]

Actions brought for the purpose of obtaining contributions for response costs or damages have a three-year statute of limitations. The statute starts running from the date of judgment in a CERCLA action to recover such costs or damages or the date of an administrative order or entry of a judicially approved settlement concerning such costs or damages.

Special Ethical Concerns for Paralegals

One of the most frequent ethical violations attorneys make is failing to meet a required time deadline, such as a statute of limitations. Paralegals often are entrusted with the responsibility of calendaring an important date on a manual or automated system in the office. As a result, it is critical that paralegals know the correct method of calculating dates, including the date from which the time limit runs and any additional time added to the deadline by statute or rule. Paralegals must make sure they confirm with the attorney their method of calculating important dates.

DIVISION OF RESPONSIBILITY FOR COSTS OR DAMAGES

In most CERCLA cases, the EPA successfully argues that individual liability cannot be properly assessed because the wastes at a particular site have been so commingled that it is impossible to ascertain which defendant is responsible for which portion of the costs or damages. For this reason, most costs or damages are assessed under CERCLA via "joint and several liability." Under this doctrine, all parties are equally responsible for costs and damages awarded. As noted previously, Section 122 of CERCLA encourages the EPA to determine whether any part was a minor, or *de minimus*, contributor to the costs or damages. The EPA usually attempts to ensure that such a minor contributor to the problem is not saddled with the entire cost and damage award.

While courts frequently agree with the EPA's argument that the liability for a release or threatened release is not severable or divisible, some courts have forced the EPA to evaluate whether waste contributed by a particular party did not contribute as significantly to the problem due to some variance in either the quantity or quality of the waste from that party. For example, if the hazardous characteristics of the waste contributed to the site by one party did not significantly contribute to the threat posed by a release or threatened release, the court might find that party less responsible for the costs and damages than other more significant contributors (see *United States v. Alcan Aluminum Corp.*[26]).

contribution action A method by which some division of liability may be made pursuant to CERCLA.

If a party to a CERCLA action determines that some division of the liability may be made, that party can bring a **contribution action**. Section 113(f) of CERCLA, part of the 1986 SARA Amendments, provides for such actions and sets forth the "equitable factors" to be considered in assessing liability.

EQUITABLE FACTORS USED IN ASSESSING LIABILITY

- The amount of waste contributed by each party
- The relative toxicity of the waste contributed by each party
- Each party's involvement in the generation, transport, treatment, storage, or disposal of the waste
- The care in handling demonstrated by the parties
- The degree of cooperation of each party with the government's attempts to protect the public and the environment

A contribution action may be brought as part of a CERCLA Section 107 cost recovery action or CERCLA Section 106 abatement action or following those actions.

In case some parties elect to settle with the EPA during an enforcement action and others do not, CERCLA contains "contribution protection" whereby a party that has "resolved its liability to the United States of a State in an administrative or judicially approved settlement shall not be liable for claims for contribution regarding matters addressed in the settlement." [42 U.S.C. sec. 9613(f)(2)]

The U.S. Supreme Court recently decided a case concerning the contribution of costs for environmental cleanup where the issue concerned the contribution of a party that had not been sued in a cost recovery action.

CASE LAW

COOPER INDUSTRIES, INC. V. AVIALL SERVICES, INC., 543 U.S. 157 (2004).[27]

SUMMARY OF CASE: A buyer of an aircraft engine maintenance business sued the seller of the business under CERCLA for contribution to the costs of environmental cleanup that the buyer voluntarily undertook at the four sites it purchased.

Justice Thomas delivered the opinion of the Court.

[T]he Comprehensive Environmental Response, Compensation, and Liability Act of 1980 (CERCLA) allows persons who have undertaken efforts to clean up properties contaminated by hazardous substances to seek contribution from other parties liable under CERCLA. Section 113(f)(1) specifies that a party may obtain contribution "during or following any civil action" under CERCLA § 106 or § 107(a). The issue we must decide is whether a private party who has not been sued under § 106 or § 107(a) may nevertheless obtain contribution under § 113(f)(1) from other liable parties. We hold that it may not.

Under CERCLA . . . the Federal Government may clean up a contaminated area itself . . . or it may compel responsible parties to perform the cleanup. . . . In either case, the Government may recover its response costs under § 107 . . . the "cost recovery" section of CERCLA. . . .

After CERCLA's enactment in 1980, litigation arose over whether § 107, in addition to allowing the Government and certain private parties to recover costs from PRPs [potentially responsible persons] also allowed a PRP that had incurred response costs to recover costs from other PRPs. More specifically, the question was whether a private party that had incurred response costs, but that had done so voluntarily and was not itself subject to suit, had a cause of action for cost recovery against other PRPs. Various courts held that [CERCLA] . . . authorized such a cause of action. . . .

After CERCLA's passage, litigation also ensued over the separate question whether a private entity that had been sued in a cost recovery action (by the Government or by another PRP) could obtain contribution from other PRPs. As originally enacted in 1980, CERCLA contained no provision expressly providing for a right of action for contribution. A number of District Courts nonetheless held that, although CERCLA did not mention the word "contribution," such a right arose either impliedly from provisions of the statute, or as a matter of federal common law. . . . Congress subsequently amended CERCLA . . . to provide an express cause of action for contribution, as codified as CERCLA § 113(f)(1).

This case concerns four contaminated aircraft engine maintenance sites in Texas. Cooper Industries, Inc., owned and operated those sites until 1981, when it sold them to Aviall Services Inc. Aviall operated the four sites for a number of years. Ultimately, Aviall discovered that both it and Cooper had contaminated the facilities when petroleum and other hazardous substances leaked into the ground and groundwater through underground storage tanks and spills.

Aviall notified the Texas Natural Resource Conservation Commission (Commission) of the contamination. The Commission informed Aviall that it was violating state environmental laws, directed Aviall to clean up the site, and threatened to pursue an enforcement action if Aviall failed to undertake remediation. Neither the Commission nor the EPA, however, took judicial or administrative measures to compel cleanup.

Aviall cleaned up the properties under the State's supervision, beginning in 1984. Aviall sold the properties to a third party in 1995 and 1996, but remains contractually responsible for the cleanup. Aviall has incurred approximately $5 million in cleanup costs; the total costs may be even greater. In August 1997,

Aviall filed this action against Cooper in the United States District Court . . . seeking to recover cleanup costs. . . .

Both parties moved for summary judgment, and the District Court granted Cooper's motion. The court held that . . . relief was unavailable to Aviall because it had not been sued under CERCLA § 106 or § 107. . . .

[T]he fifth Circuit reversed . . . holding that § 113(f)(1) allows a PRP to obtain contribution from other PRPs regardless of whether the PRP has been sued under § 106 or § 107. . . . The court held that "[s]ection 113(f)(1) authorizes suits against PRPs in both its first and last sentence[,] which states without qualification that 'nothing' in the section shall 'diminish' any person's right to bring a contribution action in the absence of a section 106 or 107(a) action." The court reasoned in part that "may" in § 113(f)(1) did not mean "may only." . . . We granted certiorari . . . and now reverse.

Section 113(f)(1) does not authorize Aviall's suit. The first sentence . . . provides: "Any person *may* seek contribution . . . *during or following* any civil action under . . . this title" (emphasis added). The natural meaning of this sentence is that contribution may only be sought subject to the specified conditions, namely, "during or following" a specified civil action.

Aviall answers that "may" should be read permissively, such that "during or following" a civil action is one, but not the exclusive, instance in which a person may seek contribution. We disagree. First, as just noted, the natural meaning of "may" in the context of the . . . clause is that it authorizes certain contribution actions—ones that satisfy the subsequent specified condition—and no others.

Secondly, and relatedly, if § 113(f)(1) were read to authorize contribution actions at any time, regardless of the existence of a § 106 or § 107 civil action, then Congress need not have included the explicit "during or following" condition. In other words, Aviall's reading would render part of the statute entirely superfluous, something we are loath to do. Likewise, if § 113(f)(1) authorizes contribution actions at any time, § 113(f)(3)(B), which permits contribution actions after settlement, is equally superfluous. There is no reason why Congress would bother to specify conditions under which a person may bring a contribution claim, and at the same time allow contribution actions absent those conditions.

The last sentence of § 113(f)(1) . . . does not change our conclusion. That sentence provides: "Nothing in the section shall diminish any person's right to bring a contribution action in the absence of a civil action under section 9605 of this title or section 9607 of this title." The sole function of the sentence is to clariy that § 113(f)(1) does nothing to "diminish" any cause(s) of action for contribution that may exist independently of §113(f)(1). In other words, the sentence rebuts any presumption that the express right of contribution provided by the enabling clause is the exclusive cause of action for contribution available to a PRP. The sentence, however, does not itself establish a cause of action; nor does it expand § 113(f)(1) to authorize contribution actions not brought "during or following" a § 106 or § 107 civil action; nor does it specify what causes of action for contribution, if any, exist outside § 113(f)(1). . . .

Each side insists that the purpose of CERCLA bolsters its reading of § 113(f)(1). Given the clear meaning of the text, there is no need to resolve this dispute or to consult the purpose of CERCLA at all. . . . Section 113(f)(1) authorizes contribution claims only "during or following" a civil action under § 106 or § 107(a), and it is undisputed that Aviall has never been subject to such an action. Avial therefore has no § 113(f)(1) claim. . . .

We therefore reverse the judgment of the Fifth Circuit. . . . ■

QUESTION

1. Do you think the Supreme Court made the right decision in this case, given the purpose of CERCLA? Why or why not?

A question left undecided in *Cooper Industries* was whether CERCLA permitted PRPs to collect costs of clean-up from other PRPs under section 107(a) of CERCLA. In a recent case, the U.S. Supreme Court decided that section 107(a) did provide potentially responsible parties with a cause of action to recover costs from other PRPs. *U.S. Atlantic Research Corp.*, 551 U.S. ___, 127 S.Ct. 2331 (2007)[28]

CITIZEN SUITS

Any "person" may file a suit under CERCLA

- against any other person (including the United States) for violations of CERCLA laws, rules, regulations, or properly issued orders.
- against any officer of the United States for failure to perform a nondiscretionary act under CERCLA (*mandamus* action). (42 U.S.C. sec. 9659)

A citizen contemplating such a suit must give the EPA and/or the alleged violator 60 days' notice prior to filing the suit.

APPLICABILITY TO FEDERAL FACILITIES

Traditionally, federal facilities, especially those associated with operations of the Department of Defense (DOD) and DOE, have sought to be exempt from environmental regulation, claiming that their activities in support of the national defense should not in any way be impeded by having to comply with environmental laws.

Clearly, the sites used by federal agencies to manufacture and store weapons and personnel over the years have created massive environmental problems. The Rocky Flats nuclear production facility and the Rocky Mountain Arsenal in Colorado are examples of federal facilities that created huge environmental cleanups. Many federal military facilities had landfills, unlined waste pits, holding ponds, drying beds, discharge into the ground, and on-site waste burning.

In response to the presence of such facilities in the United States, CERCLA contains broad waivers of sovereign immunity, allowing citizens and states to bring civil suits for recovery of cleanup costs and to require such facilities to comply with CERCLA requirements. **Sovereign immunity** is a legal doctrine that permits governments to avoid liability for their actions in certain circumstances. The antecedents of this doctrine clearly come from early law protecting the king, queen, or other "sovereign" ruler from claims by citizens.

sovereign immunity A legal doctrine permitting governments to avoid liability for their actions in certain circumstances.

Although laws vary from state to state and federal laws vary in their application of this doctrine, modern sovereign immunity laws typically protect governments from most types of liability for engaging in those activities in which they are required by law to engage for the good of the citizens. Often if a government has merely been negligent in its actions, sovereign immunity will protect that governmental entity from liability. If, on the other hand, a governmental entity has acted knowingly or willfully or in some manner as to intentionally violate the law or the rights of citizens, sovereign immunity will not shield that entity from liability.

Due to the inherent risk to human health and the environment from the types of activities in which federal agencies engage, legislators have chosen language in CERCLA that "waives," or abrogates, the protections afforded the government through sovereign immunity. An entire section of CERCLA is devoted to setting forth the compliance requirements for federal facilities, both substantively and procedurally. [42 U.S.C. sec. 9620(a)] In many ways, federal facilities must comply with the same CERCLA requirement as private facilities. Responding to these requirements, many federal agencies, such as the DOD and the DOE, have implemented extensive plans for cleanup of their facilities.

As noted at the beginning of this chapter, CERCLA has been very controversial and many suggestions have been made concerning how it can be better codified to serve the purposes for which it was intended. Most of the suggestions address the perceived arbitrary nature of assessing liability under CERCLA and the devastating nature of the amounts of money it takes to remediate a site. As of the writing of this text, there are significant problems with the funding of the Superfund and the future of CERCLA cleanup actions is uncertain. The environmental need for CERCLA and its provisions has been clearly demonstrated; and the act has allowed or required many contaminated sites to be remediated, making the United States safer for its citizens and the environment. Only time will tell whether CERCLA continues to be effective and whether its provisions will be significantly altered.

ENVIRONMENTAL LAW PARALEGAL PROFILE

Mr. Robert L. Dickson, Jr.

What types of duties do you perform in your work as a paralegal in the natural resources/environmental law fields?

The breadth of my firm's practice areas allows me to work on matters involving practically all aspects of environmental law, from federal Clean Air Act and Clean Water Act issues to local land use matters. My duties include legal and factual research; site assessment and investigation; historical research; site chronologies; preparation and review of a wide variety of regulatory, planning, and compliance documents and reports including but not limited to Environmental Impact Reports, Storm Water Pollution Prevention Plans, Water Quality Management Plans, and submittals to state and federal regulatory agencies. I frequently review files maintained by various governmental entities and prepare summary reports. I assist attorneys in performing environmental diligence for large corporate transactions. I also assist attorneys in litigation, both at the state and federal level, with all aspects of trial preparation and prosecution.

What skills are required for your work?

The ability to effectively communicate is the most important skill required for this type of work. This includes the full spectrum of business and legal communication, from computer skills to writing and speaking skills. In addition to communications skills, organizational skills are very important, as a paralegal will often be required to effectively manage many different documents in various media.

What is your favorite part of your job?

The quality of our clientele and the amazing variety of matters we work on. In one day, I may work on ten entirely distinct matters involving the whole spectrum of environmental law. Our department is truly national in scope, and I routinely get assignments from attorneys in different offices. The matters we work on are typically very complex and interesting. I have a standing assignment to monitor new federal, state, and local legislation and regulatory initiatives and analyze their potential impacts on our clients. My days are almost never routine; and the constantly evolving environmental, land use, and resources arena provides many opportunities for work on cutting-edge matters. I thoroughly enjoy the regular interaction with clients and various governmental agencies as well.

What advice do you have for paralegal students interested in environmental law?

Environmental law is not just about saving endangered species or habitats; it encompasses a truly breathtaking range of programs, statutes, and regulations. Familiarize yourself with the Web sites of the various state and federal agencies that deal with environmental issues in order to begin to develop an understanding of the practical aspects of environmental law. Internships with local regulatory agencies also can provide invaluable opportunities.

What are your tips for success?

Being successful requires a genuine interest in what you do for a living every day. Become an expert in your practice area. Develop strong research skills early on and always seek out ways to improve those skills. Familiarize yourself with the major statutory and regulatory schemes in the practice area(s) in which you work. Paralegals working in environmental law are often the principal fact gatherers and are heavily relied upon to be accurate and thorough. Always complete your assignments in a timely and accurate manner and make sure to keep your supervisors apprised of any problems as they arise, especially as gathering information from regulatory agencies can be a time-intensive process. You must be willing to work independently and be able to anticipate and plan for every contingency. Build relationships with the staff of the various agencies and municipalities you work with, as they often control access to key materials. Learn how to use every resource available to you, including libraries, databases, depositories, and news and information resources such as Lexis and Westlaw. Understanding what constitutes the universe of documents and how to access them are critical for success.

Robert L. Dickson, Jr., has worked as a paralegal for Latham & Watkins LLP in Costa Mesa, California, since 2000. Prior to obtaining his position as a paralegal, Mr. Dickson served as the firm's library assistant, a position requiring comprehensive legal research concerning environmental and regulatory issues, litigation, and other business conducted by the firm. The position also required him to maintain a full-service law library, including monitoring multiple media sources for client-related news. Mr. Dickson served in the U.S. Marine Corps Reserve as a Stinger Missile Gunner, earning the Meritorious Mast for being Top Gun at Stinger School.

SUMMARY

CERCLA was enacted to address the hazards to human health and the environment presented by inactive or closed hazardous waste sites. Otherwise known as Superfund, CERCLA picks up where the RCRA leaves off. CERCLA deals with hazardous substances, including those substances "listed" under other environmental acts. The response provisions of CERCLA are triggered by a release into the environment. The NPL prioritizes sites where there have been releases or threats of release. Types of responses include removal and remediation. As much as possible, responses also must comply with the NCP. At the completion of an RI/RS, the EPA will issue a ROD. Identifying those who have liability under CERCLA is a complex and inexact process. PRPs are identified, and their levels of contribution to the waste are assessed using many criteria. Actions attempting to assign liability under CERCLA, "contribution cases," are a frequent occurrence. The EPA is authorized under CERCLA to issue an administrative order and may agree to consent orders. The effectiveness of CERCLA has been and will continue to be debated as long as it remains law. While CERCLA may not be the most efficacious way of addressing hazardous substance release, those releases cannot be ignored.

KEY TERMS

- Abatement action
- Applicable or Relevant and Appropriate Requirements (ARARs)
- Consent decree
- Consent order
- Contaminant
- Contribution action
- Control test
- *De novo* trial
- Environment
- Facility
- Hazardous substance
- Imminently hazardous chemical substance or mixture
- Innocent purchaser defense
- Listed hazardous waste
- Modifying criteria
- National Contingency Plan (NCP)

- National Priorities List (NPL)
- Orphan share
- Potentially responsible parties (PRPs)
- Preliminary Assessment (PA)
- Primary balancing criteria
- Release
- Remedial Action (RA)
- Remedial Design (RD)
- Remedial Investigation/Feasibility Study (RI/FS)
- Remediation
- Removal
- Reportable Quantity (RQ)
- Response
- Sovereign immunity
- Superfund
- Threshold criteria
- Toxic pollutant
- Vessel

REVIEW QUESTIONS AND HANDS-ON ACTIVITIES

1. Define the terms *pollutants* and *contaminants.*
2. Define PRPs.
3. What is the Superfund?
4. What is the NCP?
5. Briefly describe several types of responses under CERCLA and the cleanup process.
6. What is a cost recovery action?
7. Research the current financial status of the Superfund. Has the federal government increased or decreased its sources of funding during the past five years?
8. Is CERCLA's system for identifying PRPs fair? Is it appropriate to hold liable those who contributed to a contamination problem many years prior to the implementation of CERCLA? Explain your answers.

9. Pursuant to the provisions of CERCLA, specially appointed trustees are authorized to recover for damages to natural resources. Is there any merit to using such a system to address other environmental recovery issues? Why or why not?

10. Does the EPA have too much authority under CERCLA to require abatement actions or other types of cleanup activities? Should one agency be given this much responsibility throughout the environmental law system? Explain your answers.

HELPFUL WEBSITES

http://www.epa.gov/superfund/sites/rods (EPA, Record of Decision System (RODS))

http://www.atsdr.cdc.gov/clist.html (Agency for Toxic Substances and Disease Registry)

http://www.epa.gov/superfund/sites/npl/npl.htm (EPA, National Priorities List Sites in the United States)

http://www.epa.gov/brownfields (EPA, Brownfields Cleanup and Redevelopment)

ENDNOTES

1. *United States v. NEPACCO,* 810 F.2d 726, 742 (8th Cir. 1986), cert. den., 484 U.S. 848 (1987).
2. *United States v. Fleet Factors Corp.,* 901 F.2d 1550 (11th Cir. 1990), cert. den., 498 U.S. 1046 (1991).
3. *United States v. Monsanto Co.,* 858 F.2d 160 (4th Cir. 1988), cert. den., 490 U.S. 1106 (1989).
4. *Long Beach Unified Sch. Dist. v. Dorothy B. Goodwin Living Trust,* 32 F.3d 1364 (9th Cir. 1994).
5. *New York v. Shore Realty Corp.,* 759 F.2d 1032, 1032 (2d Cir. 1985).
6. *United States v. Waste Indus.,* 734 F.2d 159, 164 (4th Cir. 1984).
7. *Ecodyne Corp. v. Shah,* 718 F. Supp. 1454 (N.D. Cal. 1989).
8. *Florida Power & Light v. Allis Chalmers Corp.,* 893 F.2d 1313 (11th Cir. 1990).

9. *Amcast Indus. Corp. v. Detrex Corp.,* 2 F.3d 746 (7th Cir. 1993), cert. den., 510 U.S. 1044 (1994).
10. *United States v. Cello-Foil Prods., Inc.,* 848 F. Supp. 1352 (W.D. Mich. 1994).
11. *United States v. Bliss,* 667 F. Supp. 1298 (E.D. Mich. 1987).
12. *United States v. Wade,* 577 F. Supp. 1326 (E.D. Pa. 1983).
13. *Levin Metals Corp. v. Parr-Richmond Terminal Co.,* 799 F.2d 1312 (9th Cir. 1986).
14. *United States v. Northeastern Pharmaceutical & Chem. Co.,* 810 F.2d 726 (8th Cir. 1986), cert. den., 484 U.S. 848 (1987).
15. *Kelly v. Thomas Solvent Co.,* 714 F. Supp. 1439 (W.D. Mich. 1989).
16. *United States v. Monsanto Co.,* 858 F.2d 160 (4th Cir. 1988), cert. den., 490 U.S. 1106 (1989).
17. *United States v. Montrose Chem. Corp. of California,* 22 Chem Waste Litig. Rpt. 237 (C.D. Cal. 1991).
18. *Cadillac Fairview/California, Inc. v. Dow Chem. Co.,* 840 F.2d 691, 695 (9th Cir. 1988).
19. *NL Indus. v. Kaplan,* 792 F.2d 896 (9th Cir. 1986).
20. *Brewer v. Ravan,* 680 F. Supp. 1176 (M.D. Tenn. 1988).
21. *United States v. Hardage,* 116 F.R.D. 460 (W.D. Okla. 1989), aff'd in part, rev'd in part, 982 F.2d 1436 (10th Cir. 1992), cert. den., 510 U.S. 913 (1993).
22. *Key Tronic Corp. v. United States,* 114 S. Ct. 1960 (1994).
23. *Amland Prop. Corp. v. ALCOA,* 711 F. Supp. 784 (D.N.J. 1989).
24. *Wickland Oil Terminals v. ASARCO, Inc.,* 792 F.2d 887 (9th Cir. 1986)
25. *Solid State Circuits v. United States Envtl. Protection Agency,* 812 F.2d 383 (8th Cir. 1987).
26. *United States v. Alcan Aluminum Corp.,* 964 F.2d 252 (3d Cir 1992).
27. *Cooper Industries, Inc. v. Aviall Services, Inc.,* 543 U.S. 157 (2004).
28. *U.S. Atlantic Research Corp.,* 551 U.S. ___, 127 S.Ct. 2331 (2007).

CHAPTER 8

TOXIC SUBSTANCES CONTROL ACT (TCSA)

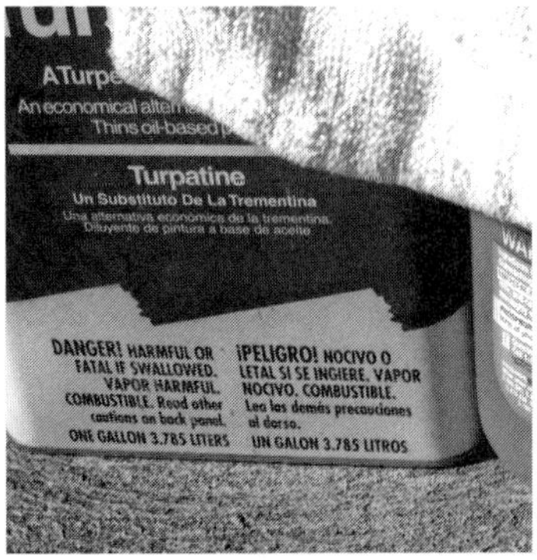

TITLE: The Toxic Substances Control Act (TSCA)

CITATION: 15 U.S.C. secs. 2601–2629 (1976)

REGULATIONS: 40 C.F.R. sec. 720, *et seq.*

PURPOSE: To control the manufacture, use, and distribution and disposal of chemical substances to protect human health and the environment

HISTORY: Part of the Superfund Amendments and Reauthorization Act (SARA) (1986)

LEARNING OBJECTIVES

After studying this chapter, the reader should be able to

- describe a premanufacture notice (PMN).
- describe PCBs and explain why they are dangerous.
- describe the TSCA Inventory and explain chemical identity.
- explain the difference between new chemicals and existing chemicals and the importance of that distinction.
- define *significant new uses.*
- describe how the EPA orders testing requirements under the TSCA.

The provisions of the Toxic Substances Control Act (TSCA) are designed to allow the EPA to gather as much information as possible about chemical substances and mixtures and then regulate the manufacture, use, and distribution of those chemicals and mixtures to protect human health and the environment against an unreasonable risk of harm.

ACTIVITIES SUBJECT TO TSCA REGULATION

disposal The discharge, deposit, injection, dumping, spilling, leaking, or placing of any solid waste or hazardous waste into or onto any land or water.

The TSCA applies to the manufacture, processing, distribution, use, or **disposal** of regulated chemicals. As you will see, while each of these categories of entities that touch chemicals and chemical mixtures have rules and regulations under the TSCA that apply specifically to their individual activities, most of the rules apply to all categories.

Manufacturing

manufacture To produce, prepare, import, or compound a toxic chemical, including the creation of substances produced coincidentally during the manufacture, processing, use, or disposal of another substance or mixture, such as by-products, coproducts, or impurities.

premanufacture notice (PMN) When a company plans to manufacture, import, or process a substance deemed to be "new," that company is required to provide the Environmental Protection Agency (EPA) with this notice, which includes detailed information concerning the substance and the proposed manufacturing operation.

The TSCA defines the term **manufacture** broadly to include the traditional, commonly accepted notions of the term, which include production of chemicals or chemical mixtures. In addition, the TSCA includes importing chemicals or chemical mixtures in the definition of *manufacture*. Extracting (removing) a chemical from another chemical substance or mixture of substances also is considered manufacturing. [40 C.F.R. secs. 704.3, 716.3. and 720.3(t)]

An entity that purchases or contracts with a chemical manufacturer also may be considered a manufacturer under the TSCA if the manufacturer produces the chemical or chemical mixture exclusively for the purchasing company and if the purchasing company designates the identity of the substance(s) and controls the amount produced and the manufacturing processes. [40 C.F.R. sec. 720.3(t)]

What does the TSCA require manufacturers to do? Generally, manufacturers must provide the EPA with data on the effects of chemicals and chemical mixtures on human health and the environment so the EPA can regulate those chemicals and chemical mixtures appropriately.

REQUIREMENTS OF MANUFACTURERS

Under the TSCA, manufacturers must

- conduct tests on chemicals they manufacture and submit data from those tests to the EPA.
- submit a **premanufacture notice (PMN)** when they are manufacturing a chemical not already on the TSCA Inventory or prior to manufacturing a chemical for a significant new use.
- avoid manufacturing PCBs.
- create and maintain reports as required by the TSCA.
- respond to subpoenas and allow the EPA to inspect their manufacturing facilities.
- demonstrate compliance with the TSCA when importing chemicals or chemical mixtures.

TSCA requirements related to the submittal of PMNs and reporting and record keeping apply only to those manufacturers that "manufacture for commercial purposes." "Commercial purposes" are defined as manufacture for

> . . . the purpose of obtaining an immediate or eventual commercial advantage for the manufacturer and includes, among other things . . .
> i. for distribution in commerce, including for test marketing
> ii. for use by the manufacturer, including use for product research and development or as an intermediate

This definition also applies to substances that are produced coincidentally during the manufacture, processing, use, or disposal of another substance mixture. [40 C.F.R. secs. 717.3(e), 712.3(h), 704.3, 716.3. and 720.3(r)]

process The preparation of a chemical substance after its manufacture for distribution in commerce in the same form or physical state as, or in a different form or physical state from, that in which it was received by the persons so preparing such substance as part of an article containing the chemical substance or mixture.

Comprehensive Assessment Information Rule (CAIR) One of the rules requiring the submittal of information pursuant to the provisions of the Toxic Substances Control Act (TSCA).

Processing

A processor under the TSCA is any person who processes a chemical substance or mixture. [TSCA sec. 3(11)] **Process** is defined in the TSCA as the preparation of a chemical substance or mixture, after its manufacture, for distribution in commerce

- in the same form or physical state as, or in a different form or physical state from, that in which it was received by the persons so preparing such substance or mixture.
- as part of an article containing the chemical substance or mixture [TSCA sec. 3(10)]

What does the TSCA require processors to do?

Requirements of Processors

Processors must

- provide the EPA with certain data under test rules.
- notify the EPA before processing a chemical for a significant new use.
- comply with EPA orders and rules.
- avoid processing PCBs unless permitted to do so by the EPA.
- comply with the reporting requirements of the **Comprehensive Assessment Information Rule (CAIR),** and record keeping and reporting requirements.
- respond to subpoenas and submit to inspections by the EPA. [TSCA secs. 5, 6, 8, and 11]

As you can see, these requirements of processors are similar to the requirements placed on manufacturers. The EPA has taken steps to enact regulations that narrow some of the requirements on certain categories of processors, since the broad definitions of *processors* and *process* and the reporting and record keeping requirements imposed place a huge burden on commerce in the United States.

Using

The TSCA does not define *use*, and the EPA has not assisted in addressing this deficiency by enacting regulations that clarify the difference between *process* and *use*.

Requirements of Users

Users, however defined, who are not also manufacturers, processors, or distributors must

- comply with applicable EPA regulations.
- refrain from using PCBs except when permitted by the EPA.
- refrain from using any chemical substance the user knows or has reason to know has been manufactured, produced, or distributed in violation of the TSCA.
- respond to subpoenas and submit to inspections by the EPA. [TSCA secs. 6, 11 and 15]

distribution The process of selling, introducing, or delivering a chemical substance into commerce or holding the mixture or article after its introduction into commerce.

The TSCA defines **distribution** (in commerce) as the process of selling, introducing, or delivering a chemical substance into commerce or holding the mixture or article after its introduction into commerce. [TSCA sec. 3(4)] *Commerce* is defined as interstate trade, traffic, transportation, or other activity that affects interstate trade, traffic, transportation, or commerce. [TSCA sec. 3(3)] To properly narrow the portion of the definition describing a distributor as someone who "holds" a mixture or an article, the EPA has enforced that portion of the requirements only against those who hold a mixture or an article for later distribution.

Requirements of Distributors

Distributors are required under the TSCA to

- comply with applicable rules and regulations.
- refrain from distributing PCBs except as permitted by the EPA.
- report "substantial risk information" to the EPA.
- respond to subpoenas and submit to inspections by the EPA. [TSCA secs. 8, 8, and 11]

Disposing

As with the term *use*, the critical term *dispose* is not defined in the TSCA.

REQUIREMENTS OF DISPOSERS

Disposers of chemicals or chemical mixtures are required to

- comply with applicable regulations.
- dispose of PCBs properly.
- respond to subpoenas and submit to inspections by the EPA. [TSCA secs. 6 and 11]

None of these requirements is surprising; and all are duplications of the requirements imposed on manufacturers, processors, users, and distributors of chemicals or chemical mixtures.

SUBSTANCES SUBJECT TO TSCA REGULATION

Chemical substances manufactured or processed for commercial purposes in the United States are subject to TSCA regulation. The TSCA places the responsibility of keeping track of these substances on the EPA. The TSCA specifies that the EPA will comply with this obviously daunting and voluminous task by keeping a list of such substances.

TSCA Inventory A list begun in 1976 by the EPA representing chemicals in commerce at the time. Since 1976, the list represents "each chemical substance which is manufactured or processed in the United States." The number of chemicals on the list presently exceeds 80,000.

TSCA INVENTORY

The list kept by the EPA pursuant to the TSCA is the **TSCA Inventory**. The Inventory keeps track of both existing and new chemicals.

THE INVENTORY LISTS REPORTABLE CHEMICAL SUBSTANCES, DEFINED AS

1) chemical substances which are 2) manufactured, imported, or processed for a commercial purpose in the United States, and 3) not specifically excluded from the Inventory.

reportable chemical substances Defined in the TSCA as chemical substances manufactured, imported, or processed for a commercial purpose in the United States and not specifically excluded from the TSCA Inventory.

ASSIGNMENT

Research the current TSCA Inventory. How many chemical substances are on the Inventory? How many have been added in the past year?

chemical substance
Defined in the TSCA as any organic or inorganic substance of a particular molecular identity, including (i) any combination of such substances occurring in whole or in part as a result of a chemical reaction or occurring in nature and (ii) any element or uncombined radical.

The initial Inventory listed such substances manufactured, imported, or processed between January 1, 1975, and June 1, 1979 (the date of the first Inventory).

To meet the first criteria for inclusion on the Inventory, a substance must be a **chemical substance**, which is defined in the TSCA as follows:

> . . . any organic or inorganic substance of a particular molecular identity, including (i) any combination of such substances occurring in whole or in part as a result of a chemical reaction or occurring in nature and (ii) any element or uncombined radical. [40 C.F.R. sec. 710.2(h)]

Statutory exclusions relating to this definition include mixtures; commercial pesticides; tobacco and certain tobacco products; nuclear source material or by-products; firing weapons and ammunition (including pistols, firearms, revolvers, shells, and cartridges); and any commercial food, food additive, drug, cosmetic, or device. [40 C.F.R. sec. 710.2(h)]

To be included on the Inventory, chemical substances must not only meet the criteria outlined above but also must be manufactured or imported for a "commercial purpose." The definition of what constitutes a "commercial purpose" is simple; it means only that a chemical substance is manufactured or imported for distribution in commerce or for use by the manufacturer or importer. [40 C.F.R. sec. 710.2(p)]

Substances Excluded from the TSCA Inventory

Certain substances have been excluded from the Inventory pursuant to the TSCA, including the following:

- Mixtures
- Chemicals manufactured or imported for a non-commercial purpose
- Chemical substances manufactured in small quantities for research and development (R&D)
- Pesticides (because they are regulated pursuant to FIFRA (7 U.S.C. sec. 136, *et seq.*)
- Articles (defined as "a manufactured item formed into a specific shape or design during manufacture which has an end-use function dependent upon its shape or design during end-use and which has no change of chemical composition during its end-use separate from the purpose of the article" [40 C.F.R. sec. 710.2(f)])
- Impurities (a "chemical substance which is unintentionally present in another chemical substance" [40 U.S.C. sec. 710.2(m)])
- By-products (a chemical substance produced without a specific commercial intent during the manufacture or processing of another chemical substance or mixture [40 U.S.C. sec. 710.2(g)])

- Chemicals produced from incidental reactions (because they are not intentionally produced for commercial purposes)
- Non-isolated intermediates (Intermediates are chemicals that are manufactured and partially or totally consumed in the chemical reaction process or that are intentionally present to affect the rate of chemical reaction by which other chemical substances or mixtures are being manufactured. *Non-isolated intermediates* are defined as "those intermediates that are not intentionally removed from the equipment in which they are manufactured.") [40 U.S.C. sec. 710.4(d)(8)])

The Inventory is not a static list—it is constantly changing as new chemicals are added. Before a new chemical can be added to the Inventory, the chemical must be screened through the PMN process, which will be discussed in detail later in this chapter. Also, Notices of Commencement of Manufacture need to be filed with the EPA prior to a chemical substance being added to the Inventory.

There also is a process to **delist** a chemical substance from the Inventory. The delisting process requires the EPA to provide notice of its intent to de-list a substance by publishing in the *Federal Register.*

With few exceptions, every four years, manufacturers and importers are required to update information concerning their chemicals listed on the Inventory. This **Update Rule** requires the manufacturers and importers to keep records that validate the information submitted to the EPA.

Another type of change that can be made to the Inventory at any time is when a manufacturer or an importer discovers that the information it submitted to the EPA so that a chemical could be listed on the Inventory is erroneous. In this situation, the entity provides Inventory correction information to the EPA. The corrections must be adequately documented and fall within one of the following categories:

- Corrections to the chemical identity of a previously submitted chemical
- Corrections to identify previously unidentified intermediates
- Corrections responsive to reporting errors identified by the EPA

With so many ways in which the Inventory can be revised, the expectation is that the EPA Inventory will accurately list and describe those chemicals that are intended for regulation under the TSCA.

The TSCA requires the EPA to maintain the Inventory. In actuality, there are two inventories. The EPA maintains one Inventory list that is

ASSIGNMENT

Review those substances that have been excluded from the TSCA Inventory. Do you think the exclusions are reasonable?

delisting When the waste generated by the treatment of a hazardous waste does not exhibit any of the characteristics for which the untreated waste was deemed hazardous, the residue waste may be delisted by the EPA. The effect of delisting is to remove many of the requirements placed on the generation, transportation, treatment, storage, or disposal of the delisted waste.

Update Rule This rule requires, with few exceptions, that every four years, manufacturers and importers update information concerning their chemicals listed on the TSCA Inventory.

confidential chemical identity A chemical formula permitted to be kept confidential under most circumstances pursuant to the Emergency Planning and Community Right-to-Know Act (EPCRA).

bona fide intent If there is a request to view a confidential chemical identity protected by the provisions of the Emergency Planning and Community Right-to-Know Act (EPCRA), that request will be granted by the EPA only if the requester can demonstrate that it has a *bona fide* intent to manufacture or import a substance for a commercial purpose.

available to the public because it does not contain any **confidential chemical identities**. The other list is a Master Inventory maintained by the EPA that includes confidential chemical identities as well as the nonconfidential chemical identities.

The TSCA requires any person intending to manufacture or import a chemical to determine whether the chemical is already listed on the TSCA Inventory. If a chemical identity is not confidential, it will be simple to determine whether the chemical is listed. However, the only way to determine with certainty whether a chemical for which one is searching on the Inventory is to have the EPA access not only the nonconfidential portion of the Inventory but also the Master Inventory so the EPA can check confidential chemical identities. Confidential chemical identities, as evidenced by their name, are intended to be confidential so not just anyone can access that portion of the Master Inventory. The EPA will access only the confidential portion of the Inventory to see whether a chemical is listed if the requester can demonstrate that it has a ***bona fide*** **intent** to manufacture or import a substance for a commercial purpose. [40 C.F.R. sec. 720.25(b)(1)]

BONA FIDE INTENT

A *bona fide* intent, submitted by the requester in writing, includes the following:

- The specific chemical identity of the chemical the entity intends to manufacture or import
- A signed statement demonstrating an intent to manufacture or import the chemical for commercial purposes
- A description of the R&D activities conducted
- The purpose for which the chemical will be manufactured or imported
- An analysis of the elements in the chemical
- An x-ray diffraction pattern (inorganic substances), a mass spectrum, or an infrared spectrum [40 C.F.R. sec. 720.25(b)(2)]

If a manufacturer or an importer determines that the chemical it intends to manufacture or import is already on the Inventory, the manufacturer or importer is free to begin manufacturing or importing the chemical. What happens, though, if a manufacturer or an importer learns that the chemical it intends to manufacture or import is not on the Inventory?

NEW CHEMICALS

Unless a "new" chemical is excluded from TSCA regulation for some reason or it is exempt from certain requirements, a manufacturer or an importer must follow the TSCA procedures set forth for "new" chemicals.

If a manufacturer or an importer discovers that it wants to manufacture or import a new chemical for commercial purposes, it must comply with the TSCA PMN requirements.

To which substances does a PMN apply? The TSCA PMN requirements apply to any **new chemical substance** and **significant new use** of an existing chemical. The idea behind the requirement for PMNs is that a manufacturer or an importer should be responsible for gathering and providing to the EPA much information concerning the new chemical and its potential effects on human health and the environment.

new chemical substance Any substance not already identified pursuant to the TSCA. The manufacture or importation of such a substance requires a premanufacture notice (PMN).

significant new use A utilization of a chemical not previously used for that purpose which triggers the requirement of a PMN.

PMN REQUIREMENTS

The PMN must include

- the identity of the chemical.
- its categories of use.
- the amounts to be manufactured or imported.
- by-products from the chemical.
- exposure of employees to the chemical.
- methods of disposal.
- test data related to the chemical's effect on human health or the environment.
- any other data regarding the chemical that is "reasonably ascertainable" by the manufacturer or importer. [TSCA sec. 5(d)]

The EPA must review the PMN within 90 days of submittal. The task of the EPA during the review period is to evaluate the chemical and determine the potential dangers to human health and the environment as a result of the chemical's manufacture, processing, distribution, use, and disposal. In making its determination, the EPA is permitted to use not only the information submitted in the PMN but also information available to the EPA from external sources and its experience with TSCA chemicals. It is easy, at times, to think of the EPA as a huge governmental entity made up of interchangeable employees.

When the role of the EPA under the TSCA is examined, however, it also is easy to see why the EPA is divided into sections and that many EPA employees specialize in a particular area of environmental regulation. The technical aspects of each section, whether it is clean water, clean air, or the TSCA, require expertise in the science and production aspects of a particular field.

If the EPA does not impose any requirements on the manufacture, processing, distribution, use, or disposal of the new chemical within the 90-day review period, the manufacturer or importer is free to begin the manufacture or importation of the chemical. Once such manufacture or importation has begun, the entity has 30 days to notify the EPA that such manufacture or import has started. The form used for this notification is the **Notice of Commencement (NOC)**. [40 C.F.R. sec. 720.102]

Notice of Commencement (NOC) A form used to notify the EPA that manufacture or importation of a chemical has begun.

Even if the 90-day period has expired, the EPA can take certain actions to intervene in the manufacture or importation of a new chemical. If it demonstrates "good cause," the EPA can delay manufacture for up to 90 days. If the EPA determines that the information it received as part of the PMN process is "insufficient" to make a proper evaluation of the risks of the chemical, the EPA can issue a proposed order to limit or prohibit manufacture of the chemical. In fact, the EPA can take almost any action concerning manufacture, including limiting, conditioning, or even prohibiting manufacture or importation if the EPA concludes that manufacture or importation "presents or will present an unreasonable risk of injury to health or the environment." (TSCA sec. 5)

Exemptions

What types of chemicals or chemical substances are excluded from the TSCA PMN requirements? The TSCA allows exemptions from PMN requirements for

- mixtures.
- pesticides covered by FIFRA.
- any food additive, drug, cosmetic, or device as defined by the Federal Food, Drug, and Cosmetic Act.
- any tobacco or tobacco product. [TSCA sec. 3(2)(B)]

These substances are exempt from PMN requirements unless they are intended for what is deemed a "TSCA use."

In addition to the exemptions from PMN requirements for the substances just described, the TSCA also exempts certain categories of chemicals. The TSCA exempts chemicals used in certain types of R&D, as well as chemicals used in test marketing. The EPA has further authority to exempt by regulation chemicals for which the EPA has determined there exists no unreasonable risk to human health or the environment.

QUESTION
Why do you think tobacco and tobacco products have been exempted from PMN requirements?

The **R&D exemption** applies to small quantities of new chemicals used only for R&D. The manufacturer must follow certain criteria to claim this exemption, including notifying all workers involved of the potential risks associated with the R&D concerning the new chemical substance. No application is associated with the R&D exemption, but EPA regulations are associated with this exemption. In addition to notifying all workers of the potential risks associated with the chemical, the manufacturer must ensure that a technically qualified individual supervises the R&D and that records are maintained concerning the R&D activities.

R&D exemption An exemption granted pursuant to TSCA for small quantities of new chemicals used only for research and development (R&D).

The **test market exemption (TME)** is available when the EPA determines that the "test market" activity does not present an unreasonable risk to human health or the environment. Pursuant to the TSCA, an entity wanting to test-market a chemical must apply for the TME.

test market exemption (TME) An exemption granted pursuant to TSCA by the EPA when the EPA determines that the "test market" activity does not pose an unreasonable risk to human health or the environment.

One of the other exemptions available under the TSCA is the **polymer exemption**. There is an expedited 21-day review for this exemption, and the exemption is available when the following three criteria are met:

polymer exemption A special exemption for certain chemical substances pursuant to TSCA.

- The chemical involved must be a "polymer" as defined in the TSCA.
- The chemical must not be specifically excluded pursuant to the TSCA.
- The chemical must have certain scientific characteristics set forth in the TSCA. (40 U.S.C. sec. 723.250)

The TSCA also provides a **low volume exemption (LVE)**. This exemption is available for a manufacturer or an importer wanting to manufacture or import a new chemical in small amounts. Volumes less than a particular amount in kilograms per year are considered low volume for the purposes of this exemption. As with other exemptions, the EPA may grant the exemption only if it determines that the substance "will not present an unreasonable risk of injury to health or the environment." [TSCA sec. 5(h)(4)] If a LVE is granted, the EPA publishes the LVE in the *Federal Register* and places the LVE on a special LVE List

low volume exemption (LVE) An exemption pursuant to TSCA available to a manufacturer or importer wishing to manufacture or import a new chemical in small amounts.

maintained by the EPA. A manufacturer or an importer granted a LVE is not required to file a NOC, and the chemical is not placed on the TSCA Inventory. After certain procedures are followed, the EPA may revoke the LVE exemption in the event the EPA receives information causing concern for human health or the environment. A similar exemption is available for low release and exposure chemicals (LOREX). This exemption differs from the LVE in that there are no maximum production requirements, but many of the procedural requirements for a LOREX are the same as for a LVE. Both exemptions require the completion of a PMN application prior to the granting of the exemption.

The TSCA also provides for other exemptions, including exemptions for

- new chemicals imported in articles.
- impurities, by-products, and non-isolated intermediates.
- chemicals formed during the manufacture of an article.
- chemicals formed incidental to the use of certain additives.

Polaroid exemption A special exemption pursuant to TSCA given to the Polaroid Corporation so the corporation could use new chemicals manufactured for its instant photography without having to comply with other TSCA requirements.

POLAROID EXEMPTION

One of the most interesting exemptions in the TSCA is the **Polaroid exemption**. This exemption is an example of the bargaining power of a large corporation. The Polaroid Corporation wanted to be able to use new chemicals manufactured for its instant photography and peel-apart technology immediately upon filing an exemption notice. Polaroid was given special permission in the TSCA [see 40 C.F.R. sec. 723.175] to manufacture those new chemicals. Until a full PMN has been filed and the process of review has been completed, however, the substances cannot be distributed in commerce. Thus, the TSCA permanently codified a request from a major U.S. manufacturer to be treated individually. There are other such provisions among the environmental laws, but they are few.

TYPES OF PREMANUFACTURE NOTICES (PMNs)

PMNs are divided into the following four categories:

- The *standard PMN*, used for a single chemical substance and submitted by a single company (the most common type of PMN submitted)

- The *consolidated PMN*, used for more than one chemical substance sharing the same molecular structures and use patterns
- The *joint PMN*, used when two companies jointly submit data, usually because one company does not have sufficient information to complete the PMN application
- The *exemption PMN*, used for polymers and low volume substances qualifying for their particular exemptions

THE PMN PROCESS

The PMN process, while frequently utilized, is complex and can be lengthy. Obviously, the best way to ensure that the PMN process will not cause a delay in the manufacture or import of a new chemical is to file a complete, detailed, and straightforward PMN form once the need for such a filing has been identified. The EPA uses a checklist to review a PMN form, and many companies make their own parallel checklist to ensure that their submittal will not be delayed because they failed to provide the necessary information.

The PMN form requires an assessment of the risk of manufacture or importation of the new chemical. This risk factor is calculated by analyzing the hazards presented by the chemical, tied with the expected exposure levels associated with the use of the chemical. This type of analysis includes scientific study of the properties of the chemical involved and the vulnerabilities of the humans and environment to which the chemical will be exposed.

Once the PMN form has been submitted, the EPA reviews the risk assessment contained therein and reviews the form to ensure that all other required technical and administrative information has been provided. As previously noted, the EPA's review period is 90 days. If the submitting company has not heard from the EPA following that 90-day period, the manufacturer is free to commence commercial manufacture of the chemical covered by the PMN.

During its review of the PMN, the EPA analyzes the information submitted and makes a determination as to whether the data is

- invalid.
- equivocal.
- valid and positive.
- valid and negative.

QUESTION
What does a finding of "valid and positive" mean? What does a finding of "valid and negative" mean?

Counterintuitively, a finding of "valid and positive" is not a good outcome; that means the EPA has determined that the chemical poses an *unreasonable* risk to humans or the environment. A finding of "valid and negative" is a positive finding; it means the EPA has determined that the chemical does not pose an unreasonable risk to human health or the environment.

In the event the EPA makes certain determinations during the review period, the EPA has the ability to take action to regulate the manufacture of the chemical that is the subject of the PMN form. The method by which the EPA takes such action is to enter an administrative order. Prior to the issuance of such an order, the EPA must find that the PMN does not provide enough information for the risk to be evaluated or that the chemical or its production creates an unreasonable risk to human health or the environment. An administrative order may limit or ban manufacture, distribution, use, or disposal of a chemical. [TSCA sec. 5(e)]

If the EPA makes a determination that the chemical poses an unreasonable risk to humans or the environment, the EPA may issue a *unilateral order*, which typically bans a chemical outright. This type of order is issued at least 45 days from the end of the review period so a manufacturer can appeal its effects.

If the EPA cannot issue an order soon enough to prevent the chemical from causing unacceptable risks, the EPA administrator may issue a proposed rule to delay, limit, or ban the manufacture, production, use, or disposal of the chemical and apply for an injunction to further prevent the expected risk. This *proposed rule* is not considered a *final agency action* for purposes of judicial appeal, so courts have not permitted appeal of such orders.

While the TSCA does not specifically provide authority for the EPA to enter into consent decrees with manufacturers, the EPA has utilized consent decrees to avoid having to be in an adversarial relationship with a manufacturer wanting to use a new chemical. By virtue of consent decrees used in this type of situation, manufacturers typically agree to restrictions on the production, distribution, and disposal of the chemical while the EPA gathers sufficient information to assess the chemical's risk and respond appropriately.

Consent orders take two forms: a "fast track" order and a "standard" order. The major difference between the two is that the fast track order is standardized and is used when the manufacturer is willing to agree to the standard terms that the order contains. If the terms of the order need to be negotiated, the standard order will be used; it takes much longer to negotiate and execute. Once signed, the order may be challenged and then amended, repealcd, or reviewed by the court system.

SIGNIFICANT NEW USES

As previously noted, a PMN is required for the use of new chemicals and for significant new uses of existing chemicals. If the EPA determines that a manufacturer intends to put an existing chemical or chemical substance to such a use, the EPA may issue a **Significant New Use Rule (SNUR)**. Pursuant to a SNUR, any entity wanting to manufacture or process a chemical for a significant new use must give the EPA at least 90 days' notice prior to such use using a **Significant New Use Notice (SNUN)**. As with a new chemical PMN, if the EPA does not respond to the SNUN within the 90-day period, the manufacturer or processor is free to put the chemical to its new use without giving further notice to the EPA.

Significant New Use Rule (SNUR) Issued by the EPA pursuant to the authority granted under TSCA, a SNUR requires the issuance of a pre-manufacture notice (PMN) for a new use of an existing chemical.

Significant New Use Notice (SNUN) Any entity wanting to manufacture or process a chemical for a significant new use must give the EPA at least 90 days' notice prior to such use through a SNUN.

In determining what constitutes a significant new use, the EPA must consider "all relevant factors." [TSCA sec. 5(a)(2)] In practice, the EPA has broadly defined a significant new use as a use that will result in increased production volume, a greater or different degree of exposure, or a different disposal method. The exemptions from the need to submit a SNUN are the same as those for submittal of PMNs. The TSCA contains reporting and compliance requirements that call for any manufacturer, importer, or processor of a chemical who believes that a chemical is being put to a significant new use to cease supplying the chemical and submit a SNUN unless permission has been obtained from the EPA to continue the manufacture, importation, or processing of the chemical.

After having received a SNUR, the EPA often utilizes the consent decree process to accomplish the same ends as those for which it uses the consent decree with respect to new chemicals. As with other types of consent decrees, once executed, a request may be made to amend or repeal the consent order or have it reviewed by the courts.

BIOTECHNOLOGY

The science of genetically engineering microorganisms is called **biotechnology**. The regulation of biotechnology by the EPA pursuant to the TSCA has been difficult due to the uncertainties involved with this

biotechnology The science of genetically engineering microorganisms.

REVIEW

A "new" microorganism is one that results from a deliberate, intergenetic combination of genetic material from organisms in different genera.

relatively new science. The EPA has chosen to assert its authority under the TCSA for this new type of technology due to the fact that the risks associated with new microorganisms are similar to those associated with new chemicals. In 1994, the EPA first published regulations addressing microorganisms. In its regulations, microorganisms are defined as "organisms classified in certain biological kingdoms (such as Protista and Fungi)." A "new" microorganism is one that is not on the TSCA Inventory and that results from a deliberate, intergenetic combination of genetic material from organisms in different genera. If all of this sounds like technical scientific jargon, it is.

Microbial Commercial Activity Notice (MCAN) A premanufacture notification form submitted prior to commercial manufacture or importation or a new microorganism for a significant new use of an existing microorganism.

In its regulations, the EPA requires a premanufacture notification form called a **Microbial Commercial Activity Notice (MCAN)**. The MCAN is to be submitted 90 days prior to commercial manufacture or importation of a new microorganism or prior to the manufacture, import, or processing of an existing microorganism for a significant new use. Upon receipt of a NOC of manufacture or import of a microorganism, the EPA places the microorganism on the TSCA Inventory.

TSCA TESTING

As previously noted, the TSCA requires manufacturers and processors to perform significant testing of their substances so that risk to humans and the environment can be assessed. The TSCA provides the EPA with authority to require testing data where the EPA determines that a chemical may present an unreasonable risk of injury to humans or the environment. Due to the extreme scientific components associated with testing of substances regulated under the TSCA, a committee of experts was appointed to make recommendations to the EPA concerning testing of TSCA substances. The **Interagency Testing Committee (ITC)** was created by law to make recommendations to the EPA concerning chemicals and chemical mixtures deserving special consideration. The chemicals or chemical substances deserving this special consideration include those that are suspected of causing or contributing to cancer, birth defects, or genetic mutations. Identification of a chemical by the ITC results in the chemical being placed on the TSCA Priority List. If the ITC identifies a chemical, the EPA must act to address the risks of that chemical within 12 months or explain why it has not done so.

Interagency Testing Committee (ITC) A body created by law to make recommendations to the EPA concerning chemicals and chemical mixtures deserving special consideration.

ITC Criteria for Identifying Chemicals

In identifying chemicals, the ITC considers the following:

- The quantities manufactured or introduced into the environment
- The amount of human exposure
- Whether the substance is similar to another chemical known to be harmful
- Any data concerning effects of the chemical
- Whether testing will assist in determining the possible risk of the chemical [TSCA sec. 4(e)(1)(a)]

There are reporting requirements for any chemical on the Priority List. The TSCA further contains a **Preliminary Assessment Information Rule (PAIR)**, pursuant to which manufacturers must submit production and exposure data on chemicals on the ITC Priority List.

Preliminary Assessment Information Rule (PAIR) A TSCA rule pursuant to which manufacturers must submit production and exposure data on chemicals on the ITC Priority List.

Test rules can be either *risk-based* or *exposure-based*. If the EPA needs testing to determine the *risk* associated with a chemical, the EPA uses testing to make a risk determination after finding that a chemical may present an unreasonable risk. The EPA may require testing if it determines

- that a chemical or chemical mixture may present an unreasonable risk to humans or the environment.
- existing data and experience associated with the chemical are inadequate to predict its risk potential.
- testing is necessary to obtain the data that will allow an analysis of the chemical's risk potential.

The first criteria requires that the EPA have some reason to make a finding that a chemical may present an "unreasonable risk." A court has found that if "all the evidence—including the industry evidence—indicates a more-than-theoretical probability of exposure," the EPA may require testing (see *Chemical Manufacturers Assoc. v. EPA*[1]). If all of the above criteria are met, this constitutes a **risk trigger**, permitting the EPA to require testing.

risk trigger If the EPA finds that a chemical may present an "unreasonable risk," that finding constitutes a "trigger," allowing the EPA to require testing of that chemical.

exposure trigger A situation where the quantity of a chemical produced and its breadth of exposure into the environment is sufficient to cause concern for human health.

Exposure Trigger

The **exposure trigger**, on the other hand, exists when the EPA determines that:

- a chemical is produced in substantial quantities.
- the substance is expected to be released into the environment in substantial quantities or there is or may be a substantial risk to humans.
- existing data is inadequate to predict the risk of the substance.
- testing is necessary to obtain the data that will allow an analysis of the chemical's risk potential.

Thus, the major difference between the risk trigger and the exposure trigger is that the exposure trigger comes into play when the quantity of the chemical produced and its consequent breadth of exposure into the environment is sufficient to cause concern. The EPA has developed scientific thresholds to determine whether an exposure is "substantial," and those thresholds determine whether a given situation meets the criteria noted earlier.

TEST RULES

If the EPA determines that the risk trigger or the exposure trigger has been met for a particular chemical or chemical substance, the EPA will publish a test rule for that chemical or substance. The EPA has broad latitude in determining what types of testing will be required and what the testing is designed to demonstrate. Typically, the EPA will require testing to include studies regarding toxicity, oncogenicity (the ability to cause cancer), reproduction, teratogenicity (the ability to cause birth defects), mutagenicity (the ability to cause mutations), neurotoxicity (the tendency of having negative effects on the neurological system), and environmental effects.

The TSCA requires that the EPA follow its usual rulemaking procedures in enacting a test rule for a chemical or chemical substance so the scope of the testing and the testing procedures required can be challenged. The entities subject to the test rule must notify the EPA within 30 days whether they will comply with the rule or seek an exemption. A failure to notify the EPA that one of those two options has been elected, coupled with continued manufacturing or processing of a chemical or chemical substance, will place the manufacturer or processor in violation of the testing rule. [40 C.F.R. sec. 790.45(e), (f)]

A case in which an EPA test rule was challenged is *Chemical Manufacturers Assoc. v. EPA*.

CASE LAW

CHEMICAL MANUFACTURERS ASSOC. V. EPA, 859 F.2D 977 (D.C. CIR. 1988).

SUMMARY OF CASE: The Chemical Manufacturers Association sought court review of a final EPA rule promulgated under the TSCA that required toxicological testing to determine the health effects of a chemical substance and imposed a duty on exporters of the substance to file notices with the EPA.

Judge Wald delivered the opinion of the Court.

Petitioners, Chemical Manufacturers Association and four companies that manufacture chemicals (collectively "CMA") seek to set aside a rule promulgated by the Environmental Protection Agency ("EPA" or "the Agency"). This Final Test Rule was promulgated under . . . the Toxic Substances Control Act ("TSCA" or "the Act"). The Final Test Rule required toxicological testing to determine the health effects of the chemical 2-ethylhexanoic acid ("EHA"), and it continues to impose on the exporters of EHA a duty to file certain notices with the EPA.

We uphold EPA's interpretation of TSCA as empowering the Agency to issue a test rule on health grounds where it finds a more-than-theoretical basis for suspecting that the chemical substance in question presents an "unreasonable risk of injury to health." This, in turn, requires the Agency to find a more-than-theoretical basis for concluding that the substance is sufficiently toxic, and human exposure to it is sufficient in amount, to generate an "unreasonable risk of injury to health." We hold, further, that EPA can establish the existence and amount of human exposure on the basis of inferences drawn from the circumstances under which the substance is manufactured and used. . . . Finally, we hold that the Agency correctly applied these standards in this case and that its findings are supported by substantial evidence. Consequently, we affirm the Final Test Rule.

TSCA provides for a two-tier system for evaluating and regulating chemical substances to protect against unreasonable risks to human health and to the environment. [T]he Act permits EPA to regulate a substance that the Agency has found "presents or will present unreasonable risk of injury to health or the environment." . . . [T]he Act empowers EPA to require testing of a suspect substance in order to obtain the toxicological data necessary to make a decision whether or not to regulate the substance. . . . The Act provides, not surprisingly, that the level of certainty of risk warranting a . . . test rule is lower than that warranting a . . . regulatory rule. . . .The Agency's interpretation of this statutory standard for testing is the central issue in this case. . . . A test rule may be set aside if it is not "supported by substantial evidence in the rulemaking record . . . taken as a whole."

EHA is a colorless liquid with a mild odor. It is used exclusively as a chemical intermediate . . . in the production of metal soaps, peroxy esters and other products used in industrial settings. EHA is totally consumed during the manufacture of these products; as a result, no products offered for sale to industry or to consumers contain EHA. . . .

EPA issued a proposed test rule on May 17, 1985. The rule proposed a series of tests to ascertain the health risks of EHA. . . . The Proposed Test Rule also addressed the question of whether humans are exposed to EHA, a question of critical importance in this case. . . . The Agency based its Proposed Test Rule on the potential danger that EHA will come in contact with the skin of workers. . . . [T]he Agency noted that approximately 400 workers are engaged in the manufacture . . . of 20 to 25 million pounds of EHA per year. . . .

CMA criticized the toxicology studies cited by the EPA and sought to show that the use of gloves by employees of companies working with EHA prevented human exposure to the chemical, thus rendering any test rule invalid. . . .

[TSCA] requires EPA to promulgate a test rule . . . if a chemical substance, *inter alia*, "may present an unreasonable risk of injury to health or the environment." The parties both accept the proposition that the degree to which a particular substance presents a risk to health is a function of two factors: (a) human exposure to the substance, and (b) the toxicity of the substance. . . . They also agree that EPA must make some sort of threshold finding as to the existence of an "unreasonable risk of injury to health." The parties differ, however, as to the manner in which this finding must be made. . . .

The . . . issue is whether, under . . . TSCA, EPA must find that the existence of an "unreasonable risk of injury to health" is more probable than not in order to issue a test rule. CMA argues that the statute requires a more-probable-than-not finding. EPA disagrees, contending that the statute is satisfied where the existence of an "unreasonable risk of injury to health" is a substantial probability—that is, a probability that is more than merely theoretical, speculative or conjectural. . . .

[W]e find that Congress did not address the precise question in issue. Examining the EPA interpretation . . . we find it to be reasonable and consistent with the statutory scheme and legislative history. Consequently, we uphold the Agency's construction of TSCA as authorizing a test rule where EPA's basis for suspecting the existence of an "unreasonable risk of injury to health" is substantial—i.e., when there is a more-than-theoretical basis for suspecting that some amount of exposure takes place and that the substance is sufficiently toxic at that level of exposure to present an "unreasonable risk of injury to health." . . .

The aim of TSCA was to make producers and users of chemical substances assume the costs of testing, so long as a more-than-theoretical basis existed for finding the presence of an "unreasonable risk of injury to health." We are persuaded that EPA's finding of potential developmental toxicity is supported by substantial evidence. . . .

We uphold EPA's interpretation of . . . TSCA as authorizing issuance of a test rule where there is a more-than-theoretical basis to suspect the presence of "unreasonable risk of injury to health." . . . The petition for review is therefore denied. ■

QUESTIONS

1. What do you think the practical difference is between a "more probable than not" standard versus an "unreasonable risk" standard?
2. Why do you think the court ruled that the standard used by the EPA in this case was correct?

Test rules must specify how data is to be collected and explain any required testing methodologies. The EPA has provided guidance in how testing is to occur by promulgating testing guidelines. The guidelines do not have the force of rule unless the actual rule promulgated by the EPA for a particular chemical or chemical substance incorporates the guidelines in the rule itself.

As previously noted, a party subject to a test rule may seek an exemption from that rule. Exemptions are granted in circumstances where it can be demonstrated that a chemical or chemical substance is "equivalent to a chemical substance or mixture for which data has been submitted" or that a chemical or chemical substance is already the subject of a test rule. If a manufacturer produces a very small amount of a chemical subject to a test rule, that manufacturer also may be granted an exemption from the rule. The EPA will deny an exemption if a timely request for exemption is not filed or if the exemption criteria cannot be met. Interestingly, even if a person is successful in obtaining

REVIEW
There is no "standing" requirement to challenge a testing rule under the TSCA. Any person can challenge such a rule.

Reimbursement Order
An order issued by the EPA pursuant to the TSCA requiring entities to tender their proper share of testing costs.

an exemption from a test rule, that person must contribute to the costs of testing incurred by those subject to the rule. If proper reimbursement is not tendered, the EPA may issue a **Reimbursement Order** requiring entities to tender their proper share of the testing costs. Companies that are going to bear the burden of testing costs frequently band together in testing "joint ventures," whereby costs are minimized and the proper testing is accomplished.

If contested, EPA test rules are subject to judicial review. "Any person" can file such a review. Unlike some of the standing requirements outlined in Chapter 1, there is no standing requirement for the filing of a judicial review of a testing rule. The appellate court will review the administrative rulemaking record concerning the rule and will not hold a new hearing to obtain additional evidence. As with most appeals, the record must contain at least "substantial evidence" for a court to overturn the EPA's rule. Thus, if a rule is reasonably supported by the administrative record, the court will find in favor of the EPA.

What does the EPA do with the test data it receives? If the test data demonstrates that the chemical or chemical substance leaves the EPA with a reasonable basis to conclude that "a chemical substance or mixture presents or will present a significant risk of serious or widespread harm to human beings from cancer, gene mutations, or birth defects," the EPA must enter rules to regulate that chemical or announce in the *Federal Register* why it has chosen not to do so. [TSCA Sec. 4(f)(2)] This standard includes the term *significant risk*, which the EPA has interpreted as presenting a population whose individual members are at a high risk from the chemical or chemical substance or when the EPA believes there is no adequate margin of safety.

If the EPA determines that a substantial risk exists, the EPA then has 180 days to determine whether it is going to regulate the chemical or substance. If a decision is made to regulate the chemical or substance, the EPA will follow the designated procedures for implementation of the regulation.

TSCA RECORDKEEPING

The EPA uses records obtained pursuant to its TSCA authority for many purposes, including decision making, monitoring of activities, and enforcement. The EPA has promulgated many rules requiring manufacturers, importers, processors, users, and disposers of chemicals to create, file with the EPA, and maintain various types of TSCA records. As part of the PMN process or other processes outlined in the TSCA, the EPA keeps all applications or forms submitted.

An example of one of these rules is CAIR. CAIR was promulgated so the EPA would receive detailed information concerning a specific group of chemical substances (19 were in the original group). CAIR has been amended to be more user-friendly from the standpoint of chemical manufacturers and processors, but it still requires that quite a bit of data concerning these chemicals be submitted by virtue of a CAIR report so the ongoing risks of the chemicals can be tracked.

In the event a chemical or mixture causes a "significant adverse reaction" to human health or the environment, manufacturers, processors, and distributors must submit a **Record of Significant Adverse Reaction**. Any allegations of adverse reaction in employees must be kept for 30 years. Allegations of such reactions from others are to be kept for five years. What is a "significant adverse reaction"? It has been defined as one that "may indicate a substantial impairment of normal activities, or long-lasting or irreversible damage to health or the environment." [40 C.F.R. sec. 710]

Record of Significant Adverse Reaction In the event a chemical mixture causes a "significant adverse reaction" to human health or the environment, manufacturers, processors, and distributors must submit this record, which is kept for 30 years.

REACTIONS TO BE REPORTED

The types of reactions that need to be reported include the following:

- Gradual or sudden changes in the composition of animal or plant life
- Abnormal numbers of deaths of organisms
- Reduction in the reproductive rate of a species
- Changes in the behavior or location of a species

REGULATION OF EXISTING CHEMICALS

This chapter has already presented the TSCA's regulation of new chemicals, but the TSCA allows the EPA to regulate existing chemicals as well in certain circumstances. If the EPA determines that the manufacture, use, or disposal of an existing chemical ". . . will present an unreasonable risk of injury to health or the environment" and those risks are not covered by another federal environmental statute, the EPA must initiate rulemaking concerning that chemical. [TSCA sec. 6(a)]

EXISTING REGULATED CHEMICALS

The existing chemicals regulated by the EPA pursuant to this authority include the following:

- Asbestos
- Chlorofluorocarbons (CFCs)
- Hexavalent chromium
- Metalworking fluids
- PCBs

Many are generally aware that PCBs are dangerous substances; but it is not widely known that through utilization of the provisions of the TSCA, the EPA has been successful in regulating the manufacture, use, and disposal of PCBs.

The EPA's regulation of asbestos was tested in *Corrosion Proof Fittings v. EPA*.[2] In that case, the EPA acted to ban asbestos by adopting a rule pursuant to the TSCA that virtually prohibited in the United States the manufacture, distribution, importation, or processing of products containing asbestos. The EPA had found that asbestos posed "an unreasonable risk to human health." The manufacturers appealed, claiming that the EPA's methodology was flawed and that this determination was not based on substantial evidence. The court found that some of the petitioners (such as a Canadian asbestos mining operation) did not have standing under the TSCA since the purpose of the act was to protect U.S. environmental interests.

However, the court found that the EPA's rulemaking procedure was flawed because it used evidence of asbestos testing (the "analogous exposure" estimates), which was not presented at the rulemaking hearing, but was considered after the rulemaking was concluded. The court found that the EPA should have reopened the rulemaking hearing to permit public comment on the analogous exposure estimates. The court also found that the EPA had failed to justify its asbestos ban because it failed to comply with the TSCA requirement that it impose the "least burdensome required regulation to protect the environment adequately."

INSPECTIONS

Section 11 of the TSCA allows the EPA to inspect establishments where chemical substances are manufactured, processed, stored, or held, as well as conveyances used to transport such substances. TSCA inspections cover records, files, papers, processes, controls, and facilities as they relate to TSCA activities. [TSCA sec. 11(b)] The TSCA does not require the EPA to obtain a search warrant before conducting TSCA inspections. However, if an entity denies entry to the EPA pursuant to a constitutional provision, the EPA must obtain a warrant before entering the premises or conveyance. As previously noted, most entities will not deny warrantless inspections due to the belief that once the EPA has obtained a warrant, it will come back for its inspection and look more closely at operations to see what a company may have been hiding by refusing warrantless entry. EPA inspections pursuant to the TSCA may be related to a specific chemical or regulation or may be intended as a general assessment of compliance with TSCA requirements.

ASSIGNMENT

Imagine you are the operator of a company and the EPA has come, without a warrant, to inspect your facility. How would you handle the situation?

Typically, the EPA follows a set procedure for TSCA inspections. The EPA will usually let a facility know an inspection is forthcoming. At the site of the inspection, the inspector will meet with officials of the facility to discuss the expected scope of the inspection. The actual inspection will then take place, after which the inspector will meet with relevant officials again to ensure that there is agreement concerning the scope of the inspection and to reveal the records, samples or other data the inspector obtained. Once the inspector has had an opportunity to analyze the data, a final report will be prepared and discussed with the appropriate facility officials.

ENFORCEMENT

The EPA is authorized to impose civil penalties, taking into account a series of factors.

FACTORS INFLUENCING CIVIL PENALTIES

- Nature of the violation
- Circumstances surrounding the violation
- Extent of the violation
- Seriousness of the violation
- The violator's role in the violation
- The violator's previous compliance history
- The violator's financial situation
- Other factors "as justice requires" [TSCA sec. 16(a)(2)(B)]

The TSCA allows imposition of additional penalties for *willful violations* and may give the violator credit for a good attitude or a good faith effort to comply with applicable regulations. The EPA has the authority to make penalties more or less severe depending on the EPA's evaluation of the decision-making criteria. Whatever civil statute of limitations exists generally applies to TSCA civil enforcement proceedings (see *3M Company v. Browner*[3]). The EPA also may impose administrative penalties for violations of applicable orders and rules, including a failure to submit required reports, applications, or forms.

One case involving TSCA enforcement is the *3M Company v. Browner* decision. In this case, 3M sought a review of a civil penalty (in the amount of $1.3 million) that the EPA assessed against it under the TSCA. The penalty was assessed based on numerous TSCA violations that occurred eight years before the complaint. 3M claimed that federal law barred imposition of penalties for any actions that occurred prior to five years before the complaint was filed. The Court of Appeals reversed the trial court's decision that the law did not apply to the TSCA; instead, the Court of Appeals ruled that the statute did apply. The Court of Appeals also determined that the claims accrued against 3M were based on the time the violations actually occurred, not on when the EPA discovered the violations.

Many civil enforcement proceedings pursuant to the TSCA are ultimately settled. These agreements typically include granting the EPA the right to inspect and audit violators and set forth remediation measures that must be undertaken.

If a settlement cannot be reached as part of a civil enforcement proceeding, the EPA may resort to an administrative hearing, at which testimony is taken and evidence is presented concerning possible violations. This "mini trial" forms the administrative record should there be an appeal of the findings at the hearing. Again, an appellate court will uphold the EPA's findings if there is "substantial evidence" in the record to support those findings.

The TSCA provides for *criminal liability* as well as civil liability. "Knowing" or "willful" violations may result in imprisonment and/or stiff monetary fines. Corporations may be found criminally liable for the actions of employees. No "corporate shield" in the TSCA protects corporations from criminal liability.

Lastly, the TSCA provides for citizen suits, which may be brought by "any person" believing that a violation of the TSCA has occurred or that the EPA has failed to perform any of its nondiscretionary duties under the TSCA.

FEATURE

Bhopal Disaster

On December 3, 1984, just after midnight, in Bhopal, India, 40 metric tons of methyl isocyanate (MIC) gas leaked from a tank at a manufacturing plant operated by Union Carbide India Limited (UCIL), which was owned by Union Carbide (51 percent) and a group of Indian financial institutions and private financial investors (49 percent total). The gas immediately killed approximately 3,800 people, and many thousands of others were disabled by the injuries they suffered from exposure to the gas. Some reports indicate that 150,000 to 600,000 people were injured, of whom at least 15,000 later died of their injuries. This incident has come to represent one of the worst industrial and environmental disasters ever to occur, primarily because of the magnitude of the loss of human life and the damage caused to the lives of those who lived.

QUESTION

Was the leak a result of sabotage by a plant employee, or was it a failure to use appropriate safety measures?

What was Union Carbide manufacturing at its plant?

The plant was built in 1969 and began manufacturing carbaryl in 1979. Carbaryl is a pesticide that was used in India to help the productivity of the agricultural industry. MIC is part of the production of carbaryl.

How did the leak happen?

The leak was caused when a large amount of water entered a tank, causing a chemical reaction that forced the chemical release valve on the tank to open and release the gas.

Safety systems were in place to prevent water from entering the tank by accident, so one independent investigation concluded that the water must have been deliberately put into the tank—that the tank was sabotaged. Other investigations concluded that "scrubbers" that should have treated the gas were being repaired and that several other safety procedures were not being used. There were even suggestions that the safety procedures and processes had been discontinued to cut costs.

Why wasn't the leak contained by the plant's safety measures?

The plant did not have systems in place to contain such a massive leak because of the safety systems that existed to prevent such a leak from ever occurring. Some reports indicated that even low-tech responses, such as blocking gaps with wet towels, were not implemented to help contain the gas.

REVIEW

UCIL paid more than $470 million in damages to the victims of the disaster. As of 2006, a reportedly $390 million is still left in the settlement fund.

How did Union Carbide respond?

Union Carbide responded immediately by sending approximately $2 million dollars in aid, sending medical equipment and supplies, sending medical experts to provide expertise, funding a vocational-technical center in Bhopal, offering to build a hospital in Bhopal, providing approximately $5 million dollars to the Indian Red Cross, setting up a charitable trust for a Bhopal hospital and providing initial funding of approximately $20 million dollars, and later providing an additional $90 million dollars to the hospital's charitable trust.

Were there lawsuits?

All legal matters concerning the incident were consolidated into the Indian Supreme Court for resolution. The government of India enacted the Bhopal Gas Leak Disaster Act in 1985, through which the government acted as the sole legal representative of the victims. Almost five years after the incident, Union Carbide and the government reached a settlement of $470 million, which was paid by Union Carbide ten days after the settlement was affirmed by the Indian Supreme Court. Interest on that settlement sum greatly increased the value of the settlement pool. By 1990, the Reserve Bank of India reported that the settlement fund, with interest, was approximately double what was needed to compensate the victims. It has been reported that approximately $390 million in interest still remains in the fund.

What are the long-term environmental effects of the incident?

The government of India has indicated that no contamination of the soil or groundwater occurred outside the plant as a result of the leak or even as a result of routine plant operations. There was some soil contamination within the plant premises, but it was not a result of the leak. The contamination in the plant was found where chemicals had been treated and disposed of as part of routine plant operations. Some studies have shown that the rates of cancer and other illnesses are higher in the areas surrounding the plant site. The site has not been cleaned up to any significant degree since the incident; and many experts are worried that the chemicals and other contaminants present on the site, if not attended to in the near future, will pollute the soil and groundwater outside the facility. ■

SUMMARY

The TSCA was enacted to control the manufacture, use, distribution, and disposal of chemical substances in order to protect human health and the environment. The TSCA uses the PMN process and the TSCA Inventory as major parts of its regulatory scheme. By providing for assessment of the risks associated with significant new uses, the TSCA ensures that new chemicals (or new uses for existing chemicals) are properly tested before their use is allowed. The EPA uses risk triggers and exposure triggers as part of its analysis of chemicals under the TSCA. The TSCA provides for the use of both civil and criminal penalties in its enforcement provisions. In conjunction with FIFRA, discussed in Chapter 9, the TSCA regulates chemical substances in the United States.

KEY TERMS

- Biotechnology
- *Bona fide* intent
- Chemical substance
- Comprehensive Assessment Information Rule (CAIR)
- Confidential chemical identities
- Delist
- Disposal
- Distribution
- Exposure trigger
- Interagency Testing Committee (ITC)
- Low volume exemption (LVE)
- Manufacture
- Microbial Commercial Activity Notice (MCAN)
- New chemical substance
- Notice of Commencement (NOC)
- Polaroid exemption
- Polymer exemption
- Preliminary Assessment Information Rule (PAIR)
- Premanufacture notice (PMN)
- Process
- R&D exemption
- Record of Significant Adverse Reaction
- Reimbursement Order
- Reportable chemical substances
- Risk trigger
- Significant new use
- Significant New Use Notice (SNUN)
- Significant New Use Rule (SNUR)

- Test market exemption (TME)
- TSCA Inventory
- Update Rule

REVIEW QUESTIONS AND HANDS-ON ACTIVITIES

1. What is the purpose of a PMN?
2. What types of chemical substances are found on the TSCA Inventory?
3. Under what circumstances are chemical identities kept confidential?
4. Name three exemptions under the TSCA.
5. What is SNUR?
6. Describe the differences between risk-based testing and exposure-based testing.
7. Find out how many chemicals are presently on the TSCA Inventory. Is it appropriate to have some chemical identities kept confidential? Why or why not?
8. Should statutes address the environmental problems of a single corporation, such as TSCA-addressed issues involved with the manufacture of Polaroid products? Why or why not?
9. Is it appropriate to regulate biotechnology as part of the TSCA? Why or why not?

HELPFUL WEBSITES

http://www.epa.gov/oppt (EPA, Pollution Prevention and Toxics)

http://www.epa.gov/pesticides (EPA, Pesticides)

http://www.epa.gov/opptintr/itc (EPA, Interagency Testing Committee Under the Toxic Substances Control Act (TSCA))

http://www.epa.gov/pesticides (EPA, Pesticides)

http://www.epa.gov/opptintr/biotech (EPA, Biotechnology Program Under Toxic Substances Control Act (TSCA))

http://www.gpoaccess.gov/cfr/about.html (GPO Access, Code of Federal Regulations)

http://www.epa.gov/opptintr/library (EPA, Prevention, Pesticides & Toxic Substances (OPPTS) Information Services)

http://www.epa.gov/opptintr/asbestos (EPA, Asbestos and Vermiculite)

http://www.epa.gov/opptintr/lead (EPA, Lead in Paint, Dust, and Soil)

ENDNOTES

1. *Chemical Manufacturers Assoc. v. EPA*, 859 F.2d 977 (D.C. Cir. 1988).
2. *Corrosion Proof Fittings v. EPA*, 947 F.2d 1201 (5th Cir. 1991).
3. *3M Company v. Browner*, 17 F.3d 1453 (D.C. Cir. 1994).

CHAPTER 9

FEDERAL INSECTICIDE, FUNGICIDE, AND RODENTICIDE ACT (FIFRA)

TITLE: The Federal Insecticide, Fungicide, and Rodenticide Act (FIFRA) (last amendment: 2004)

CITATION: 7 U.S.C. sec. 136, *et seq.*

REGULATIONS: 40 C.F.R. sec.180.1, *et seq.*

PURPOSE: To govern the use, sale, and labeling of pesticides

HISTORY: Federal Insecticide Act of 1910

Federal Insecticide, Fungicide, and Rodenticide Act of 1947

Federal Environmental Pesticides Control Act of 1972 (FEPCA)

Further amended in 1975, 1978, 1980, 1988, and 1996

LEARNING OBJECTIVES

After studying this chapter, the reader should be able to

- relate the history of FIFRA and explain how it differs from other federal environmental acts.
- describe the substances covered by FIFRA.
- describe the registration process, including
  the four criteria assessed as part of the registration process.
  unreasonable risk.
  labeling.
  cancellation.
  suspension.
- explain the purpose and effective reach of the FIFRA labeling requirement.
- describe the mechanisms used to enforce FIFRA.

HISTORY AND ANTECEDENTS OF FIFRA

Unlike many of the other environmental acts, FIFRA is almost exclusively a "federal" act in that states are given little authority to deal with the regulatory issues addressed by FIFRA. Since the enactment of FIFRA, many battles have taken place between environmentalists (represented by the EPA) on one side and farmers and chemical manufacturers on the other side. As can be noted from the frequent amendments to FIFRA, the act has been modified over time in an attempt to achieve the goal of protecting humans and the environment. In its original iteration, FIFRA dealt more with form, such as the information on pesticide labels, than it did with the substance of protecting humans and the environment. The amendments, especially FEPCA in 1972, added weight to the health and environmental issues covered by the act. The later amendments also gave the EPA additional flexibility in controlling dangerous chemicals and streamlined the appeals process.

The passage of FIFRA predated one of the more famous insecticide debacles in history. In 1948, shortly after the passage of the original FIFRA, a Swiss chemist named Paul Müller received the Nobel Prize for demonstrating that a substance called **dichlorodiphenyltrichloroethane (DDT)** had excellent qualities as an insecticide. By using DDT to control insects, countless lives were saved that would have otherwise been lost due to malaria, which is carried by mosquitoes. Unfortunately, the use of DDT also caused such serious adverse effects to humans and the environment that it was banned or the use severely restricted within about ten years of its discovery.

dichlorodiphenyltrichloroethane (DDT) An insecticide for which Paul Müller won the Nobel Peace Prize. DDT was later found to be extremely harmful.

To avoid replication of the DDT problem, FIFRA was enacted as a means to control those types of toxic substances called pesticides.

PESTICIDES

FIFRA defines a pesticide as any substance intended for "preventing, destroying, repelling or mitigating any pest" and any substance intended for use as a "plant regulator, defoliant or dessicant." [sec. 2(u), 7 U.S.C. sec. 136(u)] Note that inclusion in these definitions is dependent on knowing the *intended* use of the substance. If there is no claim, label, or advertisement contending that a substance is a pesticide (that it will do any of the things mentioned in the definitions), regardless of its effectiveness as a pesticide, it will not be considered a pesticide for the purposes of FIFRA regulation.

FIFRA defines pests as "insects, rodents, worms, fungus, weeds, plants, virus, bacteria, micro-organisms, and other animal life." [sec. 2(t), 7 U.S.C. sec. 136(t)] **Herbicides**, **insecticides**, **fungicides**, and **rodenticides** are all commonly referred to as **pesticides**. Herbicides are chemical agents used against plants—especially undesirable weeds. Insecticides, as the name implies, are used against insects. Fungicides are used against fungi; rodenticides, against rodents. All of these substances have, over the years, greatly assisted farmers and families in making the most of their crops and quality of life, respectively. You will likely use one or more of these products during your lifetime, even if merely to ward off pesky insects. Farmers have learned how to genetically engineer their crops for greater yields; but **genetic engineering** has actually increased the use of pesticides, as has the proliferation of weeds that are resistant to certain pesticides. In addition, pesticides can cause "collateral damage" to animals, plants, and other environmental targets that were not the intended targets of the pesticide. Consequently, it is important for the EPA to balance the potential harmful effects of a pesticide against its beneficial uses.

FIFRA regulates the use of pesticides in a number of ways. With few exceptions, no pesticide can be manufactured, distributed, or imported until it is registered. Pesticides must be registered with the EPA and labeled appropriately before they can be manufactured or distributed in the United States. The EPA has set up an **Office of Pesticide Programs (OPP)** that tracks the **registration** of pesticides. The registration process requires the submittal of testing results that can take millions of dollars and years to obtain. The FIFRA registration process is not as simple as the notification process for other types of chemicals under the TSCA.

herbicide A chemical agent used against plants.

insecticide A chemical agent used against insects.

fungicide A chemical used against fungi.

rodenticide A chemical substance used against rodents.

pesticide Any substance intended for "preventing, destroying, repelling or mitigating any pest" or any substance intended for use as a "plant regulator, defoliant or dessicant."

genetic engineering Manipulating the cellular structure of an organism to improve it in some manner.

REVIEW

Herbicides, insecticides, fungicides, and rodenticides are all pesticides.

Office of Pesticide Programs (OPP) The office through which the EPA tracks the registration of pesticides.

registration The process by which a pesticide is authorized for sale, distribution, and use.

REGISTRATION CRITERIA

Before a pesticide can be registered, the formula for the substance, a proposed label, and "full description of the tests made and the results thereof upon which the claims are based" must be submitted to the EPA. To be registered, the following four conditions must be met:

EVALUATING PESTICIDES FOR REGISTRATION

- The composition of the pesticide must be such as to warrant the proposed claim for it.
- The labeling and other materials for the pesticide must comply with the provisions of FIFRA.
- The pesticide will perform its intended function without unreasonable adverse effects on the environment.
- When used in accordance with common practice, the pesticide will not generally cause unreasonable adverse effects on the environment. [sec. 2(bb), 7 U.S.C. sec. 136(bb)]

unreasonable adverse effects A term defining the standard used in registering pesticides pursuant to FIFRA.

Unreasonable Adverse Effects

What does **unreasonable adverse effects** mean for the purposes of FIFRA? This term is defined as "any unreasonable risk to man or the environment, taking into account the economic, social, and environmental costs and benefits of the use of the pesticide." (Ibid) More scientific factors used in determining whether the criteria have been met include whether the pesticide is carcinogenic (capable of causing cancer) and what its effect will be on the reproductive, immunological, and neurological systems of humans. The effect of the pesticide on groundwater, wildlife, and fish also is studied. The information gathered in relation to these factors is then analyzed and a finding made as to whether the pesticide poses an "unreasonable risk."

QUESTION

What economic or social costs and benefits might affect consideration of the registration application for a pesticide?

In addition to the scientific criteria, an analysis of the four noted factors includes an evaluation of nonscientific criteria such as economic, social and environmental costs, and benefits of the pesticide.

Labeling

labeling The process of affixing warnings and information regarding pesticides to pesticide containers.

Much of the litigation involving FIFRA has been related to its **labeling** provisions. Pursuant to the present version of FIFRA, a proper label is one that contains the warnings necessary to prevent injuries to humans and the environment. Case law has demonstrated that FIFRA, a federal law, is intended to be the determining criteria in judging whether labeling is sufficient, instead of allowing claims in state courts to set different standards for pesticide labeling. Examples of this principle include the following two cases.

CASE LAW

THORNTON V. FONDREN GREEN APARTMENTS, 788 F. SUPP. 928 (S.D. TEX. 1992).[1]

Judge Rainey delivered the opinion of the court.

Before the Court is Defendant Green Light Company's Motion for Partial Summary Judgment . . . against Plaintiffs' state law claim of products liability by failure to provide adequate warning or instructions. . . .

Plaintiffs are twenty-one individuals who either resided in or worked at the Fondren Green Apartments in 1986–1987. In 1986, the interior of the apartment complex was sprayed with a pesticide known as Chlordane. The Chlordane had been repacked and labeled by Defendant Green Light Company . . . and sold to . . . another named defendant, who supervised the application of the pesticide at the complex.

In their complaint . . . Plaintiffs allege that they suffered severe injuries as a result of the indoor application of the Chlordane. Plaintiffs' claims against . . . defendants include a products liability tort claim, based on the applicable state law. It is this particular claim that forms the basis for Green Light's present motion. Plaintiffs allege that Green Light's EPA-approved label did not clearly state the possible adverse health effects from Chlordane exposure or that above-ground spraying was extremely dangerous and not allowed by law. Plaintiffs conclude that they should be able to recover against Green Light under a theory of product liability for failure to provide adequate warning or instruction.

Green Light has moved . . . to dismiss all inadequate warning claims by Plaintiffs on the grounds that the Federal Insecticide, Fungicide, and Rodenticide Act (FIFRA) . . . preempts any applicable state tort law.

. . . . [T]he majority of courts have held that FIFRA does not expressly preempt state common law. . . . Due to the large number of chemicals to be regulated, the Supreme Court considers FIFRA a general statute and not one "so comprehensive that it leaves no room for states to supplement federal law." . . . The key question when addressing actual conflict between state and federal law is whether compliance with both is physically impossible. . . . Chemical manufacturers have any number of methods of complying with both federal and state rules. . . .

When looking at a potential conflict preemption, the controlling question is whether the state law is incompatible with the goals of the federal statute. . . . The purpose of FIFRA is to regulate the registration and labeling of pesticide products such that purchasers are provided with assurances of effectiveness and safety when the product is used in accordance with its label. . . .

In the case at bar, twenty-one plaintiffs were exposed to Chlordane and sustained serious injuries, including one death, one stroke, and several continuous medical problems. The goals of the federal statute were obviously not achieved. If a state court finding in favor of Plaintiffs would encourage more complete warnings in the future, state law would not be considered incompatible with FIFRA but would in fact be helping towards the achievement of that statute's goals. As a result of this analysis, we conclude that Defendant Green Light has failed to demonstrate that FIFRA preempts Texas common law.

[I]t is recommended that Defendant Green Light's Motion for partial summary judgment be denied. ■

CASE LAW

NETLAND V. HESS & CLARK, INC., 284 F.3D 895 (8TH CIR. 2002).[2]

Kim Netland brings this action against Hess & Clark, Inc. ("Hess"), the manufacturer of the pesticide Bovinol . . . claiming damages for injury resulting from Netland's use of Bovinol on his horses. The district court granted Hess's motion for summary judgment holding that Netland's claims are preempted by the Federal Insecticide, Fungicide, and Rodenticide Act ("FIFRA") . . . because they are an impermissible challenge to Bovinol's label. For the reasons stated below, we affirm.

Netland, in the summer of 1994, following his junior year of high school, used Bovinol to control flies on his family's three horses. Margaret Netland, Netland's mother, purchased the pesticide in June 1994, from a local retail feed store for the purpose of minimizing the risk of injury to Netland from the unpredictable behavior of horses due to the annoyance of flies. The sales clerk informed Mrs. Netland that the pesticide would work for horses. Prior to giving Netland the pesticide, Mrs. Netland read the warning label and wore plastic gloves to pour the pesticide into a bathroom cleaner spray bottle. Thereafter, Netland sprayed the pesticide on his horses three to four times a week over a six-week period. Prior to riding, Netland sprayed each horse with eight to ten squirts of the pesticide and would normally ride the horse within a minute after spraying it with the pesticide. Netland did not wear any protective clothing or equipment when he used the pesticide and did not read the Bovinol label. Netland believes that he got the pesticide on his skin by touching the horses because his clothes were damp after riding.

In mid-August 1994, Netland began high school football practice and began to experience fatigue and bruising. On September 28, 1994, Netland collapsed on his way to school and was taken to his family physician. . . .

Realizing that Netland had a severe blood problem, [the physician] transferred Netland to a hematologist in Fargo, North Dakota, where he was diagnosed with acquired aplastic anemia. Over the next year, Netland's treatment consisted of large doses of steroids and approximately thirty-five blood transfusions. As a result of this treatment, one of Netland's hips failed and was replaced with a prosthesis. Netland's other hip is also at risk.

Bovinol is a registered insecticide with the . . . EPA under FIFRA and carries an EPA-approved label. . . . [T]he active ingredient in Bovinol . . . is absorbed into the human body by ingestion, inhalation, and skin absorption. The Bovinol label describes the approved and lawful uses of the pesticide, including use on cattle in animal buildings . . . in poultry houses, dog kennels and outdoor uses. . . . The label does not expressly state that Bovinol may be used on horses. The Bovinol label also contains a precautionary instruction and warning. . . .

On July 1, 1998, Netland filed a three-count complaint against Hess alleging (1) strict liability in that Bovinol was defectively designed and unreasonably dangerous, (2) failure to warn user of the dangerous characteristics inherent in the Bovinol product, and (3) negligence and breach of warranty in that Hess failed to use reasonable care in the design, manufacture, and sale of Bovinol. On January 19, 2001, Hess moved for summary judgment asserting federal preemption under FIFRA and also that Netland failed to offer admissible proof of causation. . . .

The district court granted Hess's motion for summary judgment . . . [finding] that each of Netland's claims is essentially an attack on Bovinol's EPA-approved label, and therefore preempted by FIFRA. . . .

Under FIFRA, all pesticides sold in the United States must be registered with the EPA. . . . When applying for registration, manufacturers must submit draft label language addressing a number of topics including ingredients, directions for use, and any information of which they "are aware regarding unreasonable adverse effects of the pesticide on man or the environment." . . .

Prior to registering a pesticide, the EPA must find that its labeling complies with FIFRA's requirements such as a determination that the pesticide is not misbranded, and that when the pesticide is used in accordance with its labeling that it will perform its intended function without an unreasonable adverse effect on the environment. . . . Finally, FIFRA contains an express preemption clause, which provides that a state "shall not impose or continue in effect any requirement for labeling . . . in addition to or different from those required under this subchapter." . . .

[W]e [have] held that once a label is approved FIFRA expressly provides a defense, arising from preemption, against certain state law claims . . . specifically . . . for "inadequate labeling or failure to warn." . . . It is immaterial whether an inadequate labeling or failure to warn claim is brought under a negligence or products liability theory. If a state law claim is *premised* on inadequate labeling or a failure to warn, the impact of allowing the claim would be to impose an additional or different requirement for the label or packaging. Common law claims for breach of express warranty also are preempted by FIFRA. . . .

Netland contends that his claims alleging strict liability and negligence fall outside the state law causes of action that are preempted by FIFRA. He argues that FIFRA preempts only state law claims that directly challenge the product label; therefore, FIFRA does not preempt his claims that Bovinol was defectively designed and unreasonably dangerous. . . . We agree with Netland that defectively manufactured or designed products properly labeled under FIFRA remain subject to state claims. Nevertheless, "if the state law claim is *premised* on inadequate labeling or a failure to warn," which results in the imposition of additional or different labeling requirements, the claim is nonetheless preempted regardless of the guise under which it is presented. . . . Thus it is our task to determine whether Netland's claims are essentially a challenge to Bovinol's label or the overall design of the pesticide. To guide our analysis, we must ask whether in seeking to avoid liability for any error, would the manufacturer choose to alter the label or the product. . . . After careful review of the entire record, we agree with the district court and hold that Netland's claims are preempted by FIFRA because they are an impermissible challenge to the pesticide's label. . . .

Because we find that the premise of each of Netland's claims is Bovinol's label and is therefore preempted by FIFRA, we affirm the . . . summary judgment in favor of Hess. ■

QUESTIONS FOR BOTH CASES

1. What was the main argument made by the defendant in *Thornton v. Fondren Green Apartments*? Why did that claim fail?
2. One of the arguments made by the plaintiff in *Netland v. Hess & Clark, Inc.*, was that Hess & Clark should be held to a strict liability standard. The Court determined that the strict liability argument being made by the plaintiff was premised on an argument that the labeling was inadequate or failed to warn and thus was preempted by federal law. Do you think this conclusion by the Court allowed the defendant to avoid the strict liability standard in a situation where it would have been otherwise applied?
3. Distinguish the rulings in the two cases. Why did the courts seem to make a different decision in each case?

As these cases demonstrate, consumers have found pesticide labels to be difficult to interpret. It is not only the more complicated pesticide labels that have proven confusing. Surveys conducted by the EPA in 1996 found that consumers had difficulty understanding labels for indoor insecticides, outdoor house and garden pesticides, and household hard-surface cleaners. In an attempt to assist consumers with their understanding of pesticide labels, the EPA instituted a voluntary effort called the **Consumer Labeling Initiative (CLI)**. In March 2000, CLI initiated its first project, a large-scale consumer education campaign called "Read the Label FIRST!" Since the program is voluntary, there are no compliance requirements; but the expectation is that this program as well as future programs will make it easier for consumers to read and understand the significance of pesticide labels.

ASSIGNMENT

For more information concerning the CLI, visit its website at http://www.epa.gov/pesticides/label.

Consumer Labeling Initiative (CLI) A voluntary effort to educate consumers about pesticide labels.

Types of Registration

FIFRA provides for the "conditional" registration or reregistration when a manufacturer meets certain factors. A **conditional registration** is intended to be used when data concerning the substance has not yet been provided to the EPA or when the substance has not been evaluated to determine its potential for causing unreasonable adverse effects on the environment. Many conditional registrations have been granted; in fact, conditional registrations seem to be the rule rather than the exception.

conditional registration A type of registration under FIFRA available only in certain circumstances where there appears to be little danger from a pesticide being registered.

CONDITIONAL REGISTRATIONS

Conditional registrations are authorized by FIFRA under a section entitled "Registration Under Special Circumstances." That section provides for conditional registration for:

- pesticides identical or very similar to currently registered products.
- new uses for existing pesticide registrations.
- pesticides containing active ingredients not contained in any currently registered pesticide for which data need to be obtained for registration.

QUESTION

Do you think conditional registrations are appropriate given the circumstances under which registration is sought? How is this procedure consistent with the goals of FIFRA?

The third type of conditional registration is limited in time and can be issued only when the use of the pesticide is in the public interest. Conditional registrations are considered on a case-by-case basis. When a **Notice of Rebuttable Presumption Against Registration (RPAR)** has been issued for a pesticide, conditional registration is not permitted.

Notice of Rebuttable Presumption Against Registration (RPAR) Prevents a registrant from receiving a conditional registration of a pesticide under FIFRA.

Reregistration

Reregistration of pesticides poses its own set of problems, primarily because during the five-year period a pesticide is registered, scientific advances are such that the testing that formed the basis of the original registration application is outdated. If a pesticide was registered prior to 1970, the testing done in support of the registration of that pesticide will not be considered adequate for reregistration unless the applicant can demonstrate why the testing should be considered adequate. In this situation, the applicant has the burden of proof to show that the original testing should be accepted as adequate. An applicant has only 48 months to complete the studies necessary for reregistration. Only a crisis such as the loss of a laboratory is considered sufficient to extend this time period. At the end of the review by the EPA administrator, he or she may ask for additional data, cancel or suspend the registration, or approve the reregistration.

"Me-Too" Pesticides

"me-too" pesticide A pesticide that is identical or very similar to other registered substances.

featherbedding Using the data submitted for an already-registered pesticide to register another pesticide under FIFRA.

FIFRA specifies that registration of pesticides that are identical or very similar to other registered substances (**"me-too" pesticides**) are to be expedited. [FIFRA, Section 3(c) (3)] One of the concepts in FIFRA related to "me-too" pesticides is the concept of **featherbedding**. Subsequent applicants for registration of a substance that is similar to another substance already registered often attempt to have a faster, less-costly, and easier time with registration by piggybacking on the research, testing, and expense of the original applicant (featherbedding). Once this practice was identified, FIFRA was amended to provide that if a subsequent applicant wants to rely on data submitted by the original registrant, he or she must provide "reasonable compensation" to the original applicant before the EPA administrator is allowed to use the data to evaluate the subsequent application.

QUESTION
What do you think of the concept of featherbedding, or using the data compiled by a previous registrant to get your product registered?

There have been many lawsuits over this compensation provision. As previously stated, the cost of amassing the data necessary to support a registration application successfully can be huge. Consequently, what constitutes "reasonable compensation" to the original registrant has been the source of much dispute. In *In re Ciba-Geigy Corp. v. Farmland Industries, Inc.*,[3] which was an administrative hearing, the parties attempted to clarify what constitutes reasonable compensation under FIFRA. The plaintiff, the original registrant, wanted $8.11 million for Farmland's use of its data; but Farmland wanted to pay only about

$49,000 because it contended that such a small figure represented its share of the market for the products. Ultimately, the administrative law judge created a formula he considered fair. The formula he created involved using the data producer's cost adjusted for inflation and the second registrant's market share two or three years after its initial registration.

Trade Secrets

Much of the information provided to the EPA is widely known in the pesticide industry and does not need to be protected as confidential trade secrets. At times, though, confidential information is provided to the EPA as part of the registration process; and as part of the 1972 amendments to FIFRA, provisions were added which state that trade secrets are not to be released unless necessary. If the EPA administrator intends to release trade secrets, the registrant is entitled to prior notice so a declaratory judgment preventing the release can be sought in court. In 1978, FIFRA was amended to limit the protection of trade secrets to formulas and manufacturing processes. None of these amendments has prevented litigation concerning the confidential nature of data submitted as part of the registration process. In *Ruckelshaus v. Monsanto Co.*,[4] the Supreme Court addressed the issue of how pesticide health and safety data should be classified.

CASE LAW

RUCKELSHAUS V. MONSANTO COMPANY, 467 U.S. 986 (1984).

Justice Blackmun delivered the opinion of the Court.

Over the past century, the use of pesticides to control weeds and minimize crop damage caused by insects, disease, and animals has become increasingly more important for American agriculture. . . . While pesticide use has led to improvements in productivity, it has also led to increased risk of harm to humans and the environment. . . . Although the Federal Government has regulated pesticide use for nearly 75 years, FIFRA was first adopted in 1947. Some states had undertaken to regulate pesticide use before there was federal legislation, and many more continued to do so after federal legislation was enacted. . . .

As first enacted, FIFRA was primarily a licensing and labeling statute. It required that all pesticides be registered with the Secretary of Agriculture prior to their sale in interstate . . . commerce. . . . The 1947 legislation also contained general standards setting forth the types of information necessary for proper labeling of a registered pesticide, including directions for use; warnings to prevent harm to people, animals, and plants; and claims made about the efficacy of the product. . . . In 1970, the Department of Agriculture's FIFRA responsibilities were transferred to the then newly created Environmental Protection Agency, whose administrator is the appellant in this case. . . .

. . . Congress undertook a comprehensive revision of FIFRA through the adoption of the Federal Environmental Pesticide Control Act of 1972. . . . The amendments transformed FIFRA from a labeling law into a comprehensive regulatory statute. . . . As amended, FIFRA regulated the use, as well as the sale and labeling of pesticides; regulated pesticides produced and sold in both intrastate and interstate commerce; provided for review, cancellation, and suspension of registration; and gave EPA greater enforcement authority. Congress also added a new criterion for registration: that EPA determine that the pesticide will not cause "unreasonable adverse effects on the environment."

For the purposes of this litigation, the most significant of the 1972 amendments pertained to the pesticide registration procedure and the public disclosure of information learned through that procedure. . . . The 1972 amendments . . . included a provision that allowed EPA to consider data submitted by one applicant pertaining to a similar chemical, provided the subsequent applicant offered to compensate the applicant who originally submitted the data. . . . In effect, the provision instituted a mandatory data-licensing scheme. The amount of compensation was to be negotiated by the parties, or, in the event negotiations failed, was to be determined by the EPA, subject to judicial review. . . .

Under FIFRA, as amended in 1978, applicants are granted a 10-year period of exclusive use for data on new active ingredients contained in pesticides registered after September 1978. . . . With respect to pesticides containing active ingredients that are initially registered under this Act [after September 1978], data submitted to support the application for the original registration of the pesticide . . . shall not, without the written permission of the original data submitter, be considered by the Administrator to support an application by another person during a period of ten years following the date the Administrator first registers the pesticide . . . "except . . . the Administrator may, without the permission of the original data submitter, consider any such item of data in support of an application by any other person . . . within the fifteen-year period following the date the data were originally submitted only if the applicant has made an offer to compensate the original data submitter. . . . The terms and amount of compensation may be fixed by agreement between the original data submitted and the applicant, or failing such agreement, binding arbitration under this subparagraph. . . ."

Appellee Monsanto Company (Monsanto) is an inventor, developer and producer of various kinds of chemical products, including pesticides. . . . A firm that produces an active ingredient may use it for incorporation into its own end-use products, may sell it to formulators, or may do both. Monsanto produces both active ingredients and end-use products. . . . Monsanto brought suit in District Court, seeking injunctive and declaratory relief from the operation of the data-consideration provisions of FIFRA. . . . Monsanto alleged that . . . the challenged provisions effected a "taking" of property without just compensation, in violation of the Fifth Amendment. . . . Monsanto [also] alleged that the arbitration scheme . . . violates the original submitter's due process rights. . . .

After a bench trial, the District Court concluded that Monsanto possessed property rights in its submitted data . . . [and] found that that the challenged data-consideration provisions "give Monsanto's competitors a free ride at Monsanto's expense." . . . [T]he District Court found that the compulsory binding-arbitration scheme . . . did not adequately provide compensation for the property taken. . . . The District Court therefore declared [the sections of FIFRA] unconstitutional, and permanently enjoined EPA from implementing or enforcing those sections. . . .

In deciding this case, we are faced with four questions: (1) Does Monsanto have a property interest protected by the Fifth Amendment . . . in the . . . data submitted to EPA? (2) If so, does EPA's use of the data to evaluate the applications of others . . . effect a taking of that property interest? (3) If there is a taking, is it a taking for a public use? (4) If there is a taking for public use, does the statute adequately provide for just compensation?

. . . Because of the intangible nature of a trade secret, the extent of the property right therein is defined by the extent to which the owner of the secret protects his interest from disclosure to others. . . . If an individual discloses his trade secret to others . . . his property right is extinguished. [T]he Court has found other kinds of intangible interests to be property for purposes of the Fifth Amendment. . . .

We therefore hold that to the extent that Monsanto has an interest in its . . . data cognizable as a trade-secret property right . . . , that property right is protected by the. . . . Fifth Amendment.

Having determined that Monsanto has a property right in the data it has submitted to EPA, we confront the difficult question whether a "taking will occur when EPA discloses those data . . . in evaluating another application for registration." . . . The Court has identified several factors that should be taken into account when determining whether a governmental action has gone beyond "regulation" and effects a "taking." Among those factors are: "the character of the governmental action, its economic impact, and its interference with reasonable investment-backed expectations." . . . [W]e find that the force of [the third] factor is so overwhelming . . . that it disposes of the taking question regarding those data. . . .

Monsanto knew that, for a period of 10 years from the date of submission, EPA would not consider those data in evaluating the application of another without Monsanto's permission. . . . [A]s long as Monsanto is aware of the conditions under which the data are submitted, and the conditions are rationally related to a legitimate Government interest, a voluntary submission of data by an applicant in exchange for the economic advantages of a registration can hardly be called a taking.

In summary, we hold that EPA's consideration or disclosure of data submitted by Monsanto to the agency . . . does not effect a taking. . . . We find no constitutional infirmity in the challenged provisions of FIFRA. . . . The judgment of the District Court is therefore vacated, and the case is remanded for further proceedings consistent with this opinion. ■

QUESTIONS

1. Given that the Court's opinion notes that "development of a potential commercial pesticide candidate typically requires the expenditure of $5 million to $15 million annually for several years," do you believe the Court's determination that there was no "taking" in this case was fair? Why or who not?

2. Would the underlying purpose of FIFRA been frustrated if Monsanto had prevailed in its arguments?

As this case demonstrates, the sharing and use of data as part of the FIFRA registration process has generated and will continue to generate controversy concerning the extent to which data submitted is considered to be a trade secret.

Types of Registered Use

FIFRA allows for two types of registered uses of pesticides: general use and restricted use. General use registration is preferred because it does not impose restrictions on the sale and use of a pesticide other than the restrictions and requirements generally found in FIFRA. On the other hand, a restricted use registration, as the term implies, has restrictions imposed by the EPA to mitigate identified potential harmful effects that, while not severe enough to prevent registration, require mitigation in some manner.

Commonly, pesticides are restricted when some type of restriction is placed on their use. One typical restriction is to allow a particular pesticide to be used only by users who have passed a test demonstrating their knowledge concerning the use of that pesticide. For the purposes of FIFRA, *use* means application of the substance by or under the supervision of a certified applicator. This restriction does not apply when the substance is being applied by a private applicator on his or her own land. In those instances, the applicator must take classes concerning the application of the product but does not have to take any postclass tests to determine whether he or she understands the information conveyed in the classes. The two exceptions to the restriction just identified leave holes in the effectiveness of the restriction. Other types of restrictions, although less common, include limitations on the frequency of use of a pesticide or on the locations where the pesticide may be applied. In addition, a restriction can limit the type of pest (plant, animal, or insect) upon which the pesticide may be used.

Effects of Registration

Once a pesticide is registered, the registration lasts up to five years. If a manufacturer does not request a renewal of the registration prior to the end of the initial registration period, a process for terminating the registration begins. If the EPA has not received a request for renewal of a registration at least 30 days prior to the end of the initial registration period, the EPA publishes a notice of its intent to terminate the registration in the *Federal Register*. The manufacturer then has 30 days to protest the cancellation, or the registration terminates. If the EPA is proposing cancellation of the registration and the manufacturer protests, a hearing will be held as part of the APA process. A contested cancellation case can be lengthy—taking as long as two years.

Cancellation of Registration

In a cancellation hearing, a presumption in favor of cancellation exists, so the burden of proof falls on the manufacturer to demonstrate that the risk of the substance is minimal or that other benefits outweigh

QUESTION

Do you think it is appropriate for a pesticide to continue to be sold during the hearing process? Does the possible length of the process influence your opinion? Does the fact that a presumption exists in favor of cancellation influence your opinion?

any risks. Interestingly, even though there is a presumption in favor of cancellation during the hearing process, a pesticide can continue to be sold during the hearing process.

If a pesticide is canceled, what happens to the pesticides already out in stores or the pesticides that have already been sold? FIFRA permits the EPA to continue to allow the sale and use of existing stock, but only under such conditions that will not adversely affect the environment. If a pesticide has been in use a long time, too much of the substance may be in the hands of the manufacturer, retailers, and end users for the EPA to permit continued sale and use of the product. The original provisions of FIFRA called for "indemnification" (which in this instance, means reimbursement) by the EPA for the unused product. The indemnification provision covered the manufacturer, retailers, and end users. Due to the large expense the EPA incurs with reimbursing for canceled pesticides, in 1988 FIFRA was modified to provide for the indemnification of only end users. Under extraordinary circumstances, a manufacturer or retailer may ask Congress for an appropriation to reimburse them for their stock of a canceled pesticide. Absent such extraordinary circumstances, the only recourse a retailer has is to ask the manufacturer for reimbursement. The manufacturer can refuse to reimburse a retailer or another holder of the product only when the terms of the original sale specified that there would be no reimbursement in the event of cancellation.

Suspensions

There is an alternative to the potentially lengthy cancellation hearing process. If the EPA is concerned that a pesticide presents an "imminent hazard" to human health or the environment, the EPA administrator can seek an **emergency suspension**. While the term *suspension* may not seem as harsh as the term *cancellation*, in fact, the suspension process is used in situations where the EPA believes the risk to be grave enough to require immediate action. The suspension procedure allows the EPA administrator to issue an order immediately suspending the sale, distribution, and use of a pesticide. When such an order is given, the manufacturer of the pesticide is entitled to an expedited hearing to determine if the emergency suspension was appropriate.

emergency suspension An order immediately suspending the sale, distribution, and use of a pesticide where the EPA administrator believes the pesticide poses an imminent risk.

How much risk is needed for purposes of a FIFRA suspension order? The court in *Dow Chemical v. Blum*[5] defined an emergency as a "substantial likelihood that serious harm will be experienced during the three or four months required in any realistic projection of the administrative suspension process." The court went on to identify the following five factors in analyzing that standard:

Factors Used to Analyze Risk

- The seriousness of the threatened harm
- The immediacy of the threatened harm
- The probability that the threatened harm would result
- The benefits to the public of the continued use of the pesticides in question during the suspension process
- The nature and extent of the information before the administrator at the time the decision is made

The court further held that in order to overturn an emergency suspension order, a party must demonstrate that the order was arbitrary, capricious, an abuse of discretion, or "not issued in accordance with the procedures established by law."

The option of issuing an emergency suspension order has been exercised infrequently by the EPA administrator. More often, if the administrator believes there is an imminent hazard, he or she will issue an **ordinary suspension**.

ordinary suspension An order suspending the sale, distribution, and use of a pesticide because the EPA administrator believes it to be an imminent risk. This differs from an emergency suspension in that with an ordinary suspension, the registrant has an opportunity to request a pre-order hearing.

An ordinary suspension differs primarily from an emergency suspension in that it allows the registrant to request an expedited hearing within five days of receiving notice of the administrator's *proposed* suspension action. With an emergency suspension, there is no opportunity for a hearing before the suspension is imposed—the action is taken without prior opportunity for participation by the registrant (*ex parte*). Even with an ordinary suspension, the administrator must demonstrate the existence of an imminent hazard for the suspension to be valid. The effect of the two types of suspensions is the same, but the process is different. Interestingly, courts have interpreted the term *imminent hazard* to include situations where the effect of the substance may not be felt for many years (see *EDF v. Ruckelshaus*[6]).

Enforcement

Record keeping is as important to the enforcement of FIFRA as it is to other environmental acts. Pursuant to EPA regulations, most manufacturers of pesticides keep detailed records showing the quantities sold, date of delivery, and information sufficient to identify the recipient. The EPA is entitled to inspect manufacturing or retailing facilities without prior notice upon presentation by an EPA employee of the proper credentials and a written reason for the inspection, including a statement as to whether a violation is suspected.

If a violation is found, the EPA or state agriculture department must provide written notification of any intended civil or criminal proceeding. The alleged violator is given an opportunity to respond orally or in writing prior to the filing of formal charges by the EPA or state. If the violation is minor and if it is in the public interest, the EPA or state may choose to give a written warning instead of filing a civil or criminal action. Typically, a written warning is given when a violation occurred but due care was exercised and the violation did not cause significant harm to the environment. In lieu of a written warning, the EPA also can issue a stop sale, use, or removal order or seek a seizure order from the federal court.

Civil and criminal penalties for violations of FIFRA are not as large as those for violations of other environmental acts. Civil violations range from upward of $1,000 per violation for private users/applicators to upward of $5,000 for violations by a registrant, wholesaler, retailer, or distributor. The EPA does use mitigating or aggravating factors to determine the amount of the fine requested, including the size of the business, the effect of the fine on the viability of the business, and the seriousness of the violation.

Criminal penalties may be imposed for knowing about violations of FIFRA. These fines are up to $1,000 for a user or applicator and up to $25,000 for a firm. Jail sentences may be imposed for officers of a firm or private applicators or users.

ENVIRONMENTAL LAW PROFESSIONAL PROFILE

Ms. Deanna (Sami) L. Falzone

What types of duties do you perform in your work as a paralegal in the natural resources/environmental law fields?

My work enables me to do a wide variety of tasks that include research, investigation, writing, preparation for hearings and trials, and assisting at trials. I prepare pleadings, discovery requests and responses, letters to client representatives and opposing counsel, and briefs at all levels of court. Under the supervision of an attorney, I have written articles for publication, assisted with law review articles, and prepared interoffice educational materials.

What is your favorite part of your job?

My favorite part is the variety of my assignments—working on exhibits, pre-trial pleadings and graphics, going through files at state agencies, researching new legislation. I never have a "typical" day. I also love the "digging" part—trying to find the one missing piece of information needed to support our case. I like organizing documents so they can be readily used. Working with our clients is another great perk!

What advice do you have for paralegal students interested in environmental law?

The topics in environmental law are ever-changing, and you need to be willing to learn as much as you can about the hot topic of the year.

What are your tips for success?

Success hinges on a willingness to undertake any task, work on your own with little direction, complete tasks accurately the first time, think ahead, use common sense, and build strong client relationships. I would also suggest

(continued)

building strong relationships with key contacts in the various state and federal agencies you work with. Cultivate these allies! If possible, intern with a law firm with a strong natural resources/environmental law practice. Take ownership of your assignments and love what you do!

What skills are required for your work?

You need great writing and comprehension skills, superb computer skills, good people skills, being detail-oriented, and having a flair for organization.

Sami Falzone is a paralegal with the Cheyenne, Wyoming, office of Holland & Hart, a national law firm. Ms. Falzone has been a practicing paralegal since the early 1980s, taking a break for a few years to manage a large hotel complex following litigation in which her firm represented the hotel. Ms. Falzone has, in cooperation with attorneys with whom she has worked, published a law review article entitled "Recreational Injuries & Inherent Risks: Wyoming's Recreation Safety Act" in the Land and Water Review (1993) *and assisted with the research and writing of Wyoming's Oil and Natural Gas Update, published annually in the American Bar Association's* Natural Resources, Energy and Environmental Law Year in Review.

SUMMARY

FIFRA regulates the use, sale, and labeling of pesticides. Insecticides, fungicides, and rodenticides are among the pesticides regulated by this act. FIFRA uses a registration process to analyze any possible unreasonable adverse effects that might result from the use of pesticides. In additional to analyzing such potential effects, the EPA takes into consideration the economic or social costs and benefits of a particular pesticide. The process of getting a pesticide registered is expensive and time-consuming due to the comprehensive amount of testing and information that must be provided to the EPA. Occasionally, information provided to the EPA will be deemed a trade secret and its confidentiality protected unless release is deemed necessary. The EPA may cancel or suspend pesticide registrations through various administrative or judicial processes. FIFRA also contains very specific requirements for the labeling of pesticides. These labeling requirements have been the subject of many court cases. Labeling is intended to be sufficient to warn people about the dangers of particular pesticides and to instruct them on proper use of those pesticides. FIFRA provides for the imposition of civil and criminal penalties as punishment for noncompliance with its provisions.

KEY TERMS

- Conditional registration
- Consumer Labeling Initiative (CLI)
- Dichlorodiphenyltrichloroethane (DDT)
- Emergency suspension
- Featherbedding
- Fungicides
- Genetic engineering
- Herbicides
- Insecticides
- Labeling
- "Me-too" pesticides
- Notice of Rebuttable Presumption Against Registration (RPAR)
- Office of Pesticide Programs (OPP)
- Ordinary suspension
- Pesticides
- Registration
- Rodenticides
- Unreasonable adverse effects

HELPFUL WEBSITES

http://www.epa.gov/pesticides (EPA, Pesticides)

http://www.epa.gov/pesticides/docket/#location (EPA, Pesticides Public Regulatory Docket)

http://www.epa.gov/oppt (EPA, Pollution Prevention and Toxics)

http:www.epa.gov/history/topics/fifra/index.htm (EPA, Federal Insecticide, Fungicide and Rodenticide Act)

http://www.beyondpesticides.org (Beyond Pesticides)

http://www.croplifeamerica.org (CropLife America)

REVIEW QUESTIONS AND HANDS-ON ACTIVITIES

1. Explain the role of states in the implementation of FIFRA. Is this role appropriate?

2. What are some of the ways in which pesticides are helping your quality of life today?

3. Discuss whether substances should be classified as pesticides under FIFRA based on the claims made about them and their "intended use."
4. Describe the goals of the labeling requirements of FIFRA.
5. Go to the store or your garage and find a pesticide container. Is the information provided clear and informative? Explain.
6. Discuss whether information supplied to the EPA as part of the registration process should ever be protected as a trade secret. Justify your position.
7. Review the *Ruckelshaus* decision. Discuss "takings" and their application to use of information.
8. Describe the process for cancellation of a registered pesticide.
9. Describe the two types of suspensions authorized by the provisions of FIFRA.

ENDNOTES

1. *Thornton v. Fondren Green Apartments*, 788 F. Supp. 928 (S.D. Tex. 1992).
2. *Netland v. Hess & Clark, Inc.*, 284 F.3d 895 (8th Cir. 2002).
3. *In re Ciba-Geigy Corp. v. Farmland Industries, Inc.* [Initial Decision, FIFRA Comp. Dockets Nos. 33, 34, and 41 (August 19, 1980)].
4. *Ruckelshaus v. Monsanto Company*, 467 U.S. 986 (1984).
5. *Dow Chemical v. Blum*, 469 F. Supp. 892 (E.D. Mich. 1979).
6. *EDF v. Ruckelshaus*, 439 F.2d 584 (D.C.Cir. 1971).

CHAPTER 10

EMERGENCY PLANNING AND COMMUNITY RIGHT-TO-KNOW ACT (EPCRA)

TITLE: The Emergency Planning and Community Right-to-Know Act (EPCRA) (1986)

CITATION: 42 U.S.C. secs. 11001(a)-(c)

REGULATIONS: 40 C.F.R. sec. 1400, *et seq.*

PURPOSE: To better inform and protect communities by requiring local emergency preparedness programs and facilitating dissemination of information within local communities concerning hazardous chemicals present at facilities within those communities

HISTORY: Part of the Superfund Amendments and Reauthorization Act (SARA) (1986)

LEARNING OBJECTIVES

After studying this chapter, the reader should be able to

- explain how the focus of EPCRA differs from that of other environmental acts.
- describe the importance of the emergency planning component of EPCRA.
- explain an Emergency Response Plan.
- describe the composition of the State Emergency Response Commission (SERC) and the Local Emergency Planning Committee (LEPC).
- describe the release notification requirements.
- explain how to satisfy the "community-right-to-know" requirements of EPCRA.
- describe MSDS and Form R forms.
- describe Tier One and Tier Two reporting requirements.
- define the Toxic Chemical Release Inventory Reporting requirements.
- explain what the Pollution Prevention Act (PPA) covers.

SUPERFUND AMENDMENTS AND REAUTHORIZATION ACT (SARA)

Many of the acts outlined in this text focus primarily on the role of governmental entities (such as the EPA) and businesses involved in the manufacture, processing, transportation, use, and disposal of waste or chemicals in such a way as to create a potential risk to human health and the environment. The *Emergency Planning and Community Right to Know Act (EPCRA)* has a much different focus. This act, promulgated in 1986 as part of the *Superfund Amendments and Reauthorization Act (SARA)*, is intended to generate citizen involvement and knowledge concerning certain types of hazards present in local communities.

EPCRA addresses emergency planning within local communities, contains community right-to-know reporting requirements, provides for emergency notification of chemical releases, and requires compliance with toxic chemical inventory reporting requirements. These requirements are designed to ensure that first responders to emergency incidents (primarily fire and law enforcement personnel) are not surprised and potentially injured or killed by encountering toxic substances at the scene of an emergency and that citizens can be better protected from hazards caused by an emergency situation.

Imagine a firefighter responding to a fire at a local auto body shop and using "standard" procedures to enter the premises in an attempt to put out the fire. If the business uses toxic chemicals as part of its business operations but the firefighter is not aware that dangerous chemicals are present at the site, the firefighter may be overcome by toxic fumes as he or she attempts to extinguish the flames. If, on the other hand, that same firefighter is equipped with a list of all possible toxic chemicals stored at the auto body shop and their characteristics in response to high temperatures, the firefighter can use proper protective gear when fighting the fire. Further, he or she will be able to determine whether there is a potential risk to human health caused by smoke, fluid leak, or other type of release at the emergency site and respond appropriately by evacuating the risk area or attempting to contain the source of the risk.

Modern technology, as applied to the information gleaned through compliance with EPCRA, is instrumental in assisting with EPCRA's protection of human health and the environment. For example, *geographic information system (GIS)* technology allows pinpoint correlation of the location of an emergency problem and allows first responders to identify the closest sources of aid and assistance, including fire hydrants. GIS also allows first responders to identify those who may be exposed to a risk within a particular geographical area so that protective measures can be taken. In addition, mobile weather technology permits first responders to calculate, for example, the risk area associated with a smoke plume by determining that the wind is out of the west at 5 miles per hour and that rain is expected at the emergency site within a few minutes.

ASSIGNMENT

Familiarize yourself with the GIS information available to your local emergency responders. Find out how the responders use the information.

EMERGENCY PLANNING

Responsibility for implementation of the requirements of EPCRA rests upon state and local officials as well as citizens. In each state, the governor is required to appoint a **State Emergency Response Commission (SERC)**. The SERC then designates emergency planning districts within that state. To further involve the local citizenry, EPCRA then requires the SERC to appoint a **Local Emergency Planning Committee (LEPC)** in each emergency planning district within the state. [42 U.S.C. sec. 11001 (a)-(c)]

As part of EPCRA's emergency planning requirements, the SERC gathers information from any facility that produces, uses, or stores, in certain threshold quantities, any substance listed on the EPA's "List of Extremely Hazardous Substances." For purposes of EPCRA, the threshold quantity is referred to as a **threshold planning quantity (TPQ)**. The information accumulated via this reporting requirement is stored and used by the SERC and the LEPC to assist in reducing the risk that those **extremely hazardous substances (EHSs)** will cause a risk to human health or the environment.

A facility subject to the EPCRA EHS reporting requirements must provide the SERC with the name of a representative who will act as the facility emergency response coordinator and participate in the emergency planning process. If there is any change in the coordinator or the inventory of substances located at a facility, the SERC must be notified of that change. [42 U.S.C. sec. 11003(d) and 40 C.F.R. sec. 355.30(c), (d)]

State Emergency Response Commission (SERC) A commission appointed by the governor of each state. The SERC designates emergency planning districts within the state and monitors compliance with relevant provision of EPCRA.

Local Emergency Planning Committee (LEPC) Appointed by the SERC in each emergency planning district within a state.

threshold planning quantity (TPQ) The amount of an extremely hazardous substance present in a facility at any one time that, when exceeded, subjects the facility to the emergency planning requirements.

extremely hazardous substances (EHSs) Substances causing a risk to human health or the environment that are monitored pursuant to EPCRA.

EMERGENCY RESPONSE PLANS

A large component of EPCRA's emergency planning process is the requirement that LEPCs generate an **Emergency Response Plan** for their area of coverage. This plan, which is based on all of the information reported concerning EHSs in the community, must designate

Emergency Response Plan Designates response parameters for local hazardous chemical emergency releases.

response parameters for local hazardous chemical emergency releases. EPCRA sets forth requirements concerning the contents of Emergency Response Plans, including the following:

Emergency Response Plan Provisions

- Identification of all facilities within the district subject to the emergency planning requirements of EPCRA
- Identification of all routes within the district used to transport EHSs
- Identification of all risk-related facilities in the district located near facilities such as natural gas facilities, power stations, high transmission towers, schools, or hospitals
- A description of the methods and procedures to be followed by emergency response personnel when responding to an incident within the planning district
- Designation of an emergency response coordinator and identification of all emergency response coordinators within the planning district
- A description of emergency notification procedures that will be used to notify the public and any evacuation plans to be implemented in the event of a release
- Specification of methods to determine whether a release has occurred, what the zone of danger is, and whether human life will be jeopardized
- A list of all emergency equipment and facilities within the community that can be used to respond to a release
- A description of the training program used to train emergency response personnel for releases, including a timetable for "exercising" (engaging in a mock release simulation) the emergency response plan within a district

The Emergency Response Plan is drafted by the LEPC and reviewed by the SERC for compliance with applicable EPCRA laws and regulations. In addition, the SERC should analyze the Emergency Response Plan to determine whether it is compatible with and supports the Emergency Response Plans of adjacent or nearby emergency planning districts.

RELEASE NOTIFICATION

emergency release
A release of a listed hazardous substance that is not permitted by the federal government, that exceeds the reportable quantity (RQ), and that results in exposure to humans off-site.

What constitutes an **emergency release** pursuant to EPCRA? It is the release of a listed hazardous substance that is not permitted by the federal government, that exceeds the reportable quantity (RQ) for the released substance, and that results in exposure to humans off-site. [40 C.F.R. sec. 355.40(a)] Listed hazardous substances are those on the EPA's list of EHSs, in addition to hazardous substances subject to the emergency notification requirements of the comprehensive CERCLA. The RQ is the threshold quantity that must be reported under EPCRA.

In the event of an emergency release, the owner or operator of a facility is required to notify immediately the LEPC emergency response coordinator of the area likely to be affected by the release and the SERC of any state likely to be affected by the release. This notification may be made by virtually any method, including a personal visit, a phone call, or a radio transmission. If the release relates to one of the CERCLA hazardous substances, the facility also must notify the **National Response Center (NRC)** of the release. Typically, the first thing a facility will do is call the emergency responders in the area, such as fire and law enforcement, and then make the EPCRA-required notifications as appropriate.

National Response Center (NRC) A center designed to coordinate responses to releases of hazardous substances, the NRC was established pursuant to CERCLA and is operated under the supervision of the National Response Team.

Release Notification Requirements

Whether the notification is verbal or written, certain information must be provided concerning the release, including:

- the name of any chemical substance released.
- its status or nonstatus as an extremely hazardous chemical (EHC).
- an estimate of how much has been released.
- when the release occurred and how long it lasted.
- into what type of environment the chemical was released.
- known health risks associated with the chemical(s) released, along with any known medical protocols to be followed.
- what precautions should be taken, including, potentially, evacuation.
- the name and contact information for the facility representative handling the release. [40 C.F.R. sec. 355.40(b)(2)]

In addition to immediate notification about the release as described previously, the facility must, as soon as possible following the release, submit a written notification updating the information in the original release and the steps taken following the release to that point in time. This written notification must be provided to the SERC and the LEPC.

In addition to the typical stationary site release, for which the notification requirements listed previously are applicable, EPCRA, together with CERCLA, provides different notification requirements for transportation-related releases and continuous releases. A **transportation-related release** is a release that occurs during transportation or storage

transportation-related release A release that occurs during transportation or storage incident to transportation if a shipment has not reached its ultimate destination.

incident to transportation if the shipment has not reached its ultimate destination. In the event of such a release, the owner or operator of such conveyance or facility can comply with the immediate notification requirements by providing the necessary data to an emergency operator (such as a 911 operator) or a "regular" operator.

continuous release
A release that occurs without interruption or abatement or that is routine, anticipated, and intermittent and incidental to normal operations or treatment processes.

A **continuous release** is one that occurs "without interruption or abatement or that is routine, anticipated, and intermittent and incidental to normal operations or treatment processes." If a continuous release is "stable in quantity and rate," EPCRA provides for reduced reporting requirements. "Stable in quantity and rate" means exactly what the common definition of the words would lead one to anticipate: that the release is predictable and regular in both quantity and rate of release. [40 C.F.R. sec. 302(8)(b)] Requiring only reduced reporting standards in the event of such a release is logical; the release is not really an emergency because it is, by definition, predictable. Therefore, it can be planned for and monitored in such a manner as to prevent exposure away from the release. Notification of a continuous release can be made by a phone call to the NRC pursuant to CERCLA and to the SERC and LEPC pursuant to EPCRA.

The owner or operator of the conveyance or facility from which a continuous release occurs must provide written notification of many facts associated with the release. Some of that information is similar to what is required in the notification of an emergency release, but also includes certain data particular to a continuous release. The information similar to that provided for an emergency release includes information about the company involved in the release, the number of people or types of environmentally sensitive areas potentially exposed to the release, and the name and characteristics of the hazardous substances involved in the release.

In addition, there is required information specific to a continuous release. For example, if the release occurs from a vessel (any movable conveyance, such as a boat, train, truck, or plane), the exact location must be given in terms of latitude and longitude. In addition to the EPCRA reporting requirements for continuous releases, facilities or vessels also must provide their most recent Toxic Chemical Reporting Forms as submitted to the EPA. The vessel or facility must keep all records supporting the information supplied as part of this notification for at least one year at any one of a number of types of locations as specified in EPCRA, and the forms must be made available to the EPA at its request.

COMMUNITY RIGHT-TO-KNOW REQUIREMENTS

One of the premises of EPCRA is that a community is entitled to know the amount and type of hazardous chemicals that are being stored there. Therefore, EPCRA requires the owner or operator of a facility to provide sufficient information to place the community on notice concerning such information. Two avenues are available for notifying the community of the type of chemicals being stored.

One avenue is to submit to the SERC, the LEPC, and the **local fire department (LFD)** a list of "hazardous chemicals" that exist at the facility in threshold quantities. The list must include the name of the chemical(s) and the hazard categories into which they fall.

local fire department (LFD) A fire department located within a Local Emergency Planning District.

HAZARD CATEGORIES

The hazard categories that a facility uses to further identify the risk associated with the chemical include the following:

- Immediate (acute) health hazard (designated by OSHA as "highly-toxic," "toxic," "corrosive," "irritant," and "sensitizer")
- Delayed health hazard (designated by OSHA as a "carcinogen")
- Fire hazard (designated by OSHA as "flammable," combustible liquid," "oxidizer," and "pyrophoric")
- Sudden release of pressure hazard (designated by OSHA as "compressed gas" and "explosive")
- Reactive hazard (designated by OSHA as "organic peroxide," "unstable reactive," and "water reactive")

The other reporting alternative available to a facility is to provide **Material Safety Data Sheets (MSDS)** concerning the chemicals involved. Appendix C in this text contains examples of three MSDS forms for certain types of alcohol. A review of these forms shows that the information supplied is very specific in terms of the characteristics of the substance and the proper care and handling procedures that should be used in connection with their use.

Material Safety Data Sheets (MSDS) A form detailing specific information concerning the characteristics of a chemical substance and proper care and handling procedures for that substance.

Many of the chemicals for which EPCRA reporting is required are "mixtures." Chemical mixtures can be reported by providing the qualities of the mixture itself or by providing the qualities of the individual chemicals that make up the mixture. [40 C.F.R. sec. 370.28(a)] The threshold quantity levels for mixtures are calculated for the whole mixture and do not require that the level of each chemical making up the mixture reach the threshold quantity before reporting is required.

Tier One/Tier Two
Reporting requirements pursuant to EPCRA.

REVIEW
The two tiers of reporting under EPCRA are Tier One and Tier Two.

Tier Two Confidential Location Information Sheet
If a facility believes that the location of chemical substances on its property should be kept confidential for some business purpose, that facility must submit the required information on this form, which is then available to certain committees but not to the public.

There are two tiers of reporting pursuant to EPCRA: **Tier One** and **Tier Two**. Tier One reporting requires the owner or operator of a facility to submit information concerning each hazard category as follows:

- A best estimate of the maximum quantity of hazardous chemicals in each category present at the facility at any time during the previous calendar year
- An estimate of the average daily quantity of hazardous chemicals in each category
- The general location at the facility of hazardous chemicals in each category

The information in the Tier One Report is tendered to the SERC and LEPC, is available to the public, and is used to advise emergency responders of the possible location and quantity of hazardous chemicals at a facility in the event of an emergency response.

The public also is entitled to know information typically found in the Tier Two Report, as follows:

Tier Two Report

- What the scientific and common names of a chemical are
- Whether the chemical is an extremely hazardous substance
- Whether a hazardous chemical at a facility is part of a mixture
- Whether a hazardous chemical is solid, liquid, or gas
- What the hazard categories are into which the chemical falls
- What the average amount of the chemical at the facility has been at any time or within the past year
- How the chemical is stored
- Where the chemical is stored at the facility
- Whether the owner or operator of the facility has elected to keep location information confidential for some business purpose (If location information is kept confidential, that information is submitted on a **Tier Two Confidential Location Information Sheet**, which is available to EPCRA committees but not to the public.)

The Tier Two Report is submitted to the SERC, the LEPC, and the LFD. Since the Tier Two Report contains more specific information concerning the chemicals present at a facility, it is preferred by those to whom the reports are submitted. Armed with the information contained on the tier reports, EPCRA committees and emergency responders are better prepared in the event of an emergency release of a dangerous chemical. Appendix D of this text provides reporting information that a local high school in Colorado submitted to a LERC. The information is very specific and would be extremely helpful if an emergency response were ever necessary at that location.

TOXIC CHEMICAL RELEASE INVENTORY REPORTING

Owners and operators of designated types of facilities are required pursuant to EPCRA to report certain information concerning "toxic chemicals" at their facility. The EPA identifies "toxic chemicals" by including them on a list found in EPCRA regulations [see 40 C.F.R. sec. 372.65(a)]. This list is constantly amended as new toxic chemicals are identified. If a facility releases toxic chemicals, whether intentionally or accidentally, the release must be reported annually pursuant to EPCRA requirements.

These reporting requirements apply to owners and operators of manufacturing facilities that fall into particular industrial classifications; that have a certain number of employees; and that manufacture, import, process, or otherwise use a listed toxic chemical in quantities exceeding the threshold level. For the purposes of toxic chemical release inventory reporting, Section 313 of EPCRA defines a facility as "all buildings, equipment, structures, and other stationary items which are located on a single site or on contiguous or adjacent sites and which are owned or operated by the same person." The terms *manufacture, import, process*, and *otherwise use* are broadly defined in EPCRA to ensure that potential hazards from the handling of toxic chemicals are anticipated and a proper response can be prepared and executed.

EPCRA does contain certain exemptions from toxic chemical inventory release reporting. Certain uses are exempted: use as a structural component of the facility; use in routine janitorial or maintenance activities; personal use at the facility of foods, drugs, cosmetics, or other personal items containing toxic chemicals; use for maintaining vehicles of the facility; and use of chemicals in intake water or air.

Toxic chemicals contained in articles used at the facility are not counted toward the threshold levels if certain conditions are met.

Before toxic chemical inventory reporting is required for a particular toxic chemical in use, the quantity of that chemical must reach a set threshold level. Levels are set for the manufacture, import, or processing of all toxic chemicals. Levels of toxic chemicals in mixtures and trade name products must be included in the threshold calculation. The calculation of the amount that a mixture contributes to a threshold level is dependent on what the owner or operator knows about the mixture and whether the contribution of the mixture to the threshold level is deemed to be *de minimis* (extremely minor).

In certain circumstances, EPCRA requires suppliers of mixtures to notify their customers of the presence of toxic chemicals in the suppliers' products. The determination of whether this requirement applies to a particular supplier is complex, and the notification must include certain information [see 40 C.F.R. secs. 372.45 and 372.45(b)]. If a supplier is subject to these EPCRA notification requirements and the supplier changes anything about the products it supplies that contain toxic chemicals, the supplier must amend its notice to provide sufficient information to its customers about the toxic chemical(s) involved. Suppliers must maintain records for three years that demonstrate their compliance with the notification requirements.

Toxic Chemical Release Inventory Reporting Form (Form R) This comprehensive reporting form, required in certain circumstances pursuant to EPCRA, provides sufficient data for emergency responders to know what toxic chemicals are located at a particular facility and how much risk is posed to human health and the environment from those chemicals in the event of a spill or release.

How is information communicated to comply with EPCRA requirements for toxic chemical release inventory reporting? A form aptly titled a **Toxic Chemical Release Inventory Reporting Form (Form R)** is used. The form requires the following information:

TOXIC CHEMICAL RELEASE INVENTORY REPORTING FORM (FORM R)

- The name, location, and main business activities at the facility
- Any off-site locations to which waste containing toxic chemicals is transferred
- The inclusion of whether the facility manufactures, imports, processes, or otherwise uses the toxic chemical
- The maximum quantity of the chemical at the facility at any time during the past year
- The quantity of the chemical that was released into the air, water, and land each year
- Waste treatment and disposal procedures and their efficiency
- Information concerning source reduction, recycling, and pollution prevention at the facility
- A certification from a senior manager that the Form R information is complete and accurate

In 1990, the *Pollution Prevention Act (PPA)* was passed. The requirements of the act are relevant to EPCRA because when a facility files a Form R reporting the information required by EPCRA, the facility must, pursuant to the PPA, include other information on Form R as well. The information required by the PPA, generally stated, includes information concerning source reduction and recycling activities. More specifically, for each chemical reported, the following additional PPA information must be included:

PPA INFORMATION

- The quantity of the chemical entering the waste streams before recycling, treatment, or disposal and the percentage change of that quantity from the preceding year
- The quantity of the chemical recycled and the percentage change of that quantity from the preceding year, as well as the way it is recycled
- The quantity of the chemical treated off-site and the percentage change in that quantity from the preceding year
- The estimated quantity of the chemical expected to enter the waste stream prior to recycling, treatment, or disposal over the two years following the date of the submittal of Form R
- The estimated quantity expected to be recycled over the two years following the date of the submittal of Form R
- A description of the specific source reduction practices used by the facility, such as use of different
  - equipment.
  - technology.
  - handling, recycling, treatment, or disposal processes.
  - materials.
  - management techniques such as training.
  - inventory control.
- The way source reduction ideas are obtained (e.g., from audits, employees, or management)
- The ratio of production in the year the Form R is filed to production in the prior year
- The quantity of the chemical released through accidents or other unintended methods

EPCRA requires a facility to keep many records for at least three years—for example, toxic chemical inventory reports; records justifying exemptions; receipts or manifests for chemicals transported off-site; and documentation of the handling, recycling, treatment, or disposal methods used at the facility. Those facilities for which the PPA reporting applies must maintain additional records supporting their PPA reporting.

FEDERAL COMPLIANCE WITH EPCRA

The obligation of federal facilities and operations to comply with various environmental acts has been discussed throughout this text. In 1993, President Clinton, by executive order, required federal facilities that manufactured, processed, or otherwise used listed chemicals to comply with EPCRA reporting requirements. This executive order also required federal facilities to cooperate in the development of local emergency response plans. [Executive Order 12856, 58 *Fed. Reg.* 41981 (August 6, 1993), included in this text as Appendix E]

President Clinton's order further mandated that federal agencies develop an agency-wide pollution prevention strategy and explain how that strategy will be accomplished. Pursuant to the order, federal agencies are to set voluntary goals to reduce pollution by eliminating or reducing acquisition of products containing EHSs or toxic chemicals unless those products are absolutely necessary for relevant governmental operations.

Often federal agencies such as the DOD and the General Services Administration (GSA) argue that they should not be bound by environmental laws because their activities may involve national defense and, as such, should not be limited or controlled by laws or regulations that might interfere with what they perceive to be the most efficient or effective means of operating. President Clinton's order requires the DOD and the GSA to make efforts to reduce the acquisition or use of EHSs or toxic chemicals. The order encourages creativity and innovation as well as cooperation with industry, academia, and others in an effort to find better environmental solutions to the risks surrounding federal activities.

Federal facilities meeting the EPCRA definition of *facility*, otherwise meeting EPCRA reporting requirements due to the nature of their operations, must file reports as required by both EPCRA and the PPA.

Thus, by executive order, federal facilities that, if private, would be required to comply with the provisions of EPCRA and the PPA must comply with those requirements as if they were private facilities.

TRADE SECRETS

This chapter explained that facilities can "hide" from the public (but not from certain EPCRA committees) the location of chemicals on their facility by submitting a separate form to the committees that is not available to the public. EPCRA also allows the specific identity of a chemical to be treated as confidential by a SERC, LEPC, or the LFD.

How does a facility obtain permission to keep a chemical identity confidential? A claim that a certain chemical is a trade secret must be made at the time reports are filed with the appropriate EPCRA committees, and all other required information must be provided through use of the MSDS (if applicable) and the Tier Two Report, including the generic name for any chemical claimed as a trade secret. At the time a facility claims a trade secret, the facility must notify the EPA of its intention to claim such secrecy and provide justification for its position. The EPA will make a determination as to whether the claim of trade secrecy will be upheld. If a claim is not upheld, the information concerning the relevant chemical will be made available to the public, except for location information, which, as previously discussed, may, upon request, remain hidden from the public. Also, information concerning the properties and composition of a chemical must be made available to health professionals in those circumstances where such information is a medical necessity. For trade secret information to be released in the instances just described, the request for the information must be in writing and accompanied with a written confidentiality agreement that contains confirmation that the information will be used only for the specified purpose and will not be generally disclosed.

ENFORCEMENT

Like most other environmental acts, EPCRA includes *administrative, civil, and criminal penalties* for violations of the act. EPCRA's enforcement provisions vary slightly from those in other acts because persons and entities in addition to the EPA and citizens with standing are permitted to bring enforcement actions. SERCs and LEPCs are permitted to bring such actions, as well. SERCs and LEPCs are authorized to bring civil actions against facilities that fail to participate properly in the emergency planning process, fail to designate a facility representative and/or notify the SERC or LEPC who the representative is, or fail to provide required information in a timely manner. If the SERC or LEPC is successful in its action, the court may impose civil penalties as outlined in EPCRA. Following are two recent cases dealing with civil penalties under EPCRA.

CASE LAW

WOODCREST MANUFACTURING, INC. V. U.S. ENVIRONMENTAL PROTECTION AGENCY, 114 F. SUPP. 2D 775 (N.D. IN 1999).[1]

SUMMARY OF CASE: The manufacturer of children's toys sued the EPA, alleging procedural defects in a civil penalty case under EPCRA.

Judge Sharp delivered the opinion of the Court.

In 1986, Congress passed EPCRA, largely as a response to the disaster in Bhopal India. . . . The Act required reporting of the use of certain hazardous chemicals to the EPA and to local officials and required local officials to have an emergency plan to deal with hazardous chemical releases. Companies subject to the chapter were to notify the State emergency response commission that they were subject to the requirements of the chapter no later than seven months after October 17, 1986. . . . The statute is specific about the information companies must report and the form it is to take so that communities can formulate emergency response plans.

Many small businesses were unaware of the existence of the new reporting requirements, sometimes with costly results. On May 4, 1992, an EPA inspector contacted . . . Woodcrest, a small children's toy manufacturer in Peru, Indiana, about its compliance with the statute. The inspector came out and determined that Woodcrest used several chemicals in quantities above the reporting thresholds and was therefore obligated to file the annual reports. Woodcrest alleges that it did not file the reports because it was unaware of the reporting requirement and made a good faith effort to come into compliance as soon as possible. . . . On June 23, 1992, Woodcrest sent all of the requested documents to the EPA for the three years it had failed to report. . . . Woodcrest has filed timely reports each year from 1992 to the present. Woodcrest heard nothing further from the EPA until it filed an administrative complaint January 23, 1996, asking for a civil penalty of $27,000, due to Woodcrest's failure to file the 1990 Form R reports.

Woodcrest contested the amount of the civil penalty and attempted to work with the EPA on its own. . . . [T]he ALJ [administrative law judge] ruled in favor of the EPA on June 13, 1997, finding that Woodcrest had admitted it was liable, and that a $27,000 penalty was appropriate. Woodcrest appealed to the Environmental Appeals Board (the "Board"), which affirmed the ALJ's ruling, but reduced the penalty to $24,840 based on Woodcrest's acknowledged cooperation during the 1992 inspection. Woodcrest then initiated this action alleging a number of procedural deficiencies in the EPA's handling of the matter. . . .

In EPCRA, Congress made clear its intent to allow the judicial review for any party against whom the EPA assessed a civil penalty for violation of the reporting requirements. Because Congress did not specify a standard of review in the statute, the EPA's decision is reviewed under the standard set out in the Administrative Procedure Act. . . . Under this provision, agency action should be sustained unless it is "arbitrary and capricious, an abuse of discretion, or otherwise not in accordance with the law." A decision is arbitrary and capricious if "the agency has relied on factors which Congress has not intended it to consider, entirely failed to consider an important aspect of the problem, offered an explanation for its decision that runs counter to the evidence before the agency, or is so implausible that it could not be ascribed to a difference in view or the product of agency expertise." . . . The court is not empowered to substitute its judgment for that of the agency.

Congress set out severe penalties in EPCRA for a company required to report under the reporting provisions that fails to do so, as much as $25,000 for each violation. The statute goes on to say that each day the company fails to file the required reports is an additional violation. Obviously, an unsuspecting company can accumulate enormous fines in a relatively short period of time. Woodcrest does not seem to understand that in 1992, when it discovered that it was required to report under EPCRA, it was already subject to civil penalties for each day that it had failed to file the required forms. Even if it filed the Form R's for 1988, 1989, and 1990 in 1992, when it became aware of the violation, the late filings would not have cut off its liability for the fines. Its good faith efforts to comply with the statute would only have been a factor allowing the EPA to reduce its fines. The fact that the EPA inspector may have led them to believe that they were in compliance with the statute and that there would be no consequences for their failure to report on time does not get them over the initial hurdle that their reports were not filed on time. They are caught by the maxim that ignorance of the law is no excuse.

Why the EPA chose to do nothing about the violations until 1996, and then to ask for a civil penalty of $27,000 from a company that had acted in good faith and made every effort to comply with the law for four years, is baffling. The fact remains, however, that Woodcrest violated the reporting statute and could have been fined a much higher amount, especially if the EPA had filed its assessment two years earlier, before it was time barred for the 1988 and 1989 violations.

Even if this court accepted all of Woodcrest's allegations as true . . . it would still not solve [Woodcrest's] problem that it did in fact violate the reporting statute for several years and is therefore subject to a civil penalty. . . . In spite of their good faith efforts to correct the violation, they are still subject to the civil penalties of the statute. . . .

While this Court might question the soundness of the EPA's decision to go after a company like Woodcrest after so many years of compliance, especially since this suit is likely to cost the EPA much more than they will collect in fines, it is still sadly within the discretion of the EPA to do so. In fact, this case has all the earmarks of federal bureaucratic overreaching.

There is no basis on which this court can grant the relief sought by [Woodcrest], and such is now denied. Judgment shall enter accordingly and each party shall bear its own costs. ■

QUESTIONS

1. Do you agree with the Court's decision to uphold the penalty in this case? Why or why not?
2. Why do you think the Court commented that the case had the "earmarks of federal bureaucratic overreaching"?

CASE LAW

STEELTECH, LTD. V. EPA, 273 F.3D 652 (6TH CIR. 2001).[2]

SUMMARY OF CASE: Manufacturer of metal casings sought judicial review of an EPA decision to assess civil penalties under EPCRA for manufacturer's failure to timely report use of toxic chemicals.

Judge Moore delivered the opinion of the Court.

Steeltech appeals the district court's affirmance of the civil penalty imposed by [the] EPA. . . . Steeltech has not contested its liability under EPCRA, a strict liability statute; instead, Steeltech contends that the civil penalty assessed by the EPA is excessive because the agency failed to give due consideration to the mitigating circumstances surrounding Steeltech's failure to file reports. The ALJ calculated the civil penalty by means of the Environmental Response Policy (ERP), a statement of general policy rather than a rule. Steeltech's argument is that the ALJ applied the ERP as though it were a rule, however, and that the $61,736 civil penalty imposed is excessive because Steeltech's EPCRA violations were of low gravity and caused by the firm's lack of awareness of its reporting obligations. . . . [W]e are unable to conclude that the EPA acted arbitrarily or capriciously in the present case.

. . . Steeltech manufactures iron, nickel, chromium, and cobalt-based alloy casings. Nickel, chromium, and cobalt are chemicals identified as "toxic" by federal law and thus subject to the reporting requirements of the EPCRA. Despite processing substantial quantities of these chemicals in the calendar years 1988, 1989, 1990, 1992, and 1993, Steeltech failed to file timely reports (the Form Rs required under the EPCRA) for these years and chemicals. Steeltech's failure to file timely Form Rs for the years 1988–1990 for nickel and chromium came to the attention of both Steeltech and the EPA when the EPA conducted a consensual inspection of Steeltech's facility in February 1992. Steeltech officials filed the necessary Form Rs for the years 1988–1992 the day after the inspection.

The EPA then filed an administrative complaint against Steeltech based on its failure to file timely Form Rs. . . . A hearing on the amount of the civil penalty to be assessed against Steeltech was held before [the ALJ]. . . . [T]he greater part of [the] testimony concerned Steeltech's lack of awareness of the corporation's obligation to file Form Rs under the EPCRA.

[T]he ALJ assessed a civil penalty against Steeltech. . . . Although the statute authorized a maximum possible civil penalty of $225,000 for these . . . counts, the EPA calculated an initial civil penalty of $74,736. [H]owever, the ALJ adjusted the civil penalty downward for a variety of reasons and assessed a civil penalty of $61,736. This is the amount at issue in the present case. . . . The ALJ carefully applied the ERP to the facts of this present case [in] arriving at the civil penalty assessed.

Steeltech argues that the agency acted arbitrarily and capriciously in applying the ERP to the present case at all. Steeltech's argument boils down to this: Although it admits liability for failing to comply with EPCRA, Steeltech argues that it should escape significant penalties for its multiple violations of EPCRA because, in the first analysis, all it did was fail to file some forms, and, moreover, it failed to do so only because it lacked knowledge of the law. Steeltech argues that, rather than apply the ERP, the EPA should have assessed a civil penalty somewhere in the amount of $10,000.

The ALJ . . . specifically rejected Steeltech's argument that "the ERP should not be utilized at all in calculating the penalties" and gave detailed reasons for applying the ERP. . . . [T]hus, in answer to Steeltech's argument that it was at "the other end of the spectrum" from the "most recalcitrant violator" of EPCRA, for example, the ALJ emphasized that "EPCRA is a strict liability statute; 'intent' is not an element," and that the ends of the statute are frustrated by every failure to report, irrespective of culpability. Thus, the ALJ concluded that Steeltech's lack of culpability was not a reason for departing from the ERP-recommended penalty, especially since the strict liability nature of the statute was intended to "strongly discourage ignorance of EPCRA." . . .

For these reasons, we affirm the judgment of the district court. ■

QUESTION

1. Do you think EPCRA should be a "strict liability" statute? Why or why not?

As with CERCLA, EPCRA provides for the imposition of criminal penalties for a knowing failure to report a release as required or for providing false or misleading information. [42 U.S.C. secs. 9603(b) and 11045(b)(4)] Conviction brings with it the possibility of prison and/or severe fines.

Any citizen can file a civil action if a facility fails to follow certain mandatory reporting requirements pursuant to EPCRA. A SERC or LEPC can use the same provisions to seek the same results—compliance with EPCRA reporting requirements. The administrative penalties associated with such violations accrue by the day and can be very high. Those civil penalties get even higher pursuant to EPCRA when a facility violates EPCRA provisions repeatedly.

Lastly, EPCRA allows the EPA to assess civil penalties for violations of EPCRA provisions by imposing administrative orders or by bringing civil suits to enforce compliance.

The EPA can use its authority to seek a judicial order mandating compliance with EPCRA provisions.

ENVIRONMENTAL LAW PROFESSIONAL PROFILE

Ms. Carol A. Tomaszewski

How is your job related to environmental law?

I work for the Arapahoe County Sheriff's Office and am responsible for SARA Title III compliance within our Emergency Response Area. My job involves working with business owners and managers to assist them with any questions they may have about SARA Title III compliance, working on the Emergency Response Plan, entering all of the required data into our SARA Title III computer system, making sure we comply with reporting requirements, keeping the minutes from meetings of the Local Emergency Planning Committee (LEPC), keeping current with local and national situations that might call for implementation of an Emergency Operations Plan, and much more.

What is your favorite part of your job?

I enjoy meeting and working with people most of all. I work on a daily basis with business owners/managers. I am in contact with fire agencies and assist them in meeting their needs regarding the SARA Title III software. And I work with the Sheriff's Environmental Crimes Unit to discuss the implications of a crime scene, incident, fire, or spill and the mitigation of the hazardous materials or chemical gas in the air.

This job is a constant learning experience, so it's never boring. I attend classes and seminars regarding the Emergency Preparedness and Community Right-to-Know Act (EPCRA), terrorist threats, and what the impacts might be in case of a natural or man-made disaster or terrorist attack. Pursuant to the EPCRA provisions concerning Emergency Response Plans, information required for the response plans is now included in the Emergency Response Plan required by the Department of Homeland Security. I enjoy working with the agencies in the region regarding training, sharing of information, and working together in disaster simulations. It never ceases to amaze me that something that started out as a simple Community Right-to-Know Act has now been incorporated into National Security and Response Plans!

We recently set up an Incident Command System for Katrina evacuees at the Colorado State Emergency Operations Center. I was fortunate to be part of the team and worked with the planning and communications divisions. It was a rewarding experience.

What duties do you perform in a typical day?

Every day I receive calls or e-mails regarding SARA Title III. These can be as simple as adding a chemical to the database or changing a phone number to assist a business in completing their application. I am usually working on a project for Emergency Management. We are currently updating the County Emergency Response Plan, including completely rewriting the "special needs" section (making sure those with disabilities or other special needs are accounted for and properly assisted in the event of a disaster). We have lists of resources and phone numbers in case such a need arises.

What is the most challenging part of your job?

Working on the various Emergency Response Plans and using all of the information and scenarios to come up with an all-inclusive plan for mitigation, preparedness, response, and recovery for all hazard incidents. The volume of detail necessary to "get it right" and the magnitude of the project are challenging to me.

(*continued*)

What advice do you have for paralegal students interested in working on EPCRA or environmental law issues?

Set up an internship at an agency that deals with environmental issues and environmental crimes, such as a fire agency or a law enforcement agency. Go out on actual Hazardous Materials (HAZMAT) calls. Learn firsthand how incidents are mitigated and talk with the person who will be writing the summons, whether it is a cleanup order or an actual criminal charge. Attend a SARA Title III workshop presented by the HAZMAT Team, attend a LEPC, and learn how to educate business owners/managers on their responsibilities related to proper storage and use of chemicals, including how to report their chemicals in accordance with SARA Title III reporting requirements.

Do you have any tips for success?

Learn and understand more than just the "law." Observe first responders, talk with the businesses, and study the administration of a SARA Title III website. It is important to know the law too, including what it takes to be compliant with EPCRA, from reporting chemicals and spills to knowing what needs to be in the Emergency Response Plan. Learn who has responsibility for each step in the mitigation, evacuation, and cleanup of an environmental incident.

Are special skills required for your job?

This job requires excellent communication skills and a lot of specific education in how to comply with SARA Title III reporting requirements. It is also important to be able to deal with complex information and situations, including how to respond to various types of environmental incidents from a small spill to a huge terrorist attack.

What other information or thoughts would you like to share with paralegal students interested in environmental law?

I believe the environment and protection of the environment is the responsibility of everyone. We have a beautiful world! Making people aware of the consequences of thoughtless acts and teaching people how all of us working together can keep the environment clean and safe for generations to come are noble goals. Environmental law is a means to enforce this process, and it is wonderful to be part of the solution rather than part of the problem!

Carol Tomaszewski works in the Arapahoe County Sheriff's Office in Centennial, Colorado. Ms. Tomaszewski has held her position since 2002. Prior to working for the sheriff's office, Ms. Tomaszewski worked primarily in cash management at various firms in Colorado.

SUMMARY

EPCRA was enacted to better inform and protect communities by requiring local emergency preparedness programs and facilitating dissemination of information within local communities concerning hazardous chemicals present at facilities within those communities. Provisions of SARA are the primary means by which the goals of EPCRA are realized. Emergency planning components included SERCs and LEPCs. Emergency Response Plans also are mandated. In the event that a release of a RQ of an EHS takes place, a notification process is initiated, ensuring that emergency responders are aware of the incident and of all substances within which they may come into contact. The community right-to-know requirements of EPCRA include MSDS sheets; Tier One and Tier Two Reports; and, if appropriate, a Tier Two Confidential Location Information Sheet. A reporting form, the Toxic Chemical Release Inventory Reporting Form (Form R), requires the provision of comprehensive information, supplemented by the information required by the PPA. Trade secrets are protected to a degree by EPCRA. Those communities where the provisions of EPCRA have resulted in emergency responders knowing about releases of hazardous substances and knowing the nature and quantities of the substances released can feel better about their ability to remain safe in the event of an incident.

KEY TERMS

- Continuous release
- Emergency release
- Emergency Response Plan
- Extremely hazardous substances (EHSs)
- Local Emergency Planning Committee (LEPC)
- Local fire department (LFD)
- Material Safety Data Sheets (MSDS)
- National Response Center (NRC)
- State Emergency Response Commission (SERC)
- Threshold planning quantity (TPQ)
- Tier One Report
- Tier Two Confidential Location Information Sheet
- Tier Two Report
- Toxic Chemical Release Inventory Reporting Form (Form R)
- Transportation-related release

REVIEW QUESTIONS AND HANDS-ON ACTIVITIES

1. How do SERC and LEPC interact pursuant to the provisions of EPCRA?
2. Define the term *extremely hazardous substances.*
3. What is the procedure for notification concerning a release?
4. What information is on a MSDS?
5. Describe the differences between a Tier One and Tier Two Report.
6. What is the purpose of a Toxic Chemical Inventory Reporting Form (Form R)?
7. Locate and read the Emergency Response Plan for your local community. Does it seem sufficient as an emergency planning tool? Why or why not?
8. Locate the SERC for your community. Obtain and review a MSDS sheet submitted by a local company. Would the information on the sheet assist in an emergency? Why or why not?
9. Review President Clinton's executive order in Appendix E. How does an executive order differ from a statute? From what legal source does a president derive his authority to issue an executive order?
10. Overall, does EPCRA satisfy a community's right to know what chemicals are being stored in the community and where they are stored? What other major types of information that are not covered by EPCRA might be useful to a community in an emergency situation?

HELPFUL WEBSITES

http://www.epa.gov/tri (EPA, Toxics Release Inventory (TRI) Program)

http://www.chemicalspill.org (Emergency Planning for Chemical Spills)

http://www.floridadisaster.org/cps/SERC/EPCRA.htm
(Florida Division of Emergency Management)

ENDNOTES

1. *Woodcrest Manufacturing, Inc. v. EPA,* 114 F. Supp. 2d 775 (N.D. IN 1999).
2. *Steeltech Ltd. v. EPA,* 273 F.3d 652 (6th Cir. 2001).

CHAPTER 11

NATURAL RESOURCES LAW: HOT TOPICS

When a typical citizen of the United States thinks of environmental law, he or she is most likely to think, not of the CAA, NEPA, EPCRA, or any of the other federal acts described in earlier chapters of this text. Instead, that person is more likely to think of the Endangered Species Act (ESA), which is a federal act that addresses the type of environmentalism that is seen almost every day in newspapers and magazines and on television news. The ESA, the Marine Mammal Protection Act (MMPA), and other acts that concern "natural resources" are the type of legislation that have caught the attention of the news media and, therefore, piqued the interest of people not only in the United States but also around the world.

LEARNING OBJECTIVES

After studying this chapter, the reader should be able to

- describe the types of laws that are considered natural resources laws.
- describe the Wilderness Act of 1964.
- explain the basic principles of the Marine Mammal Protection Act (MMPA) and the acts created by its amendments.
- list the basic energy sources considered to be environmentally appropriate.
- describe global warming and what is believed to cause the phenomenon.

Natural resources law encompasses land, fish, wildlife, biota, air, water, groundwater, drinking water supplies, and other resources belonging to, managed by, held in trust by, appertaining to, or otherwise controlled by the United States, any state or local government, or any foreign government (see 40 C.F.R.).

Environmental laws addressing natural resources are divided by category and include conservation (Title 16, U.S.C.), international environment and natural resources (22 U.S.C. sec. 2151), tropical forests (22 U.S.C. § 2151p-1), endangered species (22 U.S.C. sec. 2151q), prospecting (Title 30, U.S.C.), public property (Title 40, U.S.C.), natural resources and public health (Title 42, U.S.C.), and public lands (Title 43, U.S.C.).

In addition, energy laws and regulations that govern the conversion of natural resources into energy also fall into the category of natural resources law (see Title 42, U.S.C., Title 16, U.S.C., Title 30, U.S.C., and Title 10, C.F.R.).

PUBLIC LANDS AND WILDERNESS AREAS

The management of public lands in the United States is accomplished by dividing such lands into the following four classes:

Classes of Public Lands

- General public lands (managed by the Bureau of Land Management (BLM))
- National forests (managed by the U.S. Forest Service)
- National wildlife refuges (managed by the U.S. Fish & Wildlife Service (USFWS))
- National parks (managed by the National Park Service)

Wilderness areas (lands identified through criteria set forth in the Wilderness Act of 1964) can be found in any of the above-noted classes.

multiple uses The federal Bureau of Land Management (BLM) and the Forest Service are instructed to manage lands entrusted to their care for multiple uses that will best meet the needs of the American people.

The BLM and the Forest Service are instructed to manage the land entrusted to their care for **multiple uses** that will "best meet the needs of the American public." [Multiple Use, Sustained Yield Act, 16 U.S.C. sec. 531(a); Federal Land Policy and Management Act of 1976 (FLPMA), 43 U.S.C. sec. 1701 *et seq.*; National Forest Management Act of 1976, 16 U.S.C. sec.1600 *et seq.*] Many times, the "multiple uses" management has given priority to economic uses such as logging, grazing, and mineral development over other values such as wildlife and wilderness preservation. For only one class, the National Wildlife Refuges, has Congress stated that the dominant use of such lands is to be the conservation of wildlife. Other uses are to be allowed only if they are "compatible" with the designated dominant use.

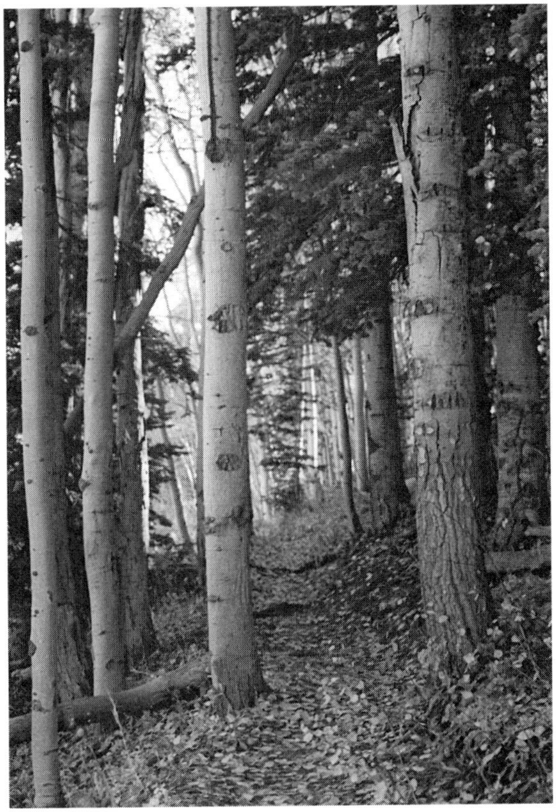

The management of two classes of lands, national parks and national wilderness areas, is extremely constrained. Managers of national parks are required "to conserve the scenery and the natural and historic objects and wildlife therein and to provide for the enjoyment of the same in such manner and by such means as will leave them unimpaired for the enjoyment of future generations." (16 U.S.C. sec.1) Managers of wilderness areas must preserve the "primeval character and influence" and "natural condition." The use of motorized equipment, permanent roads, and commercial enterprises on such lands is generally prohibited. [16 U.S.C. sec. 1131(c)]

Many other federal laws relate to the use of government lands. Pursuant to the Mining Law of 1872, citizens have the right to discover, develop, and patent hardrock mineral deposits on public lands unless the lands have been exempted from such claims. The Mineral Leasing Act of 1920 allows citizens to lease minerals.

REVIEW
National Wildlife Refuges are the only class of land for which the dominant use is stated to be the conservation of wildlife. For all other classes, economic uses have been given priority over wildlife and wilderness preservation.

FEATURE

Wilderness Act of 1964

"If future generations are to remember us with gratitude rather than contempt, we must leave them more than the miracles of technology. We must leave them a glimpse of the world as it was in the beginning, not just after we got through with it."

—President of the United States Lyndon B. Johnson on signing the Wilderness Act on September 3, 1964

In 2004, the country celebrated the fortieth anniversary of the National Wilderness Act. (16 U.S.C. secs. 1131-1136) This act was intended to protect some land within the United States in its pristine condition. The act states that it is intended

> . . . to assure that an increasing population, accompanied by expanding settlement and growing mechanization, does not occupy and modify all areas within the United States and its possessions, leaving no lands designated for preservation and protection in their natural condition. . . . [sec.2(a)]

The act creates the National Wilderness Preservation System ("System"). Upon the act's enactment, all national forest areas already classified as wilderness, wild, or canoe were automatically included in the System. The Secretary of the Interior was directed by the act to examine every roadless area of 5,000 acres or more and every roadless island within the national wildlife refuge and national park systems by September 1974 to determine whether those areas qualified for inclusion in the System. Some national forest lands were included in the act upon its enactment, and the act directs the Secretary of Agriculture to examine forest lands and determine whether they are "primitive" and therefore appropriate for inclusion in the System. In addition to the lands placed in the System at the inception of the act, later included by either the Secretary of the Interior or the Secretary of Agriculture, the act states that gifts or bequests of land within or adjacent to wilderness areas may be accepted for inclusion in the System. At present, more than 100 million acres have been included in the System. Whatever department or agency had jurisdiction over an area immediately prior to its inclusion in the System is the department or agency that continues to manage the land once it becomes part of the System. Consequently, the hundred million acres is managed by the U.S. Forest Service, the BLM, the USFWS, and the National Park Service.

What is considered a wilderness area? The act defines **wilderness** as follows:

> . . . in contrast with those areas where man and his own works dominate the landscape . . . an area where the earth and its community of life are untrammeled by man, where man himself is a visitor who does not remain; an area of undeveloped Federal land retaining its primeval character and influence, without permanent improvement or human habitation, which is protected and managed so as to preserve its natural conditions and which (1) generally appears to have been affected primarily by the forces of nature, with the imprint of man's work substantially unnoticeable; (2) has outstanding opportunities for solitude or a primitive and unconfined type of recreation; (3) has at least five thousand acres of land or is of sufficient size as to make practicable its preservation and use in an unimpaired condition; and (4) may also contain ecological, geological, or other features of scientific, educational, scenic or historical value.

wilderness Defined in the Wilderness Act of 1964 as being, *inter alia*, land that (1) generally appears to have been affected primarily by the forces of nature, with the imprint of man's work substantially unnoticeable; (2) has outstanding opportunities for solitude or a primitive and unconfined type of recreation; (3) has at least five thousand acres of land or is of sufficient size as to make practicable its preservation and use in an unimpaired condition; and (4) may also contain ecological, geological, or other features of scientific, educational, scenic or historical value.

Once an area has been included in the System, the uses of that land are extremely limited, with the intention of maintaining the wilderness character of the property. With few exceptions, no roads or permanent commercial enterprises are allowed on wilderness lands. Temporary roads, motor vehicles, motorized equipment, landing of aircraft, structures, and installations are allowed only if they are necessary to the management of the land. When 70,000 acres of the San Juan National Forest in southwestern Colorado was burned (Missionary Ridge Fire), the wilderness program manager of the U.S. Forest Service Rocky Mountain Region had to decide whether to allow helicopters to drop hay onto burned slopes to stabilize the slopes. The program manager ended up allowing use of sand bags filled with dirt and downed trees as a substitute to the intended helicopter drop, thus minimizing the intrusion of aircraft into the area, which is part of the Weminuche Wilderness.

If prior to designation as a wilderness area, motorboats and/or aircraft were used on the land, such use may continue after designation, with strict controls. Other activities, including prospecting for minerals or other resources, may be carried out on wilderness lands as long as the activities are compatible with the preservation of the wilderness nature of the land. Access rights may be granted to private citizens or states owning land completely surrounded by national forest wilderness areas, or the land can be exchanged for other federally owned land in the same state having the same approximate value. A limited number of permits are given out to hikers and

Leave No Trace Visitors to a protected wilderness are required to leave nothing of themselves behind in the wilderness.

campers each year allowing guided tours of some of the more pristine wilderness areas. The lucky people who win such a privilege are told they must leave absolutely nothing of themselves behind in the wilderness area, including bodily waste or trash of any kind. This is known as the **Leave No Trace** rule of wilderness utilization. Even these carefully controlled recreational uses are seen as "consumptive" by some people—similar to logging, mining, or grazing.

In addition to the uses described, wilderness areas have become some of the most important areas for the natural filtering and cleansing of water, which is then used to supply many of the municipal water systems in the western United States, where water is in short supply and, therefore, a very valuable commodity.

As noted earlier, more than 100 million acres have been designated as wilderness over the past 40 years. The act continues to be a mechanism whereby pristine lands are preserved by inclusion in the System. In 2002 alone, Congress designated more than 500,000 acres of federal lands in California, Colorado, Nevada, and South Dakota as wilderness. In California, the Big Sur Wilderness and Conservation Act of 2002 added 56,880 acres to the System. In Colorado, 14,000 acres were designated the James Peak Wilderness area and adjacent "protection area." The Indian Peaks Wilderness Area was also expanded by 3,000 acres. By virtue of the Clark County Conservation of Public Land and Natural Resources Act of 2002, Nevada designated more than 440,000 acres of wilderness in the Mojave Desert region of southern Nevada. South Dakota benefited by a 3,600-acre addition to the Black Elk Wilderness Area as part of the 2002 Emergency Supplemental Defense Appropriations Act. Why would wilderness designation be part of a "Defense Appropriations Act"? The designation was part of a settlement that allowed fuel to be extracted from part of the Black Hills National Forest in a different part of South Dakota.

The Wilderness Act is actively supported by a number of citizen entities, including The Wilderness Society. An organization called Forest Service Employees for Environmental Ethics (FSEEE) promotes the ethical and environmentally appropriate use of the forests and wilderness areas of the United States. Enthusiasm for preserving wilderness areas continues to thrive in the United States; and every citizen can monitor the annual progress of this program since the Wilderness Act requires that, at the opening of each session of Congress, the Secretaries of Agriculture and Interior shall jointly report to the president for transmission to Congress the status of the wilderness system. ■

PROTECTION OF FISH, BIRDS, AND WILDLIFE

As with the federal protections for public lands, federal acts protect other wildlife resources, including, for example, the ESA, the Migratory Bird Treaty Act (MBTA), and the MMPA. The chapter will address only briefly some of this national resources legislation and provide the framework for further study should you so desire.

Endangered Species Act (ESA)

One of the most commonly known natural resources laws is the Endangered Species Act (ESA). Until the late 1960s, there were no significant federal programs designed for the protection of wildlife except the MBTA (see *Missouri v. Holland*[1]). The Endangered Species Preservation Act of 1966 was essentially the first attempt by the federal government to protect the wildlife of the United States from harm. This act did not contain regulatory provisions; instead, it authorized the purchase of appropriate habitat for threatened species. Much like the recovery actions taken in the wake of the *Exxon Valdez* oil spill in Alaska in 1989 (see Chapter 3), the use of land purchases to enhance the habitats of species under duress is thought to be one way to mitigate the effects of humanity's encroachment on the natural habitat of wildlife.

In 1969, the Endangered Species Conservation Act was passed, giving continued authority for the purchase of appropriate habitat and prohibiting the importation of species threatened with worldwide extinction. Finally, in 1973, the ESA was enacted (16 U.S.C. sec. 1531, *et seq.*) This act has laid the foundation for most of the wildlife protection activities with which you are probably familiar. The ESA is intended to be comprehensive in scope and provide a wide range of protection for endangered species. As part of this new, broad protection philosophy, the ESA is designed to protect both the species and their habitats.

endangered species Any species that is in danger of extinction throughout all or a significant portion of its range.

threatened species Any species that is likely to become an endangered species within the foreseeable future throughout all or a significant portion of its range.

What is an **endangered species**? As defined in the ESA, an endangered species is "any species which is in danger of extinction throughout all or a significant portion of its range." [sec. 3(6)] A **threatened species** is defined as "any species that is likely to become an endangered species within the foreseeable future throughout all or a significant portion of its range." [sec. 3(20)] While the ESA identifies endangered and threatened species separately, in practice, not much distinction has been made in decisions concerning the safeguards imposed to protect both species categories.

The procedure set forth in the ESA to identify both endangered and threatened species involves either the Secretary of Commerce (who oversees the National Marine Fisheries Service (NMFS)) or the Secretary of the Interior (who oversees the USFWS). Under the ESA, a species can be placed on the Endangered Species List only following a procedure set forth to ensure a conservative approach to the listing of species. A petition for listing a species must be filed by a citizen under the Administrative Procedure Act (APA). The appropriate Secretary then has 90 days to decide whether a substantial case has been made for listing and up to a year to decide whether to proceed with the listing. [16 U.S.C. sec. 1533(b)(3)] In making the decision whether to list a species, the Secretary is required to rely only on the best scientific and commercial data available. In making the decision as to the **critical habitat** of a species that is listed, the standard used is the "best scientific data available . . . taking into consideration the economic impact, and any other relevant impact, of specifying any particular area as critical habitat." [sec. 4(b)] The compilation of species that have been determined to meet the criteria set forth in the ESA and thus be protected is called the **endangered species list**.

critical habitat The habitat determined to be vital to the survival of an endangered species.

endangered species list A list of all endangered species.

All federal agencies are required to implement programs to conserve endangered and threatened species. [sec. 7(a)(1)] The ESA requires such agencies to ensure that their actions are "not likely to jeopardize the continued existence of any endangered species or threatened species or result in the destruction or adverse modification" of such species' critical habitat.

As previously stated, the ESA's intention is to be conservative in the listing of species. This is due to the significant ramifications of any new listing. Mistakes have occasionally been made by listing a species too soon, only to discover later that it may not be a distinct species at all. (One example is the Preble's meadow jumping mouse, which since its listing, has been the subject of much debate because there is evidence, after much scientific study, that it is simply a variety of another common mouse.).

ASSIGNMENT

Find out what species are presently being considered for inclusion on the endangered species list. Have any species been removed from the list in the past five years? If so, which one(s)?

The ESA prohibits the "taking" of species on the endangered species list unless an **incidental take permit** has been issued pursuant to an approved **habitat conservation plan**. [sec. 10(a)] The definition of *taking* under the ESA prohibits actions that "harass, harm, pursue, hunt, shoot, wound, kill, trap, capture or collect, or attempt to engage in any such conduct" with respect to any endangered animal species. (Under the ESA, plant species are not protected to the same degree as animal species.) [Secs. 9(a)(1)(B) and (C)] As noted, the definition of *taking* includes the term *harming*. *Harming* has been very broadly defined through regulations to include any modification of habitat if that modification "actually kills or injures wildlife." Findings in subsequent case law have not required that wildlife carcasses actually be found to demonstrate that the species has been harmed. Courts have found it sufficient to show that the habitat modification has significantly impaired essential behavior patterns (see *Defenders of Wildlife v. Administrator, Environmental Protection Agency*[2]).

incidental take permit
A permit issued pursuant to the Endangered Species Act (ESA) allowing the limited taking of an endangered species from its critical habitat.

habitat conservation plan
A plan designed to protect an endangered species from inappropriate taking.

Naturally, the expansive nature of this definition has pitted environmentalists against land developers. Pursuant to typical nonenvironmental laws and regulations, landowners and developers have the right to develop property within the limitations of the land use regulations enacted by a state or local government. Such regulations usually relate to the type of land use being proposed and whatever public health, safety, and welfare conditions are placed on that type of land use. The additional layer of review and limitation imposed by the ESA on development activities has been the subject of much discussion and litigation.

In addition to conflict, the ESA requirements have also resulted in widespread cooperation in areas where endangered species are found.

Local governmental entities have banded together to create appropriate habitat conservation plans. One such example is the Natural Community Conservation Planning Program (NCCP) utilized by 5 counties, 59 local governments, federal and state governments, and private landowners to preserve the southern California coastal sage scrub habitat. Private sector developers have worked with the U.S. Department of the Interior to create programs that balance the interests of developers with concerns about the protection of endangered species. One such program is the **Safe Harbors program**. This program allows developers, in exchange for their agreement, to develop their property in a more environmentally sensitive manner that has the possibility of attracting endangered species and to retain the eventual right to develop their property in a manner that is acceptable to all concerned. Not only private sector developers, though, have found that the ESA creates roadblocks to the completion of their proposed projects.

Safe Harbors program
This program, which is part of the ESA, permits developers, in exchange for their agreement, to develop their property in a more environmentally sensitive manner that has the possibility of attracting endangered species and to retain the eventual right to develop their property in a manner that is acceptable to all concerned.

One case under the ESA with which many people are familiar is *TVA v. Hill*.[3] In 1967, the federal government began construction on the Tellico Dam on the Little Tennessee River in Tennessee. Although construction was temporarily halted through a suit pursuant to NEPA, an EIS was eventually completed and construction continued in earnest on the project. Four months later the ESA was enacted, and an enterprising student from the University of Tennessee Law School Clinic, Hiram Hill, sued under the ESA, contending that the dam was being built on a river where the snail darter fish lived. After passage of the ESA, the snail darter, a previously unknown species of perch, was placed on the endangered species list. The snail darter is a 3-inch, tan-colored fish that numbers only between 10,000 and 15,000. The Secretary of the Interior determined that the snail darter subsisted almost entirely on snails that require a clean gravel substrate to exist. The Secretary further found that "[t]he proposed impoundment of water behind the proposed Tellico Dam would result in total destruction of the snail darter's habitat" since the snail darter lives only in the portion of the Little Tennessee River that would be completely inundated by the reservoir created by the Tellico Dam. Consequently, the area affected by the Tellico Dam was deemed critical habitat of the snail darter. [40 Fed. Reg. 47505-47506] Hiram Hill took this finding by the Secretary and used it in his suit, contending that the final completion and use of the Tellico Dam would constitute a violation of the ESA since it would adversely affect the critical habitat of the snail darter.

One of the problems with Hill's suit was that construction of the dam had essentially been completed by the time the case was heard; and there was a significant question as to whether the ESA applied to completed projects. In other words, there was some concern among the environmentalists that the Court would consider the case moot because of the degree to which the dam had been completed. The Justices of the Supreme Court agreed to hear the case, however. At the oral argument on the case, the federal government tried to show that the snail darter was insignificant in light of the great benefit the dam would provide. On the other side, the environmentalists argued that the river had already been dammed in several other places and that there was no compelling necessity for the Tellico Dam to become operational since it was not needed to provide energy or any other significant benefit other than backing up water to another reservoir. The Supreme Court ruled in favor of the environmentalists, finding, *inter alia*, that

> One would be hard pressed to find a statutory provision whose terms were any plainer than those in §7 of the Endangered Species Act. Its very words affirmatively command all federal agencies "to insure that actions *authorized, funded,* or *carried out* by them do not *jeopardize* the continued existence" of an endangered species or "*result* in the destruction of modification of habitat of such species . . ." 16 U.S.C. §1536 (emphasis added). This language admits of no exception. Nonetheless, petitioner [Tennessee Valley Authority] urges, as do the dissenters, that the Act cannot reasonably be interpreted as applying to a federal project which was well under way when Congress passed the Endangered Species Act of 1973. To sustain that position, however, we would be forced to ignore the ordinary meaning of plain language. It has not been shown, for example, how TVA can close the gates of Tellico Dam without "carrying out" an action that has been "authorized" and "funded" by a federal agency. Nor can we understand how such action will "*insure*" that the snail darter's habitat is not disrupted. Accepting the Secretary's determinations, as we must, it is clear that TVA's proposed operation of the dam will have precisely the opposite effect, namely the *eradication* of an endangered species.
>
> Concededly, this view of the Act will produce results requiring the sacrifice of the anticipated benefits of the project and many millions of dollars in public funds. But examination of the

> language, history, and structure of the legislation under review here indicates beyond doubt that Congress intended endangered species to be afforded the highest of priorities . . . .
>
> . . . The plain intent of Congress in enacting this statute was to halt and reverse the trend toward species extinction, whatever the cost.
>
> Here we are urged to view the Endangered Species Act "reasonably," and hence shape a remedy "that accords with some modicum of common sense and the public weal." But is that our function? We have no expert knowledge on the subject of endangered species, much less do we have a mandate from the people to strike a balance of equities on the side of the Tellico Dam. Congress has spoken in the plainest of words, making it abundantly clear that the balance has been struck in favor of affording endangered species the highest of priorities . . . .

Thus, in that case, the ESA provided the protection to an endangered species, the snail darter, for which it was designed. Following the Supreme Court's decision in *TVA v. Hill,* Congress amended the ESA in 1978, 1979, and 1982, providing more guidance on exempted activities, but still retaining the stringent nature of the act's requirements.

Recent decisions concerning the ESA continue to uphold the authority of Congress to protect endangered species. In *GDF Realty Investments, Ltd. v. Norton,*[4] the U.S. Court of Appeals upheld application of the act to protect a very small category of wildlife: six species of invertebrates that were found only in two caves in Texas. Despite the small size of the species for which protection was sought, the Court found that the ESA "is a comprehensive program for the conservation of endangered and threatened species and the ecosystem upon which they depend." (326 F.3d at 641)

One of the interesting provisions of the act as amended creates a process for convening a committee of high-ranking government officials who have quite a bit of power to decide the fate of species. The broad range of power granted to this body has caused it to be nicknamed the **God Squad**. The committee may grant an exemption if it determines that there are no reasonable and prudent alternatives to a proposed federal action, that the action is in the public interest on a regional or national basis, and that the benefits of the action clearly outweigh the benefits of alternatives that do not jeopardize preservation of a species. This process of granting exemptions somewhat

God Squad A committee of high-ranking government officials who have the power to determine whether an exemption is granted to placing a species on the endangered species list.

mitigates the effect of the **no jeopardy rule** created by the strict provisions of the ESA. The name of this rule is taken from the provisions of the ESA which basically state that species protected by the act are to be placed in "no jeopardy" by the actions of federal agencies.

no jeopardy rule A phrase stating in common terms a rule in the ESA that no endangered or threatened species may be placed in jeopardy by the actions of a federal agency.

Another recent decision of note is *Gibbs v. Babbitt*.[5] In this case, the question was whether the ESA permitted a challenge to a regulation that limited the taking on private land of a population of red wolves that had been reintroduced on the land. The Court found that the taking of red wolves was an economic activity and that there was a sufficient substantial effect on commerce to uphold the constitutionality of the ESA. The Court noted that

> It would be perverse indeed if a species nearing extinction were found to be beyond Congress's power to protect while abundant species were subject to full federal regulatory power. Yet under the applicants' theory, the more endangered the species, the less authority Congress has to regulate the taking of it. According to this view, endangered species would lie beyond congressional protection because there are too few animals left to make a commercial difference. Such reasoning would eviscerate the comprehensive federal scheme for conserving endangered species and turn congressional judgment on its head.
>
> *Gibbs*, at p. 884

QUESTION
Has the creation of the God Squad undermined the goal of the ESA?

It is somewhat comforting to note that since the passage of the ESA and the listing of many endangered species, some of the species once placed on the list have recovered sufficiently to be removed from the list (delisted).

Other protections are in place to prohibit or regulate the commercial trade in endangered species. One such protection is the **Convention on International Trade in Endangered Species** (CITES, pronounced "sightees"). This Convention bans commercial trade in the most endangered species and severely regulates the trade in other less endangered species. This Convention has proved very difficult to enforce due to the fact that many poachers have become creative in "packaging" their product for shipping. As an example, even if a pair of crocodile shoes is intercepted in transit, it is very difficult, once the skin has been processed to make shoes, to determine the specific type of crocodile skin used to make the shoes. The success in prosecuting those who violate the Convention has come about primarily through the use of

Convention on International Trade in Endangered Species (CITES) An agreement intended to reduce the numbers of endangered species taken out of their critical habitat.

undercover law enforcement. Despite these protections, the high value of certain endangered species (such as elephants, rhinos, parrots, snowy white gyrfalcons, and grizzly bears) means they continue to be poached.

Marine Mammal Protection Act (MMPA)

Out of concern that certain species and populations of marine mammals were or were about to be in danger of depletion or extinction due to human activities, the MMPA (16 U.S.C. secs. 1631-1407) was enacted in 1972 as a means of requiring the federal government to conserve marine mammals. Congress declared that marine mammals are resources of great international significance from an aesthetic, recreational, and economic standpoint and should be protected and encouraged to develop to the extent possible in conjunction with sound resource management policies. The stated goal was to maintain the health and stability of the marine ecosystem and maintain an optimum marine mammal population within the capacity of the habitat.

The Departments of the Interior and Commerce were tasked with compliance with the MMPA. In a nutshell, the MMPA establishes a moratorium on the taking and importing of marine mammals and their by-products. The act also establishes procedures for obtaining a waiver of the moratorium and transfers management responsibility to the states. The act was amended in 1976, 1978, 1981, 1984, 1986, 1988, 1990, 1992, 1994, and 1997.

marine mammal Any mammal that is morphologically adapted to the marine environment (including sea otters and members of the orders Sirenia, Pinnepedia, and Cetacea) or that primarily inhabits the marine environment (such as the polar bear).

The act defines a **marine mammal** as "any mammal which is morphologically adapted to the marine environment (including sea otters and members of the orders *sirenia, pinnipedia* and *cetacea*), or primarily inhabits the marine environment (such as the polar bear)."

Mammals belonging to the order Sirenia are herbivorous mammals including the dugong and the manatee. The animals resemble the mythical "sirens" that look like women and, according the myths, lure mariners to their deaths by singing. These animals also are on the endangered species list.

pinnipeds From the Latin word *pinnipedia,* which means "feather or foot fin," these mammals include sea lions, seals, and walruses. They are protected by the Marine Mammal Protection Act (MMPA).

Members of the order Pinnipedia include seals, sea lions and fur seals, and walruses. These animals are called **pinnipeds** because the word *pinnipedia* translates from the Latin as "feather or fin foot." All of these animals have large finlike flippers. In addition to being protected under the MMPA, the Caribbean monk seal, Guadalupe fur seal, Hawaiian monk seal, Saimaa ringed seal from Finland, and Stellar sea lion also are on the endangered species list.

Cetaceans include whales, dolphins, and porpoises. Approximately 78 species of whales, dolphins, and porpoises are in this scientific order. Cetaceans have large heads; fishlike, nearly hairless bodies; and paddle-shaped forelimbs. Ten of these cetaceans are included on the endangered species list.

Cetacean A scientific order that includes whales, dolphins, and porpoises.

As indicated, the act prohibits, without a waiver, the "taking" of marine mammals. For purposes of this act, *taking* is defined as to "harass, hunt, capture or kill," or "attempt to harass, hunt, capture or kill" a marine mammal. Harassment of marine mammals also is prohibited, and *harassment* is defined as "an act of pursuit, torment or annoyance which has the potential to injure, or disturb by causing disruption of behavioral patterns, a marine mammal or marine mammal stock in the wild."

ASSIGNMENT

Search the Internet for an article about manatees. Are they recovering as a result of being protected by the ESA? What new protection measures are being studied?

In addition to prohibiting the taking or harassing of marine mammals, the act prohibits the taking or possession of a marine mammal product. Such products are described as "an item of merchandise which consists of, or is composed in whole or in part, of a marine mammal." Raw, dressed, or dyed fur or skin falls into this category, as do tusks, teeth, sexual organs, or any other part of a marine mammal.

Two amendments to the act in 1992 address particular problems related to marine mammals. The International Dolphin Conservation Act of 1992 is intended to "eliminate marine mammal mortality resulting from intentional encirclement of dolphins and other marine mammals in tuna purse-seine fisheries." Pursuant to this act, it is unlawful, among other things, to "sell or offer to sell, purchase, transport or ship tuna or a tuna product that is not dolphin safe."

The Marine Mammal Health and Stranding Response Act of 1992 requires the establishment of a program to "facilitate the collection and dissemination of reference data on marine mammals." In addition, strandings must be monitored, information must be collected on procedures for rescuing and rehabilitating stranded marine mammals, marine mammal tissue must be collected for analysis, and objective criteria must be developed for determining when a rehabilitated marine mammal is releasable in the wild. **Strandings** are defined as "an event in the wild in which a dead marine mammal is on a United States beach or shore, or in United States waters; or an alive marine mammal is on a United States beach or shore and either is unable to return to the water or is in need of apparent medical attention, or is in United States waters and unable to return to its natural habitat without assistance."

Stranding An event in the wild in which a dead marine mammal is on a U.S. beach or shore or in U.S. waters or an alive marine mammal is on a U.S. beach or shore and is unable to return to the water or is in need of apparent medical attention or is in U.S. waters and is unable to return to its natural habitat without assistance.

The original act built in waivers to the restrictions of the act for Indians, Aleut, and Eskimos (who live on the coast of the North Pacific Ocean), as long as any taking by such people was conducted for the sake of subsistence or for the purpose of creating and selling authentic native articles of handicraft and clothing. Procedures also exist whereby waivers can be obtained for takings for the sake of public display and scientific research.

The MMPA will continue to be amended and refined as more is learned about the human dangers to marine mammals. In the meantime, the progress in protecting these animals can be monitored through the annual report that is made to Congress at the opening of each session. Also, citizens groups such as Greenpeace monitor the activities of those who hunt marine mammals. You may have seen pictures of Greenpeace vessels placed in the path of commercial whaling ships in an effort to keep whales from being taken.

FEATURE

Greenpeace

Greenpeace is one of many environmental organizations formed by citizens to address environmental concerns. Founded in 1971 by a small group of environmental activists, Greenpeace began its first mission, which was to call attention to underground nuclear testing being performed by the United States on Amchitka, an island off the west coast of Alaska. Amchitka was the only home of 3,000 endangered sea otters; bald eagles, peregrine falcons, and other species also lived on the small island. The Greenpeace founders were not successful in reaching Amchitka before the nuclear bomb was detonated, but their expedition did succeed in gaining the attention of the U.S. public. Eventually, nuclear testing on Amchitka ended and the island was declared a bird sanctuary. Since this first trip on the boat the *Phyllis Cormack*, Greenpeace has grown into a huge international organization. Greenpeace headquarters are in Amsterdam, but there are regional offices in 41 countries.

The stated mission of Greenpeace is to "use nonviolent, creative confrontation to expose global environmental problems, and to force the solutions which are essential to a green and peaceful future." Its goal is to "ensure the ability of the earth to nurture life in all its diversity." Greenpeace is an independent organization that does not solicit or accept funds from governments, corporations, or political parties. The activities of Greenpeace are supported by 2.8 million people all over the world. Greenpeace also is careful not to accept donations that "could compromise its independence, aims, objectives or integrity." In addition to donations from individual supporters, Greenpeace accepts some grant moneys. Greenpeace believes that it has no permanent allies or enemies because it works to expose environmental threats and to find solutions to those threats. Greenpeace promotes open, informed debate about the choices available in today's society. The organization uses research; lobbying; "quiet diplomacy"; and high-profile, nonviolent conflict to pursue its goals. Many people are familiar with images of Greenpeace placing boats in the path of whaling vessels; those images have been captured by television cameras and memorialized in movies.

Greenpeace asserts that it has played a pivotal role in the adoption of:

- a ban on toxic waste exports to less developed countries.
- a moratorium on commercial whaling.
- a United Nations convention providing for better management of world fisheries.
- a Southern Ocean Whale Sanctuary.
- a 50-year moratorium on mineral exploitation in Antarctica.
- bans on the dumping at sea of radioactive and industrial waste and disused oil installations.
- an end to high-sea, large-scale driftnet fishing.
- a ban on all nuclear weapons testing.

Presently, Greenpeace is working on issues such as

- saving the oceans from overfishing and stopping threats to whales and the ocean environment.
- stopping climate change.
- phasing out fossil fuels.
- eliminating toxic chemicals.
- stopping nuclear threats.
- saying no to genetically modified organisms.
- protecting ancient forests.
- encouraging sustainable trade.

During 2004, Greenpeace dealt with a number of specific issues around the world. The organization worked to eliminate the use of fishing methods that trap dolphins. Greenpeace declared a number of victories in 2004. A United Nations treaty banning the 12 most polluting chemicals became a reality—something that Greenpeace had been campaigning for over the years. Climate change, another environmental threat identified by Greenpeace, has been declared by the Pentagon to be a greater threat than terrorism. Large corporations such as McDonald's New Zealand, Coke, Unilever, Samsung, Sony, and Puma took actions to eliminate some of the environmental threats identified by Greenpeace. Activists revealed that the underwater equivalent of rainforests—seamounts—were being destroyed by a process called bottom trawling, and Greenpeace took up the challenge of attempting to stop this type of fishing. Iceland reduced the number of whales it was going to kill from 250 to a mere 25. Greenpeace also protested the shipment of radioactive weapons grade plutonium from the United States to France. (More than 7,000 km of the plutonium was shipped across the Atlantic Ocean.) Russia finally ratified the Kyoto Protocol. The Nobel Peace Prize was awarded to a Kenyan woman named Wangari Maathai, who has worked to reforest parts of Africa (see Chapter 1).

One of the biggest challenges Greenpeace has taken on is to assist in mitigating the environmental damage caused by the massive tsunami that ravaged the Indian Ocean on December 26, 2004. In addition to assessing the situation from a strictly environmental perspective, Greenpeace is aiding in the humanitarian effort to deliver relief aid to India, Indonesia, and Thailand. Environmentalists are just beginning to assess the extent of the damage and to figure out the best ways to bring about environmental recovery in the area.

Initial analysis of the status of the environment in the area affected by the tsunami indicates that many of the habitats have been significantly damaged by the event. Coral reefs, mangroves, and wetlands appear to have suffered extensive damage, as have the facilities that were put in place to monitor those environments before the tsunami. Many of these habitats are important in and of themselves, but their importance also lies in the fact they represent the habitat for many vulnerable marine species.

Greenpeace is monitoring the efforts of the United Nations Environment Programme (UNEP), which is making a complete assessment of the environmental effects of the disaster.

One of the interesting facets of the research and analysis connected with this natural event is the extent to which human interfaces with the habitats may have contributed to the severity of the damage. For example, development along the coasts may have eroded the natural barriers to a huge ocean event such as the Indian Ocean tsunami. If such development degraded the coral reefs and mangroves that stand as natural defenses against such events, then humans may have inadvertently augmented the damage that would have been caused but for such development. Greenpeace is committed to doing what it can to ensure that redevelopment of these regions is handled in an environmentally sensitive manner and that appropriate precautions are taken so that the important ecosystems will be protected as much as possible against future damage.

As mentioned earlier, the name of the boat used by Greenpeace founders in their efforts to stop the nuclear testing on Amchitka was the *Phyllis Cormack*. On that first trip, Greenpeace founder Robert Hunter took along a book of Indian myths and legends that included some prophesies. One of the chapters was about a story that an old Cree Indian woman told. The story told of a time when the white man's materialistic lifestyle would seriously damage the earth's resources. The story went on to tell that the Great Spirit of the Indians would cause many of the Indian braves to be resurrected so they could teach the white man reverence for the land. This band of Indian braves was known as the Rainbow Warriors. In 1978, the Greenpeace ship the *Sir William Hardy* was renamed the *Rainbow Warrior*. The flagship of Greenpeace has since been known as the *Rainbow Warrior*.

Greenpeace has come to represent the nonviolent faction of activists promoting environmental responsibility throughout the world. Other groups of activists take a more revolutionary tact in making their positions known, but

Greenpeace is committed to nonviolent conflict as the method by which it presents its message. A Greenpeace banner summed up one of the philosophies of the organization: by seeking material gain, humans have damaged and continue to damage the environment to the detriment of all life. The banner read as follows:

"When the last tree is cut, the last river poisoned, and the last fish dead, we will discover that we can't eat money. . . ." ■

ENERGY SOURCES

solar energy The method of gathering energy that typically involves the use of solar panels to capture the energy of the sun and convert it to electricity.

wind energy The use of wind to make electricity, primarily through the use of wind farms utilizing turbines.

For years, environmentalists have been advocating the use of clean, renewable energy sources. Both **solar energy** and **wind energy** are considered environmentally conscious methods of producing electricity. For a time, in the 1970s, tax breaks were given for the use of solar energy as a means of encouraging the use of that energy source. In the years since, efforts have been made not only to expand the types of clean, renewable energy sources that are available for public use but also to find ways to use more efficiently the methods that are presently available. Solar energy and wind energy make up only about 2 percent of America's electricity. Other less environmentally sensitive sources of electricity, such as coal and nuclear power, make up the bulk of America's energy production methods.

Wind Energy

turbines Large bladed towers that are typically made of metal and that look like three-armed windmills. Turbines are used to produce wind energy. As the wind blows, the blades of the turbines spin, eventually producing electricity.

Wind farms, in particular, are increasing in number and size—an encouraging sign for environmentalists. More than 1 million households can be supplied by the wind farms in use today. How is wind energy produced? Wind farms use large **turbines** to produce energy. The turbines look like giant three-armed windmills made out of metal. Wind turbines are very efficient. One turbine can produce enough power to meet the needs of 500 average American homes for a full year. Modern wind turbines can be as tall as 300 feet. When the wind blows, the blades of the turbine spin, turning an electric generator that then produces electricity. The electricity produced by each turbine is collected underground and feeds into an electricity grid.

As more wind farms come into production, the cost of the energy produced from these farms continues to drop, making this energy source economical as well as appropriate from an environmental perspective. It is somewhat unusual to think of wind as a "crop"; but

essentially, that is what wind has become. Wind farmers can lease out their turbines and grow agricultural crops right up to the base of the turbines. The geography of the United States, with its open plains and mountain gaps, provides a plethora of locations where such farms can be located. The wind turbines are a familiar sight in California, but such sights are becoming more familiar across the plains in the western United States.

Solar Energy

Many parts of the United States have enough sunshine to utilize solar energy as a major source of electricity. As with wind energy, due to advancements in the methods used to produce solar energy, the cost of solar energy has decreased to the point where it is competitive with fossil fuels.

A familiar method of capturing the energy of the sun is the use of solar panels. The panels are called **photovoltaic panels** because they convert light (photons) to electricity (voltage). Another method of converting the sun's warmth to energy is the use of solar thermal systems. With these systems, the sun's heat warms water for use in businesses and homes.

photovoltaic panels Panels used to gather solar energy. They are called "photovoltaic" because they convert light (photons) to electricity (voltage).

Geothermal Energy

Geothermal energy involves the use of heat at the earth's core to generate heat and energy on the surface. Imagine using the heat from the geothermal pools at Yellowstone National Park and other locations

geothermal energy The use of heat from the earth's core to generate heat and energy on the earth's surface.

across the United States. One advantage of geothermal energy is that, unlike solar energy, geothermal energy is available 24 hours a day, 7 days a week, 365 days a year. More than 4 million homes are presently heated by geothermal energy. The use of geothermal energy reduces America's dependency on fossil fuel and nuclear energy sources.

Biomass Energy

biomass energy The type of energy that comes from the energy of the sun stored in plants as they grow.

One of the most recent and most intriguing sources of energy is **biomass energy**. What is biomass energy? It is energy that comes from plants. This may sound odd at first, but plants absorb and store the sun's energy as they grow. New techniques are being developed to extract that energy from the plant material and convert it to heat and electricity. The possibility of selling crops not only for food and other traditional uses but also for energy, provides farmers with an additional opportunity to stay in business and prosper.

There are some disadvantages to the clean, renewable power sources just described. For example, occasionally, birds are killed by flying into the wind energy turbines. Problems such as this are not the primary reason these sources are not more widely used. Traditional energy sources such as coal, oil, and nuclear power are heavily subsidized; and much of the funding for research is directed toward those sources. Environmentalists have argued for some time that traditional sources of energy emit or produce undesirable pollutants into the habitat. They argue that hydropower facilities can be very damaging to the wildlife and habitats in which the facilities exist. Heat generated from such facilities can damage the fish population in the waterways that supply the facilities, which is why heat has been designated as a pollutant under the CWA; and heat emissions from hydropower plants are carefully monitored. Similarly, the argument is made that nuclear power facilities produce large amounts of radioactive waste that will pose a danger to the environment for hundreds or thousands of years.

GLOBAL WARMING

global warming The phenomenon whereby the earth's temperature has been gradually increasing.

The primary reason that many environmentalists are concerned about the type and quality of energy sources used in the United States and around the rest of the world is that the use of traditional energy sources has created a phenomenon known as **global warming**.

There is no real debate about the fact that the earth is warmer today than it was thousands of years ago. What *has* been the subject of much debate is whether humans have caused or contributed to this warming or whether global warming is a natural, cyclical part of Earth's maturity.

Throughout history, the earth has gone through periods of varying temperature. The Ice Age, a natural occurrence, was responsible for the extinction of many species. The Ice Age resulted from a change of just a few degrees in the average temperature of the earth, but yielded dramatic environmental changes. Environmentalists claim that humans have caused the temperature of the earth to increase much faster than any natural rate of increase. Regardless of whether the increase in the Earth's temperature is a natural development or whether humans, through poor management of the earth's ecosystem, have caused the increase, the effects will be dramatic and could be drastic.

Increases in temperature cause changes in weather patterns, such as an increase in storms, which can cause flooding. Changes in the level of oceans across Earth are another danger of increasing temperature. Although Earth's temperature has risen only 5 to 9 degrees in more than 10,000 years, miniscule changes in average temperature have meant the extinction of plants and animals; and there is no scientific reason to believe there will be any change in that pattern.

How are humans causing or contributing to the acceleration of global warming? If they are causing or contributing to global warming, the theoretical causes include the buildup of **greenhouse gases** (such as carbon dioxide) through the use of fossil fuels (coal, oil, and gas) for transportation, as well as emissions from power plants. Vehicle emissions account for 20 percent of America's CO_2 (carbon dioxide) emissions, and power plant emissions account for another 36 percent of that total. What dangers does global warming pose to human health? Deadly heat waves and the spread of infectious disease (such as dengue fever, malaria, West Nile virus, and hantavirus) are thought to be linked with increased temperatures.

greenhouse gases The buildup of gases such as carbon dioxide in the earth's atmosphere, thought to be the result of the use of fossil fuels.

Whether the earth is merely experiencing a natural, if gradual, increase in temperature or the activities of humans are causing or contributing to the increase does not change the fact that any increase is likely to cause harm to life on this planet. Consequently, the existence and effects of global warming will continue to be addressed as part of the body of environmental law.

FEATURE

Kyoto Protocol

What is the Kyoto Protocol, and where did it get its name?

The Kyoto Protocol is an amendment to the United Nations Framework Convention on Climate Change. This amendment is intended to provide concrete targets for the reduction of greenhouse gas emissions because it is believed that those emissions have an adverse effect on the world climate. It is called the Kyoto Protocol or Treaty because the document was made available for signature on December 11, 1997, in Kyoto, Japan. It entered into force on February 16, 2005, without the signature of the United States.

Why was it proposed?

Some scientists believe that carbon emissions (greenhouse gas emissions) trap infrared waves in the lower atmosphere. Without the gases, the waves would be released into the upper atmosphere. When the waves are trapped in the lower atmosphere, they are believed to contribute to a rise in global temperatures, which then becomes "global warming." The Kyoto Protocol calls for limitations on the emissions of greenhouse gases, which could lessen the increase in global temperatures and reduce the damage believed to be caused by such increases in temperatures.

How does the Kyoto Protocol work?

By signing the Kyoto Protocol, industrialized nations all over the world agree that they will reduce their collective greenhouse gas emissions to a level that is 5.2 percent less than the collective emissions were in 1990. The agreed-upon level represents a 29 percent decrease from the level of emissions that would have been expected worldwide in 2010 if emissions had continued to increase at the projected rates. The provisions of the Protocol allow nations to "cap and trade" their carbon emissions. In other words, the global emissions numbers called for by the Protocol can be achieved on a percentage basis by each individual nation or one nation that intends to industrialize more than another nation can trade for the emissions credits of the less industrialized nation as long as the overall emissions level remains at the agreed-upon level.

The Protocol allows more than one country to be grouped together in "bubbles" and given a collective emissions cap. Those bubble countries will be treated as one entity in terms of compliance with the Protocol. The European Union (EU) chose to be grouped in this manner and has set up an EU Emissions Trading Scheme (ETS) that trades EU allowances. Other groups of nations have already established or will establish similar schemes for the trading of emissions

REVIEW

The Kyoto Protocol is a "cap and trade" system that allows nations all over the world to work together to reduce greenhouse gas emissions.

within their group to better comply with the terms of the Protocol. Other types of carbon markets in effect throughout the world have nothing to do with the Kyoto Protocol. Although the United States has not signed the Protocol, there are several carbon markets within the United States and 131 U.S. mayors have committed to adopt the Kyoto targets for their cities.

If a nation or bubble is found not to be in compliance with the Kyoto emissions targets, that nation or bubble must not only reduce emissions to make up the difference between its actual emissions and the agreed-upon emissions but also reduce its emissions by an additional 30 percent. The nation's or bubble's trading privileges also will be revoked.

Why hasn't the United States signed the Kyoto Protocol?

In 1997, the U.S. Senate unanimously passed a resolution stating that the United States should not be a signatory on an agreement containing binding emissions targets because it did not bind developing nations (just industrialized nations) and consequently ". . . would result in serious harm to the economy of the United States" (see Byrd-Hagel Resolution, S. Res. 98). Both Presidents Bill Clinton and George W. Bush have analyzed the Protocol; but for various reasons, neither has referred the Protocol for ratification.

What happens next?

The Protocol contains provisions allowing for its amendment, and it has been speculated that nations such as the United States might ratify the Protocol and its emissions levels if certain provisions of the Protocol are amended. Until then, those nations that have ratified the Protocol will continue to enforce it and encourage all other affected nations to join them in their battle against the effects of greenhouse gases. ■

SUMMARY

Environmental law includes various categories of laws addressing natural resources issues. Public lands have been placed in four classes and are managed based on a variety of factors, including economic uses and uses designed to protect wildlife and wilderness areas. Various acts, such as the ESA and the MMPA, have been passed to protect natural habitats and the animals that inhabit the earth. Natural resources law also addresses energy sources. Environmentally conscious energy sources, such as wind energy, are becoming more popular in an effort to avoid environmental damage caused by traditional sources of energy. The concept of global warming continues to generate concern and controversy. Whether addressing broad conservation issues or specific issues such as protection of tropical forests, natural resources law is an important and growing part of that body of law known as environmental law.

KEY TERMS

- Biomass energy
- Cetaceans
- Convention on International Trade in Endangered Species (CITES)
- Critical habitat
- Endangered species
- Endangered species list
- Geothermal energy
- Global warming
- God Squad
- Greenhouse gases
- Habitat conservation plan
- Incidental take permit
- Leave No Trace
- Marine mammal
- Multiple uses
- No jeopardy rule
- Photovoltaic panels
- Pinnipeds
- Safe Harbors program
- Solar energy
- Strandings
- Threatened species
- Turbines
- Wilderness
- Wind energy

REVIEW QUESTIONS AND HANDS-ON ACTIVITIES

1. What is the definition of *wilderness* pursuant to the Wilderness Act of 1964?
2. What is the Leave No Trace philosophy of the Wilderness Act of 1964?
3. What is the difference between a threatened species and an endangered species?

4. What is a marine mammal?
5. How is the International Dolphin Conservation Act of 1992 designed to help protect dolphins?
6. Name three sources of energy.
7. With what form of energy are photovoltaic panels associated?
8. What theory is behind the assertion that humans either cause or contribute to global warming?
9. Research and summarize a natural resources law not addressed in this chapter. What is the purpose of the law? What are its key definitions? Do you believe the law effectively addresses the purpose for which it was enacted?

HELPFUL WEBSITES

http://www.fws.gov/endangered/index.html (U.S Fish & Wildlife Service, The Endangered Special Program)

http://wilderness.org (The Wilderness Society)

http://www.fseee.org (Forest Service Employees for Environmental Ethics)

http://www.nwf.org (National Wildlife Federation)

http://www.environmentaldefense.org (Environmental Defense)

http://www.wri.org (World Resources Institute)

http://www.igc.org (Institute for Global Communications)

ENDNOTES

1. *Missouri v. Holland*, 252 U.S. 416 (1920).
2. *Defenders of Wildlife v. Administrator, Environmental Protection Agency*, 698 F. Supp. 1334 (D. Minn. 1988), aff'd in part, rev'd in part, 882 F.2d 1294 (8th Cir. 1989).
3. *TVA v. Hill*, 437 U.S. 153 (1978).
4. *GDF Realty Investments, Ltd. v. Norton*, 326 F.3d 622 (5th Cir. 2003).
5. *Gibbs v. Babbitt*, 214 F.3d 483 (4th Cir. 2000).

APPENDIX A

SELECTED PAGES FROM THE FEDERAL REGISTER

14172 Federal Register / Vol. 72, No. 57 / Monday, March 26, 2007 / Proposed Rules

ENVIRONMENTAL PROTECTION AGENCY

40 CFR Parts 260 and 261

[EPA–HQ–RCRA–2002–0031–FRL–8289–9]

RIN 2050–AG31

Revisions to the Definition of Solid Waste

AGENCY: Environmental Protection Agency.

ACTION: Supplemental Proposed Rule.

SUMMARY: The Environmental Protection Agency (EPA) is today publishing a supplemental proposal which would revise the definition of solid waste to exclude certain hazardous secondary materials from regulation under Subtitle C of the Resource Conservation and Recovery Act (RCRA). We are also soliciting comments on regulatory factors to be used to determine whether recycling of hazardous secondary materials is legitimate. The Agency first proposed changes to the definition of solid waste on October 28, 2003 (68 FR 61558). The purpose of this proposal is to encourage safe, environmentally sound recycling and resource conservation and to respond to several court decisions concerning the definition of solid waste.

DATES: Comments must be received on or before May 25, 2007. Under the Paperwork Reduction Act, comments on the information collection provisions must be received by OMB on or before April 25, 2007.

ADDRESSES: Submit your comments, identified by Docket ID No. EPA–HQ–RCRA 2002–0031 by one of the following methods:

http://www.regulations.gov: Follow the on-line instructions for submitting comments.

E-mail: Comments may be sent by electronic mail (e-mail) to *RCRA-docket@epa.gov*, Attention Docket ID No. EPA–HQ–RCRA–2002–0031.

Fax: Fax comments to: 202–566–0270, Attention Docket ID No. EPA–HQ–RCRA 2002–0031.

Mail: Send comments to: OSWER Docket, EPA Docket Center, Mail Code 5305T, Environmental Protection Agency, 1200 Pennsylvania Avenue, NW., Washington, DC 20460, Attention Docket ID No. EPA–HQ–RCRA–2002–0031. In addition, please mail a copy of your comments on the information collection provisions to the Office of Information and Regulatory Affairs, Office of Management and Budget (OMB), *Attn:* Desk Officer for EPA, 725 17th St., Washington, DC 20503.

Hand delivery: Deliver comments to: Environmental Protection Agency, EPA Docket Center, Room B102, 1301 Constitution Avenue, NW., Washington, DC, Attention Docket ID No. EPA–HQ–RCRA–2002–0031. Such deliveries are only accepted during the docket's normal hours of operation, and special arrangements should be made for deliveries of boxed information.

Instructions: Direct your comments to Docket ID Number EPA–HQ–RCRA–2002–0031. EPA's policy is that all comments received will be included in the public docket without change and may be made available online at *http://www.regulations.gov*, including any personal information provided, unless the comment includes information claimed to be Confidential Business Information (CBI) or other information whose disclosure is restricted by statute. Do not submit information that you consider to be CBI or otherwise protected through *http://www.regulations.gov* or e-mail. The *http://www.regulations.gov* Web site is an "anonymous access" system, which means EPA will not know your identity or contact information unless you provide it in the body of your comment. If you send an e-mail comment directly to EPA without going through *http://www.regulations.gov* your e-mail address will be automatically captured and included as part of the comment that is placed in the public docket and made available on the Internet. If you submit an electronic comment, EPA recommends that you include your name and other contact information in the body of your comment and with any disk or CD–ROM you submit. If EPA cannot read your comment due to technical difficulties and cannot contact you for clarification, EPA may not be able to consider your comment. Electronic files should avoid the use of special characters, any form of encryption, and be free of any defects or viruses.

Docket: All documents in the docket are listed in the *http://www.regulations.gov* index. Although listed in the index, some information is not publicly available, such as CBI or other information whose disclosure is restricted by statute. Certain other material, such as copyrighted material, will be publicly available only in hard copy. Publicly available docket materials are available either electronically in *http://www.regulations.gov* or in hard copy at the OSWER Docket, EPA/DC, EPA West, Room B102, 1301 Constitution Ave., NW., Washington, DC. The Public Reading Room is open from 8:30 a.m. to 4:30 p.m. Monday through Friday, excluding legal holidays. The telephone number for the Public Reading Room is (202) 566–1744, and the telephone number for the OSWER Docket is 202–566–0270.

FOR FURTHER INFORMATION CONTACT: For more detailed information on specific aspects of this rulemaking, contact Marilyn Goode, Office of Solid Waste, Hazardous Waste Identification Division, MC 5304P, Environmental Protection Agency, 1200 Pennsylvania Ave., NW., Washington, DC 20460 (703) 308–8800, (*goode.marilyn@epa.gov*) or Tracy Atagi, Office of Solid Waste, Hazardous Waste Identification Division, MC 5304P, Environmental Protection Agency, 1200 Pennsylvania Ave., NW., Washington, DC 20460, at (703) 308–8672 (*atagi.tracy@epa.gov*).

SUPPLEMENTARY INFORMATION:

A. Regulated Entities

Entities potentially affected by this action include about 4600 facilities in 530 industries in 17 economic sectors that generate or recycle hazardous secondary materials which are currently regulated as RCRA Subtitle C hazardous wastes (e.g., industrial co-products, by-products, residues, unreacted feedstocks). About 80 percent of these affected facilities are classified in NAICS code economic sectors 31, 32, and 33 (manufacturing), and the remainder are in NAICS code economic sectors 21 (mining), 22 (utilities), 23 (construction), 42 (wholesale trade), 44 and 45 (retail trade), 48 and 49 (transportation), 51 (information), 54 (professional, scientific and technical services), 56 (administrative support, waste management and remediation), 61 (educational services), 62 (health care and social assistance, and 81 (other services). About 0.65 million tons per year of recyclable industrial materials handled by these entities may be affected, of which the most common types are metal-bearing hazardous secondary materials (e.g., sludges and spent catalysts) for commodity metals recovery, and organic chemical liquids for recycling as solvents. This proposed rule, if promulgated, is expected to result in regulatory and materials recovery cost savings to these industries of approximately $107 million per year. Taking into account impact estimation uncertainty factors, this rule, if promulgated, could affect between 0.3 to 1.7 million tons per year of industrial hazardous secondary materials handled by 3600 to 5400 entities in 460 to 570 industries, resulting in $93 million to $205 million per year of net cost savings. More detailed information on the potentially affected entities, industries, and industrial materials, as well as the economic impacts of this

Federal Register / Vol. 72, No. 57 / Monday, March 26, 2007 / Proposed Rules 14173

rule (with impact uncertainty factors), is presented in section XVI.A of this preamble and in the "Economics Background Document" available in the docket for this rulemaking.

B. What To Consider When Preparing Comments for EPA

1. Submitting CBI. Do not submit this information to EPA through *http://www.regulations.gov* or e-mail. Clearly mark part of all information that you claim to be CBI. For CBI information in a disk or CD–ROM that you mail to EPA, mark the outside of the disk or CD–ROM as CBI and then identify electronically within the disk or CD–ROM the specific information that is claimed as CBI. In addition to one complete version of the comment that includes information claimed as CBI, a copy of the comment that does not contain the information claimed as CBI must be submitted for inclusion in the public docket. Information so marked will not be disclosed, except in accordance with procedures set forth in 40 CFR Part 2.

2. Tips for Preparing Your Comments. *When submitting comments, remember to:*

- Identify the rulemaking by docket number and other identifying information (subject heading, **Federal Register** date and page number).
- Follow directions. The Agency may ask for commenters to respond to specific questions or organize comments by referencing a Code of Federal Regulations (CFR) part or Section number.
- Explain why you agree or disagree; suggest alternatives and substitute language for your requested changes.
- Describe any assumptions and provide any technical information and/or data that you used.
- If estimating burden or costs, explain methods used to arrive at the estimate in sufficient detail to allow for it to be reproduced.
- Provide specific examples to illustrate any concerns and suggest alternatives.
- Make sure to submit comments by the comment period deadline identified above.

Preamble Outline

I. Statutory Authority

These regulations are proposed under the authority of sections 2002, 3001, 3002, 3003, 3004, 3007, 3010, and 3017 of the Solid Waste Disposal Act of 1970, as amended by the Resource Conservation and Recovery Act of 1976 (RCRA), as amended by the Hazardous and Solid Waste Amendments of 1984 (HSWA), 42 U.S.C. 6921, 6922, 6923, and 6924.

II. What Is the Scope of This Supplemental Proposal?

In today's notice, EPA is proposing to revise the definition of solid waste in order to exclude from regulation under Subtitle C of RCRA certain hazardous secondary materials sent for recycling. We are also seeking comment on certain changes to the proposed regulatory factors for determining whether recycling is legitimate. The Agency first proposed changes to the definition of solid waste, as well as regulatory criteria for legitimacy, on October 28, 2003 (68 FR 61581–61588).

The scope of the regulatory changes proposed today are as follows:

A. Exclusion for Materials That Are Legitimately Reclaimed Under the Control of the Generator in Non-Land-Based Units

This provision, with regulatory language proposed in 40 CFR 261.2(a)(2)(ii), would exclude certain hazardous secondary materials (i.e., spent materials, listed sludges, and listed byproducts) that are generated and legitimately reclaimed[1] within the United States or its territories[2] and are only handled in non-land-based units (e.g., tanks, containers, containment buildings). The exclusion would apply to hazardous secondary material that is reclaimed under the control of the generator, if the materials are not speculatively accumulated. In addition, EPA is proposing to include in 40 CFR 260.42 a requirement that the generator would be required to submit a one-time notification to EPA or the authorized state. Hazardous secondary material would be considered "under the control of the generator" under the following circumstances:

(1) It is generated and then reclaimed at the generating facility; or

(2) It is generated and reclaimed by the same company, if the generator certifies that it is under the same ownership as the reclaimer and that the owner company has acknowledged responsibility for safe management of the hazardous secondary materials; or

(3) It is generated and reclaimed pursuant to a written agreement between a tolling contractor and batch manufacturer, if the tolling contractor retains ownership of, and responsibility for, the hazardous secondary materials that are generated during the course of the manufacture.

This proposed exclusion would not include recycling practices that involve discard of materials. These practices include recycling of inherently waste-like materials (40 CFR 261.2(d)), recycling of materials that are used in a manner constituting disposal or used to produce products that are applied to or placed on the land (40 CFR 261.2(c)(1)), and burning of materials for energy recovery or used to produce a fuel or otherwise contained in fuels (40 CFR 261.2(c)(2)). This proposed exclusion is further described in section IX of this

[1] In this context, the terms "recycling" and "reclamation" are not necessarily synonymous. "Recycling typically involves a series of activities, including storage and other handling steps that culminate in the production of a valuable end product of some kind. Thus, if materials need to be reclaimed in order to produce a valuable end product, the reclamation activity can be thought of as one step in the overall recycling process. See proposed § 261.4(g). Further explanation of the term "reclamation" can be found in the preamble to the October 2003 proposal at 68 FR 61564.

[2] EPA has proposed to limit this exclusion to hazardous secondary materials reclaimed within the United States or its territories because it does not have sufficient information related to recycling activities outside of the United States or its territories to make the same general finding that it has made for materials legitimately recycled under the control of the generator. However, as noted below, EPA requests comment on whether the Agency should promulgate a conditional exclusion for exported hazardous secondary material otherwise meeting the criteria for this rule.

preamble. We note that the Agency is considering expanding its regulations for comparable fuels in a separate rulemaking.

B. Exclusion for Materials That Are Legitimately Reclaimed Under the Control of the Generator in Land-Based Units

This provision, with regulatory language proposed in 40 CFR 261.4(a)(23), would exclude certain hazardous secondary materials that are generated and legitimately reclaimed within the United States or its territories and handled in land-based units (*e.g.*, surface impoundments, waste piles). This provision requires that hazardous secondary materials managed in land-based units must be contained in such units.

C. Conditional Exclusion for Materials That Are Transferred for the Purpose of Reclamation

This conditional exclusion, with regulatory language proposed in 40 CFR 261.4(a)(24), (hereinafter referred to as the "transfer-based exclusion") would apply to hazardous secondary materials (i.e., spent materials, listed sludges, and listed byproducts) that are generated and subsequently transferred to a different person or company for the purpose of reclamation. As long as the conditions to the exclusion are satisfied, the hazardous secondary materials would not be subject to Subtitle C regulation. The conditions are intended to ensure that such materials are handled as commodities rather than wastes. They will also help guarantee that protection of human health and the environment will not be compromised in the absence of hazardous waste regulatory requirements for these materials. It is important to note that when hazardous secondary materials are generated and reclaimed within the United States pursuant to a written agreement between a tolling contractor and a batch manufacturer as defined in proposed 40 CFR 260.10, these materials would be subject to the requirements of proposed 40 CFR 261.2(a)(ii) or 261.4(a)(23) rather than the more extensive requirements of proposed 40 CFR 261.4(a)(24).

If any of the hazardous secondary materials under proposed 40 CFR 261.4(a)(24) are generated and then exported to another country for reclamation, we are also proposing that the exporter notify the receiving country of the export through EPA and obtain consent from that country before shipment of the material. This requirement is proposed to be codified in 40 CFR 261.4(a)(25). Like the previously discussed exclusion for hazardous secondary materials recycled under the control of the generator, this exclusion would not cover recycling of inherently waste-like materials, recycling of materials that are used in a manner constituting disposal, and burning of materials for energy recovery. The proposed exclusion is described in more detail in section X of this preamble.

D. Petition Process for Non-Waste Determinations

In addition to the exclusions discussed above, the Agency also is proposing a petition process, with regulatory language found in proposed 40 CFR 260.30(d), 260.30(e), 260.30(f), and 260.34, for obtaining a case-specific non-waste determination for certain hazardous secondary materials that are recycled. This process would allow a petitioner to receive a formal determination from the Agency that its hazardous secondary material is clearly not "discarded" and therefore is not a solid waste. The procedure would allow EPA or the authorized state to take into account the particular fact pattern of the recycling and to determine that the hazardous secondary material in question is not a solid waste without imposing additional requirements. The determination would be available to petitioners who could demonstrate that their hazardous secondary materials were recycled in a continuous industrial process, or that the materials were indistinguishable in all relevant aspects from a product or intermediate, or that the materials were under the control of the generator via a tolling arrangement or similar contractual arrangement. The petition process for the non-waste determinations would be the same as that for the variances from the definition of solid waste found in 40 CFR 261.31. This process and the criteria for making these determinations, are described in section XII of this preamble.

E. Legitimacy

On October 28, 2003 (68 FR 61581–61588), EPA extensively discussed our position on the relevance of legitimacy to hazardous waste recycling in general and to the redefinition of solid waste specifically. We proposed to codify in the RCRA regulations four general criteria to be used in determining whether recycling of hazardous secondary materials is legitimate. In today's action, we are proposing changes to the proposed legitimacy criteria and asking for public comment on these revisions. The changes consist of a restructuring of the proposed criteria, called factors in this proposal, by making two of these factors mandatory and two non-mandatory considerations, and providing further guidance and clarification on how the economics of recycling should be considered in making legitimacy determinations. The changes are described in section XI of this preamble.

III. What Is the Intent of This Supplemental Proposal?

Today's supplemental proposal would revise and clarify the RCRA definition of solid waste as it pertains to certain types of hazardous secondary materials that would not be considered wastes subject to regulation under RCRA Subtitle C. This notice builds on our October 28, 2003 proposal (68 FR 61558) which was initiated partially in response to decisions by the United States Court of Appeals for the DC Circuit, which, taken together, have provided the Agency with additional direction in this area.

This proposal represents an important restructuring of the RCRA regulations that distinguish wastes from non-waste materials for RCRA purposes, and that ensure environmental protections over hazardous secondary materials recycling practices. As such, it also is an opportunity for the Agency to clarify in a regulatory context the concept of "legitimate recycling," which has been and is a key component of RCRA's regulatory program for recycling, but which to date has been implemented without regulatory criteria. Today's supplemental proposal thus includes specific regulatory provisions for determining when hazardous secondary materials are recycled legitimately.

Today's supplemental proposal is de-regulatory in nature because certain recyclable materials that have heretofore been subject to the hazardous waste regulations would no longer be regulated as hazardous waste. The factors to consider for legitimate recycling codify existing principles without increasing regulation. This proposal is not intended to bring new wastes into the RCRA regulatory system.

By removing unnecessary hazardous waste regulatory controls over certain recycling practices, and by providing more explicit criteria for determining the legitimacy of recycling practices in general, EPA expects that this proposal will encourage the safe, beneficial recycling of hazardous secondary materials. This regulatory initiative is thus consistent with the Agency's longstanding policy of encouraging the recovery and reuse of valuable resources as an alternative to land disposal, while at the same time maintaining protection of human health and the environment.

It also is consistent with one of the primary goals of the Congress in enacting the RCRA statute (as evidenced by its name), and with the Agency's vision of how the RCRA program could evolve over the longer term to promote sustainability and more efficient use of resources.[3]

IV. How Does This Supplemental Proposal Relate to the October 2003 Proposal?

On October 28, 2003 (68 FR 61558), the Agency proposed to exclude from the definition of solid waste any material generated and reclaimed in a continuous process within the same industry, provided the reclamation was legitimate. "Same industry" was defined as industries sharing the same 4-digit North American Industry Classification System (NAICS) code. The basis for that exclusion was the holding in *American Mining Congress* v. *EPA* ("AMC I"), 824 F.2d 1177 (DC Cir. 1987)) that materials destined for beneficial reuse of recycling in a continuous process by the generating industry are not discarded. In order to be eligible for the exclusion, the hazardous secondary material could not be speculatively accumulated under 261.1(c)(8). In addition, the generator of such materials would be required to submit a one-time notification to EPA or the authorized State with contact information, the type of material that would be excluded, and the industry that generated the material. In the October 2003 proposal, the Agency also proposed to codify in the RCRA regulations four criteria to be used in determining whether recycling of hazardous secondary material was legitimate. We also solicited comment on a broader conditional exclusion from RCRA regulation for essentially all hazardous secondary materials that are legitimately recycled. For a discussion of public comments received on our proposed exclusion, see section IX of this preamble.

After evaluating comments received on the October 2003 proposal and conducting an independent analysis, EPA decided to restructure its approach. Following the decision of the DC Circuit Court in *Association of Battery Recyclers* v. *EPA* ("ABR")(208 F.3d 1047 (DC Cir. 2000), EPA has decided to examine the principles behind the court's holdings on the definition of solid waste, rather than trying to fit materials into specific fact patterns addressed by the court. EPA is therefore proposing (1) an exclusion for hazardous secondary materials that are generated and then reclaimed under the control of the generator; (2) a conditional exclusion for hazardous secondary materials that are generated and then transferred to another person for the purpose of reclamation; and (3) a petition process for obtaining a case-specific non-waste determination for certain hazardous secondary materials that are recycled. Today's notice also proposes a restructuring of the previously proposed legitimacy criteria and further clarification and guidance on how the economics of the recycling transaction should be considered in making legitimacy determinations. A detailed description of today's proposed regulatory changes and the reasons for not finalizing the October 2003 proposal are discussed in sections IX, X, XI, and XII of this preamble.

V. How Is Hazardous Waste Recycling Currently Regulated?

The basic regulatory provisions for defining "solid wastes" and "hazardous wastes" under RCRA are found in part 261 of Title 40 of the Code of Federal Regulations (CFR). To be subject to RCRA's hazardous waste regulatory program, a material must be a solid waste that is also a hazardous waste. A solid waste is a hazardous waste if it is explicitly listed as such (in subpart D of part 261), or if it exhibits one or more of the hazardous characteristics (as specified in subpart C of part 261).

In general, hazardous wastes are subject to RCRA's full "cradle to grave" regulatory system from the time they are generated to the time that they are ultimately disposed. However, hazardous secondary materials often can be recycled instead of being disposed, which can change how those wastes are regulated. The "definition of solid waste" regulations in part 261 in effect separate recyclable hazardous secondary materials into two broad categories—those that are classified as solid wastes when recycled, and are therefore subject to regulation under Subtitle C of RCRA if they are listed or characteristic hazardous wastes, and those that are not considered solid wastes when they are recycled, and thus are not regulated. It should be understood that the term "hazardous secondary material" as it is used in today's rule and preamble therefore refers to both categories of recyclable materials; that is, materials that are regulated as hazardous wastes when recycled, and materials that are not considered wastes when recycled.

Hazardous secondary materials that are currently not regulated as wastes when they are recycled include, for example, those which are used or reused directly as effective substitutes for commercial products, and those which can be used as ingredients in an industrial process, provided the materials are not being reclaimed. See 40 CFR 261.2(e). In essence, EPA considers these types of recycling practices to be more akin to normal industrial production rather than waste management.

In contrast, in some recycling practices, the hazardous secondary material cannot be used as is and must be significantly processed before it can be reused in a manner similar to products in commerce. In these cases, EPA has found that the material may be more "waste-like" and the hazardous secondary materials therefore have been regulated as hazardous wastes. One type of recycling that falls within this category and that is especially relevant to this rule is reclamation of certain types of hazardous secondary materials. Reclamation involves the processing of hazardous secondary materials in some way in order so that they can be used or reused. See 40 CFR 261.1(c)(4) and 40 CFR 261.2(c)(3). An example of reclamation is processing of a spent solvent to restore its solvent properties before it is suitable for reuse as a solvent. As explained elsewhere in today's preamble, this supplemental proposal would reexamine the regulatory status of these hazardous secondary materials and de-regulate a specific subset of these materials that are recycled by being reclaimed.

In the existing Part 261 regulations, EPA identified other types of recycling practices that are fully regulated because, we concluded, they involve discard of materials. These practices include recycling of "inherently waste-like" materials (40 CFR 261.2(d)), recycling of materials that are "used in a manner constituting disposal," or "used to produce products that are applied to or placed on the land,"(40 CFR 261.2(c)(1)) and "burning of materials for energy recovery" or "used to produce a fuel or otherwise contained in fuels" (40 CFR 261.2(c)(2)). Today's supplemental proposal is not intended to affect how these recycling practices are regulated.

The current regulations also provide certain specific exemptions and exclusions from the definition of solid waste for particular recycling practices. For example, pulping liquors from paper manufacturing that are reclaimed in a pulping liquor recovery furnace and then reused in the pulping process are

[3] The Agency's long-term "vision" of the future of the RCRA program is discussed in the document "Beyond RCRA: Prospects for Waste and Materials Management in the Year 2020," which is available on the Agency's Web site *http://www.epa.gov/epaoswer/osw/vision.htm.*

APPENDIX B

EXECUTIVE SUMMARY: ENVIRONMENTAL IMPACT STATEMENT

EXECUTIVE SUMMARY

INTRODUCTION

The Bureau of Land Management (BLM) has prepared this Proposed Resource Management Plan (Proposed RMP) and Environmental Impact Statement (EIS) to provide direction for managing public lands within the King Range National Conservation Area (KRNCA) planning area.

The Draft Resource Management Plan/EIS (Draft RMP) was published on January 16, 2004. This Proposed RMP/Final EIS is an abbreviated document, in that the contents of the entire Draft RMP are not reprinted. The Draft RMP may need to be referred to during review of the Proposed RMP. The Proposed RMP specifies where and under what circumstances particular uses or management activities would be allowed on public lands in the KRNCA and immediately adjacent public lands. The EIS assesses the possible environmental and social effects of implementing the Proposed RMP. The Proposed RMP is a refinement of the Preferred Alternative from the Draft RMP, with consideration given to public comments, corrections made where necessary, and rewording for clarification.

This summary provides:

- Background on the location and character of the KRNCA
- Purpose and need of the King Range RMP
- Mission and vision statements
- A summary of the public participation process
- Descriptions of each resource managed under the Preferred Alternative

BACKGROUND

The KRNCA includes approximately 58,000 acres of public and 6,000 acres of private lands, located along the rugged northern California coast about sixty miles south of Eureka and 200 miles north of San Francisco. An abrupt wall of mountains thrusts 4,000 feet above the Pacific, making the area one of the most spectacular and remote stretches of coastline in the continental U.S. The elemental beauty and ever-changing mood of the Pacific Ocean meeting the wild, undeveloped coastline, old-growth forests and rugged peaks of the King Range inspired the original NCA designation, and continues to draw people from all over the world to visit the Lost Coast of California. Visitors pursue a wide variety of activities, including hiking and backpacking eighty miles of trails, camping, beach-combing, surfing, hunting, and vehicular touring and sight-seeing on a 100+ mile network of BLM and county-maintained roads, environmental education, and wildlife viewing. Additional uses involve special forest products collection (mostly wild mushrooms) and livestock grazing by several local ranchers.

The formal plan decision area encompasses lands within the Congressionally-designated KRNCA, as well as BLM-managed lands contiguous to the KRNCA and two non-contiguous BLM parcels: one is the site of the KRNCA Project Office/Visitor Center, and the other, the Honeydew Creek Campground (see Figure 1-1 in Chapter 1). The total planning area includes approximately 68,000 acres. Formal decisions in the plan will only apply to these lands. However, a planning "area of influence" also includes the surrounding region stretching from McNutt Gulch near Petrolia in the north to Whale Gulch in the south, including the Mattole River Watershed. The plan recognizes that these nearby lands, communities, resource values, and uses are all affected by management of the KRNCA, and their use/values in turn affect management of the KRNCA.

PROPOSED ACTION

For this EIS, the proposed federal action is the adoption and implementation of an RMP for the KRNCA, to serve as a comprehensive blueprint for its future use and management over the next twenty years. The RMP is being prepared using BLM's planning regulations and guidance issued under the authority of the Federal Land Policy and Management Act (FLPMA) of 1976. The EIS is incorporated as part of this document to assess the environmental consequences associated with various alternative management scenarios. It is also included to meet the requirements of the National Environmental Policy Act of 1969 (NEPA), Council on Environmental Quality regulations for implementing NEPA (40 Code of Federal Regulations 1500-1508), and requirements of BLM's NEPA Handbook, H-1790-1.

PURPOSE OF AND NEED FOR THE KING RANGE RMP

The purpose of this RMP is to evaluate the original 1974 King Range Management Program and reaffirm and reestablish guidance, objectives, policies, and management actions for the KRNCA that reflect current issues, knowledge, and conditions. This planning effort is comprehensive in nature, evaluating existing management plans and resolving or addressing issues within the KRNCA identified through agency, interagency, and public scoping efforts. This effort also identifies the area's mission, long-range management goals, intermediate objectives, and actions and allowable uses to meet those objectives. Several additions and adjustments to the original Management Program have occurred since 1974 as environmental conditions, public needs, and management issues and strategies have changed: Rule making has been implemented through publication in the *Federal Register*; activity-level plans have been developed and implemented; and the Northwest Forest Plan (April 1994) amended all public land use plans in the Pacific Northwest, including the King Range Management Program. An additional plan amendment was made in 1998 to change management of Black Sands Beach to non-motorized use only.

This RMP analyzes the current management situation and identifies desired future conditions to be maintained or achieved, management actions necessary to achieve specific objectives, and allowable uses of the public lands. The Proposed RMP addresses and integrates all existing management plans and programs, including but not limited to: fire management; livestock grazing; threatened and endangered species; recreation and visitor services; watershed management; and transportation. The plan also meets the stated requirements of the 1970 King Range Act.

MISSION AND VISION STATEMENTS

The following mission and vision statements were developed based on the direction, intent, and spirit of the legislation and policies establishing management of the area, the KRNCA's role as a component of the BLM's National Landscape Conservation System, and input from the public during the scoping process for the plan:

> Mission Statement:
> "The BLM will manage the King Range National Conservation Area to conserve one of America's last wild and undeveloped coastal landscapes for the use and enjoyment of present and future generations."

As part of this larger mission, the BLM will:

- Provide recreation opportunities that complement the rugged primitive character that makes the area distinctive as California's Lost Coast.
- Provide for use of natural resources in a sustainable manner.
- Protect and enhance wildlife habitat with an emphasis on species dependent on old-growth forests.
- Provide healthy watersheds for aquatic species with emphasis on anadromous fisheries restoration.
- Respect community values and seek opportunities for local involvement in area conservation and use.

PLANNING PROCESS AND PUBLIC COLLABORATION

The planning process for this Proposed RMP opened with publication of the Notice of Intent in the *Federal Register* on October 11, 2002 (volume 67, no. 198). Media announcements and a planning update mailer requested public input and announced public scoping open houses, held in five cities during November 2002. The formal scoping period ended December 31, 2002, although additional comments were accepted after that date to accommodate mail and e-mail delays from a severe winter storm. A total of over 1,200 comments were compiled from the meetings and the 105 written submissions received by the deadline. These comments were recorded and categorized according to both source and topic, and were then reviewed and assessed in a scoping report published by the BLM in February 2003.

The clearest message from people who submitted comments during the scoping process was that they value the King Range for its primitive character—it represents a unique opportunity to experience the California coastline in a relatively undeveloped and natural state. This priority forms the core of this plan's vision for the future of the KRNCA, and relates to all other activities and management issues. The key planning themes identified by the public during this process fell into seven broad areas: (1) the area's primitive character and values; (2) recreation use; (3) transportation and access; (4) education and interpretation; (5) community support and involvement; (6) resource conservation and management; and (7) fire management.

In accordance with the Wild and Scenic Rivers Act (16 USC 1271-1287), a Wild and Scenic Rivers eligibility and suitability study was conducted and integrated into the Draft RMP (Appendix D). This study provides background information and compiled resource data regarding the eligibility, classification, and suitability or unsuitability of planning area river segments for potential inclusion in the National Wild and Scenic Rivers System.

The Draft RMP/EIS was published on January 16, 2004, and was open to public comment for 90 days, until April 16, 2004. During this period, five public comment meetings were held in the same cities as the earlier round of scoping: Petrolia, Eureka, San Francisco, Garberville, and Shelter Cove. A total of 33 individuals and organizations submitted formal comments at these meetings. In addition, the BLM received a total of 829 written comments from agencies (5), organizations (11), and individuals (813). Many of these written submissions contained multiple comments on different topics. Of the submissions from individuals, 95 percent (774) were standardized "form" letters which were identical or very similar in content: of these, four related to the issue of mountain bicycles and their access to the King Range; the remaining 769 form letters related to wilderness and backcountry management.

MANAGEMENT ALTERNATIVES

The basic goal of developing alternatives is to explore a reasonable range of use options and resource protection measures, for management of the KRNCA to meet a variety of public needs. Alternatives must meet the project purpose and need; must be reasonable (i.e., implementable); must provide a mix of resource protection, management use, and development; must be responsive to the planning themes; must meet established planning criteria (listed in Chapter 1); and must meet federal laws, regulations, and BLM planning policy.

Four alternatives were developed and carried forward for detailed analysis in the Draft RMP/EIS. Alternative A, continuation of current management as the "no action" alternative, was developed using available inventory data, existing planning decisions and policies, and existing land use allocations and programs. Alternatives B, C, and D were developed with input from public scoping and collaborative work among the BLM interdisciplinary planning team to represent a range of approaches to balancing use and protection of the King Range's primitive character. The vision for the future of the KRNCA, as determined through public scoping input, legislation, and other direction, involves maintaining its unique character as a vestige of undeveloped California coastline, which allows a moderate continuum of management options. Within that range, however, the alternatives represent different strategies for accomplishing that vision.

Alternative B represents the most "hands off" approach, emphasizing the utilization of natural processes wherever possible and minimizing human impacts. This would result in low levels of on-the-ground resource management, and limited recreation use focused on providing maximum opportunities for solitude and wilderness-type experiences. In the middle of the spectrum, Alternative C would provide a greater diversity of uses and approaches to management, with a broad mix of tools and moderate levels of use allowed. Alternative D would take an active approach, allowing maximum recreation use while still maintaining and enhancing resource conditions. This alternative includes the widest application of management tools and actions, and provides higher levels of recreation use with fewer opportunities for solitude than the other alternatives.

Under Alternatives B, C, and D, some management decisions are organized by geographic zones. Three zones have been delineated, which represent a consolidation, revision, and simplification of the seven original zones in the 1974 King Range Management Program. All three of the new zones allow multiple uses, but like the original zones, each emphasizes different primary resource values to be conserved and/or allowable uses available in various parts of the planning area. All public lands within the planning area are assigned to one of the three zones: Backcountry, Frontcountry, or Residential.

- Backcountry Zone – includes the western coastal slope of the King Range plus the Honeydew Creek watershed, covering 38,833 acres. It is essentially roadless, with a primary management goal focused on recognizing and managing this unique and primitive undeveloped coastal area. This zone is the core of the KRNCA and Lost Coast, providing a primary use of a wildland recreation experience to visitors while protecting resources such as old-growth forests, old-growth forest dependent wildlife, and open coastal grasslands. This environmental setting offers the greatest opportunity for both solitude and challenge, and self-sufficiency is crucial. Management activities here need to follow the "minimal-tool" concept to maintain and restore the area to a natural functioning ecosystem. Under this approach, the BLM would achieve resource management objectives with hand tools, except in emergency situations or where motorized equipment is determined through careful analysis to be the minimum necessary tool. Appropriate public use would include non-mechanized activities with no facilities other than trails and a few primitive facilities (e.g., signs, sanitary facilities) for resource protection.

- Frontcountry Zone – covers 25,661 acres and acts as the transition zone between the Backcountry Zone and surrounding private lands, and represents a broad mix of uses and tools for management. Most BLM roads and facilities are located in the southern and central parts of this zone, many functioning as "staging areas" to provide access for visitors into the backcountry. Primary uses include a more extensive array of public uses, including special forest products harvesting, fuelwood cutting, and camping in existing developed facilities. Also a primary management focus would include more intensive on-the-ground actions, such as forest stand improvement, fuels reduction work, fire break construction, or use of heavy equipment for watershed restoration. This is the zone where the most active resource restoration activities could occur. Despite the concentration of roads and facilities in this zone, many parts of the Frontcountry Zone are remote and contain minimal roads and facility developments. Examples are the areas near Cooskie Peak, Mill Creek, and Fourmile Creek in the northern part of the KRNCA. These lands were incorporated into this zone primarily because of their interface with surrounding private lands, and the need to allow for more intensive fuels management and resource restoration. No additional major public use facility developments (except trails) are proposed for these northern parts of the Frontcountry Zone under the plan.

- Residential Zone – covers 2,944 acres and represents the town of Shelter Cove, which is mostly private land except for beachfront lots and parks managed by BLM. The KRNCA's most highly developed recreation sites are in this zone, and the primary uses and management goals focus on developed recreation and resource protection. The Residential Zone also represents a place to direct non-backcountry visitors, where they can learn about the primitive character of the Lost

Coast and experience some of its values without the challenge of experiencing the Backcountry directly.

PREFERRED ALTERNATIVE AND PROPOSED RMP

The Preferred Alternative in the Draft RMP was selected by the BLM from the range of alternatives, as the best balance in managing both resources and uses of the King Range. Considerations included: environmental impacts of the alternatives; issues raised throughout the planning process; specific environmental values, resources, and resource uses; conflict resolution; public input; planning criteria, and laws and regulations. The Proposed RMP is the Agency Preferred Alternative from the Draft RMP, with changes reflecting public comment, collaboration during the preparation of this Proposed RMP, and BLM's internal comments and analysis of the entire Draft RMP.

The Proposed RMP is outlined in detail in Chapter 4. The paragraphs below highlight management guidance for each resource. The Preferred Alternative from the Draft RMP that served as the basis for the Proposed RMP is also listed:

Visual Resources Management: Alternative C

The visual quality of the rugged coastline along the King Range is one of the key reasons why many people visit the area, according to public scoping efforts. Protection of these scenic qualities also contributed to the designation of the area as a National Conservation Area. Zones within the KRNCA are categorized according to the BLM Visual Resource Management (VRM) classification system, used to ensure that any development or changes in the scenic landscape maintain or enhance the overall viewshed qualities. The proposed plan would designate the Backcountry Zone as VRM Class I; designate the Frontcountry Zone as VRM Class II and III; and designate the Residential Zone as Class IV.

Cultural and Historic Resources: Alternative D

The King Range contains substantial numbers of significant prehistoric sites and historic resources. Management efforts would reduce site deterioration and damage from other uses, as well as encourage understanding through education, outreach, and interpretive programs. The Proposed RMP would place priority on protection of cultural resources in all three zones, and would increase monitoring, site patrols, and collaboration with local Native American Tribes and individuals.

Lands and Realty: Alternative C

The BLM supported a vigorous land acquisition program in the 1970s and '80s, and most of the lands within the boundary of the KRNCA are now under public ownership. Past acquisitions have consolidated and enhanced management of the KRNCA. Acquisition is still a valuable tool for facilitating efficient and beneficial management of the area. Acquisitions are conducted on a willing-seller basis, and can be achieved through donation, purchase, exchange, or other less-than fee title transactions. The Proposed RMP includes a method for prioritizing land and interest in land acquisitions; different acquisition approaches for the three management zones; and a range of considerations for rights-of-way applications and permits. This section also identifies the need for the BLM to assert water rights and grant water rights-of-way only where watershed and fisheries values are protected.

Wilderness Characteristics: Alternative D

Management of lands with wilderness characteristics is part of BLM's multiple-use mandate, and is recognized within the spectrum of resource values and uses. With exceptions, these lands must be managed to protect these values. They are also managed for the use and enjoyment of the American people and may be devoted to the public purposes of recreation, scenic, scientific, educational, conservation, and historical use. In addition, they could augment multiple-use management of adjacent and nearby lands through the protection of watersheds and water yield, wildlife habitat, natural plant communities, and similar natural values.

The Proposed RMP would add five small parcels to the King Range Wilderness Study Area (WSA) (approximately 200 acres). These parcels were private inholdings within the WSA that have been acquired since the original Wilderness EIS was published in 1988. The KRNCA was also inventoried as part of this RMP process for additional areas with wilderness characteristics that adjoin the existing WSAs. The Proposed RMP would manage 1,465 acres adjacent to the existing King Range and Chemise Mountain WSAs for wilderness characteristics.

Wild and Scenic Rivers: Alternative D

As part of the RMP process, a review was conducted in 2003 to assess and evaluate all river segments in the planning area for eligibility for inclusion in the National Wild and Scenic River (WSR) System. Under the Proposed RMP, ten eligible river segments on nine different streams would be recommended as suitable for inclusion in the NWSRS. These include: Main Stem and North Fork Bear Creek, South Fork Bear Creek (Segments A and B), Big Creek, Big Flat Creek, Honeydew Creek, Gitchell Creek, Mattole River, and Mill Creek. The BLM would place all suitable river segments under protective management until a final decision is made by Congress.

Areas of Critical Environmental Concern: Alternative C

Areas of Critical Environmental Concern (ACECs) are areas of public land where special management attention is required to protect important natural and/or cultural resource values. The ACEC designation indicates to the public that the BLM recognizes these significant values, and has established special management measures to protect them. The Proposed RMP would continue management of the 655-acre Mattole Estuary ACEC to protect significant archaeological sites, the fragile sand dune ecosystem, and riparian areas/wildlife values in the Mattole Estuary and coastal strand south to Sea Lion Gulch. In addition, a new Mill Creek Watershed ACEC/Research Natural Area (RNA) would be established to include all public lands (approximately 680 acres) in the Mill Creek watershed. The primary features that would be protected by this designation are the water quality of this important anadromous fish stream/cold water tributary to the Mattole River, and the low-elevation old-growth Douglas fir forest.

Aquatic Ecosystems and Fisheries: Alternative C

The KRNCA contains important habitat for species listed under the Endangered Species Act (ESA), including anadromous fishes such as steelhead, coho, and chinook salmon. The overall goal for the KRNCA is to restore and maintain the ecological health of watersheds and aquatic ecosystems on public lands, and, to the extent possible, partner with other landowners to coordinate restoration efforts across watersheds. The Proposed RMP would implement upslope sediment reduction, instream habitat enhancement, riparian silviculture, and monitoring actions in the Mattole Basin in fish-bearing watersheds, as well as enhancement projects in the Mattole Estuary.

Wildlife Management: Alternative C
The Proposed RMP includes cooperative management with the California Department of Fish and Game (CDFG) and the U.S. Fish and Wildlife Service (FWS) to achieve, maintain, and enhance natural wildlife populations, protect habitat, prevent damage, and increase public education. A range of specific actions are included for six sensitive wildlife species with habitat occurring in the KRNCA, as well as other issues involving management and monitoring of wildlife populations and their habitats.

Terrestrial/Vegetative Ecosystems: Alternative C
BLM manages the vegetative resources of the King Range to promote the overall health of this diverse biogeographical region and to provide for the wide spectrum of organisms, ecosystem processes, and human resource needs that depend upon these plant communities. The overall goal for vegetation management is to produce and/or maintain a mosaic of compositionally and structurally diverse habitat types and plant communities that have historically occurred prior to the mechanized era for logging and exclusion of fire regimes in the region; approximately 1950. Specific goals, objectives, and actions in the Proposed RMP address special status species, one potential plant pathogen, and for all major habitat/vegetation types including coastal dunes, coastal scrub, grasslands, and chaparral habitats.

Forest Management: Alternative D
All of the forested lands in the planning area have been designated as a Late-Successional Reserve (LSR) under the Northwest Forest Plan, and therefore must be managed to promote late successional forest characteristics. All active forest management activities in the plan are focused in the Frontcountry Zone only, and are intended to develop more natural stand characteristics in areas that were previously harvested. Some of these previously-logged areas have burned in high intensity fires, or are at risk for future fires of stand-replacing intensity. The primary goal in silvicultural treatments would be to increase the Douglas-fir component in tanoak dominated stands, and "fireproof" this Douglas-fir component so that it has a greater chance to reach maturity. Without silvicultural treatments, most of these previously harvested stands would remain in an unnatural cycle of young forest repeatedly burned by high intensity stand replacing fires. All proposed treatments including thinning, fire salvage, and other silvicultural practices would be implemented only on sites where it can be demonstrated that they would accelerate development of late successional forest structure.

Special Forest Products: Alternative C
Special forest products collected in the King Range include wild mushrooms, fuelwood, beargrass, and other vegetative products for floral trades. Many special forest products are also associated with strong cultural meanings or roles in local communities. Under the Proposed RMP, special forest product permits would be issued for a variety of forest resources for personal collection and commercial harvesting throughout the KRNCA. Permits may be issued for such vegetative resources as but not limited to: beargrass, huckleberry, salal, mushrooms, and fuelwood. Permits may be restricted as to amount, location of collection and length of time. Additional stipulations would be identified on the permits for resource protection. The number of permits that would be issued will depend on environmental concerns and limited biological resources.

Grazing Management: Alternative C
In the northwestern corner of the King Range, livestock grazing has contributed to the ranching economy of the Mattole Valley. Grazing has also helped maintain open grasslands above the coastline.

The KRNCA currently has four active grazing leases, with associated allotments, representing a total of 2,050 AUMs; these would be maintained under the Proposed RMP. There are also several outstanding administrative issues that would to be addressed, redefining the boundary of one allotment to improve rangeland health, and administratively making four unused allotments permanently unavailable for grazing, with no change in the number of AUMs authorized.

Fire Management: Alternative C

Throughout history, fire has been one of the primary forces affecting the King Range landscape, creating and maintaining a mosaic pattern of fire-adapted ecosystems such as grasslands and chaparral. The Proposed RMP seeks to balance management for the natural dynamics of fire effects across the landscape and protection of property and resources from damage both within and adjacent to the KRNCA. The conditions associated with individual fires and the resulting tactics employed to manage those fires are too numerous to document in this plan; the appropriate management response to a specific situation must take these conditions into account along with area fire use objectives. The Proposed RMP outlines differing fire management objectives and actions in each management zone to achieve an overall management goal of developing a landscape resistant to damage associated with large scale, high intensity fires by allowing for the natural dynamic effects of fire to occur on the ecosystem, and providing an appropriate management response on all wildland fires, with an emphasis on firefighter and public safety.

Travel Management: Alternative C

The purpose of the travel management program is to provide a transportation network for public and administrative access while minimizing impacts on natural and cultural resources in the area. Area roads are designed and managed to blend with the primitive character of the KRNCA, and to allow for a diversity of uses and experiences. Limitations on use are sometimes needed to ensure safety or to protect resources from degradation due to excessive erosion. The KRNCA has a long history of travel management planning, so the Proposed RMP includes minimal changes to the existing program, most often small alterations to use patterns on specific roads.

Recreation: Alternative C

Recreation management represents one of the major challenges in the King Range, as the very qualities of pristine wilderness and remote coastal access can be degraded if too many people decide to visit at the same time. There is a strong consensus among user groups that protecting the KRNCA's unique character is a priority, yet increasing numbers of people are visiting the area seeking a wide variety of activities and experiences. The Proposed RMP considers a broad spectrum of recreation management possibilities, from facilities development to signage and permitting systems to balance access levels with opportunities for visitors to find solitude and the wilderness-type recreation experience for which the King Range is best known. As a result, the three management zones are planned for different types and levels of recreation use, so as to direct users to the parts of the KRNCA most appropriate for their interests and activities.

Interpretation and Education: Alternative A

The interpretive and educational programs in the King Range currently revolve around several major themes:

- Dynamic physical processes continue to shape the rugged isolation of the KRNCA coastline, which in turn, have created the area's special cultural and natural resource values.

- The BLM manages the KRNCA to maintain the area's undeveloped character and to protect and enhance resource values while providing a diversity of recreation opportunities for the public.
- The King Range is a very dynamic and fragile area (i.e., weather is very variable and can change rapidly, how the tides affect the beach hike, how humans impact the tidepools and other habitats).
- The King Range is located in the rural region of Southern Humboldt County. Visitors will be encouraged to travel in the area in a way that is respectful to the neighborhood.
- People will be encouraged to get to know and respect the wild, untamed character of the land and to experience the King Range on nature's terms.

A vibrant and effective interpretation and education program has already been built around these themes, and so the Proposed RMP seeks to continue implementing this program, following the "no action" continuation of current management.

ENVIRONMENTAL CONSEQUENCES

The management alternatives were developed to maximize a variety of public benefits while minimizing adverse effects on both ecosystem function and the human environment. Detailed descriptions of the direct and indirect impacts of management under the Proposed RMP for each resource are provided in Chapter 4, along with a discussion of the possible cumulative impacts that could result from actions taken in this RMP. The changes likely to result from the proposed actions are generally subtle in nature, with moderate positive impacts and mostly minor or negligible negative impacts.

CONSULTATION AND COORDINATION

As discussed above, the BLM implemented an extensive public participation process to solicit and address public input, including formal public scoping meetings and a scoping report summarizing public input. As part of this process, the BLM also met with the Shelter Cove Property Owners Association, the Garberville Rotary Club, and the Garberville Chamber of Commerce. Interagency meetings and consultations were held with the California Coastal Commission, National Marine Fisheries Service, Fish and Wildlife Service, and the State Historic Preservation Officer. Additionally, the BLM consulted and coordinated with federal, state, county, and local government elected officials and representatives, as well as the Bear River Band of Rohnerville Rancheria. Communication is ongoing and will continue through the implementation of the plan. Chapter 6 provides a discussion of coordination and consultation.

APPENDIX C

MATERIAL SAFETY DATA SHEETS

Oil and Gas Well Drilling and Servicing eTool

Drilling >> Drilling Ahead >> MSDS

This Material Safety Data Sheet (MSDS) contains information on the use and procedures for handling Caustic Soda. There are data sheets on all the hazardous chemicals used in the drilling industry. Data sheets must be supplied by the manufacturer and/or supplier each time the chemical is introduced into the workplace. See Hazard Communication: Toxic and Hazardous Substances [1910.1200]

MATERIAL SAFETY DATA SHEET

CAUSTIC SODA (NaOH)

1. CHEMICAL PRODUCT AND COMPANY IDENTIFICATION

TRADE NAME: CAUSTIC SODA (NaOH)
UN/NA (PIN) No.: 1823
CHEMICAL CLASS: Bases, alkalies (inorganic).
APPLICATIONS: Oil well drilling fluid additive. pH modifier.
EMERGENCY TELEPHONE: 281-561-1600
SUPPLIER: Supplied by a Business Unit of M-I L.L.C.
P.O. Box 42842, Houston, Texas 77242-2842
See cover sheet for local supplier.
TELEPHONE: 281-561-1509
FAX: 281-561-7240
CONTACT PERSON: Sam Hoskin

2. COMPOSITION, INFORMATION ON INGREDIENTS

INGREDIENT NAME:	CAS No.:	CONTENTS :	EPA RQ:	TPQ:
Sodium hydroxide	1310-73-2	100 %	1 000 lbs	

3. HAZARDS IDENTIFICATION

EMERGENCY OVERVIEW:

DANGER! CAUSES EYE AND SKIN BURNS. Do not get in eyes or on skin or clothing. Avoid breathing airborne product. Keep container closed. Use only with adequate ventilation. Wash thoroughly after handling. Avoid contact with water or moisture, which may generate sufficient heat to ignite combustible materials. This product is a white pellet or flake material. Slippery when wet.

ACUTE EFFECTS:

HEALTH HAZARDS, GENERAL:

Contact with this product is severely irritating to the eyes, skin, and respiratory tract and may cause severe eye injury.

INHALATION: Severely irritating to the respiratory tract if inhaled.
INGESTION: May cause burns in mucous membranes, throat, esophagus, and stomach.
SKIN: Corrosive to skin.
EYES: Corrosive to eyes.

CHRONIC EFFECTS:

CARCINOGENICITY:

IARC: Not listed. OSHA: Not regulated. NTP: Not listed.
10296 - CAUSTIC SODA (NaOH)

ROUTE OF ENTRY:

Inhalation. Skin and/or eye contact.

TARGET ORGANS:

Respiratory system, lungs. Skin. Eyes.

4. FIRST AID MEASURES

GENERAL: Persons seeking medical attention should carry a copy of this MSDS with them.
INHALATION: Move the exposed person to fresh air at once. Perform artificial respiration if breathing has stopped. Get medical attention.
INGESTION: Drink a couple of glasses water or milk. Do NOT induce vomiting unless directed to do so by a physician. Never give anything by mouth to an unconscious person. Get medical attention.
SKIN: Wash skin thoroughly with soap and water. Remove contaminated clothing. Get medical attention if any discomfort continues.
EYES: Promptly wash eyes with lots of water while lifting the eye lids. Continue to rinse for at least 15 minutes. Get medical attention if any discomfort continues.

5. FIRE FIGHTING MEASURES

AUTO IGNITION TEMP. (°F): N/D
FLAMMABILITY LIMIT - LOWER(%): N/D
FLAMMABILITY LIMIT - UPPER(%): N/D
EXTINGUISHING MEDIA:

Carbon dioxide (CO2). Dry chemicals. Foam.

SPECIAL FIRE FIGHTING PROCEDURES:

No specific fire fighting procedure given.

UNUSUAL FIRE AND EXPLOSION HAZARDS:

Upon contact with certain metals and water or moist air, hydrogen gas is generated, forming explosive mixtures with air.

HAZARDOUS COMBUSTION PRODUCTS:

Irritating gases/vapors/fumes.

6. ACCIDENTAL RELEASE MEASURES

PERSONAL PRECAUTIONS:

Wear proper personal protective equipment (see MSDS Section 8).

SPILL CLEAN-UP PROCEDURES:

Avoid generating and spreading of dust. Shovel into dry containers. Cover and move the containers. Flush the area with water. Do not contaminate drainage or waterways. Repackage or recycle if possible.

7. HANDLING AND STORAGE

HANDLING PRECAUTIONS:

Avoid handling that causes dust to generate. Wear full protective clothing for prolonged exposure and/or high concentrations. Make eye wash and emergency shower available at the work place. Wash hands often and change clothing when needed. Provide good ventilation. Provide mechanical ventilation or local exhaust ventilation.

STORAGE PRECAUTIONS:

Store at moderate temperatures in dry, well ventilated area. Keep in original container.

8. EXPOSURE CONTROLS, PERSONAL PROTECTION

		OSHA PEL:	ACGIH TLV:	OTHER:	
INGREDIENT NAME:	CAS No.:	TWA: STEL:	TWA: STEL:	TWA: STEL:	UNITS:
Sodium hydroxide	1310-73-2	2	2 C*		mg/m3

*C = Ceiling Limit

PROTECTIVE EQUIPMENT:
ENGINEERING CONTROLS: Use appropriate engineering controls such as exhaust ventilation and process enclosure to reduce air contamination and keep worker exposure below the applicable limits.
VENTILATION: Supply natural or mechanical ventilation adequate to exhaust airborne product and keep exposures below the applicable limits.
RESPIRATORS: Use at least a NIOSH-approved N95 half-mask disposable or reuseable particulate respirator. In work environments containing oil mist/aerosol, use at least a NIOSH-approved P95 half-mask disposable or reuseable particulate respirator.
PROTECTIVE GLOVES: Use gauntlet type rubber gloves.
EYE PROTECTION: Use tight-fitting goggles if dust is generated. Wear splash-proof eye goggles to prevent any possibility of eye contact.
PROTECTIVE CLOTHING: Wear appropriate clothing to prevent any possibility of skin contact. Provide eyewash station and safety shower.
HYGIENIC WORK PRACTICES: Wash promptly with soap and water if skin becomes contaminated. Change work clothing daily if there is any possibility of contamination.

9. PHYSICAL AND CHEMICAL PROPERTIES

APPEARANCE/PHYSICAL STATE: Pellets or flakes.
COLOR: White.
ODOR: Odorless or no characteristic odor.
SOLUBILITY DESCRIPTION: Soluble in water.
BOILING POINT (°F, interval): 2530 PRESSURE: 760mmHg
MELT./FREEZ. POINT (°F, interval): 604
DENSITY/SPECIFIC GRAVITY (g/ml): 2.13 TEMPERATURE (°F): 68
BULK DENSITY: 133 lb/cu. ft.; 2131 kg/m3
VAPOR DENSITY (air=1): N/A
VAPOR PRESSURE: 42 mmHg TEMPERATURE (°F): 1832
pH-VALUE, DILUTED SOLUTION: 13 CONCENTRATION (%,M): 1%

10. STABILITY AND REACTIVITY

STABILITY: Normally stable.
CONDITIONS TO AVOID: Reacts strongly with water. Avoid contact with acids.
HAZARDOUS POLYMERIZATION: Will not polymerize.
POLYMERIZATION DESCRIPTION: Not relevant.
MATERIALS TO AVOID: Organochlorine solvents, nitro and nitroso compounds, organic peroxides; aluminum, zinc, tin and their alloys.
HAZARDOUS DECOMPOSITION PRODUCTS: No specific hazardous decomposition products noted.

11. TOXICOLOGICAL INFORMATION

Component: Sodium hydroxide

TOXICOLOGICAL DATA:

24 hours. Eye. Rabbit. 1 mg Severe Irritation Corrosive effects.
24 hours. Skin. Rabbit. 500 mg Severe Irritation Corrosive effects.
LDLo. Oral. Rabbit. 500 mg/kg Acute toxicity.

TOXIC DOSE - LD 50: 1350 mg/kg (skn-rbt)

12. ECOLOGICAL INFORMATION

LC 50, 96 HRS, FISH, mg/l: 125 (Mosquitofish)

EC 50, 48 HRS, DAPHNIA, mg/l: 100

ACUTE AQUATIC TOXICITY:

This product passes the mysid shrimp toxicity test required by the U.S. Environmental Protection Agency (EPA) Region VI (Gulf of Mexico) NPDES Permit, which regulates offshore discharge of drilling fluids, when tested in a standard drilling fluid. Contact M-I's Environmental Affairs Department for more information.
This product is approved for use under the U.S. Environmental Protection Agency (EPA) Region IX (California) General NPDES Permit which regulates offshore discharges of drilling fluids. Contact M-I's Environmental Affairs Department for more information.

13. DISPOSAL CONSIDERATIONS

WASTE MANAGEMENT:

This product, should it become a waste, is hazardous by U.S. RCRA criteria.
THIS CONTAINER MAY BE HAZARDOUS WHEN EMPTY. Empty containers retain residues. All labeled precautions must be observed.

DISPOSAL METHODS:

Recover and reclaim or recycle, if practical. Should this product become a waste, dispose of in a permitted industrial landfill. Ensure that containers are empty by RCRA criteria before disposal in a permitted industrial landfill.

14. TRANSPORT INFORMATION

LABEL FOR CONVEYANCE:
PROPER SHIPPING DESCRIPTION II: Sodium hydroxide, solid, 8, UN1823, PG II
GENERAL: RQ = 1000
EMERGENCY RESPONSE GUIDE No.: 154

U.S. DOT:

UN/NA No.: 1823
U.S. DOT HAZARD LABEL: CORROSIVE (Black/white diam.) DOT17
U.S. DOT CLASS: Class 8 - Corrosive Material
U.S. DOT PACKING GROUP: II
U.S. DOT PACKAGING INSTRUCTIONS: 49 CFR 173.154; 173.212; 240

CANADIAN TRANSPORT:

TDGR CLASS: Class 8 - Corrosives
TDGR LABEL: Corrosive

SEA TRANSPORT:

UN No. SEA: 1823
IMDG CLASS: Class 8 - Corrosives
IMDG PAGE No.: 8225-1
IMDG PACK GR.: II
EmS No.: 8-06
MFAG TABLE No.: 705

AIR TRANSPORT:

UN No., AIR: 1823
ICAO CLASS: Class 8 - Corrosives
AIR PACK GR.: II

15. REGULATORY INFORMATION

REGULATORY STATUS OF INGREDIENTS:	CAS No:	TSCA:	CERCLA:	SARA 302:	SARA 313:	DSL(CAN):
NAME: Sodium hydroxide	1310-73-2	Yes	Yes	No	No	Yes

US FEDERAL REGULATIONS:

WASTE CLASSIFICATION: A hazardous waste by U.S. RCRA criteria

REGULATORY STATUS: This product or its components, if a mixture, is subject to following regulations (Not meant to be all-inclusive, selected regulations represented):

SECTION 313: This product does not contain toxic chemical subject to the reporting requirements of Section 313 of Title III of the Superfund Amendment and Reauthorization Act of 1986 and 40 CFR Part 372.

SARA 311 Categories:

1: Immediate (Acute) Health Effects

5. Reactivity Hazard

The components of this product are listed on or are exempt from the following international chemical registries:

TSCA (U.S.)

DSL (Canada)

STATE REGULATIONS:

STATE REGULATORY STATUS: This product or its components, if a mixture, is subject to following regulations (Not meant to be all-inclusive, selected regulations represented):

Illinois Right-to-Know
New Jersey Right-to-Know
Pennsylvania Right-to-Know
PROPOSITION 65: This product does not contain chemicals considered by the State of California's Safe Drinking Water and Toxic Enforcement Act of 1986 as causing cancer or reproductive toxicity, and for which warnings are now required.

CANADIAN REGULATIONS:

LABELS FOR SUPPLY:

REGULATORY STATUS:

This Material Safety Data Sheet has been prepared in compilance with the Controlled Product Regulations.
Canadian WHMIS Classification: E - Corrosive Material D2B - Other Toxic Effects: Toxic Material

16. OTHER INFORMATION

NPCA HMIS HAZARD INDEX: 3 Serious Hazard

FLAMMABILITY: 0 Minimal Hazard

REACTIVITY: 1 Slight Hazard

NPCA HMIS PERS. PROTECT. INDEX: X Ask your supervisor for guidance

USER NOTES: N/A = Not applicable N/D = Not determined

INFORMATION SOURCES:

OSHA Permissible Exposure Limits, 29 CFR 1910, Subpart Z, Section 1910.1000, Air Contaminants.
ACGIH Threshold Limit Values and Biological Exposure Indices for Chemical Substances and Physical Agents (latest edition). Sax's Dangerous Properties of Industrial Materials, 9th ed., Lewis, R.J. Sr., (ed.), VNR, New York, New York, (1997).
Product information provided by the commercial vendor(s).

PREPARED BY: Sam Hoskin

REVISION No./Repl. MSDS of: 1 / June 3, 1996

MSDS STATUS: Approved.

DATE: June 9, 1998

DISCLAIMER:

MSDS furnished independent of product sale. While every effort has been made to accurately describe this product, some of the data are obtained from sources beyond our direct supervision. We cannot make any assertions as to its reliability or completeness; therefore, user may rely on it only at user's risk. We have made no effort to censor or conceal deleterious aspects of this product. Since we cannot anticipate or control the conditions under which this information and product may be used, we make no guarantee that the precautions we have suggested will be adequate for all individuals and/or situations. It is the obligation of each user of this product to comply with the requirements of all applicable laws regarding use and disposal of this product. Additional information will be furnished upon request to assist the user; however, no warranty, either expressed or implied, nor liability of any nature with respect to this product or to the data herein is made or incurred hereunder.

Occupational Safety and Health Administration
200 Constitution Avenue, NW
Washington, DC 20210

APPENDIX D

LOCAL EMERGENCY RESPONSE COMMITTEE

Arapahoe County
Colorado's First

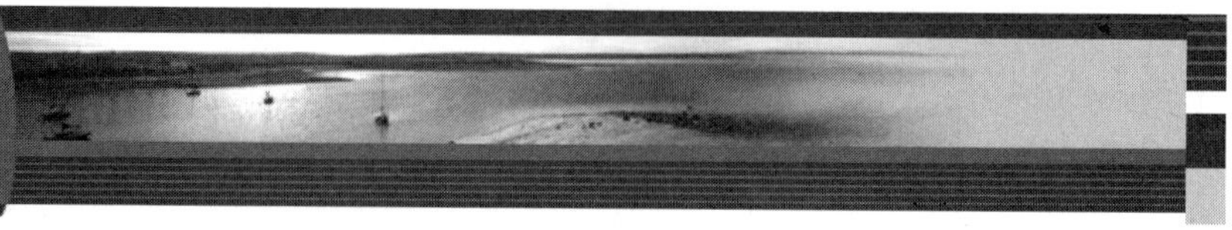

Access Account

Account Status
Change Passwd
Edit Contacts
Facility Map
Links
List Products
New Product
Reports

Log off

Contact Information

Sheriff's Office
Arapahoe County
13101 Broncos Parkway
Centennial, CO 80112
(720)874-4049
Email: LEPC

Hazardous Materials

List Products

Business Information:

Community High School
1234 Community Street
Centennial, CO
80112

Contact Information:

Frank Smith
303-344-2345

Fire Agency:

South Metro Fire

Overall NFPA Rating:

3, 4, 3, Water Reactive Chemical and Oxidixer and Corrosive

Products/Chemicals stored on location:

Product Name/Chemical	Max Amount	As of Date	
ACETIC ACID	400 Milliliters	12-05-06	
ACETIC ACID, GLACIAL	500 Milliliters	12-05-06	
ALBUMIN BOVINE	2 Ounces	12-05-06	
ALUMINUM CHLORIDE	11 Ounces	11-13-03	
ALUMINUM NITRATE	13 Ounces	12-05-06	
ALUMINUM SULFATE	7 Ounces	12-05-06	
AMMONIA	1000 Milliliters	11-04-03	Ingredients
AMMONIUM ACETATE	1 Lbs	12-05-06	
AMMONIUM CHLORIDE	3 Lbs	12-05-06	
AMMONIUM HYDROXIDE	1500 Milliliters	12-05-06	
AMMONIUM MOLYBDATE	4 Ounces	11-13-03	
AMMONIUM NITRATE	1 Lbs	12-05-06	
AMMONIUM SULFATE	1 Lbs	12-05-06	
AMMONIUM THIOCYANATE	27 Ounces	11-13-03	
ASCORBIC ACID	4 Ounces	11-13-03	
BARIUM CARBONATE	7 Ounces	11-13-03	
BARIUM CHLORIDE	2 Lbs	11-04-03	
BARIUM HYDROXIDE	6 Ounces	11-13-03	
BARIUM NITRATE	4 Ounces	11-13-03	
BARIUM SULFATE	9 Ounces	02-10-04	
BENEDICTS QUANTITATIVE SOLUTION	2 Gal	06-03-04	
BIURET SOLUTION	9 Ounces	02-10-04	
BORIC ACID	1 Lbs	11-04-03	
BROMTHYMOL BLUE INDICATOR SOLUTION	900 Milliliters	02-10-04	
BUTYL PHTHALATE	500 Milliliters	02-10-04	
CALCIUM ACETATE	4 Ounces	11-13-03	
CALCIUM CARBONATE	4 Ounces	11-13-03	
CALCIUM CHLORIDE	6 Ounces	11-13-03	
CALCIUM HYDROXIDE	11 Ounces	11-13-03	
CALCIUM NITRATE	1 Lbs	11-04-03	
CALCIUM OXIDE	9 Ounces	11-13-03	
CALCIUM SULFATE	11 Ounces	11-13-03	
CITRIC ACID	3 Lbs	11-04-03	
COBALT CHLORIDE	11 Ounces	11-13-03	
COBALT NITRATE	2 Ounces	02-10-04	
COPPER	1000 Milligrams	11-04-03	
CUPRIC CARBONATE	1 Lbs	02-10-04	
CUPRIC CHLORIDE	2 Lbs	11-04-03	
CUPRIC NITRATE	11 Ounces	11-13-03	
CUPRIC SULFATE	1 Lbs	11-04-03	
CYCLOHEXANE	500 Milliliters	11-04-03	
DEXTROSE	2 Lbs	11-05-03	
ETHYL ALCOHOL, DENATURED,	1 Gal	06-03-04	

ANHYDROUS			
ETHYLENE GLYCOL	500 Milliliters	11-04-03	
FERRIC CHLORIDE	11 Ounces	11-13-03	
FERRIC NITRATE	13 Ounces	11-13-03	
FERROUS SULFATE	2 Ounces	11-13-03	
GLYCERIN	250 Milliliters	11-04-03	
HEXANES	1500 Milliliters	11-04-03	
HYDROCHLORIC ACID	5100 Milliliters	11-04-03	
HYDROGEN PEROXIDE	750 Milliliters	11-13-03	Ingredients
INDIGO CARMINE	1000 Milligrams	03-01-04	
IODINE	18 Ounces	11-13-03	
IODINE-POTASSIUM IODIDE SOLUTION	2500 Milliliters	03-01-04	
ION EXCHANGE RESIN	16 Ounces	03-01-04	
IRON FILINGS	3000 Milligrams	03-01-04	
IRON POWDER	53 Ounces	03-01-04	
ISOPROPYL ALCOHOL	2113 Gal	06-03-04	
KEROSENE	500 Milliliters	11-04-03	
LEAD	1 Ounces	11-14-03	
LEAD NITRATE	7 Ounces	11-14-03	
LIMEWATER SOLUTION	100 Milliliters	03-01-04	
LIMEWATER TABLETS	3 Ounces	03-01-04	
LITHIUM	3000 Milligrams	11-05-03	
LITHIUM CHLORIDE	2 Ounces	11-14-03	
MAGNESIUM	1 Ounces	11-14-03	
MAGNESIUM CARBONATE	6 Ounces	11-14-03	
MAGNESIUM CHLORIDE	28 Ounces	11-14-03	
MAGNESIUM SULFATE	14 Ounces	11-14-03	
MARBLE CHIPS	70 Ounces	03-01-04	
METHYL ALCOHOL	2 Gal	11-13-03	
METHYL RED INDICATOR SOLUTION	500 Milliliters	03-01-04	
METHYLENE BLUE SOLUTION	500 Milliliters	03-01-04	
N-BUTYL ALCOHOL	800 Milliliters	11-04-03	
NAPHTHALENE	18 Ounces	11-14-03	
NICKEL	2 Ounces	11-14-03	
NICKEL CHLORIDE	42 Ounces	11-14-03	
NICKEL NITRATE	14 Ounces	11-14-03	
NITRIC ACID	1000 Milliliters	11-13-03	Ingredients
OXALIC ACID	32 Ounces	11-14-03	
PENTANE	150 Milliliters	11-05-03	
PEPSIN	2 Ounces	03-01-04	
PHENANTHROLINE	2 Ounces	03-01-04	
PHOSPHORIC ACID	2500 Milliliters	11-05-03	
POTASSIUM CHLORATE	11 Ounces	11-14-03	
POTASSIUM CHLORIDE	28 Ounces	11-14-03	
POTASSIUM CHROMATE	11 Ounces	11-14-03	
POTASSIUM DICHROMATE	1 Lbs	11-06-03	
POTASSIUM HYDROXIDE	1 Lbs	11-06-03	
POTASSIUM IODATE	1 Ounces	11-14-03	
POTASSIUM NITRATE	1 Lbs	11-06-03	
POTASSIUM PERMANGANATE	1 Lbs	11-06-03	
POTASSIUM PERMANGANATE SOLUTION	1 Lbs	11-06-03	
POTASSIUM PHOSPHATE	2 Ounces	11-14-03	
POTASSIUM THIOCYANATE	1 Lbs	11-06-03	
SALICYLIC ACID	1 Lbs	11-06-03	
SILICON	1 Lbs	11-06-03	
SILVER	5000 Milligrams	11-06-03	
SILVER NITRATE	1 Ounces	11-14-03	
SODIUM	1 Ounces	11-14-03	
SODIUM ACETATE	1 Lbs	11-06-03	
SODIUM BICARBONATE	1 Lbs	11-06-03	
SODIUM BISULFATE	16 Ounces	11-14-03	
SODIUM BISULFITE	9 Ounces	11-14-03	
SODIUM BORATE, TETRA	14 Ounces	03-01-04	
SODIUM CARBONATE	13 Ounces	11-14-03	
SODIUM CHLORIDE	28 Ounces	11-14-03	
SODIUM CHROMATE	2 Ounces	11-14-03	
SODIUM HYDROXIDE	4 Ounces	11-14-03	

SODIUM OXALATE	2 Ounces	11-14-03	
SODIUM PHOSPHATE, MONOBASIC	14 Ounces	11-14-03	
SODIUM PHOSPHATE, TRIBASIC	14 Ounces	11-14-03	
SODIUM POLYACRYLATE	14 Ounces	03-01-04	
SODIUM SULFITE	9 Ounces	11-14-03	
SODIUM THIOSULFATE	13 Ounces	11-14-03	
STARCH	16 Ounces	11-14-03	
STRONTIUM CHLORIDE	11 Ounces	11-14-03	
STRONTIUM NITRATE	18 Ounces	11-14-03	
SUCROSE	14 Ounces	11-14-03	
SULFUR	35 Ounces	11-14-03	
SULFURIC ACID	3500 Milliliters	06-03-04	Ingredients
TANNIC ACID	2 Ounces	11-14-03	
THYMOL BLUE INDICATOR SOLUTION	90 Milliliters	03-01-04	
UNIVERSAL INDICATOR SOLUTION	1450 Milliliters	03-01-04	
VINEGAR	2000 Milliliters	03-01-04	
ZINC	11 Ounces	11-14-03	
ZINC CHLORIDE	7 Ounces	11-14-03	

Copy this business's chemicals to another business
Available once business has been approved

Community High School
Lower Level

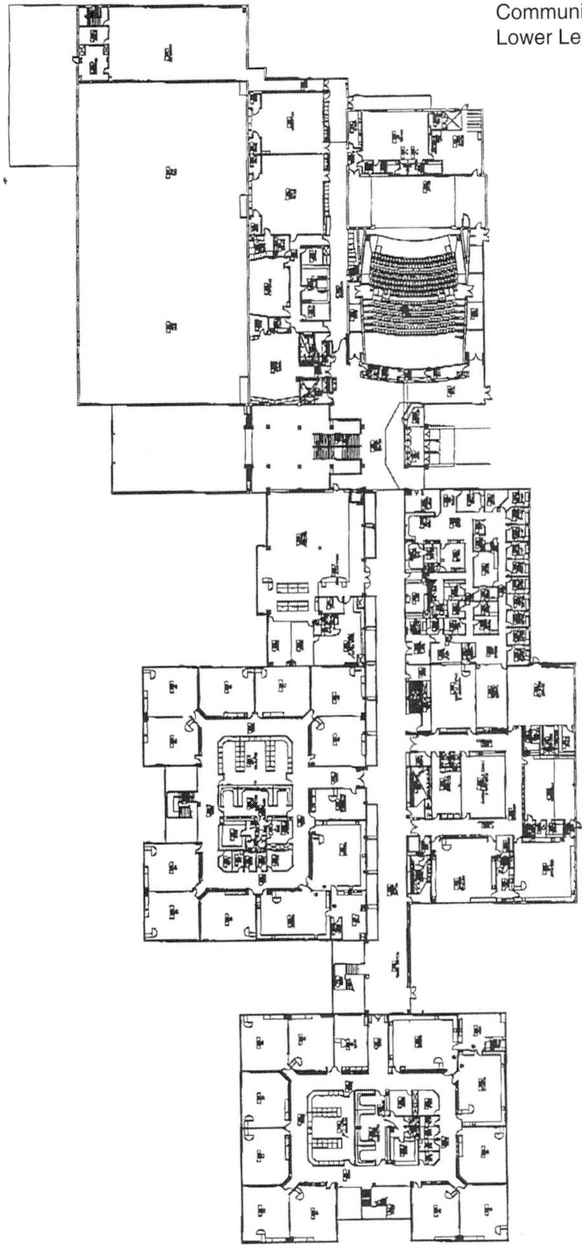

Community High School
Upper Level

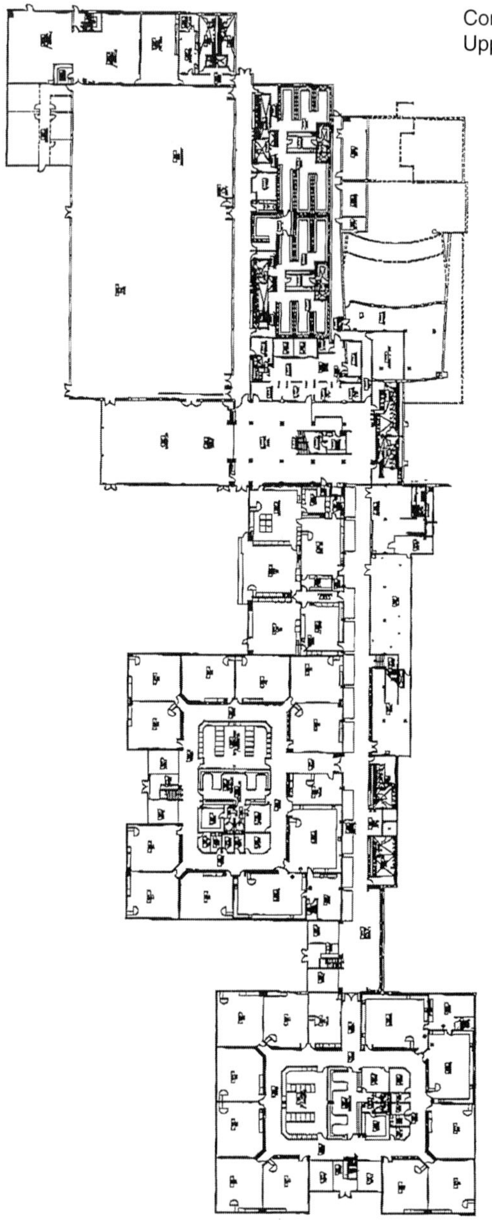

Arapahoe County
Colorado's First

Access Account

Account Status
Change Passwd
Edit Contacts
Facility Map
Links
List Products
New Product
Reports

Log off

Contact Information

Sheriff's Office
Arapahoe County
13101 Broncos Parkway
Centennial, CO 80112
(720)874-4049
Email: LEPC

Hazardous Materials

Account Status

Business Information:

Community High School
1234 Community Street
Centennial, CO
80112

Contact Information:

Frank Smith
303-344-2345

Fire Agency:

South Metro Fire

Current Certification Date: 7/10/1990

Account Status: Ready for Approval

Your application is currently under review by your local Fire Agency. You will be notified of your account status by e-mail or by mail upon the completion of your application review.

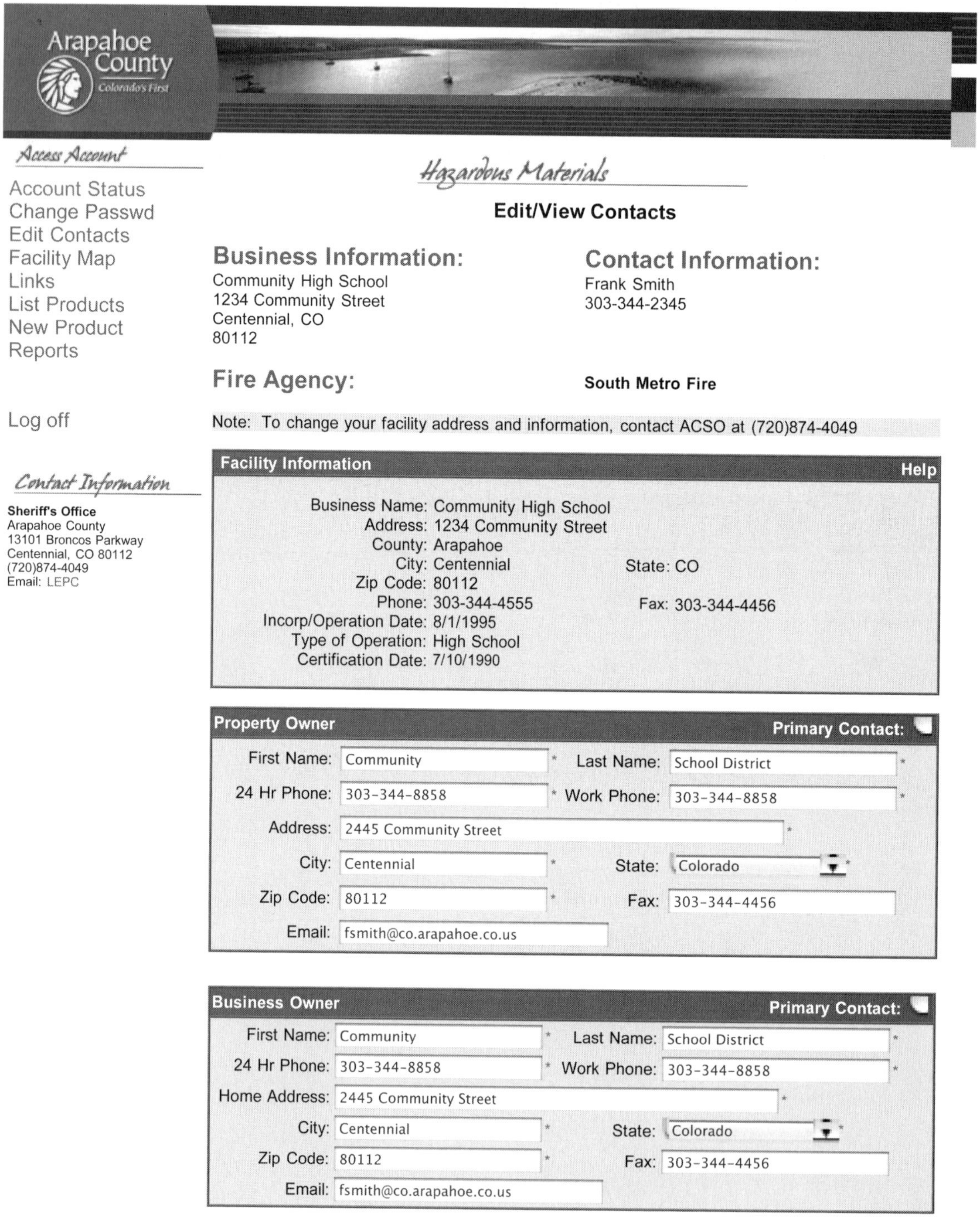

Arapahoe County
Colorado's First

Access Account

- Account Status
- Change Passwd
- Edit Contacts
- Facility Map
- Links
- List Products
- New Product
- Reports

Log off

Contact Information

Sheriff's Office
Arapahoe County
13101 Broncos Parkway
Centennial, CO 80112
(720)874-4049
Email: LEPC

Hazardous Materials

Edit/View Contacts

Business Information:
Community High School
1234 Community Street
Centennial, CO
80112

Contact Information:
Frank Smith
303-344-2345

Fire Agency: **South Metro Fire**

Note: To change your facility address and information, contact ACSO at (720)874-4049

Facility Information Help

Business Name:	Community High School		
Address:	1234 Community Street		
County:	Arapahoe		
City:	Centennial	State:	CO
Zip Code:	80112		
Phone:	303-344-4555	Fax:	303-344-4456
Incorp/Operation Date:	8/1/1995		
Type of Operation:	High School		
Certification Date:	7/10/1990		

Property Owner Primary Contact:

First Name:	Community *	Last Name:	School District *
24 Hr Phone:	303-344-8858 *	Work Phone:	303-344-8858 *
Address:	2445 Community Street *		
City:	Centennial *	State:	Colorado *
Zip Code:	80112 *	Fax:	303-344-4456
Email:	fsmith@co.arapahoe.co.us		

Business Owner Primary Contact:

First Name:	Community *	Last Name:	School District *
24 Hr Phone:	303-344-8858 *	Work Phone:	303-344-8858 *
Home Address:	2445 Community Street *		
City:	Centennial *	State:	Colorado *
Zip Code:	80112 *	Fax:	303-344-4456
Email:	fsmith@co.arapahoe.co.us		

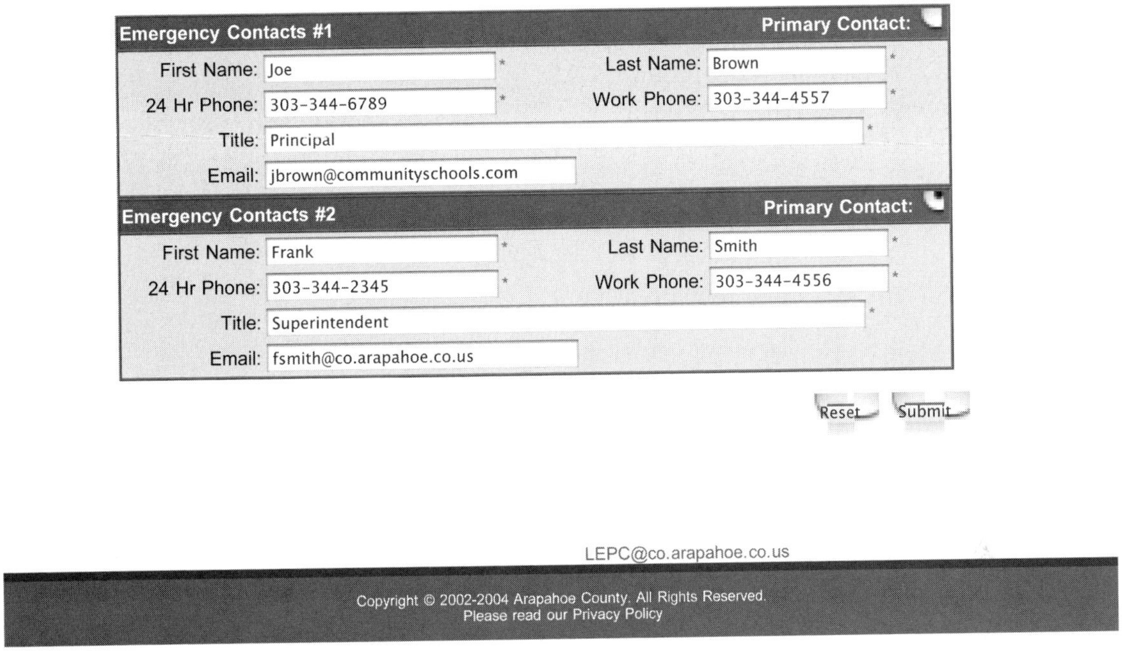

Emergency Contacts #1 Primary Contact:

First Name: Joe * Last Name: Brown *

24 Hr Phone: 303-344-6789 * Work Phone: 303-344-4557 *

Title: Principal *

Email: jbrown@communityschools.com

Emergency Contacts #2 Primary Contact:

First Name: Frank * Last Name: Smith *

24 Hr Phone: 303-344-2345 * Work Phone: 303-344-4556 *

Title: Superintendent *

Email: fsmith@co.arapahoe.co.us

Reset Submit

LEPC@co.arapahoe.co.us

APPENDIX E

EXECUTIVE ORDER, FEDERAL REGISTER

O:\EO\HTML\EOSGML~1\EO12856.SGM

Federal Register
Vol. 58, No. 150
Friday, August 6, 1993

Presidential Documents

Title 3—

The President

Executive Order 12856 of August 3, 1993

Federal Compliance With Right-to-Know Laws and Pollution Prevention Requirements

WHEREAS, the Emergency Planning and Community Right-to-Know Act of 1986 (42 U.S.C. 11001–11050) (EPCRA) established programs to provide the public with important information on the hazardous and toxic chemicals in their communities, and established emergency planning and notification requirements to protect the public in the event of a release of extremely hazardous substances;

WHEREAS, the Federal Government should be a good neighbor to local communities by becoming a leader in providing information to the public concerning toxic and hazardous chemicals and extremely hazardous substances at Federal facilities, and in planning for and preventing harm to the public through the planned or unplanned releases of chemicals;

WHEREAS, the Pollution Prevention Act of 1990 (42 U.S.C. 13101–13109) (PPA) established that it is the national policy of the United States that, whenever feasible, pollution should be prevented or reduced at the source; that pollution that cannot be prevented should be recycled in an environmentally safe manner; that pollution that cannot be prevented or recycled should be treated in an environmentally safe manner; and that disposal or other release into the environment should be employed only as a last resort and should be conducted in an environmentally safe manner;

WHEREAS, the PPA required the Administrator of the Environmental Protection Agency (EPA) to promote source reduction practices in other agencies;

WHEREAS, the Federal Government should become a leader in the field of pollution prevention through the management of its facilities, its acquisition practices, and in supporting the development of innovative pollution prevention programs and technologies;

WHEREAS, the environmental, energy, and economic benefits of energy and water use reductions are very significant; the scope of innovative pollution prevention programs must be broad to adequately address the highest-risk environmental problems and to take full advantage of technological opportunities in sectors other than industrial manufacturing; the Energy Policy Act of 1992 (Public Law 102–486 of October 24, 1992) requires the Secretary of Energy to work with other Federal agencies to significantly reduce the use of energy and reduce the related environmental impacts by promoting use of energy efficiency and renewable energy technologies; and

WHEREAS, as the largest single consumer in the Nation, the Federal Government has the opportunity to realize significant economic as well as environmental benefits of pollution prevention;

AND IN ORDER TO:

Ensure that all Federal agencies conduct their facility management and acquisition activities so that, to the maximum extent practicable, the quantity of toxic chemicals entering any wastestream, including any releases to the environment, is reduced as expeditiously as possible through source reduction; that waste that is generated is recycled to the maximum extent practicable; and that any wastes remaining are stored, treated or disposed of in a manner protective of public health and the environment;

O:\EO\HTML\EOSGML~1\EO12856.SGM
Federal Register / Vol. 58, No. 150 / Friday, August 6, 1993 / Presidential Documents

Require Federal agencies to report in a public manner toxic chemicals entering any wastestream from their facilities, including any releases to the environment, and to improve local emergency planning, response, and accident notification; and

Help encourage markets for clean technologies and safe alternatives to extremely hazardous substances or toxic chemicals through revisions to specifications and standards, the acquisition and procurement process, and the testing of innovative pollution prevention technologies at Federal facilities or in acquisitions;

NOW THEREFORE, by the authority vested in me as President by the Constitution and the laws of the United States of America, including the EPCRA, the PPA, and section 301 of title 5, United States Code, it is hereby ordered as follows:

Section 1. *Applicability.*

1- 101. As delineated below, the head of each Federal agency is responsible for ensuring that all necessary actions are taken for the prevention of pollution with respect to that agency's activities and facilities, and for ensuring that agency's compliance with pollution prevention and emergency planning and community right-to-know provisions established pursuant to all implementing regulations issued pursuant to EPCRA and PPA.

1- 102. Except as otherwise noted, this order is applicable to all Federal agencies that either own or operate a "facility" as that term is defined in section 329(4) of EPCRA, if such facility meets the threshold requirements set forth in EPCRA for compliance as modified by section 3- 304(b) of this order ("covered facilities"). Except as provided in section 1- 103 and section 1- 104 below, each Federal agency must apply all of the provisions of this order to each of its covered facilities, including those facilities which are subject, independent of this order, to the provisions of EPCRA and PPA (*e.g.*, certain Government-owned/contractor-operated facilities (GOCO's), for chemicals meeting EPCRA thresholds). This order does not apply to Federal agency facilities outside the customs territory of the United States, such as United States diplomatic and consular missions abroad.

1- 103. Nothing in this order alters the obligations which GOCO's and Government corporation facilities have under EPCRA and PPA independent of this order or subjects such facilities to EPCRA or PPA if they are otherwise excluded. However, consistent with section 1- 104 below, each Federal agency shall include the releases and transfers from all such facilities when meeting all of the Federal agency's responsibilities under this order.

1- 104. To facilitate compliance with this order, each Federal agency shall provide, in all future contracts between the agency and its relevant contractors, for the contractor to supply to the Federal agency all information the Federal agency deems necessary for it to comply with this order. In addition, to the extent that compliance with this order is made more difficult due to lack of information from existing contractors, Federal agencies shall take practical steps to obtain the information needed to comply with this order from such contractors.

Sec. 2- 2. *Definitions.*

2- 201. All definitions found in EPCRA and PPA and implementing regulations are incorporated in this order by reference, with the following exception: for the purposes of this order, the term "person", as defined in section 329(7) of EPCRA, also includes Federal agencies.

2- 202. *Federal agency* means an Executive agency, as defined in 5 U.S.C. 105. For the purpose of this order, military departments, as defined in 5 U.S.C. 102, are covered under the auspices of the Department of Defense.

2- 203. *Pollution Prevention* means "source reduction," as defined in the PPA, and other practices that reduce or eliminate the creation of pollutants through: (a) increased efficiency in the use of raw materials, energy, water, or other resources; or (b) protection of natural resources by conservation.

O:\EO\HTML\EOSGML~1\EO12856.SGM
Federal Register / Vol. 58, No. 150 / Friday, August 6, 1993 / Presidential Documents

2-204. *GOCO* means a Government-owned/contractor-operated facility which is owned by the Federal Government but all or portions of which are operated by private contractors.

2-205. *Administrator* means the Administrator of the EPA.

2-206. *Toxic Chemical* means a substance on the list described in section 313(c) of EPCRA.

2-207. *Toxic Pollutants.* For the purposes of section 3-302(a) of this order, the term "toxic pollutants" shall include, but is not necessarily limited to, those chemicals at a Federal facility subject to the provisions of section 313 of EPCRA as of December 1, 1993. Federal agencies also may choose to include releases and transfers of other chemicals, such as "extremely hazardous chemicals" as defined in section 329(3) of EPCRA, hazardous wastes as defined under the Resource Conservation and Recovery Act of 1976 (42 U.S.C. 6901-6986) (RCRA), or hazardous air pollutants under the Clean Air Act Amendments (42 U.S.C. 7403-7626); however, for the purposes of establishing the agency's baseline under 3-302(c), such "other chemicals" are in addition to (not instead of) the section 313 chemicals. The term "toxic pollutants" does not include hazardous waste subject to remedial action generated prior to the date of this order.

Sec. 3-3. *Implementation.*

3-301. *Federal Agency Strategy.* Within 12 months of the date of this order, the head of each Federal agency must develop a written pollution prevention strategy to achieve the requirements specified in sections 3-302 through 3-305 of this order for that agency. A copy thereof shall be provided to the Administrator. Federal agencies are encouraged to involve the public in developing the required strategies under this order and in monitoring their subsequent progress in meeting the requirements of this order. The strategy shall include, but shall not be limited to, the following elements:

(a) A pollution prevention policy statement, developed by each Federal agency, designating principal responsibilities for development, implementation, and evaluation of the strategy. The statement shall reflect the Federal agency's commitment to incorporate pollution prevention through source reduction in facility management and acquisition, and it shall identify an individual responsible for coordinating the Federal agency's efforts in this area.

(b) A commitment to utilize pollution prevention through source reduction, where practicable, as the primary means of achieving and maintaining compliance with all applicable Federal, State, and local environmental requirements.

3-302. *Toxic Chemical Reduction Goals.* (a) The head of each Federal agency subject to this order shall ensure that the agency develops voluntary goals to reduce the agency's total releases of toxic chemicals to the environment and off-site transfers of such toxic chemicals for treatment and disposal from facilities covered by this order by 50 percent by December 31, 1999. To the maximum extent practicable, such reductions shall be achieved by implementation of source reduction practices.

(b) The baseline for measuring reductions for purposes of achieving the 50 percent reduction goal for each Federal agency shall be the first year in which releases of toxic chemicals to the environment and off-site transfers of such chemicals for treatment and disposal are publicly reported. The baseline amount as to which the 50 percent reduction goal applies shall be the aggregate amount of toxic chemicals reported in the baseline year for all of that Federal agency's facilities meeting the threshold applicability requirements set forth in section 1-102 of this order. In no event shall the baseline be later than the 1994 reporting year.

(c) Alternatively, a Federal agency may choose to achieve a 50 percent reduction goal for toxic pollutants. In such event, the Federal agency shall delineate the scope of its reduction program in the written pollution prevention strategy that is required by section 3-301 of this order. The baseline for measuring reductions for purposes of achieving the 50 percent reduction requirement for each Federal agency shall be the first year in which releases of toxic pollutants to the environment and off-site transfers of such chemicals for treatment and disposal are publicly reported for each of that Federal agency's facilities encompassed by section 3- 301. In no event shall the baseline year be later than the 1994 reporting year. The baseline amount as to which the 50 percent reduction goal applies shall be the aggregate amount of toxic pollutants reported by the agency in the baseline year. For any toxic pollutants included by the agency in determining its baseline under this section, in addition to toxic chemicals under EPCRA, the agency shall report on such toxic pollutants annually under the provisions of section 3- 304 of this order, if practicable, or through an agency report that is made available to the public.

(d) The head of each Federal agency shall ensure that each of its covered facilities develops a written pollution prevention plan no later than the end of 1995, which sets forth the facility's contribution to the goal established in section 3- 302(a) of this order. Federal agencies shall conduct assessments of their facilities as necessary to ensure development of such plans and of the facilities' pollution prevention programs.

3- 303. *Acquisition and Procurement Goals.* (a) Each Federal agency shall establish a plan and goals for eliminating or reducing the unnecessary acquisition by that agency of products containing extremely hazardous substances or toxic chemicals. Similarly, each Federal agency shall establish a plan and goal for voluntarily reducing its own manufacturing, processing, and use of extremely hazardous substances and toxic chemicals. Priorities shall be developed by Federal agencies, in coordination with EPA, for implementing this section.

(b) Within 24 months of the date of this order, the Department of Defense (DOD) and the General Services Administration (GSA), and other agencies, as appropriate, shall review their agency's standardized documents, including specifications and standards, and identify opportunities to eliminate or reduce the use by their agency of extremely hazardous substances and toxic chemicals, consistent with the safety and reliability requirements of their agency mission. The EPA shall assist agencies in meeting the requirements of this section, including identifying substitutes and setting priorities for these reviews. By 1999, DOD, GSA and other affected agencies shall make all appropriate revisions to these specifications and standards.

(c) Any revisions to the Federal Acquisition Regulation (FAR) necessary to implement this order shall be made within 24 months of the date of this order.

(d) Federal agencies are encouraged to develop and test innovative pollution prevention technologies at their facilities in order to encourage the development of strong markets for such technologies. Partnerships should be encouraged between industry, Federal agencies, Government laboratories, academia, and others to assess and deploy innovative environmental technologies for domestic use and for markets abroad.

3- 304. *Toxics Release Inventory/Pollution Prevention Act Reporting.* (a) The head of each Federal agency shall comply with the provisions set forth in section 313 of EPCRA, section 6607 of PPA, all implementing regulations, and future amendments to these authorities, in light of applicable guidance as provided by EPA.

(b) The head of each Federal agency shall comply with these provisions without regard to the Standard Industrial Classification (SIC) delineations that apply to the Federal agency's facilities, and such reports shall be for all releases, transfers, and wastes at such Federal agency's facility without regard to the SIC code of the activity leading to the release, transfer, or waste. All other existing statutory or regulatory limitations or exemptions on the application of EPCRA section 313 shall apply to the reporting requirements set forth in section 3- 304(a) of this order.

(c) The first year of compliance shall be no later than for the 1994 calendar year, with reports due on or before July 1, 1995.

3-305. *Emergency Planning and Community Right-to-Know Reporting Responsibilities.* The head of each Federal agency shall comply with the provisions set forth in sections 301 through 312 of EPCRA, all implementing regulations, and future amendments to these authorities, in light of any applicable guidance as provided by EPA. Effective dates for compliance shall be: (a) With respect to the provisions of section 302 of EPCRA, emergency planning notification shall be made no later than 7 months after the date of this order.

(b) With respect to the provisions of section 303 of EPCRA, all information necessary for the applicable Local Emergency Planning Committee (LEPC's) to prepare or revise local Emergency Response Plans shall be provided no later than 1 year after the date of this order.

(c) To the extent that a facility is required to maintain Material Safety Data Sheets under any provisions of law or Executive order, information required under section 311 of EPCRA shall be submitted no later than 1 year after the date of this order, and the first year of compliance with section 312 shall be no later than the 1994 calendar year, with reports due on or before March 1, 1995.

(d) The provisions of section 304 of EPCRA shall be effective beginning January 1, 1994.

(e) These compliance dates are not intended to delay implementation of earlier timetables already agreed to by Federal agencies and are inapplicable to the extent they interfere with those timetables.

Sec. 4-4. *Agency Coordination.*

4-401. By February 1, 1994, the Administrator shall convene an Interagency Task Force composed of the Administrator, the Secretaries of Commerce, Defense, and Energy, the Administrator of General Services, the Administrator of the Office of Procurement Policy in the Office of Management and Budget, and such other agency officials as deemed appropriate based upon lists of potential participants submitted to the Administrator pursuant to this section by the agency head. Each agency head may designate other senior agency officials to act in his/her stead, where appropriate. The Task Force will assist the agency heads in the implementation of the activities required under this order.

4-402. Federal agencies subject to the requirements of this order shall submit annual progress reports to the Administrator beginning on October 1, 1995. These reports shall include a description of the progress that the agency has made in complying with all aspects of this order, including the pollution reductions requirements. This reporting requirement shall expire after the report due on October 1, 2001.

4-403. *Technical Advice.* Upon request and to the extent practicable, the Administrator shall provide technical advice and assistance to Federal agencies in order to foster full compliance with this order. In addition, to the extent practicable, all Federal agencies subject to this order shall provide technical assistance, if requested, to LEPC's in their development of emergency response plans and in fulfillment of their community right-to-know and risk reduction responsibilities.

4-404. Federal agencies shall place high priority on obtaining funding and resources needed for implementing all aspects of this order, including the pollution prevention strategies, plans, and assessments required by this order, by identifying, requesting, and allocating funds through line-item or direct funding requests. Federal agencies shall make such requests as required in the Federal Agency Pollution Prevention and Abatement Planning Process and through agency budget requests as outlined in Office of Management and Budget (OMB) Circulars A-106 and A-11, respectively. Federal agencies should apply, to the maximum extent practicable, a life cycle analysis and

O:\EO\HTML\EOSGML~1\EO12856.SGM
Federal Register / Vol. 58, No. 150 / Friday, August 6, 1993 / Presidential Documents

total cost accounting principles to all projects needed to meet the requirements of this order

4- 405. *Federal Government Environmental Challenge Program.* The Administrator shall establish a "Federal Government Environmental Challenge Program" to recognize outstanding environmental management performance in Federal agencies and facilities. The program shall consist of two components that challenge Federal agencies; (a) to agree to a code of environmental principles to be developed by EPA, in cooperation with other agencies, that emphasizes pollution prevention, sustainable development and state-of-the-art environmental management programs, and (b) to submit applications to EPA for individual Federal agency facilities for recognition as "Model Installations." The program shall also include a means for recognizing individual Federal employees who demonstrate outstanding leadership in pollution prevention.

Sec. 5- 5. *Compliance.*

5- 501. By December 31, 1993, the head of each Federal agency shall provide the Administrator with a preliminary list of facilities that potentially meet the requirements for reporting under the threshold provisions of EPCRA, PPA, and this order.

5-'502. The head of each Federal agency is responsible for ensuring that such agency take all necessary actions to prevent pollution in accordance with this order, and for that agency's compliance with the provisions of EPCRA and PPA. Compliance with EPCRA and PPA means compliance with the same substantive, procedural, and other statutory and regulatory requirements that would apply to a private person. Nothing in this order shall be construed as making the provisions of sections 325 and 326 of EPCRA applicable to any Federal agency or facility, except to the extent that such Federal agency or facility would independently be subject to such provisions. EPA shall consult with Federal agencies, if requested, to determine the applicability of this order to particular agency facilities.

5- 503. Each Federal agency subject to this order shall conduct internal reviews and audits, and take such other steps, as may be necessary to monitor compliance with sections 3- 304 and 3- 305 of this order.

5- 504. The Administrator, in consultation with the heads of Federal agencies, may conduct such reviews and inspections as may be necessary to monitor compliance with sections 3- 304 and 3- 305 of this order. Except as excluded under section 6- 601 of this order, all Federal agencies are encouraged to cooperate fully with the efforts of the Administrator to ensure compliance with sections 3- 304 and 3- 305 of this order.

5- 505. Federal agencies are further encouraged to comply with all state and local right-to-know and pollution prevention requirements to the extent that compliance with such laws and requirements is not otherwise already mandated.

5- 506. Whenever the Administrator notifies a Federal agency that it is not in compliance with an applicable provision of this order, the Federal agency shall achieve compliance as promptly as is practicable.

5- 507. The EPA shall report annually to the President on Federal agency compliance with the provisions of section 3- 304 of this order.

5- 508. To the extent permitted by law and unless such documentation is withheld pursuant to section 6- 601 of this order, the public shall be afforded ready access to all strategies, plans, and reports required to be prepared by Federal agencies under this order by the agency preparing the strategy, plan, or report. When the reports are submitted to EPA, EPA shall compile the strategies, plans, and reports and make them publicly available as well. Federal agencies are encouraged to provide such strategies, plans, and reports to the State and local authorities where their facilities are located for an additional point of access to the public.

Sec. 6- 6. *Exemption.*

O:\EO\HTML\EOSGML~1\EO12856.SGM
Federal Register / Vol. 58, No. 150 / Friday, August 6, 1993 / Presidential Documents

6-601. In the interest of national security, the head of a Federal agency may request from the President an exemption from complying with the provisions of any or all aspects of this order for particular Federal agency facilities, provided that the procedures set forth in section 120(j)(1) of the Comprehensive Environmental Response, Compensation, and Liability Act of 1980, as amended (42 U.S.C. 9620(j)(1)), are followed. To the maximum extent practicable, and without compromising national security, all Federal agencies shall strive to comply with the purposes, goals, and implementation steps set forth in this order.

Sec. 7-7. *General Provisions.*

7-701. Nothing in this order shall create any right or benefit, substantive or procedural, enforceable by a party against the United States, its agencies or instrumentalities, its officers or employees, or any other person.

THE WHITE HOUSE,
August 3, 1993.

[FR citation 58 FR 4198]

APPENDIX F

ACRONYM GLOSSARY

AA: Assistant Administrator

ACL: Alternate Concentration Limit

ACO: Administrative Compliance Order

ADR: Alternative Dispute Resolution

AG: Attorney General

ALJ: Administrative Law Judge

AO: Administrative Order

APA: Administrative Procedure Act

ARAR: Applicable or Relevant and Appropriate Requirement

ASTSWMO: Association of State and Territorial Solid Waste Management Officials

BACT: Best Available Control Technology

BADT: Best Available Demonstrated Technology

BART: Best Available Retrofit Technology

BAT: Best Available Technology

BCT: Best Conventional Technology

BLM: Bureau of Land Management

BOYSNC: Beginning-of-Year Significant Non-Compliers

BPJ: Best Professional Judgment

BPT: Best Practicable Technology

BTU: British Thermal Unit

CA: Corrective Action
CAA: Clean Air Act
CAIR: Comprehensive Assessment Information Rule
CAMU: Corrective Action Management Unit
CARS: Corrective Action Reporting System
CBI: Confidential Business Information
CDI: Case Development Inspection
CEI: Compliance Evaluation Inspection
CEQ: Council on Environmental Quality
CERCLA: Comprehensive Environmental Response, Compensation, and Liability Act
CERCLIS: CERCLA Information System
CESQG: Conditionally Exempt Small Quantity Generator
CFCs: Chlorofluorocarbons
CFR: Code of Federal Regulations
CGL: Comprehensive General Liability
CITES: Convention on International Trade in Endangered Species
CME: Comprehensive Ground Water Monitoring Evaluation
CMEL: Compliance Monitor Evaluation Log
CMI: Corrective Measures Implementation
CMS: Corrective Measures Study
COG: Compliance Order Guide
C/PC: Closure/Post-Closure
CSI: Compliance Sampling Inspection
CWA: Clean Water Act
DAA: Deputy Assistant Administrator
DDT: Dichlorodiphenyltrichloroethane
DOD: Department of Defense
DOE: Department of Energy
DOJ: Department of Justice
DOL: Department of Labor
DOT: Department of Transportation

DRE:	Destruction and Removal Efficiency
EA:	Environmental Assessment
EHC:	Extremely Hazardous Chemical
EHS:	Extremely Hazardous Substance
EIL:	Environmental Impairment Liability
EIS:	Environmental Impact Statement
EPA:	Environmental Protection Agency
EPCRA:	Emergency Planning and Community Right-to-Know Act
EPI:	Environmental Priorities Initiative
ERP:	Environmental Response Policy or Emergency Response Plan
ESA:	Endangered Species Act
EU:	European Union
FDF:	Fundamentally Different Factor
FEPCA:	Federal Environmental Pesticides Control Act of 1972
FFCA:	Federal Facilities Compliance Act or Federal Facilities Compliance Agreement
FFIS:	Federal Facility Information System
FIFRA:	Federal Insecticide, Fungicide, and Rodenticide Act
FIP:	Federal Implementation Plan
FOIA:	Freedom of Information Act
FONSI:	Finding of No Significant Impact
FR:	Federal Register
FS:	Feasibility Study
FSEEE:	Forest Service Employees for Environmental Ethics
FWPCA:	Federal Water Pollution Control Act
FWS:	Fish and Wildlife Service
FY:	Fiscal Year
GACT:	Generally Available Control Technology
GIS:	Geographic Information System

GSA: General Services Administration
GWM: Groundwater Monitoring
HOCs: Halogenated Organic Compounds
HON: Hazardous Organic NESHAP
HSWA: Hazardous and Solid Waste Amendments of 1984
HWDMS: Hazardous Waste Data Management System
ICS: Individual Control Strategy
ITC: Interagency Testing Committee
LAER: Lowest Achievable Emission Rate
LDF: Land Disposal Facility
LDR: Land Disposal Restrictions
LEPC: Local Emergency Planning Committee
LFD: Local Fire Department
LOIS: Loss of Interim Status
LULU: Locally Undesirable Land Use
LVE: Low Volume Exemption
MACT: Maximum Achievable Control Technology
MBTA: Migratory Bird Treaty Act
MCAN: Microbial Commercial Activity Notice
MCL: Maximum Contaminant Level
MCLG: Maximum Contaminant Level Goal
MIC: Methyl Isocyanate
MMPA: Marine Mammal Protection Act
MOA: Memorandum of Agreement
MPRSA: Marine Protection, Research, and Sanctuaries Act
MSDS: Material Safety Data Sheets
MSW: Municipal Solid Waste
MSWLF: Municipal Solid Waste Landfill
MTR: Minimum Technological Requirement
MWTA: Medical Waste Treatment Act
NAAQS: National Ambient Air Quality Standards

NAFTA: North American Free Trade Agreement

NBAR: Nonbinding Preliminary Allocation of Responsibility

NCCP: Natural Community Conservation Planning Program

NCP: National Contingency Plan

NEPA: National Environmental Policy Act

NIMBY: Not-in-My-Backyard

NIOSH: National Institute for Occupational Safety and Health

NMFS: National Marine Fisheries Service

NOC: Notice of Commencement

NOD: Notice of Deficiency

NOV: Notice of Violation

NPDES: National Pollutant Discharge Elimination System

NPL: National Priorities List

NRC: Nuclear Regulatory Commission
or
National Response Center

NSPS: New Source Performance Standards

NSWMA: National Solid Waste Management Association

OERR: Office of Emergency and Remedial Response

O&M: Operation and Maintenance

OMB: Office of Management and Budget

O/O: Owner/Operator

OPA: Oil Pollution Act

OPP: Office of Pesticide Programs

OSHA: Occupational Safety & Health Administration

OSH Act: Occupational Safety and Health Act

OSW: Office of Solid Waste

OSWER: Office of Solid Waste and Emergency Response

OUST: Office of Underground Storage Tanks

OWPE: Office of Waste Programs Enforcement

PA: Preliminary Assessment

PAIR:	Preliminary Assessment Information Rule
PCB:	Polychlorinated Biphenyl
PDWS:	Public Drinking Water System
PELs:	Permissible Exposure Limits
PICs:	Products of Incomplete Combustion
PMN:	Premanufacture Notice
POHC:	Principal Organic Hazardous Constituents
POTW:	Publicly Owned Treatment Works
PPA:	Pollution Prevention Act
PRP:	Potentially Responsible Party or Potentially Responsible Person
PSD:	Prevention of Significant Deterioration
RA:	Regional Administrator or Remedial Action
RACT:	Reasonably Available Control Technology
RCRA:	Resource Conservation and Recovery Act
RCRIS:	RCRA Information System
RD:	Remedial Design
R&D:	Research and Development
RD&D:	Research, Development, and Demonstration
RD/RA:	Remedial Design/Remedial Action
RFA:	RCRA Facility Assessment
RFI:	RCRA Facility Investigation
RI:	Remedial Investigation
RI/FS:	Remedial Investigation/Feasibility Study
RIP:	RCRA Implementation Plan
RMCL:	Recommended Maximum Contaminant Level
ROD:	Record of Decision
RPAR:	Notice of Rebuttable Presumption Against Registration

RPO: Regional Project Office
or
Regional Project Officer

RQ: Reportable Quantity

SARA: Superfund Amendments and Reauthorization Act of 1986

SCAP: Superfund Comprehensive Accomplishments Plan

SCR: Selective Catalytic Reduction

SCRAM: The State Consolidated RCRA Authorization Manual

SDWA: Safe Drinking Water Act

SERC: State Emergency Response Commission

SIP: State Implementation Plan

SNC: Significant Non-Complier

SNUN: Significant New Use Notice

SNUR: Significant New Use Rule

SOP Standard Operating Procedures

SPCC: Spill Prevention Control and Countermeasure

SPMS: Strategic Planning and Management System

SQG: Small Quantity Generator

STARS: Strategically Targeted Activities for Results

SWDA: Solid Waste Disposal Act

SWMU: Solid Waste Management Unit

TC: Toxic Characteristic

TCLP: Toxic Characteristic Leaching Procedure

TEGD: Technical Enforcement Guidance Document

TES: Technical Enforcement Support

TLVs: Threshold Limit Values

TMDL: Total Maximum Daily Load

TME: Test Market Exemption

TPQ: Threshold Planning Quantity

TRI: Toxic Release Inventory

TSCA: Toxic Substances Control Act

TSD: Treatment, Storage, and Disposal

TSDF: Treatment, Storage, and Disposal Facility

TVA: Tennessee Valley Authority

UAO: Unilateral Administrative Order

UNEP: United Nations Environment Programme

UST: Underground Storage Tank

WAP: Waste Analysis Plan

WMMA: Waste Materials Management Act

ZPO: Zone Project Officer

APPENDIX G

GLOSSARY OF WORDS

abatement action A judicial proceeding wherein the Environmental Protection Agency (EPA) asks the court to require a Potentially Responsible Party (PRP) to abate an imminent and substantial endangerment to the public health or the environment.

acid rain Rain that contains high quantities of sulfur dioxide and nitrogen oxides.

administrative adjudication An administrative hearing convened for the purpose of determining whether an agency's rules have been violated. Similar to a judicial proceeding, but adjudicated by an agency tribunal rather than a judicial officer.

Administrative Procedure Act (APA) A federal act that sets forth the procedures that agencies must follow in adopting regulations and making administrative decisions.

agency The Federal Administrative Procedure Act (FAPA) describes and defines which agencies are covered by FAPA. If an agency is not specifically excluded from the FAPA definition, that agency is governed by FAPA.

agency action Any rule, order, sanction, or failure to act taken or made by an agency.

air toxics Hazardous organic materials, metals, and other substances on a list of regulated substances kept pursuant to the Clean Air Act (CAA).

ambient air Outside air beyond (including above) the borders of an identified piece of property.

answer A pleading filed in response to a complaint in a judicial proceeding.

appeal A request that a higher court or another authority review a decision by a lower court or an administrative tribunal.

Applicable or Relevant and Appropriate Requirement (ARAR) If, to be lawful and effective, a Comprehensive Environmental Response, Compensation, and Liability Act (CERCLA) remedial action requires compliance with a provision of another environmental law, that requirement is called an ARAR.

area source As defined by the Clean Air Act (CAA), any stationary source of hazardous air pollutants that is not a major source.

arroyo A waterway or watercourse in an arid region.

attainment states States that are in compliance with (having attained) the National Ambient Air Quality Standards (NAAQS).

Best Available Control Technology (BACT) The maximum degree of reduction in pollutants achievable in light of economic, energy, and environmental factors.

Best Available Demonstrated Technology (BADT) A demonstrated technology level applicable to the discharge of toxic and nonconventional pollutants.

Best Available Retrofit Technology (BART) Pursuant to the Clean Air Act (CAA), states are required to use this level of technology to eliminate certain visible air pollution.

Best Available Technology (BAT) A technology level applicable to the discharge of toxic and nonconventional pollutants.

Best Conventional Technology (BCT) A technology level applicable to the discharge of conventional pollutants.

Best Practicable Technology (BPT) The minimum level of required treatment for pollutants.

Best Professional Judgment (BPJ) The use of scientific analysis of the type, amount, location, and other relevant conditions connected with a proposed discharge.

beyond a reasonable doubt The standard of proof in criminal cases.

bio-accumulation The consequence of the release of polychlorinated biphenyls (PCBs) into the environment and the food chain. If released, PCBs, which are extremely hazardous to human health and the environment, accumulate in the environmental media and the food chain.

biomass energy The type of energy that comes from the energy of the sun stored in plants as they grow.

biotechnology The science of genetically engineering microorganisms.

***bona fide* intent** If there is a request to view a confidential chemical identity protected by the provisions of the Emergency Planning and Community Right-to-Know Act (EPCRA), that request will be granted by the EPA only if the requester can demonstrate that it has a *bona fide* intent to manufacture or import a substance for a commercial purpose.

burden of proof The responsibility of one or the other parties to litigation to produce evidence to prove a fact in dispute.

by a preponderance of evidence A standard of proof that requires a party to produce slightly more evidence than their opponent.

bypass The intentional diversion of waste effluent from a treatment facility.

carcinogen Any substance known to cause cancer or contribute to the production of cancer.

cases and controversies A phrase describing, collectively, the restraints on federal jurisdiction, such as a prohibition against advisory opinions.

categorical exclusion A means by which the need for an environmental assessment (EA) is bypassed. If a category of actions do not individually or cumulatively have a significant environmental impact, an agency may determine that a categorical exclusion applies, thus bypassing the need for an EA in a particular situation.

Cetacean A scientific order that includes whales, dolphins, and porpoises.

characteristic waste A waste exhibiting at least one of four hazardous characteristics: (1) ignitability, (2) corrosivity, (3) reactivity, or (4) toxicity. A characteristic waste may exhibit more than one of the four hazardous characteristics.

chemical substance Defined in the Toxic Substances Control Act (TSCA) as any organic or inorganic substance of a particular molecular identity, including (i) any combination of such substances occurring in whole or in part as a result of a chemical reaction or occurring in nature and (ii) any element or uncombined radical.

chemical substances and mixtures A substance regulated pursuant to the TSCA or any other environmental act that regulates such substances or mixtures.

closure The ceasing of operations at a facility pursuant to an approved closure plan and in compliance with all applicable regulatory requirements.

commerce clause A section of the Constitution that allows regulation of commerce between the states.

common law A body of case law based on generally accepted legal principles adopted from England and modified over the years.

complaint The initial pleading in a litigation proceeding.

Comprehensive Assessment Information Rule (CAIR) One of the rules requiring the submittal of information pursuant to the provisions of the TSCA.

conditional registration A type of registration under the Federal Insecticide, Fungicide, and Rodenticide Act (FIFRA) available only in certain circumstances where there appears to be little danger from a pesticide being registered.

confidential chemical identity A chemical formula permitted to be kept confidential under most circumstances pursuant to the Emergency Planning and Community Right-to-Know Act (EPCRA).

consent decree An order entered by a federal court. This term is part of CERCLA.

consent order An agreement outside of a court proceeding. This term is part of CERCLA.

Consumer Labeling Initiative (CLI) A voluntary effort to educate consumers about pesticide labels.

contained-in rule The rule stating that material that is contaminated with hazardous waste also is regulated as hazardous waste.

container Defined in the Resource Conservation and Recovery Act (RCRA) as any portable device for storing or handling hazardous waste.

contaminant Any substance that will cause or may reasonably be anticipated to cause harmful health effects.

contempt of court When a party to a court proceeding fails or refuses to abide by an order of court, that party may be held in contempt of court.

contingency plan A plan to be followed in response to an environmental emergency such as a fire, an accident, or a chemical release.

continuous release A release that occurs without interruption or abatement or that is routine, anticipated, and intermittent and incidental to normal operations or treatment processes.

contribution action A method by which some division of liability may be made pursuant to CERCLA.

control test Any person who arranged for disposal of hazardous substances owned or possessed by such person is deemed to have sufficient control to be considered an owner or operator pursuant to CERCLA.

Convention on International Trade in Endangered Species (CITES) An agreement intended to reduce the numbers of endangered species taken out of their critical habitat.

corrosivity A characteristic of hazardous waste that involves wastes at either the high or low end of the pH scale.

cost-benefit analysis A fiscal analysis for a proposed project designed to produce a ratio of costs for that project, taking into consideration the degree to which spending money to implement a particular procedure or to purchase particular equipment will benefit the environment, balanced by the effect such expenditure will have on the fiscal viability of the entity proposing to implement the project.

Council on Environmental Quality (CEQ) Three individuals appointed by the President of the

United States and confirmed by the Senate. Their job is to assist the President in assessing the quality of the environment, determining whether federal agencies are complying with the requirements of the National Environmental Policy Act (NEPA), and suggesting new national policies to preserve and improve the environment.

cradle-to-grave A term used to describe the intent of the RCRA to control hazardous wastes from their creation (cradle) to their disposal (grave).

criteria information Concentration limits (numerically) necessary to support a designated use.

criteria pollutants Carbon monoxide (CO), sulfur dioxide (SO_2), nitrogen dioxide (NO_2), ozone (O_3), lead (Pb), and particulate matter (PM10).

critical habitat The habitat determined to be vital to the survival of an endangered species.

D wastes Characteristic wastes are identified by a three-digit number preceded by a "D," and are typically referred to as "D wastes." Wastes with an ignitability characteristic are designated as D001 wastes, wastes with a corrosivity characteristic are designated as D002 wastes, wastes with a reactivity characteristic are designated as D003 wastes, and wastes with a toxicity characteristic are designated as D004 through D043 wastes, depending upon their composition.

damages Money payments for injuries.

defendant A party against whom a legal action is brought.

delisting When the waste generated by the treatment of a hazardous waste does not exhibit any of the characteristics for which the untreated waste was deemed hazardous, the residue waste may be delisted by the EPA. The effect of delisting is to remove many of the requirements placed on the generation, transportation, treatment, storage, or disposal of the delisted waste.

***de minimis* party** A party identified as a potentially responsible party (PRP) at a Superfund site whose contribution to the amount or toxic effects of the substances at that site is minimal in comparison to the contributions of other PRPs. If the PRP is the owner of the facility, to be considered a *de minimus* party, the owner cannot have allowed generation, treatment, storage, or disposal at the facility; cannot have contributed to any release at the facility; and cannot have purchased the property knowing it had been or was being used for the generation, transportation, treatment, storage, or disposal of hazardous substances.

***de novo* trial** A "new" trial not based on the record from a lower tribunal.

derived-from rule A rule providing that residue from the treatment of *listed* hazardous wastes is considered hazardous waste regardless of whether the resulting residue is, in fact, hazardous. The residue from *characteristic* hazardous wastes is considered hazardous only when the residue exhibits a hazardous waste characteristic.

dichlorodiphenyltrichloroethane (DDT) An insecticide for which Paul Müller won the Nobel Peace Prize. DDT was later found to be extremely harmful.

discarded material Material that is abandoned, recycled, or inherently wastelike. A solid waste is defined as any "discarded material" not subject to exclusion.

discharge The accidental or intentional leaking, spilling, pumping, pouring, emitting, emptying, or dumping of hazardous waste into or onto any land, water, or air.

discovery Information exchanged by parties to a legal proceeding.

disposal The discharge, deposit, injection, dumping, spilling, leaking, or placing of any solid waste or hazardous waste into or onto any land or water.

disposal facility A facility where hazardous waste is intentionally placed into or on land or water and where waste will remain after the facility is closed.

distribution The process of selling, introducing, or delivering a chemical substance into commerce or holding the mixture or article after its introduction into commerce.

effluent A liquid waste source emanating from a point source.

EPA lists Lists of hazardous wastes developed by the EPA assigning a number to various types of specific hazardous wastes.

emergency release A release of a listed hazardous substance that is not permitted by the federal government, that exceeds the reportable quantity (RQ), and that results in exposure to humans off-site.

Emergency Response Plan Designates response parameters for local hazardous chemical emergency releases.

emergency suspension An order immediately suspending the sale, distribution, and use of a pesticide where the EPA administrator believes the pesticide poses an imminent risk.

endangered species Any species that is in danger of extinction throughout all or a significant portion of its range.

endangered species list A list of all endangered species.

environment Air, land, water, and all living things on Earth.

environmental assessment (EA) The beginning of the process found in the National Environmental Policy Act (NEPA) to determine the impact of certain proposed federal actions.

environmental elitism The practice of locating dangerous environmental activities in areas of low income or minority populations not having significant resources to speak out on the issue.

environmental impact statement (EIS) A detailed analysis of the environmental impact of a proposed federal action. Follows the environmental assessment (EA) as part of the NEPA process.

environmental justice Ensuring that minority or low-income populations are not unduly exposed to environmental hazards and that such populations are given a forum in which to voice their comments concerning a potential hazard.

Environmental Protection Agency (EPA) The federal agency tasked with administering and enforcing most of the federal environmental acts.

environmental racism The practice of locating dangerous environmental activities in areas where minority populations do not have significant resources to speak out on the issue.

existing chemical A chemical substance listed on the Toxic Substances Control Act (TSCA) Inventory.

exposure-based test rules Rules based on the extent to which a chemical poses a risk of exposure into the environment.

exposure trigger A situation where the quantity of a chemical produced and its breadth of exposure into the environment is sufficient to cause concern for human health.

extremely hazardous substances (EHSs) Substances causing a risk to human health or the environment that are monitored pursuant to EPCRA.

F wastes General classes of compounds listed as hazardous by the Environmental Protection Agency (EPA).

facility All buildings, equipment, structures, and other stationary items located on a single site or on contiguous or adjacent sites owned, operated, or controlled by the same person or entity. For some reporting purposes in environmental law, the term also includes motor vehicles; rolling stock; aircraft; and any land, structures, or appurtenances or improvements used for the treatment, storage, or disposal of waste.

featherbedding Using the data submitted for an already-registered pesticide to register another pesticide under FIFRA.

Federal Implementation Plan (FIP) If the Environmental Protection Agency (EPA) is not satisfied that a state has successfully enacted a State Implementation Plan (SIP) for the preservation of air quality in that state, the federal government may enact its own plan (FIP) for that state.

fill material Any material used to replace liquid with dry land or to change the elevation of a body of liquid.

Finding of No Significant Impact (FONSI) A FONSI finding is a conclusion by a federal agency that a proposed action will not have a significant impact on the environment. Such a finding is one of the possible conclusions reached as part of the evaluation process set forth in the National Environmental Policy Act (NEPA). The NEPA process includes the completion of an environmental assessment (EA), which can be used to make a FONSI determination.

Form R A particular reporting form used as part of the Toxic Inventory Form under the Emergency Preparedness and Community Right to Know Act (EPCRA). The form is used to report releases of toxic chemicals into the environment.

Freedom of Information Act (FOIA) A federal act giving the public access to records kept by governmental bodies and agencies.

fundamentally different factor (FDF) A type of variance given under the Clean Water Act (CWA) when a discharger can demonstrate that factors applied to determining the technology-based standards for its facility are fundamentally different from the factors considered when the Environmental Protection Agency (EPA) developed the effluent limitations guidelines for the type of facility the discharger is operating.

fungicide A chemical used against fungi.

Generally Available Control Technology (GACT) The technology generally available to reduce air emissions at a facility.

generator Any person whose act or process produces hazardous waste or whose act first causes a hazardous waste to become subject to regulation. All generators must acquire a generator identification number from the EPA and comply with regulations governing their activities found in the RCRA.

genetic engineering Manipulating the cellular structure of an organism to improve it in some manner.

geothermal energy The use of heat from the earth's core to generate heat and energy on the earth's surface.

global warming The phenomenon whereby the earth's temperature has been gradually increasing.

God Squad A committee of high-ranking government officials who have the power to determine whether an exemption is granted to placing a species on the endangered species list.

greenhouse gases The buildup of gases such as carbon dioxide in the earth's atmosphere, thought to be the result of the use of fossil fuels.

habitat conservation plan A plan designed to protect an endangered species from inappropriate taking.

hard look A term used by the U.S. Supreme Court to describe the type of analysis that should be given not only to the evaluation of a National Environmental Policy Act (NEPA) matter but also to any court review of an environmental issue.

hazardous chemicals Chemicals that constitute a hazard to human health or the environment as determined by federal law. Most chemicals are considered hazardous.

Hazardous Organic NESHAP (HON) The first set of technology standards meeting the Maximum Achievable Control Technology (MACT) standards under the Clean Air Act (CAA).

hazardous substance A material listed in the CERCLA that invokes the need for a facility to comply with certain release notification requirements.

hazardous waste As defined in the Resource Conservation and Recovery Act (RCRA), hazardous waste is a solid waste, or combination of solid wastes, which, because of its quantity, concentration, or physical, chemical, or infectious characteristics may: (1) cause, or significantly contribute to, an increase in mortality or an increase in serious, irreversible, or incapacitating reversible, illness; or (2) pose a substantial threat or potential hazard to human health or the environment when improperly transported, treated, stored or disposed of, or otherwise managed.

hazardous waste discharge The accidental or intentional leaking, spilling, pumping, pouring, emitting, emptying, or dumping of any hazardous waste into or onto land, air, or water.

herbicide A chemical agent used against plants.

household waste Any solid waste including but not limited to garbage, trash, and sanitary waste in septic tanks derived from households (single-family or multifamily), hotels and motels, bunkhouses, ranger stations, crew quarters, campgrounds, picnic grounds, and day-use recreational areas.

ignitability A characteristic of hazardous waste that is capable during handling of starting a fire or exacerbating a fire once started.

imminently hazardous chemical substance or mixture A chemical substance or mixture that poses an immediate potential threat to human health or the environment.

incidental take permit A permit issued pursuant to the Endangered Species Act (ESA) allowing the limited taking of an endangered species from its critical habitat.

incinerator A regulated facility for disposing of hazardous waste by burning it at an extremely high temperature.

individual control strategies (ICSs) Standards set for bodies of water that, even with the application of technology-based limitations, will not meet the state's water quality standards.

industrial user A company that discharges effluent into a municipal sewer or storm water drainage system.

influent A liquid waste stream that flows from a point source into a publicly owned treatment works (POTW) or another permitted source.

injunction A court order to do (or refrain from doing) a specific act.

injury in fact A showing that a person has suffered from individual, concrete harm rather than a speculative future harm.

innocent purchaser defense A defense available to a current owner or operator of a facility who can demonstrate that, at the time of purchase, it did not know and had no reason to know that hazardous materials had been handled at a site.

insecticide A chemical agent used against insects.

Interagency Testing Committee (ITC) A body created by law to make recommendations to the EPA concerning chemicals and chemical mixtures deserving special consideration.

interim status A term used in the Resource Conservation and Recovery Act (RCRA) to describe a facility that was already treating, storing, or disposing of hazardous was when the RCRA took effect. Such facilities were required under the RCRA to file Part A of the RCRA treatment, storage, and disposal (TSD) permit application. Until such facilities received a full TSD permit, the facilities were known as interim status facilities.

K wastes Industry-specific or process-specific wastes listed as hazardous by the Environmental Protection Agency (EPA).

labeling The process of affixing warnings and information regarding pesticides to pesticide containers.

Land Disposal Restrictions (LDR) To protect human health and the environment, some wastes require treatment prior to disposal in land-based facilities. These restrictions are known as Land Disposal Restrictions.

landfill A disposal facility where hazardous waste is placed in or on the land.

leachate Any liquid, including suspended components in the liquid, that has percolated through or drained from hazardous waste.

Leave No Trace Visitors to a protected wilderness are required to leave nothing of themselves behind in the wilderness.

liner A layer of natural or synthetic materials that surrounds the bottom and sides of a surface impoundment, landfill, or landfill cell. A liner is intended to prevent or restrict the escape of hazardous waste, hazardous waste components, or leachate.

listed hazardous waste A hazardous waste determined by the EPA to meet one or more factors such as toxicity, persistence, degradability, potential for accumulation in tissue, flammability, corrosivity, or another hazardous characteristic. Wastes are listed in four groups designated as F wastes, K wastes, P wastes, and U wastes.

Local Emergency Planning Committee (LEPC) Appointed by the State Emergency Response Commission (SERC) in each emergency planning district within a state.

local fire department (LFD) A fire department located within a Local Emergency Planning District.

locally undesirable land uses (LULUs) Any potentially hazardous manufacturing, processing, or disposal facility in the vicinity of a developed area.

low volume exemption (LVE) An exemption pursuant to TSCA available to a manufacturer or importer wishing to manufacture or import a new chemical in small amounts.

Lowest Achievable Emission Rate (LAER) A standard based on the most stringent limitations contained in a state's State Implementation Plan (SIP) or the most stringent limitation achieved in practice for a similarly situated facility, whichever is more stringent.

low volume exemption (LVE) An exemption pursuant to the Toxic Substances Control Act (TSCA) available to a manufacturer or an importer wanting to manufacture or import a new chemical in small amounts.

MACT hammer MACT is Maximum Achievable Control Technology as defined in the Clean Air Act (CAA). The MACT hammer requires the Environmental Protection Agency (EPA), in certain circumstances, to issue a permit under the CAA even when it has not set all relevant emissions standards related to the types of activities covered by the permit.

major federal action A federal action that may have major environmental ramifications and, thus, may be subject to regulatory requirements under the National Environmental Policy Act (NEPA).

major modification The permit granted for any operation that poses a potential environmental threat designates specific procedures to be used in that operation and sets specific emission levels for each criteria pollutant involved in the operation. Any operational or physical change in a plant that causes a certain level of change in emissions will be considered a major modification, thus invoking the application of various regulatory requirements.

major source As defined in the Clean Air Act (CAA), a stationary source, or group of stationary sources, having the potential to emit a specified number of tons per year of any single pollutant, or a specified number of tons per year of any combination of hazardous air pollutants.

manifest A document used to keep track of hazardous waste shipments. Consisting of six parts, a manifest is created by a hazardous waste generator and must follow each load of hazardous waste from the generator through transportation to its ultimate disposal destination.

manufacture To produce, prepare, import, or compound a toxic chemical, including the creation of substances produced coincidentally during the manufacture, processing, use, or disposal of another substance or mixture, such as by-products, coproducts, or impurities.

marine mammal Any mammal that is morphologically adapted to the marine environment (including sea otters and members of the orders Sirenia, Pinnepedia, and Cetacea) or that primarily inhabits the marine environment (such as the polar bear).

Material Safety Data Sheets (MSDS) A form detailing specific information concerning the characteristics of a chemical substance and proper care and handling procedures for that substance.

Maximum Achievable Control Technology (MACT) Standards based on existing technology as well as the level of control achieved by sources in each source category demonstrating the best results in eliminating pollutants.

maximum contaminant level (MCL) The maximum level of a drinking water contaminant under the Safe Drinking Water Act (SDWA).

maximum contaminant level goal (MCLG) As part of the 1986 amendments to the Safe Drinking Water Act (SDWA), the standard previously known as the recommended maximum contaminant level was redesigned as the maximum contaminant level goal and represents the level of a contaminant at which no known or anticipated adverse effects on the health of persons occur and that allows an adequate margin of safety.

"me-too" pesticide A pesticide that is identical or very similar to other registered substances.

Microbial Commercial Activity Notice (MCAN) A premanufacture notification form submitted prior to commercial manufacture or importation of a new microorganism or a significant new use of an existing microorganism.

mixture rule A rule holding that any nonhazardous waste that is mixed with a hazardous waste becomes a part of the hazardous waste due to the fact that such mixing has occurred.

modifying criteria State acceptance and community acceptance of a remedy pursuant to CERCLA.

multiple uses The federal Bureau of Land Management (BLM) and the Forest Service are instructed to manage lands entrusted to their care for multiple uses that will best meet the needs of the American people.

National Ambient Air Quality Standards (NAAQS) The maximum levels of pollutants allowed in the ambient air (air outside the boundaries of one's fence line).

National Contingency Plan (NCP) A plan designed to address responses to releases of hazardous substances.

National Institute for Occupational Safety and Health (NIOSH) The research institute designed to assist the Occupational Safety & Health Administration (OSHA) set exposure limits for workplace substances.

National Pollutant Discharge Elimination System (NPDES) Pursuant to the Clean Water Act (CWA), this system determines, through the permitting process, the types and amounts of pollutants discharged into waters and streams. The process includes the following: the filing of an application, certification by the state, Fact Sheet or Statement of Basis, opportunity for the public to provide comment, and issuance or denial of a permit.

National Priorities List (NPL) A list prioritizing the releases or threats of release of hazardous materials in the United States for the purpose of allocating financial and administrative assistance. This list is compiled by the EPA pursuant to CERCLA. The list is comprised of uncontrolled hazardous substance releases that are priorities for long-term remedial evaluation and response.

National Response Center (NRC) A center designed to coordinate responses to releases of hazardous substances, the NRC was established pursuant to CERCLA and is operated under the supervision of the National Response Team.

navigable A term used in the definition of waters of the United States to mean "deep and wide enough to afford passage for ships."

negligence A breach of a duty to another person that causes an injury.

negligence per se A situation where conduct is treated as negligence even when there is no actual evidence concerning a breach of duty.

new chemical substance Any substance not already identified pursuant to the TSCA. The manufacture or importation of such a substance requires a premanufacture notice (PMN).

new source As defined in the Clean Air Act (CAA), construction of a new source, or modification to an existing source, that will produce a significant increase in emissions of pollutants.

New Source Performance Standards (NSPS) Standards applicable to new source discharges.

no jeopardy rule A phrase stating in common terms a rule in the ESA that no endangered or threatened species may be placed in jeopardy by the actions of a federal agency.

nonattainment states States that do not meet the National Ambient Air Quality Standards (NAAQS).

nonpoint source A source of pollutant that is not quantifiable or not easily quantified. Examples include runoff from a farm or a city street.

Notice of Commencement (NOC) A form used to notify the EPA that manufacture or importation of a chemical has begun.

Notice of Rebuttable Presumption Against Registration (RPAR) Prevents a registrant from receiving a conditional registration of a pesticide under FIFRA.

Not-in-My-Back-Yard (NIMBY). This syndrome reflects a common view of citizens living or working near a proposed facility that may pose an environmental threat. The phrase basically means that the citizens don't want such a facility anywhere near where they are. In response to this syndrome, many local governments have begun providing a forum in their facility siting process for citizens to make a public record of their concerns.

Notice of Proposed Rulemaking (NPRM) Pursuant to the Federal Administrative Procedure Act (FAPA), this type of notice to the public is required whenever an agency is considering or has proposed a rule on a subject within its rule-making authority. This notice is published in the *Federal Register.*

nuisance A tort that results from an annoyance or a disturbance that unreasonably interferes with the enjoyment of property.

Occupational Safety and Health Act (OSH Act) The federal environmental act enacted to protect the workplace environment.

Occupational Safety & Health Administration (OSHA) The federal agency tasked with the administration and implementation of the Occupational Safety and Health Act (OSH Act).

Office of Pesticide Programs (OPP) The office through which the EPA tracks the registration of pesticides.

offset A reduction in current emissions that is equal to or exceeds the amount of proposed new emissions.

operator The person responsible for overall operation of a facility. Pursuant to federal environmental laws, the definition of *person,* and consequently the definition of *operator,* is quite broad.

ordinary suspension An order suspending the sale, distribution, and use of a pesticide because the EPA administrator believes it to be an imminent risk. This differs from an emergency suspension in that with an ordinary suspension, the registrant has an opportunity to request a pre-order hearing.

orphan share Waste contributed by parties that are either defunct or bankrupt at the time of a CERCLA enforcement action.

owner The person who owns a facility, either in whole or in part. The broad definition of *person* in federal environmental law leads to the term owner also being defined broadly.

Part A and Part B permit application Two parts or types of an application required in certain circumstances pursuant to the RCRA. Upon passage of the RCRA, existing treatment, storage and disposal (TSDs) facilities (also known as interim status facilities) were required to file this application with the EPA for a permit to continue to do business until they received their full operating permit.

permissible exposure limits (PELs) A standard representing the maximum amount of any substance to which someone may be exposed in the workplace as set by the Occupational & Safety Health Administration (OSHA).

person An individual, a partnership, a corporation (including a government corporation), an association, a firm, a joint stock company, a federal agency, a state, an arm or political subdivision of a state, a municipality, or an interstate body.

personal stake A distinct and palpable injury to a plaintiff in a court proceeding and a causal connection between the injury and the challenged conduct.

pesticide Any substance intended for "preventing, destroying, repelling or mitigating any pest" or any substance intended for use as a "plant regulator, defoliant or dessicant."

photovoltaic panels Panels used to gather solar energy. They are called "photovoltaic" because they convert light (photons) to electricity (voltage).

pinnipeds From the Latin word *pinnipedia,* which means "feather or foot fin," these mammals include sea lions, seals, and walruses. They are protected by the Marine Mammal Protection Act (MMPA).

plaintiff The party bringing a litigation action.

plume blight Impairment of visibility as a result of plumes, which are identifiable columns obscuring visibility.

point source As defined in the Clean Water Act (CWA), any discernible, confined, and discrete conveyance, including but not limited to any pipe, ditch, channel, tunnel, conduit, well, discrete fissure, container, rolling stock, concentrated animal feeding operation [such as a feed lot], or vessel or other floating craft, from which pollutants are or may be discharged.

Polaroid exemption A special exemption pursuant to TSCA given to the Polaroid Corporation so the corporation could use new chemicals manufactured for its instant photography without having to comply with other TSCA requirements.

police power The power of governments to make laws to protect the health, safety, and welfare of citizens.

pollutant Dredged spoil; solid waste; incinerator residue; sewage; garbage; sewage sludge; munitions; chemical wastes; biological materials; radioactive materials; heat; wrecked or discarded equipment; rock; sand; cellar dirt; and industrial, municipal, and agricultural waste.

polychlorinated biphenyls (PCBs) Substances regulated pursuant to the Toxic Substances Control Act (TSCA).

polymer exemption A special exemption for certain chemical substances pursuant to TSCA.

potentially responsible parties (PRPs) Parties identified by the EPA as potentially responsible for the cleanup of hazardous substances pursuant to CERCLA.

Preliminary Assessment (PA) Part of the process established pursuant to the National Environmental Policy Act (NEPA), this initial assessment assists in determining whether a proposed action may require further investigation to learn whether the action poses an environmental risk.

Preliminary Assessment Information Rule (PAIR) A TSCA rule pursuant to which manufacturers must submit production and exposure data on chemicals on the ITC Priority List.

premanufacture notice (PMN) When a company plans to manufacture, import, or process a substance deemed to be "new," that company is required to provide the Environmental Protection Agency (EPA) with this notice, which includes detailed information concerning the substance and the proposed manufacturing operation.

preponderance of evidence A standard of proof that requires a party to produce slightly more evidence than their opponent.

prevention of significant deterioration (PSD) PSD is a standard for new sources of air pollution located in attainment areas. The new sources must comply with a permit program designed to maintain the air quality at approximately the same level as before the new source was added.

primary balancing criteria Long-term effectiveness, reduction, short-term effectiveness, implementability, and cost are criteria to be considered once threshold criteria are met.

primary standards A category of standards under the Safe Drinking Water Act (SDWA). These standards relate to contaminants that might cause adverse effects on people's health.

process The preparation of a chemical substance after its manufacture for distribution in commerce in the same form or physical state as, or in a different form or physical state from, that in which it was received by the persons so preparing such substance as part of an article containing the chemical substance or mixture.

proposed action Pursuant to the National Environmental Policy Act (NEPA), a proposed action is an idea, a goal, or a project for construction of a facility or implementation of some sort of operation being actively considered by a federal agency. A proposed action requires further study to determine what potential environmental risk the proposed activity presents.

proximate cause The act (or failure to act) without which an injury would not have occurred; the event that produces an injury without an intervening cause.

public drinking water system (PDWS) A system for the provision to the public of piped water for human consumption if such system has at least 15 service connections or regularly services at least 25 individuals. It also includes any collection, treatment, storage, and distribution facilities under the control of the operator of such a system and any collection or pretreatment storage facilities not under such control that are used primarily in connection with such a system.

R&D exemption An exemption granted pursuant to TSCA for small quantities of new chemicals used only for research and development (R&D).

reactivity A characteristic of hazardous waste that has the characteristic of reacting violently or exploding during handling or management.

reasonable person test This is part of the test for negligence, and is based upon whether a person of ordinarily prudent care would have exercised that care under the particular circumstances of a case.

Reasonably Available Control Technology (RACT) A technology standard pursuant to the Clean Air Act (CAA) requiring facilities to use air cleaning technology reasonably available to facilities of that type and with the same type of emissions.

recommended maximum contaminant level (RMCL) The standard renamed the maximum contaminant level goal. This standard represents the level of a contaminant at which no known or anticipated adverse effects on the health of persons occur and that allows an adequate margin of safety.

record All data, documents, information, and testimony compiled during any administrative or judicial proceeding.

Record of Decision (ROD) This document must be prepared whenever an agency makes a decision or recommendation concerning an action proposed pursuant to the National Environmental Policy Act (NEPA).

Record of Significant Adverse Reaction In the event a chemical mixture causes a "significant adverse reaction" to human health or the environment, manufacturers, processors, and distributors must submit this record, which is kept for 30 years.

regional haze The technical term for what is more commonly known as smog. A general film impairing visibility over a large area.

registration The process by which a pesticide is authorized for sale, distribution, and use.

Reimbursement Order An order issued by the EPA pursuant to the TSCA requiring entities to tender their proper share of testing costs.

release Any spilling, leaking, pumping, pouring, emitting, emptying, discharging, injecting, escaping, leaching, dumping, abandoning, or disposing of any hazardous chemical, extremely hazardous substance, or other hazardous substance into the environment.

Remedial Action (RA) Part of the remedial action process described in CERCLA. This portion of the remedial process involves the design of the remedial action and the implementation of that design.

Remedial Design (RD) *See* Remedial Action (RA).

Remedial Investigation/Feasibility Study (RI/FS) A two-part process designed to ensure that there is enough information to analyze the possible remediation alternatives for a site containing hazardous substances so a permanent cleanup plan can be finalized.

remediation A lengthy response following the initial response action related to the cleanup of a hazardous materials release. The intent of remediation is to effect a permanent cleanup of the contaminated site.

removal An action in response to an environmental emergency. A removal is intended to contain the problem and reduce the immediate risk to human health and the environment.

reportable chemical substances Defined in the TSCA as chemical substances manufactured, imported, or processed for a commercial purpose in the United States and not specifically excluded from the TSCA Inventory.

Reportable Quantity (RQ) The amount of hazardous substance which triggers a reporting requirement under CERCLA.

response An action resulting in removal or remediation pursuant to CERCLA.

risk assessment The process of evaluating risk.

risk-based testing rules Testing rules designed to assess the risk associated with the use of a chemical.

risk management An area of management consisting of the evaluation of risks that might affect the successful operation of an entity's activities, attempting to minimize or mitigate those identified risks, and ensuring that sufficient funds or insurance are available to compensate for any losses.

risk trigger If the EPA finds that a chemical may present an "unreasonable risk," that finding constitutes a "trigger," allowing the EPA to require testing of that chemical.

rodenticide A chemical substance used against rodents.

rulemaking The administrative process by which an agency develops a rule or regulation as required by law.

rule or regulation As defined by the Federal Administrative Procedure Act (FAPA), an agency statement or action with "future effects designed to implement, interpret, or prescribe law or policy."

rules of evidence The rules governing the information that may be presented to a court or an administrative tribunal. These rules specify what information can be presented and in what form.

Safe Drinking Water Act (SDWA) Enacted in 1974, this act represents federal controls on the water used in municipal water systems. The act's provisions apply to water in public drinking water systems, underground hazardous waste injection wells, and some aquifers.

Safe Harbors program This program, which is part of the ESA, permits developers, in exchange for their agreement, to develop their property in a more environmentally sensitive manner that has the possibility of attracting endangered species and to retain the eventual right to develop their property in a manner that is acceptable to all concerned.

scoping This portion of the environmental impact statement (EIS) process includes identifying and addressing significant issues related to a proposed action, including the range of possible actions, alternatives, and possible environmental impacts related to the alternatives.

secondary standards A category of standards under the Safe Drinking Water Act (SDWA). These standards relate to contaminants that might affect the appearance or odor of the water.

Section 106 enforcement action This type of action is named for the section of the Comprehensive Environmental Response, Compensation, and Liability Act (CERCLA) from which it is taken. Pursuant to this section, the Environmental Protection Agency (EPA) may order responsible parties to undertake an emergency removal action or to effect a remedial cleanup of a contaminated site.

significant new use A utilization of a chemical not previously used for that purpose which triggers the requirement of a PMN.

Significant New Use Notice (SNUN) Any entity wanting to manufacture or process a chemical for a significant new use must give the EPA at least 90 days' notice prior to such use through a SNUN.

Significant New Use Rule (SNUR) Issued by the EPA pursuant to the authority granted under TSCA, a SNUR requires the issuance of a premanufacture notice (PMN) for a new use of an existing chemical.

siting criteria Criteria used by regulators, the regulated entity, and the public as part of the approval process for a new or modified landfill.

small quantity generator (SQG) As defined in the RCRA, a small quantity generator is one that generates more than a certain minimum quantity of hazardous waste but less than a certain maximum quantity of hazardous waste. SQGs have slightly relaxed regulatory storage and transportation time limits compared to larger generators.

solar energy The method of gathering energy that typically involves the use of solar panels to capture the energy of the sun and convert it to electricity.

solid waste As defined in the RCRA, a solid waste is broadly defined as any garbage, refuse, sludge from a waste treatment plant, water supply treatment plant or air pollution control facility and other discarded material, including solid, liquid, semisolid, or contained gaseous materials resulting from industrial, commercial, mining and agricultural activities, and from community activities. The definition does not include solid or dissolved material in domestic sewage or solid or dissolved material in irrigation return flows or industrial discharges that are point sources subject to permitting requirements pursuant to the Clean Water Act (CWA).

sovereign immunity A legal doctrine permitting governments to avoid liability for their actions in certain circumstances.

spill prevention control and countermeasure plans (SPCC) Plans that require facilities to be prepared for the worst-case spill.

standing to sue No person may bring an action in court unless that person has standing to sue, which is determined by the application of numerous criteria, such as whether the person has a personal stake in the outcome of the litigation.

state Any state in the United States, in addition to the District of Columbia, the Commonwealth of Puerto Rico, Guam, American Samoa, the United States Virgin Islands, the northern Mariana Islands, and any other territory or possession over which the U.S. government has jurisdiction.

State Emergency Response Commission (SERC) A commission appointed by the governor of each state. The SERC designates emergency planning districts within the state and monitors compliance with relevant provision of EPCRA.

State Implementation Plan (SIP) Enacted by each state based on standards set by the Clean Air Act (CAA). Requirements vary depending on whether the state has met the National Ambient Air Quality Standards (NAAQS).

statute A rule of general applicability passed by the legislative branch of a government.

storage facility A facility that holds hazardous waste for a temporary period, at the end of which period the waste is treated, disposed of, or moved elsewhere for additional storage.

stranding An event in the wild in which a dead marine mammal is on a U.S. beach or shore or in U.S. waters or an alive marine mammal is on a U.S. beach or shore and is unable to return to the water or is in need of apparent medical attention or is in U.S. waters and is unable to return to its natural habitat without assistance.

strict liability A liability for damages as a result of engaging in an activity even when there is no proof that the liable party breached a duty while engaging in that activity. This is a very common liability standard in environmental law due to the hazardous nature of many activities related to environmental law.

Superfund The name given to the Comprehensive Environmental Response, Compensation, and Liability Act (CERCLA) and to the fund originally designated by that act to assist with the cleanup of contaminated sites.

surface impoundments Any natural or human-made excavation or diked area designed to hold hazardous wastes containing or consisting of free liquids. Pits, ponds, and lagoons are types of surface impoundments.

tanks Stationary devices made primarily of non-earthen materials that provide structural support, typically for the storage of liquids.

technology-based standards These standards typically require the use of particular equipment deemed to be appropriate to achieve the applicable emissions standard.

test market exemption (TME) An exemption granted pursuant to TSCA by the EPA when the EPA determines that the "test market" activity does not pose an unreasonable risk to human health or the environment.

threatened species Any species that is likely to become an endangered species within the foreseeable future throughout all or a significant portion of its range.

threshold criteria The overall protection of human health and the environment and compliance with Applicable or Relevant and Appropriate Requirements (ARARs).

threshold planning quantity (TPQ) The amount of an extremely hazardous substance present in a facility at any one time that, when exceeded, subjects the facility to the emergency planning requirements.

Tier One/Tier Two Reporting requirements pursuant to EPCRA.

Tier Two Confidential Location Information Sheet If a facility believes that the location of chemical substances on its property should be kept confidential for some business purpose, that facility must submit the required information on this form, which is then available to certain committees but not to the public.

tort A civil, as opposed to a criminal, wrong.

total maximum daily load (TMDL) The amount of pollutants a certain body of water can tolerate without exceeding applicable water quality standards.

Toxic Chemical Release Inventory Reporting Form (Form R) This comprehensive reporting form, required in certain circumstances pursuant to EPCRA, provides sufficient data for emergency responders to know what toxic chemicals are located at a particular facility and how much risk is posed to human health and the environment from those chemicals in the event of a spill or release.

toxicity A characteristic of hazardous waste that is likely to leach hazardous concentrations of certain toxic constituents into groundwater under mismanagement conditions.

Toxicity Characteristic Leaching Procedure (TCLP) The method by which the toxicity of a material is analyzed. In a laboratory, the material being tested is mixed with an acetic acid solution for a specific period of time. The acetic solution is then checked for certain heavy metals and organic compounds. If the compounds or heavy metals are detected in the solution in quantities greater than the limits prescribed in the RCRA, the material will be considered a hazardous waste due to its toxicity.

toxic pollutant Any pollutant as defined by the Clean Water Act (CWA) deemed toxic to human health or the environment.

transportation-related release A release that occurs during transportation or storage incident to transportation if a shipment has not reached its ultimate destination.

transporter A person engaged in the off-site transportation of hazardous waste by air, rail, roadway, or water.

treatment facility A facility that qualifies for purposes of the RCRA if its operator uses any method, technique, or process, including neutralization, designed to change the physical, chemical, or biological character or composition of any hazardous waste so as to neutralize such waste or so as to recover energy or materials resources from the waste or so as to render such waste nonhazardous or less hazardous; safer to transport, store, or dispose of; or amenable for recovery, amenable for storage, or reduced in volume.

treatment, storage, and disposal (TSD) facility Pursuant to the RCRA, such hazardous waste facilities are strictly regulated in areas such as design, construction, operation, and closure.

trespass to land This tort occurs when there is an unlawful entry onto another's real property. The tort does not require that a person set foot on someone else's property; sending noxious odors or water onto someone else's property can be considered trespass to land.

trial The forum in which a lawsuit is adjudicated.

TSCA Inventory A list begun in 1976 by the EPA representing chemicals in commerce at the time. Since 1976, the list represents "each chemical substance which is manufactured or processed in the United States." The number of chemicals on the list presently exceeds 80,000.

turbines Large bladed towers that are typically made of metal and that look like three-armed windmills. Turbines are used to produce wind energy. As the wind blows, the blades of the turbines spin, eventually producing electricity.

underground storage tank (UST) The Resource Conservation and Recovery Act (RCRA) contains a separate program for the regulation of such tanks.

Uniform Hazardous Waste Manifest A document that accompanies hazardous waste at all times from its generation through its disposal.

unmanifested waste Waste accepted at a treatment, storage, and disposal (TSD) facility without a manifest.

unreasonable adverse effects A term defining the standard used in registering pesticides pursuant to FIFRA.

Update Rule This rule requires, with few exceptions, that every four years, manufacturers and importers update information concerning their chemicals listed on the TSCA Inventory.

vessel Any craft used as a means of transportation on water.

waste minimization A requirement of generators pursuant to the RCRA that efforts be made to reduce the volume and risk associated with hazardous materials.

waste pile Any noncontainerized accumulation of nonflowing hazardous waste.

water quality standards Standards established by states for waters within their jurisdiction. The standards consist of two elements: use classifications and water quality criteria.

waters of the United States All waters in which the United States has an interest, including navigable waters of the United States, interstate waters and their tributaries, and waters that may be used in commerce.

wilderness Defined in the Wilderness Act of 1964 as being, *inter alia*, land that (1) generally appears to have been affected primarily by the forces of nature, with the imprint of man's work substantially unnoticeable; (2) has outstanding opportunities for solitude or a primitive and unconfined type of recreation; (3) has at least five thousand acres of land or is of sufficient size as to make practicable its preservation and use in an unimpaired condition; and (4) may also contain ecological, geological, or other features of scientific, educational, scenic, or historical value.

wind energy The use of wind to make electricity, primarily through the use of wind farms utilizing turbines.

INDEX

D

E

F

G

H

I

J

K

L

M

N

O

P

R

S

T

U